6.98   6 AM

D1244741

EAGLES OF THE
THIRD REICH

0 11557 03405 9

Other titles in the Stackpole Military History Series

THE AMERICAN CIVIL WAR
Cavalry Raids of the Civil War
Pickett's Charge
Witness to Gettysburg

WORLD WAR II
Armor Battles of the Waffen-SS, 1943–45
Army of the West
Australian Commandos
The B-24 in China
Backwater War
The Battle of Sicily
Beyond the Beachhead
The Brandenburger Commandos
The Brigade
Bringing the Thunder
Coast Watching in World War II
Colossal Cracks
D-Day to Berlin
Exit Rommel
Flying American Combat Aircraft
  of World War II
Fist from the Sky
Forging the Thunderbolt
Fortress France
The German Defeat in the East, 1944–45
German Order of Battle, Vols. 1, 2, and 3
Germany's Panzer Arm in World War II
Grenadiers
Infantry Aces
Iron Arm
Luftwaffe Aces
Messerschmitts over Sicily
Michael Wittmann, Vols. 1 and 2
The Nazi Rocketeers
On the Canal
Packs On!
Panzer Aces
Panzer Aces II
The Panzer Legions
Retreat to the Reich
Rommel's Desert War
The Savage Sky

A Soldier in the Cockpit
Stalin's Keys to Victory
Surviving Bataan and Beyond
Tigers in the Mud
The 12th SS, Vols. 1 and 2

THE COLD WAR / VIETNAM
Flying American Combat Aircraft:
  The Cold War
Land with No Sun
Street without Joy

WARS OF THE MIDDLE EAST
Never-Ending Conflict

GENERAL MILITARY HISTORY
Carriers in Combat
Desert Battles

EAGLES OF THE THIRD REICH

Men of the Luftwaffe in World War II

Samuel W. Mitcham, Jr.

STACKPOLE
BOOKS

This book is dedicated to my lovely wife, Donna P. Mitcham

Copyright © 1988 by Samuel W. Mitcham

Published in paperback in 2007 by
STACKPOLE BOOKS
5067 Ritter Road
Mechanicsburg, PA 17055
www.stackpolebooks.com

All rights reserved, including the right to reproduce this book or portions thereof in any form or by any means, electronic or mechanical, including photocopying, recording, or by any information storage and retrieval system, without permission in writing from the publisher. All inquiries should be addressed to Stackpole Books, 5067 Ritter Road, Mechanicsburg, PA 17055

Cover design by Tracy Patterson

Printed in the United States of America

10 9 8 7 6 5 4 3 2 1

Library of Congress Cataloging-in-Publication Data

Mitcham, Samuel W.
  [Men of the Luftwaffe]
  Eagles of the Third Reich : men of the Luftwaffe in World War II / Samuel W. Mitcham, Jr.
      p. cm. — (Stackpole military history series)
  Originally published under the title: Men of the Luftwaffe. 1988.
  Includes bibliographical references and index.
  ISBN-13: 978-0-8117-3405-9
  ISBN-10: 0-8117-3405-6
  1. Germany. Luftwaffe—History—World War, 1939–1945. 2. World War, 1939–1945—Aerial operations, German. I. Title.

D787.M56 2007
940.54'4943—dc22

                                                2007003011

Table of Contents

Introduction

Are wars fought by men and machines, or are they fought by men with machines? Since history is truly argument without end, this question is somewhat moot, but for purposes of this book I adopt the second premise, since the machines themselves were (and are) the products of men. In other words, I believe that the Luftwaffe lost the war because of human failure, rather than because of technological failure. This is not to say that the technological failure did not occur—quite the opposite. I in no way intend to minimize the contributions of those who study the technological aspects of the air war in Europe; I very much respect and admire them. However, it is my opinion that the human factor was (and is) primary in war—just as war itself, in the larger sense, must be regarded as a human failure. For example, the technical reasons why the British Spitfires and Hurricanes were superior to the Heinkel 111s and Messerschmitt 110s during the Battle of Britain are significant questions, but perhaps a more significant question might be: "Why were the German combat pilots still saddled with obsolete He-111s and Me-110s as late as 1940?"

The purpose of this book is to look at the men behind the airplanes, i.e., to examine the fundamental causes of the Luftwaffe's demise. The war has now been over for more than sixty years. The technology of the 1940s has been relegated to museums for decades, but the causes of the Luftwaffe's defeat are still with us. One only has to listen to a debate in the American Congress to understand that. If those who do not study the past are indeed condemned to relive it, then this book should serve as a warning to the leaders, strategists, and technicians of today.

Acknowledgments

First and foremost, I wish to thank Mr. Harry R. Fletcher and the staff of the Albert F. Simpson Historical Research Center, Air University, Maxwell Air Force Base, Alabama, for all their kind and very professional help.

Thanks also go to the staff of the United States National Archives, Washington, D.C., for providing photographs; to Paula Leming, Professor of Foreign Languages at Henderson State University, for help in translating; and to Dr. Claude Sumerlin of H.S.U. for proofreading and advice. Appreciation is also extended to Drs. Charles D. Dunn and Joe T. Clark for their support, and to Dr. Gene Mueller for assisting in the acquisition of material on the Condor Legion. Gratitude is also extended to the staff of Huie Library, H.S.U., and most especially to Mrs. Barbara Roberts, who has for years been plagued by my insatiable demands for interlibrary loans.

CHAPTER 1

The Secret Air Force

Although it would not officially exist for more than two years, the Luftwaffe can trace its birth to 11 A.M. on January 30, 1933, when Adolf Hitler was sworn in as chancellor of Germany. Later that day he appointed Hermann Goering, the number two man in the Nazi party, as minister without portfolio and Reich commissioner of aviation (*Reichskommissariat für die Luftfahrt*) in the new government. Actually Goering was minister of aviation and commander-in-chief of the secret German air force. In many ways his personality dominated the Luftwaffe throughout its existence.

Hermann Goering, author Matthew Cooper later wrote, "was an enigma. He was as much the stuff of which heroes are made as are villains. He was a remarkable combination of contradictions . . . He was both energetic and lazy; realistic and romantic; brutal and kind; brave and cowardly; refined and coarse; intelligent, vain, humourous and ruthless . . . [an] inspiration to some, an object of ridicule and detestation to others."[1]

Hermann was born in Marienbad Sanitarium at Rosenheim, Bavaria, on January 12, 1893, the fourth son of Heinrich Ernst and Franiszha "Fanny" Goering. His middle name was Wilhelm, after Kaiser Wilhelm II, whom he was destined to serve in World War I. Hermann grew up in Bavaria. A headstrong and rebellious youth, he was educated at various boarding schools: the Karlsruhe Military Academy and the prestigious Gross-Lichterfelde Cadet Academy near Berlin, where he underwent officer training. He was gazetted *Leutnant* (second lieutenant) in the Prince Wilhelm (112th Infantry) Regiment at Muelhausen in March 1912.[2]

When World War I broke out in the fall of 1914, young Goering's regiment was sent to the western front, where he was commended for initiative and daring. He soon fell ill, however, and was recovering in the military hospital at Freiburg when a visit from Lt. Bruno Loerzer changed his entire life.

Young Loerzer, who had formerly served in the 112th Infantry, had left the Muelhausen regiment to become a pilot trainee at Freiburg and was now scheduled to join an air force unit at Ostend, Belgium. Loerzer's adventurous tales so excited Hermann Goering that he decided to apply for a transfer and join his friend there as an aerial observer. When the transfer was refused and he was ordered to rejoin his regiment, Goering headed for Ostend anyway—in direct disobedience of orders. Naturally the commander of the Muelhausen regiment demanded his immediate court-martial.

Fortunately for Goering, he had friends in high places. His godfather (and his mother's lover) was Ritter ("Knight," or "Sir") Hermann von Epenstein, a rich half-Jewish aristocrat who had received his knighthood title from Kaiser Wilhelm II. Ritter von Epenstein used his influence at court to intercede in Hermann's behalf. The court-martial proceedings were quietly dropped, and he was soon officially transferred to the air service.

From the beginning, Hermann Goering proved himself to be an incredibly brave airman. "Goering's belief . . . ," Manvill and Fraenkel wrote, "was that nothing could happen to harm him. He was, quite literally, insensitive to physical danger."[3] As an aerial observer with the 25th Air Detachment during the Battle of Verdun in 1915, Goering and his pilot, Loerzer, both won the Iron Cross, 1st Class, and were personally decorated by Crown Prince Friedrich Wilhelm. In June, Lieutenant Goering returned to Freiburg as a pilot-trainee and in October was posted to the 5th Jagdstaffel (Fighter Squadron) as a fighter pilot. Three weeks later, he was shot down by a British Sopwith. Had he not been fortunate enough to crash-land next to a German field hospital, he would have bled to death. Observers later counted sixty bullet holes in his airplane. It took months for his shattered thigh to heal.

Goering spent his convalescent leave at his godfather's Mauterdorf Castle in the summer of 1916, where he fell in love with Marianne Mauser, the daughter of a local landowner, and proposed marriage to her. Their engagement remained unofficial, however, because of her parents' objections. Herr Mauser looked upon Goering as a man without any prospects except an early death, and it appeared he was right: Hermann returned to the western front in late 1916.

His new unit was the 26th Fighter Squadron, which was commanded by Bruno Loerzer and was headquartered at their old regimental station of Muelhausen. Here Goering came into his own. By mid-1917 he had shot down seventeen enemy airplanes and had been named commander of the 27th Fighter Squadron at Yseghem, in the Flanders sector. In recognition of his leadership, Kaiser Wilhelm decorated him with the *Pour le Merite* after only fifteen victories, instead of the normal twenty-five. Goering had already been awarded the Zaehring Lion with Swords, the Karl Friedrich Order with Swords, and the Hohenzollern House Order with Swords, 3rd Class.[4]

The leading German ace, of course, was Baron Manfred von Richthofen, the commander of the 1st Jagdgeschwader (Fighter Wing), who scored eighty victories. The "Red Baron" was killed on April 21, 1918, by a lucky machine-gun burst from Roy Brown, an unassuming Canadian ace with a nervous stomach.[5] Richthofen was replaced as wing leader by Capt. Wilhelm Reinhardt, who was killed in a flying accident on July 3. Most people expected the new commander to be Ernst Udet, a member of the squadron who had over fifty kills and was Germany's leading surviving air ace. Everyone was surprised when Hermann Goering was given the prestigious command.[6]

Goering (by now a captain) led Jagdgeschwader Richthofen Number 1 very well. Although at first resented by some of the pilots, he soon gained their confidence and made lifelong contacts. Among his subordinates were four of his future generals: Wolfram von Richthofen, a future field marshal and a cousin of the Red Baron; Ernst Udet; and lieutenants Karl Bodenschatz and Kurt von Doering. All except Doering played significant roles in the future Luftwaffe. Goering ran his victory total to twenty-two before the armistice was signed. On Goering's orders the wing smashed their aircraft at Darmstadt, rather than surrender them intact to the Allies as they had been ordered to do.

In December, Goering rejoined his mother in Munich. Here his unofficial engagement to Fräulein Mauser quietly came to an end. "What have you got now to offer my daughter?" Herr Mauser wrote to Hermann.

"Nothing," the unemployed Goering telegraphed back.[7] And that was the end of that.

Like many ex-officers, Goering was embittered by the Treaty of Versailles, which the victorious Allies forced Germany to sign. Among other things, the "Versailles Dikta" (dictate) limited the size of the German Army to 100,000 men (of which 4,000 could be officers) and completely outlawed military aviation and the elite General Staff. The former commander of the Richthofen wing briefly joined the Freikorps in 1919, before leaving war-torn and revolutionary Germany in disgust. He began a career as a barnstormer in Denmark and Sweden. It was here he met and fell in love with Karin von Kantzow (nee von Fock), the beautiful wife of a Swedish army captain. She soon left her husband for Goering, and they lived together for several months before her divorce was secured. They were finally married in Munich on February 3, 1923.

Hermann Goering returned to Germany in 1922 and enrolled in the University of Munich as a history and political science student. Here he met the second and last hero of his life. The first had been his half-Jewish godfather; the second was Adolf Hitler, head of the infant *Nationalsozialistische Deutsche Arbeiter Partei* (the National Socialist German Workers' Party, also known as the NSDAP or Nazi party).

Goering's career in the rise of the Nazi party (1922–32) is fascinating, but beyond the scope of this book. One incident is germane, however: on November 9, 1923, during Hitler's attempt to seize power in Bavaria during the so-called Beer Hall Putsch, Goering took part in the march in Munich and, in front of the Feldennhalle, was shot by the police, who were firing high-velocity 7.9mm slugs. The bullet struck him in the upper right thigh, just inches from the groin. He fell to the pavement and got dirt in the wound, causing further medical problems.[8] Given morphine to relieve the terrible pain, he soon became a drug addict. He was also never able to control his weight after this.

When Goering took office in early 1933, the Treaty of Versailles was still in effect. It had never been scrupulously observed, however. Gen. Hans von Seeckt, the creator of the Reichsheer (as the 100,000-man army was called), had insisted that 180 of the 4,000-man officer corps be chosen from the former air service. Under his tutelage Germany made a covert agreement with the Soviet Union and set up a secret air training base at Lipetsk, Russia. He also set up secret air organizations and an air training office in the *Truppenamt* (troop office), as the clandestine General Staff was called, and placed Maj. Helmut Wilberg in charge of it. By the time Adolf Hitler and Hermann Goering rose to power, there were a number of undercover aviation squadrons in Germany. They did not amount to much and would not have lasted a week in a war with a major power, such as France, but they could be used to form the nucleus of an air force and provided a reservoir of trained personnel from which the Luftwaffe could draw.[9]

In 1933, Hermann Goering held a multitude of offices. In addition to being Reich commissioner of aviation and Hitler's chief deputy, he was president of the Reichstag and minister of the interior of Prussia, and would soon be prime minister of Prussia, Reich forest master (*Reichsforestmeister*), Reich game warden (*Reichsjaegermeister*), and chief plenipotentiary of Hitler's Four Year (economic) Plan. Hitler was planning to call an election for March 5. Therefore, prior to that, Goering had to purge the Berlin and Prussian police forces of their anti-Nazi elements and replace them with people he could depend on. He had neither the time nor inclination to concern himself with the day-to-day building of the Luftwaffe. This he left to his deputy, the state secretary for aviation.

The best-qualified man for this post was Helmut Wilberg, at that time a major general. A highly capable and technically proficient General Staff officer, Wilberg had been a military pilot since 1910. He had been adjutant in the Inspectorate of Flight Troops prior to the First World War. During the conflict he had commanded the 2nd Flying Detachment, had been the chief aviation staff officer to Field Marshal von Mackensen's headquarters, and had been commander of flying units attached to the First and Fourth armies. He emerged from the war with a whole laundry list of medals, including the Knights Cross of the Hohenzollern House Order with Swords, the Iron

Cross, 1st and 2nd Classes, the Bavarian Military Order of Merit with Swords, the Mecklenburg Military Cross of Merit (2nd Class), the Mecklenburg Military Cross for Distinguished War Service (2nd Class), the Austro-Hungarian Military Cross of Merit (3rd Class), plus Turkish and Bulgarian decorations. From 1920 to 1929 he was chief of the Air Organization and Training Office in the Truppenamt, before doing troop duty as commander of the Prussian 18th Infantry Regiment. Now he was inspector of ordnance (arms) in the Defense Ministry.[10] Unfortunately he had one disqualifying characteristic: he was Jewish.

Hermann Goering did not share the anti-Semitism that characterized most of the rest of Hitler's followers. In private he commented that Jews were much like other people, just "a bit smarter," and they had their good and bad, like any other group. Hitler's anti-Semitic outbursts usually left Goering depressed for hours.[11] Unfortunately, Wilberg's background was too Jewish for even Hermann Goering to be able to hide. He continued to protect Wilberg, however, and even promoted him to general of flyers (*General der Flieger*), but appointing him state secretary was out of the question.[12] Instead, he turned to Erhard Milch, the director of Lufthansa.

Perhaps the most enigmatic character to come out of the Third Reich was Erhard Milch, who was deputy commander-in-chief of the Luftwaffe in its earlier days and who, even more than Goering, deserves credit for its initial construction. Milch was in many ways difficult to categorize: he was arrogant, yet sensitive; selfish, yet patriotic. Looked down on by his peers as a civilian, he nevertheless became a field marshal and was the second-ranking man in the Luftwaffe for much of his career. Most strangely, he was a Nazi whom Hitler personally decorated with the coveted Gold Party Badge, even though Milch's father was a Jew.[13] This meant that Erhard Milch himself was half Jewish under Hitler's racial laws and should have been sitting in a concentration camp according to the rules of the Third Reich, instead of at Goering's right hand.

Milch was born on March 30, 1892, in Wilhelmshaven, on Germany's northwestern coast, the son of naval pharmacist Anton Milch.[14] Milch, which means "milk" in German, was considered a Jewish name by the Nazis. The Nazi racial investigators later produced photographs of tombstones in Jewish cemeteries, complete with the Star of David, bearing the name Milch. Indeed, one of Milch's brothers became a Jew.[15] There is, however, no evidence that Erhard himself seriously embraced any religion except belief in the Kaiser and, later, his own personal ambition.

Anton Milch left the navy in the 1890s and established his own chemist's business in Gelsenkirchen, a town in the Ruhr. His wife left him in the 1900s and returned to her native Berlin, taking her children with her. Erhard graduated from the Joachimsthal public school in Berlin in January 1910, and promptly volunteered for active duty with the Imperial Navy. His application for that branch was turned down because of his Jewish ancestry,[16] so he joined the 1st Foot Artillery Regiment at Koenigsberg instead. After eight months' training, he was sent to the Anklam Military Academy. He graduated first out of 120 cadets and received his commission as a second lieutenant on August 18, 1911.[17]

Second Lieutenant Milch returned to duty with the 1st Foot Artillery in the latter part of 1911. He took a course (probably in gunnery) at the famous Jueterbog Artillery School in 1913 and was engaged in gunnery practice with his unit in West Prussia when World War I broke out.[18] Milch was a battalion adjutant in the 1st Foot Artillery when it helped repulse the Russian invasion of East Prussia in 1914. Later he fought in the bitterly won German victory at Weeden on the eastern front, before being detailed to the 204th Artillery Reconnaissance Battalion on the western front in July 1915. He was promoted to first lieutenant on August 18, 1915.[19]

Erhard Milch spent most of the next two years as an aerial observer on the western front. His aircraft was an unarmed Albatross B, operating between Metz and Verdun—a very hazardous job indeed. Unlike many of his contemporaries, Milch survived the hell that was Verdun, the Somme, and other bloody battles of World War I. In June 1917, he was transferred to Lille as deputy commander of the 5th Air Detachment, where he had better aircraft and less danger. Selected as a candidate for the General Staff in 1918, he was briefly given command of the 9th Company, 41st Infantry Regiment, near Arras. This Memel unit had already suffered heavy losses against the British, but Milch missed the bitterest of the fighting. After two months of frontline experience, he returned to the air service as an intelligence officer in July, 1918. He was promoted to captain in August,[20] but the war ended before he could be transferred to the War Academy for General Staff training.

Milch's last assignment in the 1914–18 war was commanding officer, 6th Fighter Squadron, a post he held even though he could not fly himself. A few weeks later, the kaiser abdicated, the Second Reich collapsed, and Erhard Milch's world fell apart. He returned to Germany, embittered by defeat. He reported to XVII Corps Headquarters at Danzig, where he spent several weeks dissolving left-wing soldiers' councils and engaging in disarmament work, activities which were hardly calculated to improve his attitude. Then, in April 1919, he became commander of the 412th Volunteer Flying Squadron, which Irving described as "a motley collection of patriots, soldiers and mercenaries."[21] This unit was dissolved under the terms of the Treaty of Versailles, and Milch himself left the military service on January 31, 1920.[22]

There is no reason to believe that Milch was not absolutely sincere in his idealistic belief in Imperial Germany. Its destruction, however, caused a fundamental change in him: idealism in Erhard Milch was extinguished forever. From this period on, Milch became more and more the slave of his own ruthless ambition.

It is unclear whether or not Milch applied for one of the 4,000 officers' slots allowed Germany by the Treaty of Versailles, but if he did, he was not accepted. Young Milch did not immediately take off his uniform, however, but joined the East Prussian Freikorps instead. He was soon invited to form a police air unit at Koenigsberg, which he did. He promptly moved his new command from the East Prussian capital to the former zeppelin airfield at Seerapen, away from the revolutionary influences then sweeping the cities. Much to his surprise, he was actually expected to perform police duties with his paramilitary force. His unit was assigned to put down a wave of burglary in the port area of Koenigsberg. After one of his men was killed by a criminal, Milch ordered his men to shoot prowlers on sight and shoot to kill. They did. The burglaries soon ended.[23]

The Allies forced Germany to dissolve her police air squadrons in March 1921, so Milch, now almost twenty-nine, left the constabulary and entered the civilian job market for the first time. He landed a position with Lloyd Ostflug (Lloyd Eastern Airlines) as head of their Danzig office. Lloyd was owned by Professor Hugo Junkers and Gotthard Sachsenberg, a former naval aviator. Soon Milch became business manager of the Danzig Air Mail Service, a subsidiary of the Junkers-Sachsenberg operation. Milch, however, was still haunted by the Treaty of Versailles. The French forced the mail service to close, and Milch was out of business for seven months. He was finally reemployed as an executive with Junkers Airways, Limited, in May 1922.[24]

The former captain rose rapidly in the Junkers organization and, before long, was director of its central administration. He successfully expanded Junkers' operations by skillfully negotiating a financial arrangement with the Polish national airlines. Junkers was soon flying to Warsaw, Lemberg, and Krakow. Eventually the young executive had aircraft flying to Bucharest, Rumania, South America, and the United States. Milch went to America himself and visited the Ford plant at Detroit and other concerns. He was impressed by what he saw and was virtually the only high-ranking Nazi to appreciate the industrial potential of the United States. He also understood the folly of Hitler's declaration of war against the U.S. in December 1941, but this is getting ahead of our story.

In late 1925, the Weimar Republic dictated that Germany's two major airlines—Junkers Airways and Aero-Lloyd—must merge into a single, national airway. To the astonishment of almost everybody, Milch was named one of the three directors of the new super-airline, and he was the only director to come from the Junkers firm. Later he froze out the other two directors, Otto Merkel and Martin Wronsky, and, on September 5, 1929, became commercial director (chief executive officer) of Lufthansa, the German national airline. He was thirty-six years old.

Under the energetic and ruthless Milch, Lufthansa established regular passenger service with Paris (1926), Marseilles (1927), and Spain (1927). Eurasia, a Lufthansa system, started flying to China in 1930, four years after another Lufthansa auxiliary line was established in South America. By 1933 regular Lufthansa commercial and passenger flights were landing in Rome, Latvia, Estonia, and Russia.[25]

Meanwhile, Hitler's political revolution was taking shape in Germany, and Milch, very much aware of his Jewish ancestry and the threat it posed to him if Hitler won power, was not slow to ingratiate himself with the future Fuehrer and his lieutenants. He first met Hitler in 1930 and was quickly impressed with Hitler's grasp of aviation and aerial warfare and with his overall program, with its attractive combination of nationalism and socialism.[26] By 1932, Lufthansa aircraft were placed at Hitler's disposal free of charge for his election campaigns. Lufthansa (i.e., Milch) was also depositing 1,000 Reichsmarks a month into the personal account of Reichstag President Hermann Goering, who spoke out loudly in favor of Lufthansa interests and appropriations in the German national legislative body.[27] Milch's help in the Nazi party's "time of struggle" was not forgotten. When Hitler came to power in 1933, Milch became the Nazis' first secretary of state for aviation.

Milch did not really want to accept a formal position with the government at first, perhaps fearing that Hitler would be unable to consolidate his power. When Hermann Goering offered him the post of state secretary of Prussia in late 1932, Milch turned it down. Indeed, it took a personal appeal from Hitler to convince Milch to accept the job as state secretary for aviation. Initially, however, there was no Aviation Ministry. Goering's official title was Reich commissioner of aviation, and Milch was named his deputy.[28]

Not sharing Hitler's prejudices, Goering used to say: "I am the one to determine who in the Luftwaffe is a Jew and who is not!" Milch's background, however, could not be ignored entirely, so Goering invented an elaborate cover story for his new deputy. An "investigation" revealed that Milch's mother had carried on an adulterous affair with Baron Hermann von Bier, a minor aristocrat, for years. Frau Milch, a pure-blood "Aryan," signed an official document to this effect, and Erhard's birth certificate was reissued with von Bier listed as his father. Goering then closed the file, strongly forbidding any further investigation of Milch's racial background.

That ended the matter, for official purposes anyway. Thereafter, there were few men in Nazi Germany who were more verbally anti-Jewish than Erhard Milch. Even so, the whispers about Milch's ancestry continued until the end of the Third Reich.[29]

Milch never developed a personal relationship with Hermann Goering. He had, after all, been paying the fat man bribes for years and did not look upon him with a great deal of respect. Down the road, Milch planned to take charge of the Air Ministry and the Luftwaffe himself. Goering would go the route of Junkers, Merkel, and Wronsky and be sacrificed to the ambition of Erhard Milch, or at least that was the plan. First, however, he had to consolidate his own power and create the Luftwaffe.

Milch began his program by dividing the Reich Aviation Ministry (RLM) into a Central Branch, the Air Command Office (LA), the General Air Office (LB), the Technical Office (LC), the Luftwaffe Administrative Office (LD), and the Luftwaffe Personnel Office (LP). The Air Command Office was the most important subdivision and was, in effect, the clandestine General Staff of the Luftwaffe. It was subdivided into the Operations Branch (LA-I), the Organization Branch (LA-II), the Training Branch (LA-III), the Flak Artillery Branch (LA-IV), and the Supply Branch (LA-V), plus signals and medical departments. To officer the RLM, Milch and Goering had to depend on the coordination of General of Infantry (later Field Marshal) Werner von Blomberg, the minister of defense. Fortunately for them, Blomberg was not a selfish man, and he recognized the importance the air force would have in the future. In 1933 alone he transferred 550 officers with aviation experience to the RLM (including his entire air operations staff), followed by about 4,000 junior officers and NCO volunteers.[30] More than that, Blomberg did not take this as an opportunity to rid the army of marginal or inefficient officers, as a lesser man might have done. Instead, Blomberg transferred many of his best men to the Luftwaffe. Some of these, including Col. Albert Kesselring, made the move with reluctance; others were happy to be back in aviation. Many of the capable General Staff officers Blomberg shipped to the Luftwaffe had no previous aviation experience at all. The list of army officers sent to the new branch included Col. Hans-Juergen Stumpff, an excellent chief of personnel; Lt. Col. Walter Wever, the new chief of the Air Command Office; Col. Wilhelm Wimmer, who took charge of the Technical Office; and Capt. Baron Wolfram von Richthofen, the new chief of the Development and Testing Branch in the Technical Office and one of Wimmer's two principal assistants. Also transferred to the Luftwaffe were colonels Hugo Sperrle, Hellmuth Felmy, and Ludwig Wolff; lieutenant colonels Hans Geisler, Max von Pohl, Wilhelm Speidel, and Helmuth Volkmann; majors Paul Deichmann, Joseph Kammhuber, Hans Jeschonnek, Herhudt von Rohden, Kurt Student,

Otto Hoffmann von Waldau, and Karl Heinrich Bodenschatz; and captains Andreas Nielsen, Hermann Plocher, Joseph "Beppo" Schmid, and Hans Seidemann.

State Secretary Milch realized that the number of air units he could activate depended on two factors: 1) the production of aircraft; and 2) the number of trained crews the aviation schools could produce. Unfortunately, there were no military aviation schools in Germany in 1933, and the German aircraft industry was very small. To build the Luftwaffe would require money. (Hitler estimated the cost at thirty million reichsmarks; it would actually cost three billion reichsmarks over the next six years.) Milch obtained the funds through Dr. Hjalmar Horace Greeley Schacht, the president of the Reichsbank. Schacht funneled the money to RLM through the Metal Research Company (MEFO), the Autobahn Air Transport Office, the Air Depot of the Volunteer Labor Service, Lufthansa, the South German Lufthansa Company, the Glider Research Institute, and others. Meanwhile, Milch busily expanded the Luftwaffe's training program. In the spring of 1933 he established the Flying School Command within the Aviation Ministry. Subordinate to the Air Command Office, it was responsible for supervising military aviation courses given in commercial flying schools, as well as making preparations for the establishment of military flight training schools.[31] The next year Sports Flyers, Ltd., a civilian organization, was placed directly under the command of the state secretary and, in effect, became a paramilitary training organization. The president of Sports Flyers, Ltd., was simultaneously named inspector of reserve flyers. He was none other than Bruno Loerzer, Goering's World War I comrade (and more recently a cigar salesman), who was destined to become a colonel general in the Luftwaffe.

To build the new military training facilities and to enlarge the capacity of the "civilian" schools, Milch had to provide them with aircraft, which meant he had to greatly expand the German aviation industry. Using MEFO funds, he converted locomotive firms such as Gotha and A.T.G., and shipbuilding concerns, such as Blohm and Voss, into factories for the production of aircraft and aircraft components. Existing aviation firms, including Dornier, Heinkel, Fieseler, Arado, Messerschmitt, and Junkers, were given lucrative government loans to expand their factories and production capabilities.[32] When Hitler took power in January 1933, there were 4,000 skilled workers in the German aircraft industry. The number grew to 20,000 by February, 1934, and stood at almost 72,000 by June, 1935. By the end of 1933 there were an estimated two million workers employed in other aspects of the Luftwaffe's buildup, including the construction of airfields, barracks, bases, military housing, factories, training schools, and other facilities.

Hugo Junkers, Milch's former employer, presented problems. The former professor of thermodynamics had invented and patented a full-cantilevered flying wing in 1910. Then he left his university and entered the new field of aerodynamics. He invented the Juno diesel engine for trucks and airplanes and turned the Juno Works into a multimillion dollar operation. By the fall of 1933 he owned two airplane companies. Unfortunately, he was an idealist and a visionary who thought aviation should be used for peaceful purposes only. He built passenger planes and went into a violent rage when it was suggested that his firm design bombers. Milch instantly and ruthlessly turned on his former mentor, who was of no further use to him. He had the old man arrested, threatened with prosecution, and interrogated for six hours at a time. Junkers, the father of twelve, was forced to sell 51 percent of his airline, factories, and other aviation assets to the Third Reich, and he only escaped prosecution on trumped-up charges of treason by dying on February 3, 1935. Junkers was replaced by Dr. Heinrich Koppenberg, who later also fell out of Milch's favor and was sacked by the state secretary.[33]

On January 1, 1934, the "Rhineland Program" was launched secretly. Its objective was to create an air force of more than 4,029 aircraft—a force that would impress the Allies by pure numbers. The air force thus created was called the "Risk Luftwaffe" (*Risikoluftwaffe*), because it was designed to convince any potential enemy that attacking Germany would be risky. In keeping with this idea, the Risk Luftwaffe was bomber-heavy. It was to include 822 bombers, 590 reconnaissance aircraft, 251 fighters, 51 dive-bombers, and 149 naval aircraft, for a total of 1,863 first-line airplanes. It also included 1,760 trainer aircraft, 89 communications aircraft, and 309 miscellaneous airplanes (mainly experimental prototypes). Many of these planes were obsolete, as Milch and Goering knew. The fighters, for example, were Arado 64s and 65s (Ar-64s and Ar-65s) and Heinkel 51s (He-51s)—all biplanes— but they would have to do until the next generation of aircraft could be put into production. Besides, time was an important factor here. Germany, after all, could hardly expect to keep such a large-scale military buildup secret indefinitely. The Risk Luftwaffe was to be ready by September 1935.[34]

As the Luftwaffe grew in strength, it became necessary to set up its basic territorial and unit organizations. The territorial organization was established on April 1, 1934, when six senior air offices were established. Later called *Luftkreise* (Air Service Commands), they were corps-level units, headquartered at Koenigsberg (I), Berlin (II), Dresden (III), Muenster (IV), Munich (V), and Kiel (VI) (Sea). Each Luftkreis included a senior air commander (*Hoeherer Fliegerkommandeur*), who was in charge of all aviation units in the Luftkreis; two or three Air Administrative Area Commands (*Luftgaukommandos*); a Signal Communications Command; an Air Service Area Medical Battalion; and a Procurement and Supply Group. They also had authority over all civilian airfields and the right to issue orders pertaining to civil air defense. Later, in 1935 and 1936, the Luftkreise commanders were made responsible for the flak artillery units in their areas (under the senior flak artillery commander). They were also responsible for personnel replacement in their zones, and in 1935 they added replacement battalions to their organizational charts. In 1936 these were enlarged to replacement regiments (*Fliegerersatzregimente*). The Luftkreise (under various names) were the basic territorial units of the Luftwaffe and remained responsible for flak artillery defense and personnel (including pilot) replacement through much of the war.[35]

To command the Luftkreise, Goering and Milch induced three Reichsheer retirees to join the Luftwaffe: lieutenant generals Hans Halm, Edmund Wachenfeld, and Leonhard Kaupisch. All were capable administrators who were immediately promoted to general of flyers. Konrad Zander, a retired naval officer, was also promoted to general of flyers and placed in command of Luftkreis VI at Kiel, where the naval aviation units were concentrated. Two younger Luftwaffe officers, Col. Hugo Sperrle and Maj. Gen. Karl Schweickhard, both of whom had previously been transferred from the army by Blomberg, were given command of Luftkreise, but they were not promoted.[36]

During the period of the Risk Luftwaffe, the German Air Force organized its basic combat aviation units, which were to remain standard throughout the Second World War. The basic unit was the Geschwader, which was roughly equivalent to a U.S. Air Force wing. Wings included 100 to 120 aircraft and were commanded by majors, lieutenant colonels, colonels, and occasionally by major generals. Wings were designated by their aircraft type. Thus the 1st Fighter Wing was *Jagdgeschwader* 1 (abbreviated JG 1), the 51st Bomber Wing was *Kampfgeschwader* 51 (or KG 51), and so forth. Twin-engine fighter wings were designated "Destroyer Wings" (*Zerstorergeschwader* or ZG). Training wings (*Lehrgeschwader*) could be composed of any type of aircraft.

Each wing had a staff squadron (*Stabsstaffel*) and three (later four) groups (*Gruppen*) of thirty to thirty-six airplanes per group. Normally commanded by majors or lieutenant colonels, each group had a staff squadron and three combat squadrons (*Staffeln*). Groups were designated by Roman numerals. Thus II/StG 1 was the II Group, 1st Stuka Wing (*Stukageschwader* 1). Squadrons (nine to twelve airplanes each) were given arabic designations (1, III/JG 3, for example, referred to the 1st Squadron, III Group, 3rd Fighter Wing). As in the wings and groups, the number of aircraft actually in the typical squadron declined considerably as the war progressed.

Squadrons were further subdivided into sections (*Ketten*) of three or four aircraft each. A fighter section was called a *Schwarm* and normally consisted of four aircraft.

On March 9, 1935, Germany announced to foreign military attachés that the Luftwaffe had officially come into being on March 1.[37] One week after the announcement, on March 16, Hitler renounced the military clauses of the Treaty of Versailles and announced plans to create an army of thirty-six divisions. The Luftwaffe and the German Armed Forces (*Wehrmacht*) had come out of the closet.

CHAPTER 2

Command Fragmentation

Although he never officially held the title, the first chief of the General Staff of the Luftwaffe was Lt. Gen. Walter Wever, the chief of the Air Command Office from September 1933, to June 3, 1936. He may have been the most capable officer in the Luftwaffe's history and was remembered by all who knew him as a leader of incredible foresight and genius.

Walter Wever was born in 1887 in the province of Posen, which was handed over to Poland by the Treaty of Versailles in 1919. Wever joined the Imperial Army as an infantry *Fahnenjunker* (officer-cadet) in 1905. He spent the first year of World War I as a platoon leader on the western front. In 1915 he was promoted to captain and became a member of the General Staff, where he distinguished himself. In early 1917 he was assigned to the staff of Field Marshal Paul von Hindenburg and Gen. Erich von Ludendorff. He was partially responsible for originating the concept of elastic defense, which broke the back of a French offensive in the Chemin des Dames sector in the latter stages of the war. Wever became Ludendorff's adjutant and, after the armistice, was assigned to the Truppenamt (the clandestine General Staff). Highly respected by Col. Gen. Hans von Seeckt, the commander of the Reichsheer, Wever was promoted to major in 1926 and to lieutenant colonel in 1930. He was chief of the Training Branch of the Reichsheer when he was selected for assignment to the Luftwaffe in 1933. General Blomberg moaned that he was losing a future chief of the General Staff of the Army when Wever left to join the air force.

Colonel Wever quickly immersed himself in his new duties and mastered them as no one else ever would. One of his staff officers, future Lt. Gen. Andreas Nielsen, later wrote of him:

> Greeting his new assignment with enthusiasm, Wever devoted his full attention to the new mission with typical zeal. His quick intelligence, his remarkable receptiveness toward the developments of modern technology, and his vast store of military experience soon enabled him to grasp the fundamental concepts of his mission. He worked untiringly to exploit the unusually favorable circumstances

provided by the time in order to create a military instrument equal to the other Armed Forces branches for the defense of the nation.[1]

General Wever was "a firm adherent of National Socialism."[2] Unlike the Allied political leaders and most of his peers, Wever was intelligent enough to take the time to read *Mein Kampf,* and Hitler's book became his strategic bible. From it, he learned that Hitler wanted no war of revenge against France and Britain. Russia, the Fuehrer wrote, was Germany's main strategic enemy. Therefore, Wever concluded, the Luftwaffe must be built for a war against the Soviet Union.

Wever believed it was far more economical to destroy the enemy's weapons at their sources, rather than on the battlefield. He wanted a bomber with sufficient range to reach Russia's industrial heartland and beyond—as far as the Ural Mountains, 1,500 miles east of Germany's easternmost airfields. Col. Wilhelm Wimmer, the chief of the Technical Office, agreed wholeheartedly. The result was the "Ural Bomber," a four-engine strategic aircraft. By 1936, the prototypes of two promising models were ready for test flying: the Ju-89 and the Do-19. The Dornier model had sufficient range (1,800 miles, as opposed to 1,240 for the Junkers prototypes), but both lacked speed. Dissatisfied, Wever ordered the aircraft industry to design future bombers with greater horsepower. Under Wever's inspired leadership, research and development on the strategic bomber continued unabated, despite Goering's initial opposition.

In the critical area of handling people, Wever was a master. He managed to work in perfect harmony with such difficult men as Milch, Goering, and Sperrle. Unfortunately, his ability as a flyer was less laudatory. He did not become a pilot until 1933 and had fewer than 200 hours in his logbook when, on June 3, 1936, he flew to Dresden to deliver a speech to the cadets of the Air War Academy. In a hurry to return to Berlin to attend the funeral of Gen. Karl von Litzman, a hero of the eastern front in World War I, Wever skipped the preflight inspection of his He-70—an aircraft with which he was not thoroughly familiar. Every pilot knows how dangerous such an omission is. Because he did not check his aircraft, he did not notice that his aileron lock was still engaged. The ensuing flight was very short. The fully fueled Heinkel hit the ground near the runway and exploded, killing Wever instantly. When he heard the news, Goering broke down and wept like a baby. Although it would not be apparent for some time, his death ended the Luftwaffe's chances for winning a strategic air war. Wever was replaced by Lieutenant General Kesselring.

✠

Albert Kesselring was born in Marktsheet, Bavaria, on November 20, 1885, the son of a local teacher who had married a cousin. He grew up in Wunsiedel and attended the Latin School at Bayreuth. Kesselring apparently never explained why he decided upon a military career, but on July 20, 1904, almost as soon as he graduated from Bayreuth, he enlisted in the 2nd Bavarian Foot Artillery Regiment as a *Fahnenjunker*. He attended the War Academy at Munich for two years, and was duly commissioned *Leutnant* on March 8, 1906. He spent the next eight years with his regiment in the garrison town of Metz, except for attending an artillery course in Munich in 1909–10.[3]

Two events occurred at Metz that shaped Kesselring's future career. First, he became interested in flying. There were four balloon companies at Metz, and Kesselring saw their value in reconnaissance and as a platform for directing artillery fire. He trained as a balloon observer and became adjutant of the balloon battalion.

The second event was much less happy. In 1911 Kesselring became the victim of an arranged marriage. His father received at least 30,000 marks in the bargain; Lieutenant Kesselring received Pauline Anna Kayssler, a woman for whom he was unsuited. They might have grown to care for each other (other arranged marriages have worked), but unfortunately, Pauline's mother was part of the bargain. By the marital agreement, she lived with the couple until her death, which occurred long after Albert became a general officer. She made Albert's life miserable; however, Kesselring's Catholic religion prohibited divorce. Albert escaped his unhappy domestic life by burying himself in his career. The service caused frequent and sometimes long separations, which Kesselring regretted not at all. There were no children from the union, although they did adopt a son.

Kesselring went to war with his unit in 1914 and spent the bulk of the next four years engaged in positional warfare on the western front. He was promoted to captain in 1915 and was transferred to the artillery staff of Crown Prince Rupprecht's Sixth (Bavarian) Army in Flanders. In early 1917 he was named adjutant of the Bavarian 3rd Artillery Regiment and, in April, he displayed great courage and skill in rallying disorganized units and in blunting the Anglo-Canadian attacks on Vimy Ridge and Monchy-le-Preux. For his conduct he was recommended for appointment to the General Staff. The appointment was approved without his even having to attend the war academy: a rare mark of distinction indeed in the Imperial German Army.

During the last two years of the war, Kesselring served as General Staff officer to the 2nd Bavarian Landwehr Division on the eastern front, in the Quartermaster's Branch of the II Bavarian Corps on the western front, and as chief intelligence officer with the III Corps in northern France, a post he held when Germany capitulated. In the chaos following the abdication of the kaiser, he was operations officer (I-a) to the deputy commander of the III Corps at Nuremberg and assisted in organizing Freikorps units in northern Bavaria. He was a right-wing German nationalist then and remained so until the day he died.[4]

Captain Kesselring considered leaving the army in the early 1920s, but found his prospects none too good in the disrupted civilian economy. He was selected for the 100,000-man Reichsheer and assigned to the 7th Bavarian Artillery Regiment. From 1919 to October, 1922, he commanded a succession of artillery batteries at Amberg, Erlangen, and Nuremberg. After finishing his initial command duty, Kesselring was promoted to major and assigned to the Truppenamt. He worked in the T-4 (Training) Department, where he was involved in the secret training of airmen in the Soviet Union. Later he was with the T-2 (Operations) Department, before being transferred to the staff of Wehrkreis VII (Military District VII) at Munich in 1929.[5]

During his General Staff tour, Kesselring increased his already good reputation as an organizer and a diplomat. He had a certain charm and developed an ability to get his own way. He had set a firm foundation for his career and advanced rapidly thereafter. He was promoted to lieutenant colonel on February 1, 1930, and assigned to the Army Personnel Office three months later.[6] For a time he was Reichswehr commissioner for retrenchment and simplification, a job which involved cutting down the armed forces' bureaucracy and eliminating unnecessary paperwork—a responsibility which Kesselring seems to have thoroughly enjoyed.[7] Then, on February 1, 1932, he received a prize appointment: commander of the 4th Artillery Regiment at Dresden. He was promoted to full colonel later that year. Then, in 1933, Hitler came to power and Kesselring's career took a radical turn. He was transferred, somewhat against his will, to the embryonic and still-secret Luftwaffe in October 1933. Here he was responsible for budgeting, housing, construction, food, and clothing. Since the Luftwaffe had few bases and troop barracks and was expanding rapidly, his was an extremely important assignment, which he carried out with remarkable efficiency. He also underwent pilot training during this period, and he also became an admirer of Adolf Hitler and the Nazi regime. He was promoted to major general on October 1, 1934, and lieutenant general on April 1, 1936. On June 9, 1936, he was named chief of the General Staff of the Luftwaffe, replacing General Wever.[8]

Kesselring played a major role in the construction of the Luftwaffe ground establishment and in the creation of the parachute corps during his one-year tenure as chief of the General Staff. He later gained a reputation as a military genius for his conduct of ground operations in Italy in 1943 and

1944. Kesselring, however, was much less farsighted than his predecessor and, in early 1937, he recommended that the development of the four-engine bomber be halted because the airplane was very costly in raw materials, especially critical metals.[9] Also, the fuel requirements were high for oil-poor Germany. Each machine would require an average of six tons of fuel per air operation.[10] Unfortunately for the Luftwaffe, this recommendation was acted upon.

While Kesselring must bear much of the blame for cancelling the "Ural Bomber" program, State Secretary Milch must also share the responsibility. When Col. Paul Deichmann, then chief of Branch I (Operations) of the Luftwaffe General Staff, heard of the proposed cancellation of the four-engine bomber, he at once asked for an appointment with Goering to try to talk him into reversing himself. Milch, however, quickly denounced Deichmann's far-sighted arguments as "pure fantasy." With available resources, Milch said, the Luftwaffe could produce about 1,000 four-engine bombers, or several thousand two-engine bombers instead. Goering remarked that the Fuehrer asked him *how many* bombers he had, not *what type* he had, and accepted Milch's arguments.[11] Col. Kurt Pflugbeil, the inspector of bomber forces, also pleaded for the four-engine bomber, but was also turned down. "And Milch personally ensured that Dornier's and Junkers' prototypes were consigned to the scrap-heap," Bekker charged later.[12] As a result, Germany had no suitable strategic bombers with which to attack the Soviet Union's factories in World War II, nor with which to support the U-boats in the North Atlantic, or to conduct long-range attacks against Allied naval convoys bound for Britain or the Soviet Union. Meanwhile the Anglo-Americans devastated Germany's urban areas—with four-engine bombers.

Ironically enough, Goering's order to halt all work on the four-engine bomber was issued on April 29, 1937. A Technical Office report dated April 26 (and reflecting aircraft status as of March 15) listed both the Ju-89 and Do-19 as "SV"—ready for testing.[13] The prototypes of both models were scrapped.

In addition to the loss of four-engine bombers, Wever's death also led to a dangerous command fragmentation that would hamper the Luftwaffe for the rest of its existence. The direct causes of this fragmentation were the personalities of Hermann Goering and Erhard Milch.

Hermann Goering, the commander-in-chief of the Luftwaffe, was fully acceptable to the senior air force officers for a number of reasons. Because he was a holder of the *Pour le Merite* and the last commander of the 1st Fighter Wing "Richthofen," he was looked upon as a comrade as well as a superior.

He was optimistic, humorous, and generally respected by his men. Not blood-thirsty by nature, he did not want a war—and certainly not before the Luft-waffe was fully prepared for it. Also, he made no attempt to involve himself in the day-to-day activities of the Luftwaffe, and—until 1940—he was the man closest to Adolf Hitler: a fact that was of immeasurable use to the German Air Force. His main role in the Luftwaffe's expansion was in the procurement of funds. When the minister of finance turned down a request for money, Wever and his successors would simply turn the matter over to Goering, who would go directly to the Fuehrer.

"Here it is!" Goering would exclaim later, when he returned with the approved appropriation. "The Fuehrer is surprised that we're so modest. He expected us to ask for a lot more. Incidentally, once and for all, money is no object. Remember that!"[14] He would then turn on his heel and leave. It would be hard for anyone *not* to like a boss like that.

After 1934, Goering's energy diminished greatly. His wife had died of cancer in 1931. Lonely for some time, Hermann met and fell in love with Emmy Sonnemann, a generous, big-hearted, natural blonde, who was an actress with the Weimar National Theater. They were married on April 10, 1935. Emmy was as unlike the first Frau Goering as can be imagined. Where Karin had pushed Hermann to work harder for the Fuehrer, Emmy encour-aged his natural tendencies to laziness and luxurious living. Whereas Karin was a rabid Nazi, Emmy was definitely not. One gets the impression that she did not take Hitler and his crowd very seriously. She consistently refused to disassociate herself from her Jewish friends. Every time Goering returned home after another wave of Jewish persecution shook Germany, Emmy would meet him at the door with a list of Jews she wanted Hermann to help. Shak-ing his head, Goering would present the list to his adjutant, knowing full well that the news of his "influence" would reach Hitler's ears via Gestapo Chief Heinrich Himmler and others.[15]

In the meantime, Goering constructed his own palace, named "Karin-hall" in honor of his first wife, on a 100,000-acre private estate he acquired for himself in East Prussia. Life was now thoroughly enjoyable for Hermann Goering. He ballooned to about 300 pounds, gorging himself on his favorite dish (blinis with caviar, smothered with whipped cream), chased down with champagne or expensive wine. These gastronomic orgies were usually fol-lowed by a fit of dieting and exercise, the positive results of which were almost immediately negated by a midnight raid on his well-stocked refriger-ator. To make matters worse, he went back on drugs. This time it was para-codeine, a mild morphine narcotic. By the end of 1937, he was taking up to ten pills a day.[16] With his many posts, his indulgent wife, his natural love of luxury, and his drug habit, Goering had little time for the Luftwaffe.

Milch, of course, knew all of this. Like Goering, Milch loved both luxury and power. His advancement had been rapid. Commissioned colonel in the Reichswehr in 1933, he was promoted to major general on March 24, 1934, lieutenant general on March 28, 1935, and general of flyers on April 20, 1936. Meanwhile, he carefully cultivated Adolf Hitler. The chancellor had even personally conferred the Golden Party Badge on the half-Jewish Milch in a special cabinet meeting—a rare, special sign of favor. Meanwhile, Goering's spies in the RLM informed him that Milch privately referred to himself as the minister of aviation—implying that Goering was merely a figurehead whom Milch would someday replace. The fact that Milch was regarded as the future minister by Defense Minister Blomberg, SS Chief Heinrich Himmler, Nazi party chief Rudolf Hess, and others did nothing to mitigate Goering's suspicions.[17]

Nothing came of the behind-the-scenes plotting as long as Walter Wever was alive. The dynamic chief of the General Staff of the Luftwaffe had kept friction at a minimum, skillfully placating both Milch and Goering and still getting his own way. This happy situation changed radically with his death, when Goering appointed Lt. Gen. Albert Kesselring to the vacant post.

Although undoubtedly capable as an administrator and as a tactician, Kesselring lacked the strategic genius of Walter Wever. He also lacked Wever's ability (and inclination) to deal with the ambitious Milch. He and the deputy C-in-C of the Luftwaffe clashed almost immediately. Milch demanded that Maj. Hans Jeschonnek, the commander of the III Training Group at Greifswald, be court-martialled because of the high number of flying accidents taking place there. Kesselring steadfastly refused. Furthermore, Kesselring joined the growing list of General Staff officers who demanded Milch be restricted exclusively to civil aviation. At one point, Kesselring even accused Milch of high treason for divulging too much information about the Luftwaffe's strength to the British during a trip he took to England.[18]

For his part, Milch could never understand the generals' attitude toward him. He, after all, held the same rank as they did—if not higher—and he understood the complex areas of aircraft production and business negotiations, which they at first did not. He took his title literally and considered himself Goering's deputy in all matters, including those involving the General Staff. He also had a talent for manipulation and internal political intrigue, which he used against his enemies to the maximum extent possible.

The generals' attitudes are easy to understand. Milch was younger than most of the other air force generals who had been transferred from the army by Blomberg. He also lacked their command experience and General Staff training. True enough he had the initial advantage of vastly superior technical aviation knowledge, but the bright newcomers applied themselves to their new field and were gradually closing the technical gap between themselves and Milch. They looked down on the state secretary, whom they considered a civilian who owed his appointment to political considerations. Goering, of course, was also a civilian, but they accepted him, because he held the keys to promotions and never tried to run the Luftwaffe on a day-to-day basis, as Milch did. Whispers about Milch's Jewish ancestry could also be heard in the halls of the ministry. Milch responded by filling ministerial appointments with his own people, insofar as that was possible. Insecure and sensitive, he surrounded himself with yes-men. Worse than that, he refused to cooperate with the chief of the General Staff, whoever that might be.

Goering—no professional officer himself—feared both sides in the power struggle (i.e., both Milch and the General Staff). He had only briefly commanded an air wing eighteen years before, and the Luftwaffe was full of men who were technologically and professionally better qualified than he. He should have stepped in and settled the dispute between Milch and the General Staff, but instead he encouraged it—a prime example of divide and rule. With Milch and the General Staff at each others' throats, neither could threaten Goering, who realized that he was technologically inferior to either faction. Hermann thus protected his own position, even though he did irreparable damage to the Luftwaffe in the process.

Kesselring soon tired of the constant bickering and backbiting and resigned as chief of staff in 1937. He was given a promotion and a territorial command (Luftkreis III at Dresden) and was succeeded for one year by Gen. Hans-Juergen Stumpff, the chief of the Personnel Office. Stumpff never wanted the post and indeed was not the first choice. The appointment had been offered to two army officers—Lt. Gen. Franz Halder and Col. Alfred Jodl—but both declined because they did not want to work with (or against) Milch.[19]

In early 1937, Goering announced the reorganization of the Air Ministry into military and civilian branches. The General Staff was to be in charge of the High Command of the Luftwaffe (*Oberkommando der Luftwaffe*, or OKL), but Milch retained control of the General Air Office, the Central Branch, and the inspectorates, and would simultaneously be inspector general of the Luftwaffe. This organizational setup was obviously unworkable and Milch said so. "You are ruining the Luftwaffe this way," he warned Goering. "Somebody has to be in charge of everything. If I don't do it, then you will have to . . . but you won't!"[20] Milch submitted his resignation, but Goering refused to accept it. "Look here, Milch," he said, "I'm not demoting you because you failed, but because you've succeeded *too* well. The Party keeps telling me that it's Milch who does all the work. And . . . I won't stand for that!"[21] At a time when revolutionary developments were being made in the fields of aircraft design, radar, jet engines, and rocket propulsion, the leading men of the Luftwaffe were preoccupied with jealousy, power struggles, and petty personnel disputes. The division of authority and the internal strife continued until 1944.

The Luftwaffe's internal situation deteriorated even further in 1937 and 1938, when Goering removed three offices from Air Ministry and General Staff control and placed them directly under the minister (i.e., Goering himself). These were the Personnel Office (under Gen. Ritter Robert von Greim), the Office of the Chief of Air Defense (Gen. Otto Guenther Ruedel), and the Technical Office (Maj. Gen. Ernst Udet). Since Goering had no interest in their daily operations, these changes in effect made these offices independent of any control or outside supervision. It was tantamount to total command fragmentation and paralysis of many important functions. Before June, 1936, there was only one center of power in the Luftwaffe and that was Milch. After this date there were two (Milch and Kesselring, followed by Stumpff). By January 1938, there were five: Milch, Stumpff, Udet, Greim, and Ruedel. In the cases of Greim and Ruedel, it mattered little. Greim was a capable personnel officer and Ruedel, the former inspector of antiaircraft artillery, needed no supervision in the Air Defense Office.[22] The Technical Office, however, was another matter entirely.

In June 1936, Goering had replaced the competent Gen. Wilhelm Wimmer (whom he disliked) with Colonel Udet, his old friend from the Richthofen wing. He made Udet's office independent of Milch and Stumpff in 1937 and expanded it into the Office of Supply and Procurement in 1938.[23]

Ernst Udet was a military adventurer and the leading German ace to survive World War I. Born in Frankfurt-am-Main on April 26, 1896, he attended school in Munich before joining the 26th Infantry Division as a motorcycle dispatch rider. Young Udet was a war volunteer, rather than a soldier, so he managed to secure a discharge in the fall of 1914. He immediately reported to an aviation replacement unit but was not accepted for pilot's training because he was too young. He was not to be blocked, however. His father, Adolf Udet, paid 2,000 marks to Gustav Otto, the owner of the Otto Works in Munich, so that young Ernst could take his private pilot's training. He rejoined the service as an enlisted pilot with the 9th Reserve Flying Detachment on June 15, 1915, and was soon sent to the western front with the 206th Artillery Flying Detachment. He was promoted to lance corporal (*Gefreiten*) on September 21, 1915.[24]

Initially Udet flew for an artillery observer and was awarded the Iron Cross, 2d Class, for bravery in the Vosges sector. Later he spent seven days in the stockade for losing an aircraft due to his own carelessness. Nevertheless he was promoted to sergeant (*Unterofzzier*) and was transferred to the 68th Field Flying Detachment in Flanders as a fighter pilot in late 1915.[25]

Udet wrote his memoirs, *Mein Fliegerleben*, in 1934. In many ways it was very frank.[26] He tells, for example, how he froze in his first aerial combat and was almost shot down as a result. He soon managed to master his fear, however, and shot down his first airplane, a French Farman, on March 18, 1916.

After his first victory, Udet was assigned to the 15th Fighter Squadron. He did not score his second kill until October 12, and did not become an ace (i.e., did not register his fifth kill) until April 24, 1917. Meanwhile, he was commissioned second lieutenant of reserves on January 22, 1917. On August 5, 1917, Udet was named commander of the 37th Fighter Squadron. Here he came into his own. On February 18, 1918, he scored his twentieth victory when he shot down a Sopwith Camel near Zandvoorde. After that victory Capt. Manfred von Richthofen offered him command of the 11th Fighter Squadron, part of his famous 1st Fighter Wing. He led this unit for the rest of the war, scoring forty-two more victories and winning the *Pour le Merite* in the process.[27] When the Red Baron was killed in action on April 21, 1918, he was succeeded by Capt. Wilhelm Reinhardt, who was killed in a flying accident soon after. Most people expected Reinhardt to be replaced by Ernst Udet; everyone (including Udet) was surprised when Capt. Hermann Goering was given the prestigious command instead. Initially suspicious of Goering, Udet and he soon became fast friends.

After the armistice, Udet smashed his airplane and returned to Munich, where he worked for Gustav Otto as an automobile mechanic. On Sundays he worked for a POW relief organization by putting on exhibition dogfights against Ritter Robert von Greim, until Greim flew into a high-power line. The knight survived the crash, but his Fokker was a write-off and a replacement could no longer be obtained. Then Udet went to work as a pilot for the Rumpler Works, which had instituted air service between Vienna and Munich.[28]

Udet was dissatisfied with civilian life in the Weimar Republic. When members of the Allied Control Commission confiscated his airplane, Udet worked in the construction of sports aircraft until 1925, when he moved to Buenos Aires as a stunt pilot and sports flyer. This was followed by a trip to East Africa, a barnstorming tour of the United States, and a hunting trip to the Arctic. He returned to Germany about the time Hitler came to power.

Nothing in Udet's background or training qualified him for higher-level General Staff assignments. He also lacked the patience, maturity, toughness, and self-discipline necessary for such a post. He did not even want to join the Luftwaffe, but old comrade Goering insisted. He was inducted into the air force as colonel on special assignment on June 1, 1935. His promotion was rapid. He was successively named major general (April 20, 1937), lieutenant general (November 1, 1938), general of flyers (April 1, 1940), and colonel general (July 19, 1940).[29]

Udet's first major assignment came on February 10, 1936, when he succeeded his friend and stunt-flying partner, Ritter von Greim, as inspector of fighters and dive-bombers. Only four months later, on June 9, 1936, he succeeded Wimmer as chief of the Technical Office, which became the Office of Supply and Procurement in 1938. This bureau was responsible for aircraft and weapons development, procurement, and supply for the Luftwaffe. Udet converted it into a hopelessly bureaucratic organization, in which Udet himself tried to direct twenty-six separate departments in between wild parties, drunken sprees, drug abuse, and womanizing. Udet smoked to excess, drank far too much, periodically ate only meat, and took drugs—especially ones with depressing side effects. Department heads were not able to see their boss for weeks at a time, and critical decisions were made by default.[30] The entire office became a hotbed of in-fighting and political intrigue. As a result, Germany's technological advantage in aviation stagnated and was eventually overtaken by the Allies. The "second generation" of German aircraft, including the Me-109 fighter, the He-111 bomber, and others, had been developed under the guidance of Milch and began coming off the assembly lines in 1936. The next generation of German aircraft never fully developed, due to Udet's mismanagement. The Luftwaffe's loss of the Battle of Britain in 1940 was a direct result of this technological failure, but more about this later.

The Luftwaffe was reorganized again in early 1939, causing even more harm to the air force. The High Command of the Luftwaffe (OKL), which was headed by the chief of the General Staff (Stumpff and, later, Jeschonnek), was separated from RLM, but not entirely. The chief of the General Staff was made solely responsible to Goering, although he had to inform Milch about operational matters. All departments of the General Staff not directly concerned with operations were to be absorbed by RLM. The chief lost control of communications and partial control of training. Two new organizations were created: the Office of Signal Communications (Maj. Gen. Wolfgang Martini) and the Office of Training (Lt. Gen. Bernard Kuehl), which controlled no fewer than fourteen inspectorates. The chief of personnel (Greim) was directly responsible to Goering for officer appointments, but in all other matters was subordinate to Milch. The Office of Air Defense was once again placed under the state secretary. In addition, Milch retained the post of inspector general of the Luftwaffe, which enabled him to inspect units in the field and meddle in the affairs of the General Staff. The Office of Supply and Procurement (Udet) remained independent of both the General Staff and Milch.

Map 1: Europe, 1939

Hans-Juergen Stumpff was a stopgap appointment as chief of the General Staff. A congenial Pomeranian and a veteran General Staff officer, he was a good administrator but was unsuited for the post of chief, and he knew it. He had enjoyed being personnel director but did not like being in the middle of the battle of intrigue for control of the Luftwaffe. He tried to straighten out the organizational mess but failed. He was relieved when he was succeeded by Hans Jeschonnek, the former chief of operations of OKL. Stumpff took over the Office of Air Defense—ironically enough under Milch. Meanwhile, Jeschonnek became the fourth chief of the General Staff in four years.

Jeschonnek was born on April 9, 1899, in Hohensalza, East Prussia (now Inowroclaw, Poland), the son of an assistant secondary schoolmaster. His oldest brother, Paul, had been one of the rising stars of the secret aviation arm of the Reichswehr until he was killed in an air accident at Rechlin in 1929. Hans' own youngest son, Gert, served in the German Navy in World War II and later held several important posts in the West German Navy.

At the age of fifteen and one-half, Hans Jeschonnek volunteered for service in World War I. He attended the elite cadet school at Gross-Lichterfelde, received his commission, underwent pilot training, and joined the 40th Fighter Squadron in 1917. He scored two aerial victories prior to the armistice. In 1919 he took part in the fighting against the Poles in Upper Silesia as a member of the 6th Cavalry Regiment. After this he joined the Reichsheer. In 1923 he was assigned to the Army Ordnance Department as a member of the staff of Capt. Kurt Student in the Inspectorate of Arms and Equipment, one of the camouflaged air branches of the Reichswehr. In this office he studied aircraft development in neighboring countries, including Sweden, the Netherlands, and Switzerland. After that he underwent clandestine General Staff training and graduated at the head of his class in 1928.

Lieutenant Jeschonnek was assigned to Inspectorate 1 of the Reichswehr Ministry in April, 1928. Actually he worked for Lt. Col. Hellmuth Felmy in the inspectorate for the clandestine air units. On January 30, 1933, he was named adjutant to his friend, Erhard Milch, the state secretary for the Reich Commissariat of Aviation. Next he did a tour of troop duty and was in the 152nd Bomber Wing in March 1934, when he was promoted to captain.

Hans Jeschonnek was an extremely bright young officer and a thorough professional who impressed all who came into contact with him with his military bearing. After 1934 he was promoted rapidly—in fact, far too rapidly. It had taken him seventeen years to advance from second lieutenant to captain. In the next eight years he would be promoted to colonel general—the second-highest rank in the service (excluding the rank of Reichsmarschall, which Hitler created for Hermann Goering in 1940 and which was held only by him). Jeschonnek was successively promoted to major (1935), lieutenant colonel (1937), colonel (1938), major general (1939), general of flyers (1940), and colonel general (1942). The grade of lieutenant general he skipped entirely.

Meanwhile, Jeschonnek made a deadly foe. Shortly after he assumed command of the III Training Group of Air Administrative Area I, which was stationed at Greifswald, Erhard Milch tried to have him court-martialled. Why the two fell out is not known. Once good friends, they were now bitter enemies. Jeschonnek, however, was protected by Kesselring, who virtually told Milch to mind his own business. As we have seen, there was no love lost between those two, either.

Jeschonnek was assigned to General Staff duties in 1937 and was named chief of the operations staff of the OKL in 1938. He became chief of the General Staff on February 1, 1939. His appointment came as a surprise to many. It is true that Wever looked upon him as a potential successor, but then Wever had not planned on dying so suddenly.

Did Hermann Goering appoint Jeschonnek to this post because of his known antipathy for Erhard Milch? We will never know for sure, but it was almost certainly a factor. Stumpff had tried to work with Milch, but it was certain Jeschonnek would not. Another factor was that Goering believed he could work more easily with young men than with older officers, many of whom were his seniors and who had definite views on matters of high command, were not prone to compromise, and felt they owed little or nothing to Hermann Goering. Goering felt threatened by strong-willed officers such as Kesselring, Greim, Richthofen, and, of course, General Milch.

Hans Jeschonnek's position was difficult from the beginning. He found it hard to force his views on generals so senior to him in age, rank, and experience. He often felt it necessary to make concessions, especially when dealing with Kesselring, Sperrle, and Baron von Richthofen. Jeschonnek also lacked the gift of winning the cheerful and enthusiastic support of his subordinates, with whom he tended to be too reserved or sarcastic. "Despite his keen intellect," Suchenwirth wrote, "Jeschonnek . . . lacked an understanding of human nature, the cardinal attribute of a leader."[31]

As if all of this were not enough, Jeschonnek also had difficulties in dealing with Goering's "inner circle." This group included Gen. Bruno Loerzer; Paul "Pilli" Koerner, the state secretary for the Four Year Plan; Gen. Karl Bodenschatz, the chief of the Ministerial Office and Goering's liaison officer to Fuehrer Headquarters; Alfred Keller, the commander of Luftkreis IV; and Col. Bernd von Brauchitsch and Lt. Col. Werner Teske, Goering's adjutants. None of these men liked either Milch or Jeschonnek, whom they looked upon as rivals for power. This group formed a sort of collateral High Command and was sarcastically referred to as the "Little General Staff." Their power was very real, however, because Goering took their advice all too often. Frequently Goering would go to his hunting lodge in Rominten, or to Karinhall, or to his castle at Veldenstein in Upper Franconia, and would issue orders to the various commands through his adjutants, bypassing Jeschonnek completely. This situation frustrated and confused the young chief of the General Staff. And no wonder! It would be difficult to design a command arrangement more disunified and fragmented than that of the Luftwaffe. It was, in reality, virtually leaderless, and would remain so for the rest of its existence.

As if the lack of clear leadership were not enough, the Luftwaffe's production program got completely out of hand after the Sudetenland crisis of September, 1938. Hitler brought Europe to the brink of war that month, before the Allies backed down at the last moment, signed the Munich accords, and abandoned Czechoslovakia to the mercies of Nazi Germany. However, during this crisis, Hitler, for the first time, saw that he might eventually have to fight Great Britain, whether he wanted to or not. He asked Goering what the Luftwaffe's chances were of winning an air war against England. Goering turned the problem over to General Felmy, the commander of Luftwaffe Group 2 (later 2nd Air Fleet).

Hellmuth Felmy, who was born in Berlin on May 28, 1885, was a veteran of thirty-four years' service. He joined the Imperial Army as a *Fahnenjunker* in the 61st Infantry Regiment in 1904. Commissioned second lieutenant in 1905, he went to flight school in 1912 and underwent General Staff training at the War Academy in Berlin the following year. During World War I he commanded air squadrons at the front and was engaged in setting up colonial air units. During the Reichswehr era (1919–32) he alternated between infantry and aviation assignments and was deeply involved in the secret air force. He was commander of the 17th Infantry Regiment when he transferred to the Luftwaffe in 1933. In the air force he had been commander of the aviation schools in the Berlin area (1933–35), the senior air commander, Munich (1935–36), and commander of Luftkreis VII (1936–38). After slow promotions in his early career (typical of a small army), he advanced rapidly in the 1930s. He was promoted to first lieutenant (1913), captain (1914), major (1931), lieutenant colonel (1933), colonel (1936), major general (1937), lieutenant general (February 1, 1938), and general of flyers three days later.[32] Regarded as a solid General Staff and commanding officer, Felmy could be counted on to give Goering the correct answer—not necessarily the one he wanted to hear.

Felmy set up a special staff under his personal direction and thoroughly analyzed the problem. His investigations ended with a three-day "war game," which resembled a modern-day CPX (command post exercise). After completing his staff study, Felmy reported back to Goering on September 22. His long memorandum concluded that "with our present available resources . . . a war of annihilation against England appears to be out of the question."[33] Three weeks later, on October 14, 1938, Hitler ordered a major armaments program to deal with the possibility of a two-front war. The Luftwaffe was given priority under this program and was ordered to expand 500 percent.

The Luftwaffe General Staff studied the program and estimated that, in practice, this meant the production of 45,700 airplanes by the spring of 1942. The program (later dubbed the "Hitler Program") would cost an estimated sixty billion reichsmarks—about equal to the total amount spent on rearmament by all of the military branches between 1933 and 1939. Clearly it was impossible. Udet was among those who opposed it, stating that the mere fueling of the more than one hundred aircraft wings the program would create would require Germany to import about 85 percent of the world's current output of aviation fuel. Joseph Kammhuber, the chief of the Organizations Branch of RLM, came up with an alternative plan, which cut the Fuehrer's requirements by two-thirds.[34]

Lieutenant Colonel Kammhuber was one of the brightest young General Staff officers Defense Minister Werner von Blomberg had transferred to the Luftwaffe in 1933. A native of Burgkirchen, Upper Bavaria, he had entered the service as a private upon the outbreak of World War I and spent four years in Bavarian infantry units. Promoted to second lieutenant in 1917, he was selected for the Reichsheer, trained for the secret General Staff in Stettin and Berlin between 1926 and 1929, and did his pilot's training at the secret German air base in Russia in 1930. He served on the operations staff of the clandestine General Staff until 1933, when he joined the Organizations Department of RLM. After a year's troop duty as commander of a night fighter group, he had returned to the Air Ministry as chief of the Organizations Branch in 1937. After the war he became the commander of the West German Air Force.[35]

Summoned by State Secretary Milch on November 28, the RLM heads met, without Goering. One by one they declared even the Kammhuber Program unworkable. Stumpff, then still chief of the General Staff, suggested that it be adopted as an interim target. Milch suggested that he and Kammhuber go to Goering and put the idea to him. Colonel Jeschonnek, then chief of operations of the General Staff, objected to this. "In my view it is not our duty to betray the Fuehrer's ideas like this!" he snapped. For some reason, Milch then replied: "All right, Jeschonnek, you come along with me to the Field Marshal!" This was a terrible mistake on Milch's part. Goering, as always anxious not to disagree with Hitler, sided with Jeschonnek. Milch returned to RLM and announced that, even if Hitler's program could not be carried out, every department chief would have to do his utmost to see that as much of it as possible was achieved. Kammhuber demanded to know where the resources were to come from. He received no answer. "Thereafter," he remarked later, "the Luftwaffe drifted."[36]

Seeing disaster on the horizon, a disgusted and angry Joseph Kammhuber applied for transfer and was sent to Braunschweig as chief of staff of the 2nd Air Fleet. It was left to the incompetent Udet to try to carry out a program which even he knew was impossible.

CHAPTER 3

Spain: The First Battle

The Luftwaffe's first campaign dates from July 17, 1936—just three weeks after the death of General Wever. On that date Jose Sanjurjo, Francisco Franco, and other dissatisfied Spanish generals launched a coup against the Spanish government in Madrid. The success of the coup was mixed. The Army of Africa in Spanish Morocco went over to Franco, and soon the Nationalists had overrun the entire colony. However, the attempted takeover failed in Madrid, Barcelona, and most of the coastal cities, where the rebel forces were massacred. Then Gen. Jose Sanjurjo was killed in a plane crash, leaving Franco in charge of the entire rebellion.

General Franco, then forty-four, was the extremely tough former commander of the Spanish foreign legion. Once he had personally shot and killed a legionnaire for mocking his high-pitched voice. Franco now faced a serious problem. He had planned on ferrying his troops across the Strait of Gibraltar via Spanish naval ships, but the sailors remained loyal to the Republic. They rebelled, killed their officers, and left Franco isolated in Morocco. The Spanish air force also remained loyal to Madrid. Although they held a large part of northern Spain, the rebel footholds in southern Spain were soon reduced to enclaves around Seville, Granada, and Cadiz[1] (see Map 2). Unless Franco could get his main combat troops to the mainland, the surviving rebel forces would soon be wiped out and the rebellion doomed. The pro-Fascist Franco had no choice but to seek outside aid. He sent delegations to Rome and Berlin, to appeal to Benito Mussolini and Adolf Hitler for help.[2]

Hitler received Franco's delegation on July 25 at Bayreuth, where he was attending the Wagner festival. Goering, Milch, and Adm. Wilhelm Canaris, the chief of military intelligence, all favored intervention. Without bothering to consult the Foreign Ministry (then headed by Baron Konstantin von Neurath), Hitler promised to send aid. The next day twenty Ju-52 transports took off for Seville and Tetuan, Spanish Morocco. During the next month they conducted the first military airlift in history. Meanwhile, on the evening of July 25, Special Staff W (*Sonderstab W*) was set up in Berlin under Lt. Gen. Helmut Wilberg to supervise the German military aid mission to Spain, while Lt. Col. Walter Warlimont was soon dispatched to Franco's headquarters to take charge of all German military and economic involvement in Spain. By the end of the month six He-51 fighters and twenty 20mm antiaircraft guns had been dispatched by sea from Hamburg.[3] As summer turned into fall, German military involvement escalated. In August, army major Ritter Wilhelm von Thoma, who later commanded the Afrika Korps at El Alamein, arrived in Spain to train Nationalist troops. Later that year he assumed command of the German panzer forces in Spain, which eventually totalled four tank companies. These, however, were never part of the Condor Legion.[4]

Franco's Nationalists were unable to win a quick victory over the Republicans (or Loyalists), and soon French and Soviet air units were flying in support of the government. The Soviet military aid was massive and included a large number of excellent tanks. The Fuehrer viewed the Russian involvement as a threat to the peace of Europe, so in late October he decided to activate the Condor Legion. It was set up to direct all German air and antiaircraft forces in Spain. The units of the legion, which eventually totalled 4,500 men, assembled at Stettin and Swinemuende and sailed through the Baltic Sea and the English Channel to Seville. The pilots and air crews flew thirty-three aircraft from Germany to Rome to Sardinia and joined the ground crews, communications troops, and previously transported aviation forces in Spain. They suffered no losses en route.

The first commander of the Condor Legion was a big, ugly, heavy-jowled bear of a man named Hugo Sperrle. The son of a brewer, he was born in Ludwigsburg, Wuerttemburg, on February 2, 1885. He joined the 8th Wuerttemburg Infantry Regiment as a *Fahnenjunker* in 1903 and remained with his unit for years. He became a second lieutenant about a year after joining the 8th, was promoted to first lieutenant in 1913, and became a captain in late 1914. He was training as an artillery spotter when World War I broke out.

Sperrle did not distinguish himself in the Great War to the degree that Goering, Udet, and Loerzer did, but he still compiled a solid record in that conflict, where he specialized in aerial reconnaissance. He first served as an aerial observer with the 4th Field Flying Detachment (*Feldfliegerabteilung*). Later he underwent pilots' training and led the 42d and 60th Field Flying Detachments and the 13th Field Flying Group, before assuming command of the Air Observers' School at Cologne. When the war ended he was officer-in-charge of all flying units attached to the seventh Army on the western front. After the kaiser fell, Sperrle promptly joined the Luettwitz Freikorps and commanded its aviation detachment. In 1919 he was named one of the 180 former aviators in the 4,000-man officer corps of the Reichsheer.

Back in the infantry, Captain Sperrle served on the staff of Wehrkreis V (Military District V) at Stuttgart (1919–23), in the Defense Ministry (1923–24),

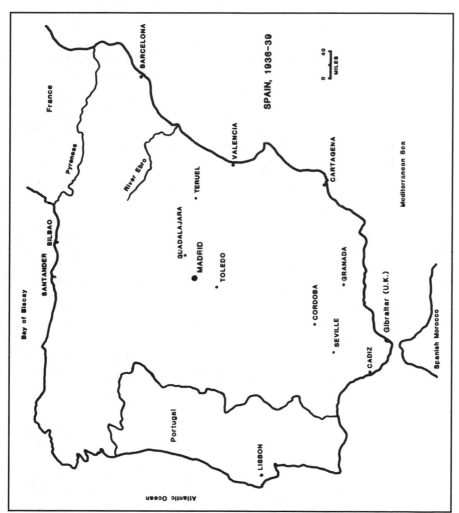

Map 2: Spain, 1936–39

and with the 4th Infantry Division at Dresden (1924–25). He maintained his interest in aviation and underwent secret advanced flight training at the clandestine German base at Lipetz, Russia, in 1928. He also made at least two trips to England to observe Royal Air Force displays.

Sperrle's career as a ground officer continued to make steady if unspectacular progress. He served on the General Staff in the Reichswehr Ministry (1925–29), was promoted to major (1926) and lieutenant colonel (1931), and spent four years as commander of III Battalion, 14th Infantry Regiment (1929–33). From October 1, 1933, until the unofficial end of his army career, the bear-like Sperrle was commander of the 8th Infantry Regiment.[5]

Sperrle resumed his aviation career on April 1, 1934, when, as a full colonel, he was placed in charge of the 1st Air Division of the still-secret German air force. He also held the office of commander of army aviation. His territorial responsibilities included the city of Berlin.[6] Sperrle was thus well placed to assume a prominent role in the emergence of the Luftwaffe when Hitler decided it was time to openly defy the Allies and denounce that section of the Treaty of Versailles which prohibited Germany from having an air force.

In March, 1935, Hitler announced the existence of the Luftwaffe to the world, and Sperrle was officially transferred to the Luftwaffe. Initially in charge of II Air District (Luftkreis II), his previous aviation experience gave him a tremendous advantage over most of his peers. On October 1, 1935, he was promoted to major general and named commander of Luftkreis V, headquartered at Munich.[7] He was already one of the leading figures of the air force when the Spanish civil war broke out.

Sperrle organized the Condor Legion into three air squadrons: one bomber, one fighter, and one naval air squadron, as well as two antiaircraft batteries (one heavy and one light). In January, 1937, an experimental bomber squadron was established to try out new aircraft. It was integrated into the legion in April, 1937. The Condor Legion grew to the size of a reinforced wing during the campaign, but it never exceeded 5,500 men.[8] Table 1 shows its composition and unit designations at the height of its strength.

Although assigned to support Republican ground units, Sperrle was responsible only to General Franco and thus held rank equivalent to an air theater commander. Both by necessity and design he did considerable experimenting with aircraft, formation organization, and combat tactics while commander of the legion. Most of the Luftwaffe tactics used in the Second World War were developed in Spain.

Despite the fact that Germany took elaborate measures to keep the existence of the legion secret, the strong-willed Sperrle flouted its presence in Spain. Of peasant stock, Sperrle nevertheless had a taste for luxury which

TABLE 1: ORGANIZATION OF THE CONDOR LEGION, 1938

Designation	Function/Composition
S/88	Operations Staff
K/88	Bomber Group (4 squadrons), plus a flight of dive-bombers
J/88	Fighter Group (4 squadrons)
A/88	Air Reconnaissance Squadron
AS/88	Naval Air Squadron
F/88	AntiAircraft Battalion
	1st Battery: 88mm AA guns
	2d Battery: 88mm AA guns
	3d Battery: 88mm AA guns
	4th Battery: 20mm AA guns*
	5th Battery: 20mm AA guns*
	6th Battery: 88mm AA guns**
	7th Battery: Ammo columns
	8th Battery: 88mm AA guns
	9th Battery: Training unit (for Spanish troops)
Ln/88	Luftwaffe Signal Communications Battalion
	1 telephone company
	1 radio company
	1 flight security company
	1 aircraft reporting company
P/88	Air Armaments Group (inc. an aircraft park)
San/88	Medical Battalion
W/88	One meteorological service battalion

*Included three 20mm AA gun platoons and a 37mm AA gun platoon
**Originally a searchlight battery
Source: Drum MS.

would finally prove to be his undoing in 1944. He set up his headquarters at Seville, confiscated the best hotel in the city for his own use, and flew the swastika flag over it. He repeated this procedure later, when he moved his HQ to Burgos. He also reserved the best brothels for his troops, who marched to them—much to the amusement of the Spanish prostitutes. The legionnaires' recreation time was very short, however, because the war heated up in October. The Soviet Union had shipped the Republicans forty-two Ilyushin 15 (Il-15) biplane fighters and thirty-one modern Il-16 monoplane fighters,[9] which were superior to anything the legion had. Sperrle, however, developed superior tactics, and the quality of his volunteer pilots was higher than that of the Republican pilots. Fairly typical was 1st Lieutenant Kalderak, who flew a He-46 reconnaissance plane. Quite without permission, he trained himself as a fighter pilot in his spare time. One day he took up a He-51 biplane fighter and shot down three French Brequet bombers in one minute. Bureaucrats in RLM tried to contest his victories on the grounds that he had no fighter license, but to no avail. Kalderak was killed in action shortly thereafter.[10]

The first major action of the Condor Legion took place at Toledo. Here, Nationalist General Varela had been surrounded since July 20, and by September his men had eaten their last mule and their perimeter was very small. Captains Henke and Baron Rudolf von Moreau of the legion nevertheless dropped critical supplies to the beleaguered garrison, despite heavy enemy fire. They repeated the performance six times and enabled the garrison to hold out until Franco could rescue it on September 27.[11]

Next, the legion turned its attention to the coastal ports, in an effort to stop the flow of arms to the Republicans. On November 15, Sperrle personally led a thirty-four-aircraft attack on the Red naval fleet at Cartagena. The fleet quickly put to sea to escape destruction, although two vessels were sunk by German bombs. The port city and harbor were engulfed in flames and were unusable for some time. No German casualties were suffered in this operation. The next evening, Sperrle attacked Madrid.[12]

Franco reached the suburbs of Madrid on November 7. The Republican government fled to Valencia, but their troops—reinforced by Soviet tanks, artillery, and the now famous International Brigades—rallied. Out-numbered 37,000 to 12,000,[13] Franco was checked, but he refused to give up the battle. Casualties were heavy on both sides as the Fascists tried to slug their way into the capital city. By December, 1936, the Nationalists were pinned down in extremely heavy fighting in the university quarter and other sections of Madrid. Sperrle was also having his problems. The Heinkel 51s—his main fighters—were proving inferior to the Communist aircraft, which were gradually establishing air superiority over the Spanish capital. Sperrle offset this dangerous situation with superior tactics. He ordered three German fighters to engage the enemy fighters until the Reds were low in fuel. As the Loyalist aircraft landed at their bases to refuel, Sperrle's bombers—which had been circling the battle at a higher altitude—dived on the Red bases. Several Republican squadrons were destroyed in this manner.[14] Nevertheless, superior tactics could not make up for inferior machines indefinitely. The Condor Legion did not succeed in overcoming the Red air forces until the Me-109 fighters arrived in Spain in 1937, and in December 1936, Sperrle had to tell

Franco that the Condor Legion would only support his forces in the Madrid area during the hours of darkness.[15]

Sperrle meanwhile determined that the Ju-52 was unsuitable as a bomber. One problem was its bombsight, which proved entirely unsatisfactory. In fact, the Luftwaffe never did develop a bombsight comparable to the American models and thus was never able to develop the pinpoint bombing accuracy the United States Air Force obtained during the Second World War.[16] The Ju-52 was eventually replaced as a bomber by the Ju-87 "Stuka" dive-bomber and the twin-engine He-111 bomber. The He-46 and He-70 "Blitz" were also scrapped as reconnaissance aircraft and replaced with the Dornier 17 (Do-17), which doubled as a long-range bomber. Sperrle was also disappointed with the performance of this airplane, which lacked protective armament and required too much maintenance time per hour of operation. It was replaced by the He-111 in early 1937.[17] The He-59 and He-60 seaplanes both proved too slow and vulnerable, so Sperrle used them mainly in night missions.[18]

The first chief of staff of the Condor Legion was Lt. Col. Alexander Holle, who later rose to the rank of colonel general and commanded the 4th Air Fleet on the eastern front in 1944. He apparently did not work well with the opinionated Sperrle, however, and was replaced in January, 1937, with an officer of great intelligence, courage, and arrogance. An extremely dominant personality, this officer was destined to play an extremely important role in the development of the strategic and tactical doctrines of the Luftwaffe. He won some of its greatest victories and, to a large degree, his influence was a major factor in its disastrous strategic defeat. His name was Baron Wolfram von Richthofen.

The younger cousin of the famous Red Baron of World War I, Wolfram was born in Barzdorf, Silesia, on October 10, 1895. After attending cadet school at Gross-Lichterfelde, he entered the Imperial Army on March 3, 1913, as an officer-cadet in the 4th Hussar Regiment. Richthofen was commissioned second lieutenant on June 19, 1914, and served with the cavalry until September 6, 1917, when he transferred to the flying corps. Richthofen's service up until this point was exclusively on the eastern front.

The younger Baron von Richthofen did his pilot's training with the 14th and 11th Reserve Air Detachments and was assigned to combat duty with the 1st Fighter Wing on March 27, 1918. His first commander was his famous cousin, who was killed less than a month after Wolfram arrived at the unit. His last commander was Hermann Goering.

During his short tour as a fighter pilot, Wolfram was credited with eight victories in aerial combat.[19] Although nowhere near the totals of his cousins

Manfred (eighty kills) and Lothar (forty victories),[20] it was still a respectable showing.

Defeat had less effect on Wolfram than it did on many of his contemporaries. He left the army on February 29, 1920, with the honorary (*charakteristik*) rank of first lieutenant and enrolled in the Hanover Technical School as an engineering student. He received his engineering diploma in 1924 and continued to do post-graduate work after reentering the service. He received his advanced degree in engineering from Hanover in 1929.[21]

Richthofen entered the Reichswehr on November 1, 1923, as a second lieutenant in the Prussian 11th Cavalry Regiment, then headquartered in Berlin. He received an adjusted date of rank of January 1, 1916, which enabled him to be promoted to first lieutenant (permanent rank) on April 1, 1925.[22] The following year he was permitted to fly again under the Paris Air Agreement. He took part in many civilian air competitions in the late 1920s and was, in fact, a member of both the secret German air force and the General Staff.

Lieutenant von Richthofen was officially posted four times in the three years between 1927 and 1929, probably to hide his aerial activities from the Allied high commissioners. He was officially assigned to the 13th Cavalry Regiment, the Wuerttemberg 5th Medical Company, the T-3 Section of the Reichswehr (Defense) Ministry, and the 5th Artillery Regiment. Finally, on April 1, 1929, only two months after his promotion to captain, he was officially given a "leave of absence" from active duty. Actually he never left the service. The leave was arranged to avoid overtly violating the Treaty of Versailles. In reality, Richthofen was attached to the Italian General Staff in Rome, where he became a close friend of Air Marshal Italo Balbo, a pioneer of Italian military aviation. Richthofen learned a great deal from this dynamic and capable aviator, who was destined to be shot down and killed over Tobruk in 1940, the victim of his own trigger-happy antiaircraft gunners.[23]

Richthofen learned more in Italy about the employment of large air units than it was possible to learn in Germany at that time. Upon his return to Germany in late 1932, the thirty-seven-year-old captain was assigned to the Prussian 6th Motorized Detachment so he could gain firsthand experience with the kind of mobile units he would one day be called upon to support.[24] It was his last assignment in the army. Hitler came to power on January 30, 1933, and Goering transferred Richthofen to the secret Luftwaffe as chief of the Development and Testing Branch.

Richthofen rose rapidly in the new air force. He was promoted to major on June 1, 1934, and to lieutenant colonel on April 1, 1936. His real rise to high command, however, can be dated to the outbreak of hostilities in Spain.

"The history of the Spanish Civil War," Gen. of Flyers Karl Drum later wrote, "is inseparable from the career of Freiherr [Baron] von Richthofen in Spain."[25] As chief of testing and development, Richthofen was naturally interested in the performance of the new German aircraft models in actual combat. He went to Spain himself in December, 1936, to supervise the employment of the new Me-109 fighters, the He-111 and Do-17 bombers, and the Hs-123 dive-bombers. Here he came into close contact with General Sperrle for the first time. They got along extremely well, and no one was particularly surprised when Richthofen replaced Holle as chief of staff of the Condor Legion in January, 1937.

With the departure of Richthofen, Udet lost his most competent assistant, a man whose absence would cost him dearly in the years ahead. Richthofen, however, now had his first opportunity to really distinguish himself, and he quickly took advantage of it. Not only was he extremely efficient, but he was also a very skillful diplomat and negotiator. He was already thoroughly conversant in Italian, and he quickly mastered Spanish as well. Not unnaturally, the Spanish Nationalist commanders were impressed by his efforts and the speed with which he learned their language, to the point where he was soon able to carry on technical military discussions in Spanish. Generalissimo Franco especially respected the capable Silesian pilot. "One can say without exaggerating that he was soon the acknowledged spokesman of the Condor Legion," wrote Drum. "At the same time, the relationship between General Sperrle and his chief of staff was an unusually cordial one. The two men complemented each other perfectly, and their excellent teamwork contributed a great deal to the position of respect which the Legion established for itself in Spain."[26]

As Sperrle's chief of staff, Richthofen came to appreciate the value of close air support for ground forces. He especially was impressed with the performance of the dive-bomber, which he had been extremely skeptical of as head of the Testing and Development Branch. On June 9, 1936, Richthofen had gone so far as submitting a memorandum calling for the discontinuance of the Stuka dive-bomber,[27] but his proposal had been rejected by Udet. Before the end of the Spanish civil war, Richthofen would become one of its strongest advocates.

In January 1937, Sperrle came up with a plan to capture Madrid and end the war. It called for a two-prong attack, with one wing cutting the Valencia highway, while the other severed the road to Barcelona. The Fascist assault forces would then link up southeast of the capital city, encircling the main Loyalist garrison, which would be pinned down by frontal attacks. Franco, who held Sperrle in high esteem, liked the idea and ordered it implemented.[28]

The plan was good, but its execution was poor, because the two wings did not attack at the same time. The Spanish managed to cut the Madrid-Valencia highway on February 13, but, when Franco's other wing did not attack on schedule, garrison commander General Miaja concentrated his reserves on the Valencia highway. By February 24 he had reopened the road, although it remained under Fascist artillery fire.

The second prong of the offensive was formed by the Italian Corpo Truppe Volontarie (C. T. V.), under the command of Italian general Mario Roatta. Roatta did not start until March 8. To further complicate matters, he did not reveal his plans to Sperrle and Richthofen until the last moment, thus hampering his own air support. On March 11, after making good progress, the vanguard of the four Italian divisions lost its head and was routed at Guadalajara by an inferior number of Republicans, who were well supported by Soviet tanks. Madrid was saved for the Loyalists, at least for the time being. Again checked, Franco turned his attention to northern Spain and the Basque country around Asturia.[29]

In the weeks that followed, the Condor Legion was used mainly in close air support operations for the Nationalists. Sperrle's men flew in support of the rebel drive on Bilbao, a city in northern Spain, which fell on June 19, after a long and bitter fight. The legion was then rushed back to Madrid, where a Red counteroffensive threatened to break the siege. This offensive was not completely halted until July 12; even then the Estremadura highway—the Nationalists' lifeline—was threatened. Franco responded by attacking again on July 25, in what became known as the Battle of Brunete. Well supported by the Condor Legion, including the flak batteries used in a ground support role, he routed the Loyalists' vanguards and destroyed the wedge aimed at the Estremadura highway. The closely packed defenders were slaughtered by Sperrle's bombers, which were well protected by the newly arrived Me-109 fighters. The Loyalists estimated their own losses at 30,000. General Drum considered Brunete the decisive battle of the civil war.[30]

The Nationalists had split the Loyalist forces in half in 1936 but had been unable to eliminate the northern pocket on the Bay of Biscay. Unable to take Madrid, Franco again turned his attention to this sector upon the strong recommendations of Sperrle and Richthofen. The tactical plan for the battle was drawn up by Baron von Richthofen. The offensive began in late March 1937.[31]

During this campaign, Sperrle introduced another innovation: the Fascist terror raid. On April 26 he attacked the Basque town of Guernica with He-111 and Ju-52 bombers, which dropped incendiary and high-explosive bombs, while He-51 fighters strafed the fleeing and unarmed civilian inhabitants, clearly in violation of international law. Some 1,654 civilians were killed and 889 were wounded.[32] "Guernica," Fletcher wrote later, ". . . has since become a synonym for Fascist brutality in Spain."[33]

Sperrle apparently never received so much as a mild reprimand for Guernica. Certainly the deaths of a few hundred Spanish civilians was of little concern to him. Besides, Franco could not repudiate his actions, even if he was so inclined, which is highly doubtful. In fact, for years after the war, it was a crime in Franco's Spain to say that Guernica was bombed by Nationalist forces. The generalissimo would not risk losing the Condor Legion, which he desperately needed for his autumn offensive on the northern front.

The mountainous terrain, with its deep valley, steep slopes, and poor road network, offered innumerable advantages for the defenders. The attackers were led by General Vigon, the commander of the Navarre Corps and a man of great determination. Closely supported by Sperrle and Richthofen, he pushed his way through the mountains and reached the coast near Torrelavega, west of Santander, on August 25. This victory cut off the retreat of 70,000 Republicans, who were forced to surrender. Although surviving elements continued to resist fiercely, the Loyalist northern front was doomed after Torrelavega. The last pocket of resistance was wiped out at Gijon on October 21.[34]

Meanwhile, a conflict between Sperrle and Lt. Gen. Wilhelm von Faupel, the German chargé d'affaires in Spain, reached its head. Faupel had had a long career in the Imperial Army. He had served in the Freikorps in the 1919–20 period and was a military advisor to several South American countries in the 1920s. Considering himself an expert on Latin affairs, Faupel recommended that Hitler send three full infantry divisions to Spain—a proposal which Warlimont strongly objected to. Hitler ruled in favor of Warlimont, but Faupel continued to interfere in Spanish military affairs, much to the annoyance of Franco and his confederates. He also tried to interject himself into the business of the strong-willed Hugo Sperrle, and a series of bitter disagreements ensued. The feud reached such proportions that Hitler decided to replace both men, but not at the same time, to preserve appearances. Faupel was recalled on August 20.[35]

Ten days after Gijon fell, Sperrle formally gave up command of the Condor Legion and returned to Germany as a hero. He had been promoted to lieutenant general on April 1. Seven months later, on November 1, 1937, he was advanced to the rank of general of flyers. On February 1, 1938, he assumed command of Luftwaffe Group 3, which was redesignated 3rd Air Fleet in February, 1939.[36] Sperrle led the 3rd for the rest of his career.

Maj. Gen. Helmuth Volkmann succeeded Sperrle as commander of the Condor Legion. An army officer since 1908, he had been transferred to the Luftwaffe as a colonel in 1934. Volkmann picked his own chief of staff, Maj. Hermann Plocher, who had been with the Condor Legion since 1936. Baron von Richthofen remained in Spain until the end of 1937, when he returned to Germany and received a special promotion to colonel. He was given command of the 257th Bomber Wing on April 1, 1938,[37] but his adventures in the Iberian peninsula were not over, as we shall see.

The main problem General Volkmann faced was the issue of whether the Condor Legion should remain in Spain or not. Due to casualties, and wear and tear on equipment caused by months of heavy fighting, the legion was no longer a first-class fighting unit. Volkmann favored continuing the war, but demanded that the legion be reequipped and properly resupplied, or else that it be returned to Germany. His 150 aircraft were in poor condition, and too many were obsolete models. His flak guns, especially the 88s, were worn out after firing hundreds of rounds (many of them in support of ground troops), and only sixteen of his thirty fighters were serviceable. Volkmann flew to Berlin and presented his case very effectively. He won the support of Col. Gen. Wilhelm Keitel, the commander-in-chief of the Armed Forces High Command (*Oberkommando der Wehrmacht*, or OKW), who was then at the height of his influence. Volkmann also warned that the withdrawal of the Condor Legion would have a disastrous effect on the morale of the Nationalists. His arguments were well taken, and the legion was virtually rebuilt. The He-51 was fully superseded as a fighter by the excellent Messerschmitt 109 (Me-109), which shot down twenty-two enemy airplanes in a five-day period in July, without suffering a single casualty.[38] Meanwhile, the Ju-87 Stuka dive-bombers arrived in Spain in strength, and the He-111 and Do-17 twin-engine bombers became more numerous, while new flak artillery arrived to replace worn-out pieces. Supply operations were also stepped up, and the Condor Legion had no further trouble in that area for the rest of the war.[39]

✠

Neither side was able to win a decisive victory in 1938, but the tide gradually turned against the government. Franco repulsed a major Republican offensive in the Teruel sector and then drove through the Aragon to the Mediterranean, with the objective of splitting Republican Spain in two. Well supported by the Condor Legion, he reached the sea near Vinaroz on April 14, cutting off the Valencia government from its forces in Catalonia. Two days later, forty He-111s bombed the Red fleet, harbor facilities, and oil refineries at Cartagena. Although they dropped eighty-two tons of bombs on their targets, one bomber was shot down and several others were seriously damaged by heavy antiaircraft fire. Volkmann decided not to renew the attack, as he had only twenty-seven operational bombers on April 18.

Franco now made a serious tactical mistake. Instead of pursuing the disorganized and shaken enemy north into Catalonia—as Volkmann and Plocher strongly urged—he turned south and drove on Valencia. This "Mediterranean offensive" led to one brutal air battle after another for the Condor Legion. It scored an impressive number of victories but also suffered serious casualties and loss of equipment. Volkmann's headquarters was also bombed and strafed by forty airplanes but, remarkably, no one was hurt.[40]

While Franco's advance on Valencia slowly gained ground, the enemy in Catalonia recovered, as Volkmann and Plocher had predicted. On July 25 the Republicans launched a major offensive across the River Erbo, and Franco turned north to meet the new threat. This began the Battle of the Erbo, which lasted until November 15.

During this battle, significant numbers of Ju-87 Stuka dive-bombers were used in combat for the first time. The Stuka (an abbreviation for *Stukampfflugzeug*, or "dive-bomber") could drop one 1,000-pound or two 500-pound bombs on a target with much greater accuracy than a horizontal bomber and was highly successful in Iberia, Poland, and France, but it would prove to be extremely vulnerable to enemy fighters in the Battle of Britain. Its vulnerabilities were not yet apparent, however, and the Luftwaffe—chiefly influenced by Richthofen—came to over-rely on this strictly tactical aircraft.

Also during the Erbo campaign a young lieutenant named Werner Moelders changed fighter tactics forever. Moelders had replaced Adolf Galland as commander of the 3rd ("Mickey Mouse") Squadron of J/88 in July, 1938. He soon devoted his considerable talents to the problems of fighter tactics in Spain.

Until this point, Luftwaffe tactics (and those of air forces throughout the world) were based on the outmoded tactics of World War I, which had been built around slow biplanes. Moelders was not bound by these old ideas. He invented the "Finger Four" formation, based on the Schwarm of four aircraft. There were two *Rotten* of two aircraft each. Each *Rotte* could operate independently in defense or attack, but could cooperate with the other *Rotte*. The *Rotte* leader flew in the forward position, with the other aircraft protecting his rear. The rear aircraft flew 600 feet behind the leader, so that both pilots could concentrate on finding the enemy, rather than concentrating on maintaining a tight formation, as the British did early in the war. The British were extremely vulnerable, because they were too busy avoiding colliding with their neighbors, rather than looking for the Germans. After they were mauled by the Luftwaffe in the French campaign, the R.A.F. adopted Moelders' tactics.

When both *Rotten* flew together, the aircraft usually adopted the "Finger Four" formation, so called because it resembled the extended fingers of a hand. Again the space between airplanes was considerable, so that maximum attention could be devoted to looking for the enemy. This formation also allowed for maximum visibility, cooperation, maneuverability, and concentration of firepower. This formation is still used by the high-powered aircraft of the U.S. Air Force today, except the distance between aircraft is far greater.

The brilliant Moelders, who was a gifted aviator as well, used his new tactics to maximum advantage and became the leading German ace in the Spanish civil war. Since it was standard procedure for Condor Legion fighter pilots to be rotated back to Germany as flight school instructors after they had shot down five airplanes, Moelders took to hiding his victories. He had fourteen kills before his deception was discovered and he was sent home as an inspector of fighter units for RLM.

The Battle of the Erbo was virtually won by November 1, when Col. Wolfram von Richthofen succeeded Volkmann as commander of the Condor Legion. Volkmann's relief was not at all unexpected. He had quarrelled frequently with Berlin over its lack of support for the legion and had lost faith in the possibility of a Nationalist victory in Spain. Baron von Richthofen named Lt. Col. Hans Seidemann his chief of staff. Volkmann's chief of staff, Plocher, now a lieutenant colonel, returned to Berlin as chief of plans and mobilization for the Luftwaffe General Staff, a post he held until the end of 1939. He would have more than enough to keep him busy before that year was out. For Plocher the war would end in the Netherlands on May 10, 1945, when, as a lieutenant general, he surrendered his 6th Parachute Division to the Canadian army. He was forty-four years of age. After the war he worked for the United States Air Force's Historical Division and wrote three of the most detailed manuscripts in existence on the air war in Russia. Tragically, he died of leukemia before he could write a proposed history of the Condor Legion: an irreplaceable historical loss.

Volkmann, who had been promoted to lieutenant general on April 1, 1938, also returned to the fatherland, where he was promoted to general of flyers and named commandant of the Air War Academy. Unhappy in the Luftwaffe, he transferred back to the army on August 28, 1939, as a general of infantry. He took charge of the 94th Infantry Division, then forming in Saxony. Despite the fact that he was one grade too high in rank for such a command, Volkmann led his unit in the French campaign. He was killed in an automobile accident on August 21, 1940, at the age of fifty-one.[41]

Major General von Richthofen directed the Condor Legion in the closing operations on the Erbo with his usual skill and efficiency. When the fighting ended on November 16, the Reds and Loyalists had lost 15,000 men killed and another 55,000 wounded and/or captured. They had also lost 35 tanks, 60 guns, 400 machine guns, and 300 aircraft.[42] Government power in north-central Spain was broken, and its northwestern forces were permanently cut off from the rest of the armies in eastern Spain.

Following their victory on the Erbo, Franco and his insurgents turned northward for a major offensive against Catalonia in the northeast. He divided his forces into five Spanish corps of three divisions each, plus an Italian corps of four divisions. These units faced twenty Red divisions, all of which were at one-half to one-third their authorized strength.

The supremacy of the Messerschmitt 109 fighter over the Loyalist Curtiss and Rata aircraft (from the United States and Russia, respectively) had by now been clearly established. Richthofen had forty-five Me-109s in his J/88 fighter group and forty He-111 bombers in his K/88 bomber group, as well as a squadron of dive-bombers. He also controlled a reinforced Luftwaffe flak battalion, which lent heavy artillery support to Franco. In all, Richthofen contributed 98 operational aircraft to the offensive, compared to 146 for the Nationalist Air Force and 134 for the Italians. The Reds had about the same number of fighters as their opponents, but had only about a dozen operational bombers left.[43]

Bad weather forced Franco to postpone the start of the offensive until December 23. When the attack began, the Condor Legion was given the task of supporting the Moroccan and Navarre Corps. This was the largest offensive of the Spanish Civil War. The legion bombed and strafed Loyalist positions and artillery emplacements just before the insurgent infantry units struck. Fighting was bitter and lasted for days, but the Navarre Corps slowly pushed forward and took Tarregona on January 14, 1939. A third of the Red Catalonian Army had been encircled.

The victory at Tarregona left Richthofen free to attack and harass government forces throughout the Catalonian coastal plain. German airmen shot up supply lines, sunk transports, and generally disrupted the enemy's rear, while Franco pursued his beaten enemies. On the 21st and 22nd Richthofen bombed Barcelona, in order to prevent its relief by the Reds. The major Spanish Mediterranean port fell on January 26.

The Condor Legion was given only twenty-four hours' rest following the fall of Barcelona, while its ground support units repaired the airfields at Lerida and Sabadell; then the legion was sent on pursuit operations in the Pyrenees. Franco's Nationalist troops were advancing all along the front by January 27. Their objective was to crush the Loyalist forces in the Pyrenees region and thus seal off Red Spain from France—its only land bridge to the rest of the world and its main supply line. Richthofen's men attacked trains, ships, and fighters heading to and from France and again disrupted Red supply lines.

By now, Richthofen had learned that the He-51, although obsolete as a fighter, made an effective low-level bomber, strafer, and ground support airplane. He armed them with clusters of small, twenty-two-pound incendiary bombs known as "flambos." A flambo consisted of a can filled with a mixture of high-octane aviation fuel and motor oil, connected to a small fragmentation bomb. Fighter pilot Adolf Galland called it an "early prototype of the modern napalm bomb."[44] The legionnaire pilots dropped them on retreating Republicans with deadly effect.

By February 1, Doctor Negrin, the Republican minister of defense, was making peace overtures to the Nationalists, and he even suggested a possible surrender. Franco, however, had little interest in such proposals now, as total victory was within his grasp.[45]

At dawn on February 6, the fighters of the Condor Legion launched a surprise attack on the last major Republican airfield in Catalonia. They destroyed twenty-five Curtiss and Rata aircraft on the ground. This blow eliminated the Loyalist air force in Catalonia. By February 10, Nationalist forces reached the French border all along the line, and the conquest of Catalonia was complete. Meanwhile, the Condor Legion was in action over Valencia, which it raided on the 10th.

Manuel Azana, the president of the Spanish Republic, had fled to Paris and could not be persuaded to return to Madrid. The defense of the Republican capital fell to Dr. Negrin, who was preparing a last-ditch stand. On February 27, Great Britain and France extended official diplomatic recognition to Franco, which prompted the resignation of Azana. Dr. Negrin took charge and placed the command of the remains of the central army under pro-Communist Colonel Modesto. Other elements of the Popular Front, led by Colonel Casado, demanded Negrin resign. Finally, on March 5, the Republican navy mutinied and sailed to Algiers (French territory) with three cruisers and eight destroyers. Colonel Casado in Madrid was openly calling for an honorable surrender, while Richthofen bombed Madrid, Toledo, and Valencia in an effort to speed up the Republican capitulation.[46]

Franco took advantage of the Loyalists' confusion by returning to the offensive on March 26. He was closely supported by the low-level attacks of the Condor Legion. Toledo soon fell, and the Reds were in full retreat. Ten thousand prisoners were captured the first day. By 10 A.M. on March 27, white flats were already appearing in Madrid. Franco ordered Richthofen to halt his attacks on the fleeing Republicans, to prevent needless loss of life. The government surrendered on March 29, 1939. The Spanish Civil War was at an end. The Condor Legion left Spain on May 28, 1939, and returned to Germany, where it was greeted by Field Marshal Goering and where it was disbanded. Most of its members were incorporated into the 53d Bomber Wing, the 9th Flak Regiment, or the 3rd Air Signal Regiment, all of which were authorized to wear the "Condor Legion" cuff on the sleeves of their uniforms.[47]

During the conflict, the Condor Legion had registered 386 aerial victories. Only seventy-two of its aircraft had been shot down by enemy fighters or antiaircraft fire. It had sunk fifty-two enemy ships and had dropped 21,046 tons of bombs on enemy targets.[48] It lost only 420 men killed, of which an estimated 50 percent died "as a result of careless driving on the torturous winding roads in the mountains of Spain." Army colonel (later colonel general) Erwin Jaenecke, the chief of staff of Special Staff W, later described the Condor Legion's casualties as "ridiculously low," especially in view of the thousands of German aviators reported as killed by the world's news media.[49]

The Luftwaffe in general and Baron von Richthofen in particular had learned a great deal during the Spanish Civil War. The German Air Force had gained some two hundred crews and had learned the technological value of the He-111, Do-17, Ju-86, Ju-87, Ju-52, Me-109, Hs-123, and other aircraft. It had acquired valuable experience in formation flying, night action, combat navigation, tactics, and organization. A remarkable number of these men distinguished themselves during World War II. Six of the legion's pilots shot down more than 100 enemy airplanes: Herbert Ihlefeld (123 kills), Walter Oesau (115 kills), Moelders (115), Gunther Luetzow (103), Adolf Galland (103), and Reinhard Seiler (100).

Ihlefeld, a sergeant in Spain, shot down nine airplanes in the civil war and rose to the rank of colonel, commanding the 52nd Fighter Wing. He survived the war. Oesau also rose to the rank of full colonel and commanded the 1st Fighter Wing. He was killed during an attack on an American bomber formation near Aachen on May 11, 1944. Both Moelders and Galland became generals of fighters. Luetzow became a full colonel and commanded the 4th Air Division in Italy. One of the first jet pilots, he was reported missing in action in 1945. Other former legionnaires also distinguished themselves. Col. Baron Hans-Henning von Beust, who commanded the 2nd Squadron of K/88—the bomber group—became the general of bomber forces in the last month of the war. Lt. Col. Baron Siegmund-Ulrich von Gravenreuth flew bombers in Spain and later sank a number of warships and transports in World War II, before he died in an accident in 1944. Maj. Martin Harling-hausen, the naval air squadron commander (AS/88), personally accounted for twenty-six enemy ships before assuming command of the II Air Corps in February, 1943.[50] Other legion pilots had successes almost as noteworthy. Two of the legion's three commanders became field marshals—and the Luftwaffe only had six in its history.

In Spain, the Condor Legion firmly adopted the fallacious idea that fast, well-armed bombers could protect themselves against enemy fighters in day-light bombing operations, as well as the fateful strategy of emphasizing close air support for ground forces, at the expense of a well-balanced program for strategic aerial warfare. As a result, Germany never developed a long-range bomber or long-range fighter and instead emphasized the manufacturing of medium bombers and dive-bombers, while neglecting fighter production. Wolfram von Richthofen was a leader in the movement for close air support. In Spain, he had instituted a system whereby air controllers were sent into the forward battle zones to direct air strikes from the ground. This system was to result in the Luftwaffe's greatest victories in the years 1939–42; it also contributed to its neglect of strategic warfare, which was to lead (indirectly) to its greatest defeats.

In 1957, retired general of flyers Karl Drum wrote a monograph on the Spanish campaign for the United States Air Force Historical Division. This work has never been published because of some misconceptions Drum had about the German command structure in the civil war. His conclusions about Richthofen and his impact on German air strategy and doctrine during World War II, however, are worth quoting in full, because of his firsthand knowledge and his depth of insight into Richthofen's overall influence on the Luftwaffe and the air war against the Allies. He wrote:

> Luftwaffe command circles, both before and during the Second World War, were greatly influenced by the strong personality of Frei-herr von Richthofen. The units under his command during World War II . . . were always the ones sent into action at the critical point in the ground operations. In his own method of operation, in the organization of his staffs and their subordinate agencies, and in the command of his units, von Richthofen was a firm adherent of "close-support tactics at all costs." Without exception he employed all his units in close-support operations on behalf of the Army, regardless of their degree of combat readiness or their suitability and usefulness for this type of operation. This also applied to anti-

aircraft artillery. Again and again he employed them in large-scale operations requiring the participation of all available forces. The resultant attrition of forces, the losses, and the consequent need for replacements were all at the expense of other sectors of the front and other areas of operation; in the last analysis, of course, they made deep inroads into the substance of the Luftwaffe as a whole. It cannot be denied that von Richthofen's methods brought some spectacular results. Though often limited in terms of time and area, these results were undeniably tangible and thus very welcome to the Army, which, after all, benefited most by them. The inevitable consequences of this state of affairs was that close-support tactics were strongly propagated within the Luftwaffe and, during lengthy periods throughout the war, were applied as a general practice, often against the better judgment of the commanders in charge and the leaders of the individual units.

After the Battle of Britain, the first negative aspects of this development began to become apparent on the Eastern Front, during the autumn of 1942. Although they suffered tremendous losses at the front, the Russians were able to make them up and even to reinforce their strength because their industries, their oil refineries, their transport and communications networks, and their supply system in the hinterland had hardly been subjected to air attack, not even at a time when the German bombers would have been fully capable, in terms of range and strength, of delivering destructive blows against these targets.

In 1943, when it was apparent to all concerned that a fundamental error had been committed, it was too late to change the method of employment of the Luftwaffe. While close-support tactics had been employed by choice up to this point, after 1943 they continued to be employed by necessity, since the overall military situation permitted nothing else. This was true not only of the Eastern Front but also of all the other theaters of operations and the home front. From this time on, von Richthofen's influence began to diminish, and the method of employment he developed in Spain was recognized to be out of date. It would, of course, be unfair to von Richthofen as a personality to evaluate his very real accomplishments in Spain and during World War II and his many contributions to the general field of "coordinated operations of the Luftwaffe and Army" exclusively from the point of view of the negative aspects described above. After all, it was the responsibility of the Luftwaffe's top-level command to keep the tactical employment of the air units within a reasonable limit without losing sight of the need for strategic air operations as well.

Author Raymond L. Proctor, who interviewed many of the Luftwaffe commanders who survived the war, stated that these men felt the experiences of the Spanish civil war produced both positive and negative results. Many of these men, he said, felt the negative results outweighed the positive.[51] This author emphatically agrees with this assessment.

The Richthofen who returned from Spain was described by Suchenwirth as "ruthless" and "as demanding as a prima donna." His influence vastly exceeded his rank. Certainly the young Col. Hans Jeschonnek, the new chief of the General Staff of the Luftwaffe, was utterly unable to stand up to his dominant personality.[52] Richthofen made his views felt in every respect and guided the Luftwaffe down the path of close air support, at the expense of strategic aerial warfare. The Luftwaffe's failure to strike an appropriate balance between the two spheres was the underlying cause for its defeat in the Battle of Britain and its ultimate demise, as Drum suggested. In other words, the Battle of Britain was effectively lost in Spain, as we shall see.

CHAPTER 4

The Buildup and the Outbreak of the War

While the Condor Legion was helping win the Spanish civil war for the Nationalists, the Luftwaffe High Command was muddling its way through the last days of peace without taking advantage of them.

Hans Jeschonnek was a National Socialist who had blind faith in the Fuehrer. He believed Hitler would be able to secure Germany's national objectives without a general European war. Trusting Hitler's genius, he did not plan for a war against Great Britain because Hitler said that he did not want a war against England. Unfortunately for Germany, it did not occur to Jeschonnek that Hitler might not have a choice: Britain might declare war on Germany, as she had done in 1914. Without taking this possibility into account, Jeschonnek "prepared for a lightning war without so much as a sideward glance," wrote Suchenwirth.[1] He was totally convinced that any war would be of short duration. Lt. Col. Hermann Plocher, now chief of the Organizational Branch of the Luftwaffe General Staff, stressed the need for a buildup in depth for both aircraft and personnel, to ensure a continuous flow of pilots and machines to replace losses in combat. Jeschonnek disagreed with this concept, however. He insisted that if war came everything the Luftwaffe had was to be committed immediately—including much of the training establishment. The Luftwaffe would go into the war ready to fight a tactical conflict, but not a strategic one; it was equipped for breadth, not depth.

Lt. Col. Paul Deichmann, the chief of staff of the Training Office at OKL, was upset when he heard of Jeschonnek's plans. He was already distressed at the acute shortage of pilot training schools, but Jeschonnek had turned down his requests for additional men and funds. The training schools already had to rely on the National Socialist Flying Corps to give primary flight instruction to their pilots. Even then German pilots were sent to the wings with only 160 hours of flying time—less than half that of their British and American counterparts. They lacked training in night flying, advanced navigation, and other fields.[2] Now Jeschonnek was raiding the training establishments of their indispensable instructor pilots as well. Deichmann protested, but Jeschonnek rejected his appeal. Now, if war came, the training program would be crippled from the first day of the conflict.

Meanwhile, the Luftwaffe organized itself for war. The peaceful annexation of Austria in March, 1938, brought to light the critical weakness of the Luftwaffe system: its territorial nature made it unsuitable to highly mobile air operations. Goering therefore ordered a major reorganization. By July 1, 1938, the old Luftkreise had been reorganized as Luftgaue (Air Administrative Area Commands) or had been upgraded into Luftwaffe Group or Luftwaffe Command Headquarters. The group and command HQs controlled not only the territorial units but also directed combat units, which were now being organized into air divisions. Table 2 shows the territorial organization of the Luftwaffe in 1938.

On April 1, 1939, Luftwaffe Groups 1, 2, and 3 and Luftwaffe Command Austria were redesignated 1st, 2nd, 3rd, and 4th Air Fleets, respectively. Their commanders, in order, were Kesselring, Felmy, Sperrle, and Gen. Alexander Loehr, the former commander of the Austrian air force. Luftwaffe Command East Prussia was subordinated to the 1st Air Fleet, as were the recently formed

TABLE 2: LUFTWAFFE TERRITORIAL ORGANIZATION, JULY 1938

Luftwaffe Group 1	Berlin
Luftgau III	Berlin
Luftgau IV	Dresden
Luftgau VIII	Breslau
Luftwaffe Group 2	Braunschweig
Luftgau VI	Muenster
Luftgau X1	Hanover*
Luftwaffe Group 3	Munich
Luftgau VII	Munich
Luftgau XII	Weisbaden
Luftgau XIII	Nuremberg
Luftwaffe Command Austria	Vienna
Luftgau XVII	Vienna
Luftwaffe Command East Prussia	
Luftgau I	Koenigsberg

*Headquarters, Luftgau XI, was transferred to Hamburg on April 1, 1939.
Source: Suchenwirth MS 1969.

1st and 2nd Air Divisions. The 3rd and 4th Air Divisions were assigned to 2nd Air Fleet, while the 5th and 6th Air Divisions came under the control of the 3rd Air Fleet. Two special divisions, the Training Division (*Lehrdivision*) and the 7th Air Division (the parachute unit), remained under the direct control of OKL and were not assigned to the air fleets. Fourth Air Fleet controlled the units of the former Austrian air force (which had been small) and had no divisions initially.[3]

There was no uniform establishment for an air division. Each had at least one fighter wing and two or three bomber wings; some also had a dive-bomber wing. Eventually every division was given a long-range (strategic) reconnaissance squadron and an air signal battalion.

The Lehrdivision had grown out of the II Group, 152nd Bomber Wing, in Greifswald. It was officially formed on August 1, 1938, and by June, 1939, consisted of two training wings, a flak artillery regiment, and the Luftwaffe Signal Communications Training Regiment. The division cooperated closely with the Luftwaffe testing stations, various manufacturing firms, and the Technical Office until the outbreak of the war; then it was relieved of its training mission and sent into combat.

The 7th Air Division, which was established on June 1, 1938, included the 1st Parachute Regiment (headquartered at Stendal), the 16th Infantry Regiment (transferred from the army), and the 1st and 2nd Special Duty Bomber Wings, equipped with Ju-52 transports. The 7th Air Division was commanded by World War I ace General of Flyers Kurt Student, who was also inspector of parachute and airborne forces.[4]

The propaganda machines, both of Germany and other nations, pictured the Luftwaffe in 1939 as a war machine of overwhelming strength. They did such a good job that almost fifty years have not shaken this image. In fact, the Luftwaffe had many glaring weaknesses, as the insiders on the General Staff knew. The vital question remains: did Adolf Hitler know of the Luftwaffe's weaknesses?

According to Col. Nikolaus von Below, Hitler's Luftwaffe adjutant, all air problems until far into the war were handled by a simple tête-à-tête between Hitler and Goering. Jeschonnek, as chief of staff, could only urge Goering to inform the Fuehrer of the true nature of the situation. Apparently Jeschonnek did not do so; and even if he did, it is certain that Goering did not tell the Fuehrer.

Would Hitler have behaved differently in 1939 if he had known that it was impossible for the Luftwaffe to annihilate the R.A.F. and wage a successful strategic air war against the United Kingdom? Would he have tried to reach a genuine understanding with British Prime Minister Neville Chamberlain on the Danzig issue in 1938 or 1939, instead of going to war so lightly? We will never know the answers to these questions for sure, of course, but they do point out the dangers of the Goering-Hitler relationship, which had benefited the Luftwaffe so greatly in its early years.

Despite the chaos in the Technical Office, the intriguing, backbiting, plotting, and confusion in the OKL and RLM, the inexperience in the General Staff, the general disorientation caused by a too-rapid expansion, and the lack of leadership at the top, the Luftwaffe entered World War II with an impressive array of aircraft, at least by 1939 standards.

In August 1939, there were thirteen combat-ready bomber wings in the Luftwaffe. The standard bomber was the twin-engine He-111, a medium bomber. It was manufactured at the Heinkel plant at Oranienburg, which had been designed by Albert Speer, Hitler's favorite architect, in 1936. The first He-111 rolled off the assembly line in early 1937. It could carry 2.2 tons of bombs and had performed well in Spain. Its speed was only about 250 miles per hour, and its maximum range was only about 740 miles. Considered virtually invincible in 1937, it would be looked upon almost as a sitting duck on the western front by 1941. Nevertheless it would remain the backbone of the German bomber arm throughout the war.[5]

The other major medium bomber was the Do-17, which was also used as a long-range reconnaissance aircraft. Dubbed the "Flying Pencil," it had a 1.1-ton bomb carrying capacity. Its speed and range were similar to that of the He-111, except for the F model (the Do-17F), which had a range of nearly 1,000 miles.

Germany had no long-range bomber in 1939, although one was under development: the twin-engine Junkers 88. Udet and Milch had already informed Goering that the Luftwaffe would reach its ultimate strength of 5,000 Ju-88s in April 1943—about the time the Luftwaffe originally expected to go to war. Unfortunately, Udet and the Air General Staff had added the requirement that the Ju-88 be able to dive. As a result, its weight increased from six tons to more than twelve tons, with a corresponding decline in range and speed. Goering had proposed to Milch, Udet, and Koppenberg that the Ju-88 replace the He-111 as the standard bomber after the first prototype came off the assembly lines in September 1938. Milch opposed this move on the grounds that the air brakes and structural strengthening required to make it a dive-bomber severely cut its performance. He was overruled by Goering, who ordered Koppenberg to oversee its manufacture.

The structural, design, and technical problems which Milch pointed out came to light only after the production models came off the assembly lines in 1939. The Luftwaffe bomber program never really got back on track as a result. Although about fourteen thousand Ju-88s were manufactured by the end of the war, the bomber never achieved its full potential, due to the added weight, which cut its speed and reduced its range to about twelve hundred miles. It was still highly maneuverable, however, and was used mainly as a night fighter in the last years of the war.

Besides the glaring lack of a long-range bomber, the Luftwaffe bomber arm went into war poorly trained. It lacked night bombers, radar guidance systems, bombs larger than 1,000 pounds, modern armaments, air-to-air communications, and good bombsights. It was also short of trained commanders at every level—the natural result of a too-hasty buildup.

The Luftwaffe dive-bomber units were equipped with the Ju-87 Stukas which had done so well in the Spanish civil war. They had been adopted on the recommendation of Udet and had gone into series production in 1937. About five thousand were manufactured during the war. The vulnerability of the Stuka to modern fighters was not recognized until 1940. Only eight groups of Stukas were ready for war in August, 1939.

The most numerous airplane manufactured by Nazi Germany was the Me-109 of which 30,480 were produced between 1939 and 1945. This single-engine fighter went through several models, the most important of which was the Me-109G, which had more power than earlier models. The Me-109E was the most important fighter in the 1939–41 period. It was small, fast, climbed rapidly, and had good maneuverability. Armed with two machine guns under each wing and a 20mm machine gun which fired through the propeller hub, it was superior to anything the Poles, French, Dutch, or Belgians sent up against it. Later models had even more firepower. It was, however, slightly inferior to the British Spitfire and definitely inferior to the Hurricane.

Between 1941 and 1945 the Me-109 was gradually replaced as a fighter by the Focke-Wulf 190, but never completely. The Me-109 was also widely used as a fighter-bomber in the East, especially after 1942. In August, 1939, the Luftwaffe had five single-engine fighter wings and eighteen and one-third independent groups at its disposal. Almost all of these were equipped with Me-109s, although a few groups still flew obsolete biplanes.

The Me-109, which had a range of only 365 to 400 miles, was unsuited for the mission of escorting bombers. For this purpose the Luftwaffe adopted the Me-110, a twin-engine fighter, in 1938. When war broke out in Poland, the Luftwaffe had ten twin-engine fighter groups. Long-range and short-range reconnaissance units in 1939 were equipped with a few Do-17s and a variety of obsolete aircraft, including He-45 and H-46 biplanes. Many of these units were attached to the army during the Polish campaign. The

Luftwaffe also mustered 552 tri-engine Ju-52 transports when the war began.[6]

✠

"No serious thought was entertained in intermediate or high levels of the Luftwaffe command that the war with Poland was imminent," then-colonel Wilhelm Speidel, the chief of staff of the 1st Air Fleet, wrote after the war. "This was all the more the case because the existing weaknesses and inadequacies in the training, equipment, and operability of the field forces were too well known and were dutifully reported repeatedly to the higher levels of command."[7]

It was not until Hitler summoned the leading commanders and staff officers of the armed services to the Obersalzberg on August 23, 1939, that the true gravity of the international crisis burst upon them. Speidel and the others left the conference in "undisguised consternation."[8]

The German plan was as follows: the Third Army would attack westward from East Prussia and link up with the Fourth Army, advancing eastward from Pomerania, cutting the Polish Corridor. Meanwhile, to the south, Army Group South would advance on Warsaw, spearheaded by the Tenth Army. One and a half million German soldiers were committed to action against Poland. In the West, Col. Gen. Ritter Wilhelm von Leeb's Army Group C would cover the German rear from a possible attack by the French and British. Table 3 shows the German Army Order of Battle in August 1939, and Map 3 shows the Polish campaign and the initial dispositions of the major air and army units.

The Luftwaffe deployed rapidly behind the army. Kesselring's 1st Air Fleet was given the mission of supporting Army Group North, while Loehr's 4th Air Fleet supported Army Group South, the main thrust of the German invasion. To the west, Felmy's 2nd Air Fleet covered Army Group C's northern sector and was charged with the air defense of northwestern Germany. Sperrle's 3d Air Fleet had the same responsibility for southwestern Germany.

First Air Fleet initially had the bulk of the German strength on August 31, 1939: 795 aircraft, of which 519 (or 65.3 percent) were bomb carriers. Its principal subordinate units were the 1st Air Division (Lt. Gen. Ulrich Grauert) and Air Command East Prussia (Gen. of Flyers Wilhelm Wimmer), which included Lt. Gen. Helmut Foerster's Luftwaffe Training Division, the Lehrdivision. Foerster was charged with the task of supporting the Third Army in East Prussia, while the 1st Air Division supported the Fourth Army.

To the south, 4th Air Fleet had 507 aircraft, of which 360 (or 71 percent) were bomb carriers. Loehr's air fleet included the 2nd Air Division (Lt. Gen.

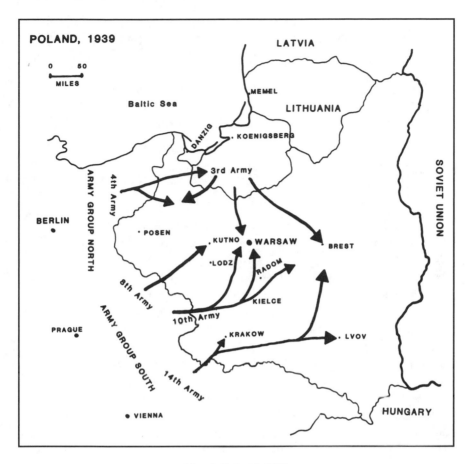

Map 3: Poland, 1939

Bruno Loerzer) and *Fliegerfuehrer z.b.V.*, or Special Purposes Air Command, under Major General Baron von Richthofen. Loerzer was charged with supporting Army Group South, while Richthofen had a special mission: supporting the panzer-heavy Tenth Army, the spearhead of the German advance.

All totalled, the "Operational Luftwaffe" (1st and 4th Air Fleet) had 1,302 aircraft, of which 879 were bomb carriers (bombers, dive-bombers, and ground attack aircraft). The rest were fighters, reconnaissance, and transport planes. Also on the eastern front were 123 aircraft (mainly reconnaissance planes) under the direct control of OKL; 288 reconnaissance aircraft attached to the army; and 216 fighter aircraft under Luftgaue I (Koenigsberg), III (Berlin), IV (Dresden), VIII (Breslau), and XVII (Vienna).[9] These were responsible for the air defense of eastern Germany.

It is interesting to note that the Luftwaffe concentrated its strength in the north, while the German Army concentrated in the south. This was because

TABLE 3: ORDER OF BATTLE OF THE GERMAN ARMY, SEPTEMBER 1, 1939

Army Group North	Col. Gen. Fedor von Bock
Third Army	Gen. Georg von Kuechler
Fourth Army	Gen. Gunther von Kluge
Army Group South	Col. Gen. Gerd von Rundstedt
Eighth Army	Gen. Johannes Blaskowitz
Tenth Army	Gen. Walter von Reichenau
Fourteenth Army	Gen. Wilhelm List
Army Group C	Col. Gen. Ritter Wilhelm von Leeb
Army Detachment A	Col. Gen. Baron Kurt von Hammerstein*
Fifth Army	Gen. Curt Liebmann
First Army	Gen. Erwin von Witzleben
Seventh Army	Gen. Friedrich Dollmann

*Still in formation. Army Detachment A was not activated until September 10, 1939.

the primary mission of the Luftwaffe during the first two days of the campaign was to destroy the Polish air forces, not to support the ground units. It was to assume this mission only after air supremacy had been clearly established.

On the western front, 2nd Air Fleet deployed the 3rd Air Division (Maj. Gen. M. Putzier) and the 4th Air Division (Lieutenant General Keller), while the 3rd Air Fleet controlled the 5th Air Division (Maj. Gen. Ritter von Greim) and the 6th Air Division (Maj. Gen. Otto Dessloch). Second Air Fleet had 309 aircraft (165 bomb carriers) and 3rd Air Fleet had 264 airplanes, of which 120 were bomb carriers. Another 153 aircraft were attached to the army units on the western front, while 150 fighters under Luftgaue VI (Muenster), XI (Hamburg), VII (Munich), XIII (Nuremberg), and XII (Wiesbaden) provided fighter defense for western Germany. In all, there were 876 aircraft in the West of which only 285 (or 32.5 percent) were bomb carriers.[10] Table 4 shows the disposition of the 2,985 first-line aircraft the Luftwaffe had on September 1. Table 5 shows the Order of Battle for the 1st and 4th Air Fleets.

The Luftwaffe was opposed by three Polish air divisions, which were subordinate to the army, as Poland had no separate air force. The Polish 1st Air Division (1st, 5th, 6th Air Regiments) and 3rd Air Division (2nd, 3rd, and 4th Air Regiments) were headquartered at Warsaw, while the 2d Air Division (7th and 8th Air Regiments) was still in the process of forming in the interior. The main non-divisional unit was Naval Air Group Putzig, a mixed force of seven

TABLE 4: ORDER OF BATTLE OF THE LUFTWAFFE, SEPTEMBER 1, 1939

Unit	Aircraft	Bomb Carriers	% Bomb Carriers
1st Air Fleet	795	519	65.3
1st Air Division	(444)	(309)	
Lw Cmd East Prussia	(324)	(210)	
Air Fleet units	(27)	(0)	
4th Air Fleet	507	360	71.0
2d Air Division	(315)	(240)	
Air Cmd z.b.V.	(183)	(120)	
Air Fleet units	(9)	(0)	
(Total, operational LW:	1,302	879	67.5)
Under OKL	123	18	
Attached to army	288		
Home Air Defense, East	216		
TOTAL, EASTERN FRONT:	1,929	897	46.5
2d Air Fleet	309	165	53.4
3d Air Division			
4th Air Division			
3d Air Fleet	264	120	45.5
5th Air Division			
6th Air Division			
Attached to army	153		
Home Air Defense	150		
TOTAL, WESTERN FRONT:	876	285	32.5
Naval Air Units	180		
LUFTWAFFE TOTAL:	2,985	1,182	39.6

Source: Speidel MS.

bomber, fighter, reconnaissance, and antiaircraft squadrons, located in the Baltic sector.[11]

The principal tactical unit of the Polish air forces was the group. Each group had two to four squadrons, which had ten to twelve aircraft each. Upon mobilization, these units came under the direct operational control of

TABLE 5: ORDER OF BATTLE, 1ST AND 4TH AIR FLEETS, SEPTEMBER 1, 1939

1st Air Fleet: General of Flyers Kesselring
   Chief of Staff: Col. Wilhelm Speidel
   1st Air Division: Lt. Gen. Ulrich Grauert
      KG 1 (-)
      KG 26 (-)
      KG 27
      StG 2 (-)
      ULG 2
      ZG1(-)
   Lehrdivision: Lt. Gen. Helmut Foerster
      LG 1
      KG 2
      KG 3
      UStG 1
      UJG 1
   Luftgau I (Koenigsberg)
   Luftgau III (Berlin)
   Luftgau IV (Dresden)

4th Air Fleet: Gen. of Flyers Alexander Loehr
   Chief of Staff: Col. Guenter Korten
   2nd Air Division: Lt. Gen. Bruno Loerzer
      KG 4
      KG 76
      KG 77
      UZG 76
   Air Command z.b.V.: Maj. Gen. Baron von Richthofen
      StG 77 (-)
      SLG 2 (-)*
      UZG 2
Luftgau VIII (Breslau)
Luftgau XVII (Vienna)

*2nd Stuka Training Wing.
Source: Speidel MS.

the army or the navy. The Polish air force had ten reconnaissance groups, seven fighter groups, five fighter-bomber groups, and six groups of liaison aircraft. In all, they had 935 airplanes, including 350 reconnaissance planes, 300 fighters, 150 fighter-bombers, and 135 liaison aircraft. A large number of their planes were obsolete. The main Polish fighter was the PZL P.11, which was made by the National Aviation Plant (Panstwowe Zaklady Lotnicze) in Warsaw. These high-wing monoplanes dated back to 1931. They were armed with only two light machine guns and had an operational ceiling several thousand feet below the Messerschmitts. The P.11 was also about one hundred miles per hour slower than the Me-109.

Poland did have a modern medium bomber, the P.37 "Elk." Unfortunately, the Polish bomber arm had just begun to modernize, and only thirty-six Elks had reached the groups.

In addition to its obsolete aircraft and lack of centralized command, the Polish air forces were handicapped by poor dispositions. Each of the six Polish armies was given one fighter group, one reconnaissance group, and one balloon company, under an air unit commander. In all, the army and naval air forces had 165 of the available fighters, 265 recon aircraft, 100 liaison airplanes, 30 naval reconnaissance planes, and 10 naval defense aircraft. This left only 150 fighters for the defense of the Polish cities, industrial regions, and rear areas. Of these, sixty were located in the general vicinity of Warsaw, twenty in the Deblin area, thirty around Gdynia (the Polish Baltic Sea port), and forty in the various industrial regions. These fighter units were under the control of the chief of air forces at Polish GHQ in Warsaw.

World War II began at 4:40 A.M. on September 1, 1939. There have been a great many misconceptions about the Luftwaffe's success on that day. Many people believe that the Polish air forces were destroyed on the ground in the first few hours of the campaign. This simply is not true. The Polish leadership recognized that war was a distinct possibility, if not actually imminent. They did not keep their air units concentrated in their large peacetime bases; rather, with the international situation at the boiling point, they took the elementary precaution of dispersing their air units to ninety tactical airfields throughout the country. They thus saved most of their airplanes from the initial German onslaught.

The Poles lost control of the air battle before it began, because the Polish ground services were extremely primitive. No Polish air signal corps existed. This fact was of critical importance, for Polish air units had to depend on army signal units, which had no specialized training in aerial communications. The Polish tactical airfields were not even served by telephones. The Polish air command simply did not have the communications to contact— much less control—their small units, which were now scattered all over the country. Much like the Polish army, the Polish air units operated in "penny packets," which were swamped one by one by the Wehrmacht. Except in the vicinity of Warsaw, where Polish communications were at their best, Polish aviators never achieved a single important concentration against the Luftwaffe.

The weather was poor throughout Poland on the morning of September 1, but it was especially bad in the zone of the lst Air Fleet, where most of the Luftwaffe's striking power was concentrated. At Warsaw, for example, the cloud ceiling was 600 feet and visibility was less than three-quarters of a mile. Lacking proper instrument training, the Luftwaffe's plans for a synchronized takeoff of all operational air forces were upset. Only a few units actually took off on schedule and the planned large-scale attack deteriorated into a series of actions by individual units. Only four groups of the Lehrdivision (the best-trained unit in the Luftwaffe) took off on schedule. The bulk of the 1st Air Division was simply grounded in eastern Pomerania. Only I Gruppe, 1st Bomber Wing, took off on schedule. In all, only five of Kesselring's fourteen and one-third initial attack groups took off on time: hardly the overwhelming attack the German propaganda machine pretended it was. Yet it was successful, because the Polish Air Command was simply not able to exercise more than the slightest control over its own units.[12]

In the south the weather was somewhat better. Operating out of bases in Silesia and Bohemia, Loehr's air fleet attacked Polish airfields and ground installations in the vicinity of Lvov, Krosno, Krakow, Chenstochau, Kattowitz, Moderovka, Kielce, and Radom. Other units attacked the Polish railroad system and successfully disrupted the mobilization of the Polish army.

The most successful attack took place at Krakow, where the main base of the Polish 2nd Air Regiment was located. Here 60 He-111 bombers from the 4th Bomber Wing dropped forty-eight tons of bombs on the airfield, which was then attacked by 30 Stukas, followed by 100 Do-17s, which came in at treetop level. The air base was completely smashed. However, only a few Polish airplanes were destroyed, and most of these were second-line trainers or inoperable aircraft that had been unable to move into the interior.

While 2nd Air Division flew these missions, Baron von Richthofen's Special Purposes Air Command was providing close air support for the Tenth Army. Due to the closeness of their tactical airfields to the front lines, Richthofen's three dive-bomber groups and one ground attack group (352 aircraft) were able to fly multiple missions in direct support of the ground units. In all, the Fliegerfuehrer z.b.V. flew thirteen group-sized missions and delivered 139 tons of bombs on targets assigned by Luftwaffe liaison officers attached to the army. Polish troop concentrations and marching columns were attacked repeatedly. Near Wielun, thirty Stukas caught a Polish cavalry brigade in the open. At Udet's suggestion, sirens had been attached to the fixed landing gear of the Stukas. When they dived, these sirens (dubbed "the trumpets of Jericho") emitted a high-pitched scream. Coming in at an angle of 80 degrees, they released 550-pound bombs and fired their two 7.92mm Rheinmetall machine guns into the helpless cavalry formations. The results, General Speidel wrote later,

> were highly satisfactory and led to the complete disorganization of the Polish ground forces thus attacked. Entire Polish units disintegrated, the troops fleeing in wild disorder from the burning settlements, only to come under repeated air attack in their wild eastward flight. The impressions of the first day of combat thus revealed clearly that the new close support air arm had supported the army's advance decisively and in numerous cases had made the advance possible at all.[13]

Richthofen's division only lost one aircraft that whole day. Sixteen others were damaged by Polish defensive fire. Fourteen undamaged Me-110s had to make forced landings because of faulty navigation—they simply got lost on their first combat missions and could not find their way back to base.

About noon the weather broke over northern Poland and the 1st Air Fleet got into the battle in strength during the afternoon. Kesselring committed seven groups from Luftwaffe Command East Prussia and thirteen from 1st Air Division—twenty groups in all. They attacked Polish ground service installations, ammunition depots, railroad facilities, trains, and troop concentrations. Five Stuka groups dive-bombed Polish shipping and attacked the Polish Baltic Sea ports and naval bases on Cape Hela, in support of the German Navy. Polish airfields at Graudenz, Thorn, Bromberg, Gnesen, Posen, Putzig, Lida, Warsaw-Okecie, Warsaw-Molotov, Goclav, Polck, Biala, and Brest were attacked, some of them twice. Several presumed Polish headquarters were bombed and strafed. The major ammunition depot at Rembertov was blown up, and Polish radio stations at Babice and Lacy were destroyed at the request of Army Group North, which intercepted coded messages from them. After these stations were neutralized, there was a noticeable interruption in transmissions from the Polish High Command.[14]

The only serious resistance offered by the Polish air force came when ninety He-111s from 1st Air Fleet attacked the Okecie airfield near Warsaw and the nearby PZL airframe works. They were met by about thirty P.11 fighters at point-blank range. Some of the German bomber pilots were so unnerved that they broke formation and jettisoned their bombs over the countryside. Fortunately for the Heinkels, the escorting Me-110s promptly joined the battle. Firing their two 20mm cannon and four machine guns, they shot down five of the Polish fighters in a matter of minutes. It was the first air-to-air combat of the war.[15]

Kesselring later estimated that only thirty Polish airplanes were destroyed on the ground in the first day of the campaign. Because of the failure of the Polish air forces to form a coherent defense, only 44 percent of the air fleet's combat missions were flown against it, while 56 percent of the missions were flown in support of the German Army and Navy.[16] With their decentralized organizational policy and their failure to appreciate the need for effective air signal communications, the Polish air units had virtually taken themselves out of the battle before it even began. Elements of the Polish air forces continued to offer sporadic resistance until September 14–17, when they crossed the frontiers into Lithuania, Russia, and Rumania. They never played a significant role in the campaign.

✠

By the afternoon of September 2, the General Staffs of the 1st and 4th Air Fleets had concluded that the Polish air forces had been only partially neutralized but were nevertheless thoroughly paralyzed. In fact, Kesselring's chief of staff noted, they were not even able to *find* the Polish air force. From that point on, operational sorties in direct and indirect support of ground forces were given the highest priority. Indirect support missions involved disrupting Polish mobilization by attacking the Polish railroad system. This interdiction was soon applied to the highway system as well. Several Polish units found themselves unable to reach the front; others were unable to advance or retreat. The Polish armies lost much of their already limited mobility. At the front, Polish troop concentrations and defensive positions were subjected to repeated aerial bombardment before they were attacked by the army. Supply lines were also pulverized. Resupply could only take place at night, when it was possible at all.

Meanwhile, aided by its air umbrella, the German Army surged forward. On September 3 the third and fourth armies linked up, cutting off much of the Polish Pomorze army in the Polish Corridor, which had until then separated East Prussia from Pomerania and the rest of the Reich. To the south, Reichenau's Tenth Army crossed the Warta and advanced on Warsaw, while List's Fourteenth Army fought its way through the Polish Carpathians and advanced to the Vistula. The Luftwaffe assigned their dive-bomber and bomber missions to smaller and smaller units, down to flight level, to give better support to the army. Fighter and twin-engine fighter units, no longer needed as bomber escorts, were also assigned low-level ground support missions.

After the cutting of the corridor, air combat units were gradually transferred from the 1st Air Fleet to the 4th Air Fleet, which was supporting the main drive on Warsaw. The first transfer took place on September 6, when the 26th Stuka Wing was assigned to Loehr and another Stuka group was sent to Richthofen. The next day, Headquarters, 1st Air Division, was assigned to 4th Air Fleet, and 1st Air Fleet was gradually phased out of the battle. After Britain and France declared war on September 3, Goering became increasingly anxious about the safety of western Germany, where the Ruhr industrial region lay vulnerable to enemy air attack. We know now that he need not have worried, but, given the information available to him at the time, his concerns were certainly justifiable. As a result, combat aviation units were transferred to the zone of the interior as early as September 12, much to the disgust of General von Richthofen. Meanwhile, the land battle reached its climax. Kuechler's Third Army pushed southward from East Prussia to invest Warsaw from the north, while Reichenau encircled and destroyed five Polish infantry divisions and a cavalry brigade (the bulk of the Krakow army) at Radom. Polish Galicia was quickly overrun and Gen. Heinz Guderian's XIX Motorized Corps of Army Group North poured into north-eastern Poland and into the Polish rear. The Polish government fled to Lvov, while Polish resistance everywhere began to deteriorate. On September 10 the Poznan army, heroically led by Gen. Tadeusz Kutrzeba, launched a surprise attack against the weak German eighth Army, which was covering the left flank of the main drive. This attack caused the German High Command some bad moments and the 30th Infantry Division was almost overrun. The German ground commanders reacted quickly, however, and reinforced General Blaskowitz to a strength of six corps. With these new units he was able to quickly encircle Kutrzeba, trapping elements of twelve Polish infantry divisions and three cavalry brigades in the Kutno Pocket—a full one-third of the entire Polish land force.[17] About 150,000 Polish soldiers surrendered. General Kutrzeba later remarked that "every movement, every troop concentration, every line of advance came under pulverizing bombardment from the air. It was just hell on earth.[18]

Meanwhile, Richthofen pushed his Special Purposes Air Command to the limit of its ability and succeeded brilliantly. He was assigned the mission of supporting the Eighth Army at Kutno and played a major role in breaking the back of the Polish attack. Gradually reinforced (see Table 6), he was in charge of the bulk of the Luftwaffe's forces still in combat in Poland after the Kutno Pocket collapsed on September 17. Then he was given the mission of subduing the most important remaining center of Polish resistance: the city of Warsaw.

The Polish capital had come within Richthofen's zone of operation during the first week of the campaign, when Reichenau neared the city from the southwest. A firm believer in the terror raid since his days in Spain, Richthofen ordered Colonel Seybold, the commander of the 77th Bomber Wing, to bomb

TABLE 6: UNITS ASSIGNED TO FLIEGERFUEHRER Z.B.V. (RICHTHOFEN), SEPTEMBER 3–30, 1939

Date(s)	Units
3–4 Sept.	II/StG 2
4 Sept.	I Battalion, 23rd Flak Regiment*
6 Sept.	HQ, LG 2, controlling two Stuka groups
8 Sept.	StG 77
	III/KG 51
9 Sept.	II and IWKG 77
11 Sept.	I/StG 1
11–16 Sept.	III Battalion, 1st Parachute Regiment*
14–15 Sept.	I Battalion, 3rd Flak Regiment*
20 Sept.	I/KG 77
22–30 Sept.	I/ZG 76
	I/LG 2 (Me-110s)
	I/JG 76
23–26 Sept.	IV/KG 1 (Ju-52s)
24 Sept.	IV/LG 2 (Stukas)

*For airfield protection.

Source: Speidel MS.

the ghetto area of Warsaw. Seybold, however, had scruples against attacking defenseless civilian targets. The next day, September 11, he disobeyed orders and "on his own authority and in agreement with his sub-commanders . . . diverted the group designated for this attack to targets of military importance in Warsaw." Furious, Richthofen relieved Seybold of his command, effectively ruining his military career.[19] The tenor raid on Warsaw had to be postponed indefinitely, however, because a nervous Goering began to withdraw the He-111s to the western front the next day. Once again, Richthofen was very angry: he wanted to use the bombers to drop flambos on Warsaw.[20]

By September 22 Warsaw was tightly invested by the Third and Eighth Armies, and Richthofen was again calling for an all-out annihilating terror raid against the city. His recommendation was turned down, but when Polish resistance showed no signs of slackening, OKL approved the raid.

Richthofen struck the Polish capital at 8 A.M. with 1,150 airplanes. Eleven percent of the bombs that fell were incendiaries. They were dropped by thirty Ju-52 transports. Two men in each plane hurled the two-pound fire bombs out of the cargo door with ordinary potato shovels. The fires which resulted caused such dense clouds of smoke that it was impossible for German observers to identify any detail in the city, either by ground or aerial observation. The aiming of the bombs was extremely inaccurate, of course, and some fell within German lines, causing friendly casualties.

General Blaskowitz was furious. He quickly called Richthofen to account, but the baron refused to call off the raid just because German soldiers were being killed. Their argument reached such proportions that Hitler himself had to be called in. At the joint Army-Luftwaffe Command Post the Fuehrer ruled that the Luftwaffe was to operate as before. Special Purposes Air Command flew 1,776 sorties against the city and pulverized it with 560 tons of high-explosive bombs and 72 tons of incendiaries. Smoke clouds over Warsaw reached heights of 18,000 feet. That night the glow from the burning city could be seen for miles—all quarters of the city were on fire. All the Germans lost was two Stukas and a Ju-52, shot down by Polish antiaircraft fire.

The next morning Richthofen was told that the Luftwaffe was to operate against Warsaw only at the direct request of the Eighth Army. Apparently these orders came directly from Goering. No such request was forthcoming from the disgusted Blaskowitz, so Richthofen, on his own initiative, attacked the nearby city of Modlin with 450 aircraft. He was preparing to raid Warsaw again on September 27, when white flags appeared. Polish General Juliusz Rommel surrendered the city unconditionally, so Richthofen attacked Modlin again, this time with 550 aircraft. Rather than endure such an attack again, the city surrendered later that day. All totalled, Richthofen had dropped 318 tons of bombs on the city on September 26 and 27.

The last seat of Polish resistance, the naval base at Hela, surrendered on October 1, and the last sporadic resistance ended on the 6th. The campaign had lasted thirty-six days, during which the Polish army of more than a million men had been completely destroyed. The Luftwaffe had lost only 285 aircraft during the campaign and was, in fact, stronger at the end of the battle than when it began. The lion's share of the credit for the victory went to the two new arms of the German armed forces: the panzer branch and the Luftwaffe. For the first time in history an air force, operating as an independent service, had played a decisive role in a ground campaign. The Luftwaffe leadership's mood was euphoric. Their arm had come through its first trial of combat with flying colors, and it seemed to be invincible. In their eyes—and in the eyes of the world—it was, at least for the moment.

During the Polish campaign, the tactical air support methods Wolfram von Richthofen had perfected in Spain had been completely vindicated on a larger scale, or so it appeared to Goering, Jeschonnek, and most of the rest of the Luftwaffe. Despite his relatively junior rank, Richthofen continued to be a dominant force in the Luftwaffe, with unfortunate results. Even now no effort was being made to develop the strategic potentialities of the German Air Force.

Despite the magnitude of its success, there were a number of deficiencies in the Luftwaffe, as some of the more astute General Staff officers noted. Training was inadequate in many areas, especially in instrument flying and bomb aiming. In fact, the Luftwaffe had been built so rapidly that, prior to Poland, some of the newly formed units had never practiced with live bombs at all. General Speidel concluded: "Weaknesses were noticeable in unit commanders and all officers, because most of them lacked theoretical and practical experience." He also wrote: "Inadequacies became apparent everywhere due to the too-speedy build-up, in which emphasis was on numbers rather than quality."[21] It was too late to do much about it now, however; they were already in the middle of a world war.

Lt. Gen. Martin Harlinghausen, the anti-shipping expert who commanded the naval air squadron of the Condor Legion and was later Air Commander Atlantic.

Harlinghausen (left) with Field Marshal Erhard Milch, the state secretary for aviation and deputy commander-in-chief of the Luftwaffe.

Erich Hartmann (right), who shot down the incredible total of 352 enemy airplanes. He is seen here with his rear gunner, Heinz Merten.

An American two-engine bomber is shot down over Toulon, 1943. UNITED STATES MILITARY ACADEMY

General of Flyers Joseph Kammhuber,
the first general of night fighters.

General of Fliers Beppo Schmidd (center), a long-time Nazi and personal friend of
Hermann Goering, was a terrible failure as chief of intelligence of the Luftwaffe.

A Ju-88. This Junkers aircraft was used in a variety of roles, including bomber, dive-bomber, night-fighter, and reconnaissance aircraft.

The Moelders brothers: Werner (third from the left), the first general of fighter forces, and Victor (second from the right), who was shot down over Britain in 1940.

The Me-163 Komet, one of the first jet fighter airplanes.

Col. Hajo Hermann, fighter ace and innovator who invented the "wild boar" fighter tactics that wreaked havoc on Allied bombers.

Field Marshal Albert "Smiling Al" Kesselring, the second chief of the General Staff of the Luftwaffe.

A Messerschmitt Me-262 jet fighter after its capture by American forces, 1945.

Johannes Steinhoff, commander of the 77th Fighter Wing in Sicily. He ended the war as a jet fighter pilot with 176 victories.

Hugo Sperrle, commander-in-chief of the 3rd Air Fleet, in 1944.

A Ju-88 night fighter is shot down over France, 1943.

Lt. Gen. Adolf "Dolfo" Galland, the second general of fighter pilots.

Left to right: Colonel Stolle, commander of a flak regiment; General of Infantry Hans Zorn, commander of the XXXXVI Panzer Corps; and Luftwaffe General Ritter Robert von Greim, commander of the 6th Air Fleet—on the Eastern Front, 1943.

Col. Gen. Ritter Robert von Greim (left) shakes hands with Col. Guenther Luetzow (right) while Col. Walter Oesau looks on. Luetzow shot down 115 enemy aircraft during his career; Oesau shot down 127.

A Junkers Ju-88 bomber.

Lt. Ernst Udet of the Richthofen Fighter Wing. He shot down 62 aircraft during World War I and later served, less effectively, as head of the Luftwaffe's technical and air armaments office.

Maj. Walter "Nowi" Nowotny, commander of the first jet fighter unit. He scored
258 confirmed kills—255 of them on the
Eastern Front—before being killed in
action in November 1944, a month
before his twenty-fourth birthday.

Alfred "Bomber" Keller, who commanded Imperial Germany's 1st Bomber
Wing during World War I. At the age of
fifty-eight, he personally led his fighter
squadrons into action at Dunkirk in
1940.

CHAPTER 5

Blitzkrieg

The war on the western front began with a whimper. Hitler categorically forbade the Luftwaffe to take any offensive action at all against the Western alliance, and small wonder: in September, 1939, France had 110 divisions available for use against Germany. Behind the West Wall, Germany had only thirty divisions to defend 300 miles of frontage. Only a dozen of these were first-class units, and none were panzer. Fortunately for the Third Reich, France and Great Britain let the opportunity pass; they did not help their Polish ally at all.

By the second week in October, Hitler was demanding the army launch a major offensive in the West during the winter of 1939–40. Col. Gen. Walter von Brauchitsch, the commander-in-chief of the army, and Gen. Franz Halder, the chief of the General Staff of the army, both favored waiting until the spring of 1940, but Hitler would not listen. He demanded that the Army General Staff prepare an offensive plan for a winter attack. Halder therefore presented an unimaginative rehash of the Schlieffen Plan of 1914. It called for an advance through the Low Countries with the bulk of the panzer and motorized divisions on the right (northern) flank. Hitler did not like it, but could not come up with a viable alternative, so he ordered its execution. The weather would not cooperate, however, and the attack was delayed time after time. Then, on January 10, 1940, the plan was compromised altogether—by members of the Luftwaffe.

On January 9, 1940, over a beer at the Officers' Mess in Muenster, Maj. Helmut Reinberger complained to his friend, Maj. Erich Hoenmanns, about the long train ride he had to face the next day in order to attend a staff conference at Cologne. Hoenmanns, a World War I aviator and commandant of the nearby airfield at Loddenheide, needed some flight time and wanted to visit his wife at Cologne, so he offered to fly Reinberger to the conference. Even though he was carrying secret plans concerning the offensive, Reinberger accepted the invitation—a clear violation of security regulations.

The weather was bad the following morning when the majors took off. Hoenmanns got lost and then accidentally shut off the fuel supply to his Me-108 communications plane, an aircraft which he had only flown once before.

They crash-landed near the Belgian town of Mechelensur-Meuse, about twelve miles north of Maastricht. Neither major smoked, so they had no matches. Reinberger was unable to burn his top-secret documents before he was seized by Belgian gendarmes.[1]

Hitler was beside himself with rage when he heard the news the next day. "It is things like this that can lose us the war!" he snapped.[2] No one in Germany knew whether or not Reinberger had destroyed the top-secret documents. The Fuehrer summoned Goering at once and, for the first time, gave his designated successor a devastating rebuke. He even considered relieving Goering of command of the Luftwaffe.

In keeping with his character, Goering found scapegoats immediately. He sacked Gen. Hellmuth Felmy, the commander of the 2nd Air Fleet, and his chief of staff, Colonel Kammhuber, even though they were completely innocent of any wrongdoing. Kammhuber would overcome this blot on his record and go on to greater things, but Felmy, who was already out of favor due to his frank appraisal on the capabilities of the Luftwaffe vis-à-vis the R.A.F., would not. He lived in forced retirement until the spring of 1941, when he was placed in charge of Special Staff F in Greece and later in the Caucasus. Gradually working his way back into the good graces of the Nazi High Command, he later commanded the army's LXVIII and XXXIV Corps in the Balkans (1943–45). Kammhuber, on the other hand, was allowed to remain on active duty. He was named commander of the 51st Fighter Wing (the "Edelweiss Wing"), which he led with considerable distinction in the Western campaign, until he was shot down and captured near Paris on June 3.[3] Hoenmanns and Reinberger were both sentenced to death in absentia, but the sentence was never imposed, because they spent the rest of the war in prison camps, mainly in Canada.

Goering was still shaken on January 12, when he summoned Kesselring into his presence. "You will take over 2nd Air Fleet," he told the former chief of staff, ". . . because I have nobody else." Kesselring later remembered that Goering was more depressed that day than he ever saw him, even in the darkest days of the war.[4] Kesselring retained Wilhelm Speidel as his chief of staff. General Stumpff assumed command of the 1st Air Fleet in Poland, and the capable Maj. Gen. Heinz-Hellmuth von Wuehlisch soon became 1st Air Fleet's chief of staff.

It is interesting to note that one of the applicants for the command of 2nd Air Fleet was Erhard Milch. He had no intention of giving up his other posts, but felt he needed command time to improve his standing and better his position. His appointment, however, was blocked by his bitter enemy, Jeschonnek.

On January 13, the day after Kesselring received his appointment, Holland and Belgium began to mobilize on a massive scale. Obviously they expected a German invasion—a sure tip-off that the plan had been compromised. The Belgian General Staff ordered its units not to resist if the French army crossed the frontiers.[5] Hitler had no choice but to cancel the invasion, at least for the time being.

✠

Hitler's next invasion did not come in the west, but in the north. Correctly fearing that Britain planned to occupy northern Norway to cut off Germany's vital iron ore supply, he ordered the Wehrmacht to seize both Norway and Denmark. The invasion began on April 9.

Initially Hitler planned to invade Sweden, as well as her neighbors. Goering did not learn of these plans until March, but when he did he immediately went to Berchtesgaden and stood up to Hitler for perhaps the only time in his life. Sweden, it will be recalled, was the home of Goering's first wife. He had lived there, off and on, during the 1920s, and his stepson, now fighting against the Russians in Finland as a volunteer, was a Swede. In anguish, Hermann told Hitler that he had given his word to King Gustav of Sweden through Count Eric von Rosen (his former brother-in-law) that Nazi Germany would never violate Swedish neutrality. Should Hitler invade Sweden, he would have to insist that the Fuehrer accept his resignation.

Hitler saw that Goering was serious. He ordered OKW to shelve its plans to attack Sweden, even though he was not at all pleased about it. Hitler toyed with the idea of invading Sweden later in the war, but he never did. So much for the myth of Scandinavian neutrality. Of the four countries in that region, only Sweden escaped the ravages of war, and it was spared only because an obscure German aviator fell in love with a beautiful Swedish woman on a cold winter's night in 1920.

The invasion of Denmark presented no problems, because it had a land frontier with Germany. It was overrun in a matter of hours by General of Artillery (formerly General of Flyers) Leonhard Kaupisch's XXXI Army Corps. The invasion of Norway was another matter altogether. Norway had to be overcome by a combination airborne and seaborne invasion under the general direction of Gen. Nikolaus von Falkenhorst's Group XXI (formerly XXI Army Corps, later redesignated the Army of Norway).[6] Luftwaffe general Hans Geisler's X Air Corps was assigned to support the invasion. For this task he was given 1,000 aircraft, including 290 He-111s, 40 Ju-87s, 30 Me-109s, 70 Me-110s, 70 reconnaissance and coastal aircraft, and 500 Ju-52 transports.[7] As was the case in Poland, some 340 of the transports were taken from the pilot training schools. The rest of the Ju-52s belonged to Student's 7th Air, the world's first parachute division. Geisler's principal subordinate units were the 4th, 26th, and 30th Bomber Wings and the 1st Special Purposes Bomber Wing (*Kampf-geschwader z.b.V. 1*, or KG z.b.V. 1), a transport unit.[8]

The invasions of Norway and Denmark were the first battles in which parachute troops were employed. Unlike in the United States and Great Britain, these troops were members of the air force, not the army. On April 9 they seized Aalborg and Vordingborg in Denmark and Stavanger and Dombas in Norway. But, the planned parachute operation against Oslo had to be cancelled due to bad weather. Oslo fell after a flight of Ju-52s, covered by Me-110s, simply landed at the previously unoccupied Fornebu Airfield and off-loaded an infantry battalion, despite Geisler's efforts to recall it.[9]

The Norwegian campaign seemed all but over on April 10, but it was not. The Royal Navy intervened between April 15 and 19, landing British and French troops at Namsos and Andalsnes and near Narvik, sinking seven German destroyers in the process. Narvik in northern Norway was the main iron ore port and was the key objective of the campaign. It was held by 4,600 men under Lt. Gen. Eduard Dietl, the commander of the 3rd Mountain Division. Dietl's situation was critical. More than half of his men were sailors (the crews of the sunken destroyers), who had no training in land warfare.[10] Badly outnumbered and cut off by sea, the Luftwaffe supplied Dietl by air while Falkenhorst dealt with the Allied landings and prepared a campaign to relieve Narvik.

Meanwhile, the headquarters of the newly formed 5th Air Fleet took command of the Luftwaffe forces in Norway. Its commander was Erhard Milch. The half-Jewish Nazi wanted his command time, but he did not actually want to leave Germany, the seat of power. He tried to direct operations in Scandinavia from Hamburg, and Hermann Goering actually had to order him to go to Oslo, promising to recall him when the invasion of France began. Milch's HQ did not begin to move to Norway until April 24. When the invasion of France began three weeks later, Milch returned to Germany (where he received his Knights Cross) and was succeeded by Hans-Juergen Stumpff. General of Flyers Alfred Keller, the former commander of the IV Air Corps, shortly thereafter took command of the 1st Air Fleet in Poland.[11]

The Luftwaffe played a decisive role in the conquest of Norway. It attacked the British ground forces and the Royal Navy, forcing them to withdraw from Namsos and Andalsnes, and supported Falkenhorst's relief expedition to Narvik. After the Allies finally forced Dietl out of the city on May 28, the Ju-52s continued to resupply him. Several of them had to make one-way trips, crash-landing on frozen lakes to bring vital supplies and reinforcements to the trapped mountain troops. A high proportion of the 127 aircraft the Luftwaffe lost in Scandinavia were transports. The Norwegian campaign did not end until June 8, when the British evacuated Narvik and returned home. England needed all of the troops she could muster by that time, because her forces in France had been smashed, and Paris was on the verge of falling to Nazi Germany.

✠

After Halder's original plan had been compromised by the unlucky majors, a new plan had been proposed by Lt. Gen. Erich von Manstein, the brilliant chief of staff of Rundstedt's Army Group A. This military genius spotted the decisive weakness in the enemy's dispositions: their failure to properly cover the Ardennes, a hilly and heavily wooded region which was considered too difficult for armored operations.

Manstein's plan consisted of three stages (see Map 4). First, Fedor von Bock's Army Group B (Sixth and Eighteenth Armies) would invade the Netherlands and Belgium. Second, the Allies would commit their mobile reserves against Bock, thinking his was the main attack. Third, Gerd von Rundstedt's Army Group A would launch the real main attack, spearheaded by Panzer Group Kleist (under General of Cavalry Ewald von Kleist), with half of Germany's ten panzer divisions, plus three motorized divisions. According to the Manstein Plan, Kleist would quickly drive through the main French defenses on the Meuse River in the vicinity of Sedan before the Allies could react. Then he would drive to the English Channel, cutting off the main French and British forces in Belgium. Meanwhile, to the south, Leeb's Army Group C would keep the French forces along the Maginot line occupied with diversionary attacks.

The Luftwaffe, as usual, was assigned the task of supporting the armies. Kesselring's 2nd Air Fleet, consisting of I Air Corps (Ulrich Grauert), IV Air Corps (General Keller), the Air Landing Corps (consisting of the 7th Air and 22nd Air Landing Divisions under General Student), and the 9th Air Division (Lt. Gen. Joachim Coeler), was to support Army Group B. Sperrle's 3rd Air Fleet, including Loerzer's II and Greim's V Air Corps, was to support army groups B and C. As in Poland, most of the Stukas and ground attack aircraft were directed by Baron von Richthofen, now the commander of the VIII Air Corps. This unit was initially attached to the 2nd Air Fleet, but it would be transferred to the south on the third day of the invasion to furnish direct support to the main attack. The II Flak Corps (Maj. Gen. Otto Dessloch) and the I Flak Corps (Gen. Hubert Weise) were assigned to the 2nd and 3rd Air Fleets, respectively, to provide air defense for both ground forces and Luftwaffe installations.

Between them, Kesselring and Sperrle had some 4,000 aircraft, including 1,120 He-111, Do-17, and Ju-88 bombers, 324 Ju-87 Stukas, 42 Hs-123 ground

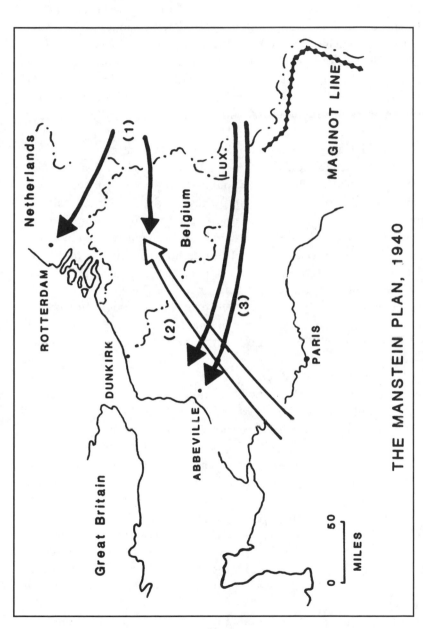

THE MANSTEIN PLAN, 1940

Map 4: The Manstein Plan. Erich von Manstein's brilliant plan consisted of three parts: Army Group B attacks the Low Countries (1), drawing in the Allied mobile reserves (2). Then Army Group A delivers the real main attack through the Ardennes (3). The plan worked exactly as planned.

attack biplanes, 1,106 Me-109 fighters, and 248 Me-110 twin-engine fighters, plus about 600 reconnaissance and 500 transport aircraft. They faced 1,151 British, Belgian, French, and Dutch fighters and 1,045 Allied bombers and ground-attack aircraft. They outnumbered their enemy about 2,840 to 2,200 in combat aircraft, excluding 1,200 R.A.F. airplanes still stationed in England for home air defense. Most of these would remain in Britain throughout the campaign. These figures are somewhat misleading, however, because the main French fighters (Curtiss 75A Hawks, Bloch 152s, and Morane-Saulnier 406s) were all inferior to the Me-109 and were fifty to seventy-five miles per hour slower than the Messerschmitt.[12] Also, the commander of the French air force was already thoroughly intimidated by the Luftwaffe.

The French commander, Gen. Joseph Vuillemin, was a distinguished World War I ace who was "liked by his soldiers, but whose own 'ceiling' was regrettably lower than that to which his planes could ascend in the skies."[13] In August, 1938, he went on a five-day tour of Luftwaffe installations, where, guided by Milch and that master showman, Udet (who had worked briefly in Hollywood), he was the victim of an elaborate hoax. Visiting airfield after airfield, he saw hundreds of fighters and bombers and was given astonishing (and completely false) production figures. Many of the aircraft Vuillemin saw were the same planes he had seen before: they were being shuttled from airfield to airfield, to deceive him into thinking that the Luftwaffe was much stronger than it actually was. The ruse worked. Vuillemin, thoroughly shaken, reported back to his government that the French air force could not last a week against what he had seen.

The rest of the French leadership was no more astute than Vuillemin, and some were much worse. Gen. Maxime Weygand, the former French chief of staff and still a major influence in the army, said time and time again: "You can't hold the ground with planes."[14] Gen. Maurice Gamelin, the French commander-in-chief, shared Weygand's views. His principal subordinate, Gen. Alphonse-Joseph Georges, commander of the north-east front (extending from Dunkirk to the Swiss border), described the German adoption of panzer tactics as a terrible blunder. "Their tanks will be destroyed in the open country behind our lines if they can penetrate that far, which is doubtful," he said.[15] Two months before Hitler struck, Georges told General Visconti-Prasca, the Italian military attaché to Paris, that he wanted the Germans to attack, and that he would willingly give Germany a billion francs if they would attack without delay.[16]

The Allies did indeed have some significant advantages. They outnumbered the Germans in men and in tanks (by 3,432 to 2,574, excluding obsolete French Renault and British light tanks). Many of the French tanks were superior to the best panzers in firepower and armament, although they were inferior in speed, range, and maneuverability. Unfortunately for the Allies, more than half of the French tanks were scattered among forty infantry support tank battalions, deployed from the English Channel to the Mediterranean Sea.[17]

French morale was also very poor. The French had sat in their fortifications for nine months, waiting for German power to collapse by itself. Valuable training time was wasted. Discipline grew lax, suicides occurred with alarming frequency, and alcohol abuse was rampant. They were simply not ready for the offensive when it burst upon them on May 10, 1940.

As was their custom, the Luftwaffe began the campaign with a devastating series of attacks against the enemy air bases. At dawn six wings of He-111s and Do-17s (more than three hundred aircraft) bombed twenty-two airfields in northern France, Belgium, and the Netherlands. On the first day of the offensive the Dutch air force was nearly annihilated, the Belgian air force was virtually eliminated, and the French Armée de l'Air was badly stung. The next day R.A.F. bases in France were also smashed. By the evening of May 11, Luftwaffe reports indicated that the Anglo-French forces had lost 1,000 aircraft. By the next day, the R.A.F. and French air units in northern France had lost half their airplanes. This was enough for Vuillemin, who sent most of his units to the interior and dispersed them. As a result, the French air force was scattered everywhere, but had no real strength anywhere. The Luftwaffe was able to gain superiority over them at critical points and times throughout the campaign.[18]

Meanwhile, the two armies of Bock's Army Group B (Kuechler's Eighteenth and Reichenau's Sixth) invaded Holland and Belgium, respectively. German paratroopers seized key positions and bridges in an effort to quickly penetrate the frontier defenses. These forces were under Student's Air Landing Corps (later redesignated XI Air Corps) and had the mission of capturing two positions of critical importance: Eben Emael, the vital Belgian fortress on the Albert Canal, and the Moerdijk Bridge, sixteen miles south of Rotterdam, the key to a quick victory over Holland. Table 7 shows the order of battle of the Air Landing Corps.

Eben Emael and the three adjacent bridges at Veldwezelt, Vroenhoven, and Canne were attacked by Assault Group Koch, a specially trained parachute engineer unit led by Capt. Walter Koch, a very brave officer from the 1st Parachute Regiment. Koch had been a member of the Prussian Security Police prior to joining the service as a second lieutenant in 1935 or 1936. He was only twenty-nine years old when he led the attack on the seemingly impregnable Belgian fortress, which was garrisoned by 1,000 men. It featured concrete walls, flood gates, machine guns, field artillery, antiaircraft guns, and searchlights. It had one major weakness, however: it had a flat roof.

TABLE 7: ORDER OF BATTLE, AIR LANDING CORPS,
MAY 10, 1940

Air Landing Corps: Lt. Gen. Kurt Student
7th Air Division: Student
    1st Parachute Regiment
    I Battalion, 2d Parachute Regiment
    16th Infantry Regiment
    KG 6 z.b.V. (a transport wing)
22nd Air Landing Division: Lt. Gen. Count Hans von Sponeck
    II Battalion, 2d Parachute Regiment
    47th Infantry Regiment
    65th Infantry Regiment
    KG 2 z.b.V. (a transport wing)
Air Support Formations: Major General Putziger
    4th Bomber Wing (He-111s)
    26th Fighter Wing (Me-109s)
    51st Fighter Wing (Me-109s)
    26th Destroyer Wing (Me-110s)
Corps Units:
    9th Special Air Group
    11th Special Air Group
    12th Special Air Group

Koch's men approached the fortress in eleven DFS-230 gliders, which had been released over Germany several minutes before. Their approach was silent and their landing on the roof completely surprised the sleepy garrison. Soon eighty-five parachute engineers were on the roof, where they crippled the rooftop gun emplacements and artillery periscopes with hollow charges (*Hohlladungen*), used here for the first time. Gun ports and other openings were attacked with flame throwers; other paratroopers tossed explosives down the ventilating shafts and threw 110-pound charges down the staircases. In all, fourteen Belgian guns were knocked out. Despite counterattacks by the Belgians, Koch's men took the upper gallery of the fortress, making the entire complex useless. It was finished off the next day by combat engineers from the rapidly advancing Sixth Army.

The fall of Eben Emael broke the Belgian Albert Canal line and forced the Belgian army to retreat to the west, pursued closely by the Sixth Army. Perhaps more important, the fall of Eben Emael had a tremendous psychological effect on the Belgians. They never managed to completely regain their equilibrium and were forced to surrender within three weeks.

Meanwhile, a parachute battalion landed near the railroad and highway bridges at Moerdijk in the Netherlands. Because the bridges were more than one mile long, two companies were dropped north of the bridges and two came down in drop zones south of it. This coup effectively separated "Fortress Holland" (i.e., the core region of Holland, including the major cities of The Hague, Rotterdam, and Amsterdam) from the French and British armies. Later that afternoon the French 25th Infantry Division, the spearhead of the French Seventh Army, advanced to Breda, ten miles south of the bridges, but they were attacked by the Luftwaffe and were "flattened." The next day the 25th Infantry, now reinforced by elements of the French 1st Light Mechanized Division, was attacked and beaten back by the 9th Panzer, the SS Verfuegungs Motorized Division, and the SS Leibstandarte Adolf Hitler (Motorized) Regiment. Fortress Holland could not be reinforced; it would have to hold out on its own.

Further north, at The Hague, the attempt to seize the Dutch capital met with disaster. Many paratroopers landed in the wrong places. Thirteen Ju-52s, carrying infantrymen from the 22d Air Landing Division, tried to land at Valkenburg Airfield, and eleven of them were shot down. Lt. Gen. Count Hans von Sponeck, the divisional commander, was critically wounded. Kesselring quickly cancelled the operation and diverted the second assault wave—which was already in the air—to Rotterdam.

Rotterdam was the key to the defense of Fortress Holland. The Luftwaffe seized the Willems Bridge here on May 12 in a unique manner. A dozen Heinkel seaplanes, carrying a total of 150 men, landed on the Lek River and seized the vital bridge, which they held against repeated Dutch attacks. The Dutch even sent the destroyer *Van Galen* up the river to shell the bridge and the nearby Waalhaven Airport (which had been captured by the paratroopers), but the *Van Galen* was sunk by the Luftwaffe before it could interfere with the operation. The vanguard of the 9th Panzer Division arrived the next day, and by May 14 the Dutch resistance began to weaken.

Surrender negotiations at Rotterdam began on the morning of May 14, but the Dutch were in no hurry. They still outnumbered the Germans, held most of the city, and were helping their allies by stalling like this. Kuechler's Eighteenth Army, after all, could not join Bock in Belgium until Holland capitulated.

They did not know that Kesselring had ordered a massive air raid for 3 P.M. that afternoon. At 2:15 P.M., the Luftwaffe signals unit at Waalhaven sent a message to the 2d Air Fleet, asking that the bombing be postponed. However, 100 He-111s had already taken off. They had wound in their trailing antenna and could not be contacted by wireless; however, they had been instructed to fly to secondary targets if they saw red signal flares. This is where the tragedy began. Due to the smoke of burning buildings and Dutch antiaircraft fire, only forty-three of the bombers saw the red flares. Fifty-seven Heinkels dropped their high-explosive (HE) bombs on the city.

HE bombs do not normally cause major fires, but some of these hit a margarine warehouse, causing a major blaze which spread quickly. The Rotterdam water mains were broken, so there was no water in the fire hydrants. Citizen fire brigades, with their antiquated two-wheel hand pumps, could not handle the flames, which devastated 1.1 square miles in the center of Rotterdam. Nine hundred eighty people were killed and 78,000 were left homeless.[19]

The horrified Dutch supreme commander, Gen. Henri Winkelman, surrendered early that evening with his army virtually intact. German fire engines were dispatched from as far away as the Ruhr to save what was left of Rotterdam. Meanwhile, Kuechler and his men turned south, where the French, British, and Belgians were still trying to stave off defeat. Kurt Student was not with them, however; he had been hit in the head by a stray bullet and almost killed. Major General Putziger, the corps air units commander and former commander of the 6th Air Division, assumed temporary command of the 7th Air Division. He, in turn, was succeeded as transport commander by Maj. Gen. Wilhelm Suessmann.

✠

The Allies had been thoroughly deceived by the strength and fury of Bock's attack. Thinking that Army Group B's advance was the main one, General Gamelin committed his main forces—the French First and Seventh Armies and the British Expeditionary Force (B.E.F.)—to the north, in Belgium and the Netherlands. Hitler was overjoyed. "When the news came through that the enemy were moving forward along the whole [northern] front I could have wept for joy," he recalled later. "They had fallen into the trap. It was vital that they should believe that we were sticking to the old Schlieffen Plan, and they had believed it!"[20] Now, as planned, Panzer Group Kleist struck to the south, spearheaded by Guderian's XIX Motorized Corps. Supported by the Stukas of Richthofen's VIII Air Corps, Guderian broke across the Meuse on the morning of May 13. "The assault proceeded as if it had been a training exercise," Guderian said later.[21]

The French sector at Sedan was held by two Class B divisions: the 55th and 71st Infantry of the X Corps. The corps commander, General Gransard, called them "fat and flabby men in their thirties who had to be re-trained."[22] The key to holding the sector rested with the French artillery. General Georges had reinforced the already strong X Corps Artillery, and on May 13 the 71st Division had three artillery groups and the 55th had seven. However, they had almost no antiaircraft guns. Richthofen's mission, then, was to neutralize this potent force.

Instead of launching one large raid (as Sperrle proposed), Guderian persuaded Richthofen to carry out a constant, though less intensive, aerial bombardment. As a result, the French batteries were paralyzed by the constant threat of air attack. The Stukas did little real damage, but their effect on French morale was "enormous," according to General Gouhard. The artillery especially "went to ground."[23] The Stukas continued to make passes over French positions even after they had dropped their bombs, their "trumpets of Jericho" screaming. Throughout the day about two hundred Stukas, covered by several fighter wings, flew multiple missions in the Sedan sector. French artillery fire slackened while the panzer engineers began building bridges across the Meuse. Then the panic began. Rumors circulated through shaken French artillery channels that strong panzer forces had broken through. This was not true. Only the German infantry and combat engineers had crossed the river, using rubber assault boats. Not a single bridge had been completed and not a single tank had crossed the Meuse. Nevertheless the X Corps' and 55th Division's artillery commanders abandoned their command posts and headed for the rear, followed by most of their men. Naturally this panic affected the other branches, especially the ill-trained infantry. The rout was on.

The next afternoon the R.A.F. joined the battle. They hoped to destroy Guderian's bridges across the Meuse before XIX Corps could cross the river in strength. The Luftwaffe was ready for them, however. The entire area was crowded with flak from 20mm, 37mm, and 88mm guns. The approaches to the bridgehead were protected by the fighter gruppen. The German fighter pilots flew 814 sorties that day and shot down more than ninety British and French aircraft on May 14, which became known as *Tag der Jagdflieger*—the "Day of the Fighter Pilot." It was the Luftwaffe's most successful day of the French campaign.[24] Of the seventy-one British Battle and Blenheim bombers committed to the attack on the bridgehead, thirty-nine were shot down—56 percent of the total. That evening they tried again, this time with strong fighter support. Of the twenty-eight Blenheims committed, five were shot down and two others crash-landed in France.[25] The bridges were not damaged. The tanks continued to roar across, heading towards the English Channel. The next morning, French prime minister Paul Reynaud called British prime minister Winston Churchill, who had replaced Neville Chamberlain only five days before. "We are beaten," Reynaud said bluntly. "We have lost the battle."[26]

He was right. Under pressure from the Luftwaffe and the Panzertruppen, the French Ninth Army was disintegrating. That night seventy-eight

British heavy bombers took off from England and bombed the Ruhr for the first time, setting several oil plants on fire. They returned to base without loss.[27] Apparently they hoped to force the Luftwaffe to pull back some of its flak guns and fighter planes for the defense of the fatherland. If so, it did not work. The Luftwaffe continued its tactical support missions all along the front.

The Manstein Plan was working out exactly as its creator said it would. Panic broke out in Paris on May 16, and Brussels fell to the Sixth Army on May 17, the same day that Gamelin recommended to Reynaud that he seek an armistice. On May 19 Reynaud sacked Gamelin and replaced him with General Weygand, but the move did little good. The next day Guderian's spearhead reached the English Channel near Abbeville, cutting off the B.E.F. and the First and Seventh French Armies with their backs to the sea. Almost simultaneously, the R.A.F. abandoned its last airfield in Belgium and flew back to England. Only 66 of its original 261 fighters had survived the ten-day air battle. The French campaign was won. Hitler was already mapping out the peace terms he would offer the defeated Allies.

At this point, Hermann Goering made one of the worst of the many mistakes he would make in the Second World War: he let success go to his head. On May 23, as Ewald von Kleist's tanks closed in on Dunkirk, Goering was sitting at a heavy oak table near his command train. A dispatch arrived with the news that the Allied forces in Flanders were all but surrounded near Dunkirk. Goering banged his fist on the table with delight. "This is a wonderful opportunity for the Luftwaffe!" he exclaimed. "I must speak to the Fuehrer at once." In the ensuing telephone conversation, he assured Hitler that the Luftwaffe alone could destroy the enemy. Hitler, perhaps wishing to conserve his panzer strength for the drive on Paris, consented. Goering even persuaded him to withdraw some of the tank units a short distance, so that they would not be in danger of being hit by a misdirected bomb.

Milch, Kesselring, Jeschonnek, and Maj. Gen. Alfred Jodl (the chief of operations of OKW) all opposed the plan. When a very sarcastic army general told him that the panzers had been halted, Wolfram von Richthofen rushed back to his headquarters (a children's convalescent home at Proisy) and telephoned Jeschonnek immediately. These orders must be revoked immediately, he cried: "Unless the panzers can get moving again at once, the English will give us the slip. No one can seriously believe that we alone can stop them from the air!"

"You're wrong," Jeschonnek replied. "The Iron One [Goering] believes it."[28]

The Luftwaffe lacked the necessary prerequisites for the operation. The air units were nearly exhausted after two weeks of continuous action, they had no advanced airfields, and they had lost about a thousand aircraft to enemy fighters, ground fire, and normal maintenance problems. It was too late for discussion now, however: Goering had committed himself.

For the first time, over Dunkirk, the Luftwaffe met large numbers of British Spitfires flying at a maximum speed of 370 miles per hour—13 mph faster than the best German fighter, the Me-109. The Messerschmitts did dive better and had a 2,000-foot fighter ceiling, but they were much less maneuverable than their British opponents—a critical disadvantage in aerial combat. The Stuka dive-bombers were almost helpless against the new R.A.F. fighters. In short, for the first time, the Luftwaffe met pilots as good as their own in aircraft as good or better than their own. As a result, they were unable to halt the British evacuation. Some 40,000 French troops were captured when Dunkirk fell on June 4, but 338,226 British and Allied soldiers had been saved. It was the first serious loss of prestige for the Luftwaffe.

Less than three weeks later the French capitulated. Despite Dunkirk (the importance of which had not yet been recognized by the Germans), the Luftwaffe had again distinguished itself. It had lost 1,389 airplanes, including 521 bombers, 122 Stukas, 367 fighters, 213 transports, and 160 reconnaissance aircraft. The Belgian and Dutch air forces had been almost totally wiped out, and the R.A.F. had lost 854 of its 1,873 frontline airplanes—more than 45 percent of its strength. The Allied losses to the Luftwaffe totalled well over 3,000 planes by June 4.[29]

The most successful Luftwaffe ace of the campaign was Capt. Wilhelm Balthasar, a squadron leader in JG 27. Balthasar, who had scored seven kills as a member of the Condor Legion (including four in a wild, six-minute combat), shot down twenty-three enemy airplanes and destroyed thirteen more on the ground. He had shot down nine airplanes on June 6 alone. Later he commanded III/JG 3 in the Battle of Britain and the 2nd Fighter Wing "Richthofen" in the West (1940–41). Known for his chivalry in battle, he was killed on July 3, 1941, when his overstressed wing suddenly collapsed during a tight turn in a battle against Spitfires. In accordance with his wishes, he was buried in Abbeville, France, next to his father, a World War I captain who had been killed in action in 1915 when Balthasar was ten months old. Balthasar had forty victories at the time of his death.

Werner Moelders also distinguished himself in this campaign by shooting down thirteen enemy aircraft before June 5, when he was surprised by a French fighter near Compiegne. Shot down and promptly captured, he spent the next few weeks as a prisoner of war, but returned to his wing after the French surrender.[30]

And what had happened to the French air force? Between May 10 and June 12, it had received 1,131 new aircraft—668 of which were fighters.

French air power had actually increased during the campaign, General Vuillemin later admitted that his air force had received more aircraft during the campaign than it had lost to enemy action. After the armistice, there were 4,200 military airplanes in the unoccupied zone of France, and the Italian Control Commission in North Africa found 2,648 modern French airplanes. More than 700 of these were fighters—many of them of recent manufacture.[31] It is hard to escape the conclusion that the French air commanders lost their nerve after the first Luftwaffe attacks and abandoned both their allies and their own troops to their fate. As for the Luftwaffe, it had covered itself with glory once again. Reward day was not long in coming.

On the evening of July 19, in the Opera House in Berlin, Hitler promoted a dozen generals to the rank of field marshal. The highest honors, however, went to Hermann Goering. Hitler himself read the citation: "For his mighty contribution to victory, I hereby appoint the creator of the Luftwaffe Reichsmarschall of the Greater German Reich, and award him the Grand Cross of the Iron Cross."

Goering was now the only holder of the highest decoration in the land and the only holder of the highest military rank in German history, and a hitherto unheard of rank at that. That night he celebrated in his usual style, throwing a lavish party for a few friends at the Leipziger Palace, his Berlin residence. The meal included pâté de foie gras from Paris, several different-colored vodkas from Poland, roast salmon from Danzig, Moselle from Trier, goose with Chateau Haut Brion from Veldenstein, Viennese torte with Chateau d'Yquem, as well as Napoleon brandy and French liqueurs. Everyone got quite inebriated. Goering promptly forgot all about the war, concentrating most of his energies on hunting art treasures. From then until 1945, except for very brief periods, the Luftwaffe was almost leaderless. Air fleet commanders frequently had to journey to Rominten to see Goering, where the most important business was discussed in breaks during stag hunts.[32]

Goering was not the only one rewarded on July 19. Sperrle, Kesselring, and Milch were promoted to field marshal. Richthofen was awarded the Knights Cross and advanced to general of flyers, completely skipping the rank of lieutenant general. Ulrich Grauert was promoted to colonel general. Ritter von Greim became a general of flyers, as did Hans Jeschonnek, who, like Richthofen, bypassed the rank of lieutenant general. Others receiving promotions that day included Alfred Keller, Stumpff, Ernst Udet, and Hubert Weise, all of whom became colonel generals. Hans Geisler became a general of flyers, and a score of lesser lights received promotions and/or high decorations. Except for Goering, these men had little time to rest on their laurels, however, for England had not yet been subdued. Here, for the first time, some of the weaknesses of the German Air Force would be made apparent, and the Luftwaffe (and the Reich) would suffer its first major defeat.

CHAPTER 6

The Air War against Britain, 1939–42

The air war against the United Kingdom can be divided into two major periods: 1) the years 1939–41, when Germany was essentially on the offensive, and 2) the 1942–45 period, when the aerial offensives were conducted largely (but by no means exclusively) by the Royal Air Force and its American ally. The first period can be subdivided into a number of phases: 1) antishipping operations; 2) the Battle of France; 3) the Battle of the Channel; 4–6) the three phases of the Battle of Britain; and 7) the period of stalemate, when Hitler and the Luftwaffe leaders knew that England could not be bombed into submission but had to keep up a harassing action for reasons of prestige. The air war against Britain did not begin with the Battle of Britain, as many of today's Americans think; rather, it began with the start of the war.

Initially, before the invasion of France, Germany's air war against Britain was waged against the Royal Navy and the merchant marine. Two commanders directed these operations: Maj. Gen. Joachim Coeler and Lt. Gen. Hans Ferdinand Geisler. Geisler's chief of operations, Maj. Martin Harlinghausen, also distinguished himself in these operations. Appropriately enough, all three of these men were ex-sailors.

Joachim Coeler was born in Posen (now Poznan, Poland) in 1891 and entered the navy as a cadet in 1912. He joined the 1st Navy Air Unit (*Marine Flieger Abteilung*) as an ensign in 1915 and became a fighter pilot. Later he commanded the naval bomber school at Putzig until the armistice. He remained in naval aviation during the Reichswehr period and, after a tour of duty with the German mission in Tokyo (September 1934, to March 1935), was transferred to the Luftwaffe as a staff officer with Luftkreis VI (Sea) in 1935. In 1936 he was promoted to colonel and named inspector of naval aviation. In 1939, Coeler was promoted to major general and named commander of Naval Air Group West (*Seeluftstreitkraefte West*), headquartered in Kiel. For the first six months of the war he was subordinate to the High Command of the Navy (OKM).[1]

When the war began, Coeler had 228 aircraft under his command—mostly obsolete He-59 and He-60 seaplanes, some floatplanes, and a few Stukas and Me-109s that had been specially adapted for naval support operations. Coeler made the most of his limited resources and conducted an aggressive mine-laying campaign against the British navy and merchant marine. He was so successful that, by mid-December, his slow, obsolete aircraft had been responsible for sinking about one hundred thousand tons of British shipping. As a result, his command was upgraded to 9th Air Division on February 1, 1940, and placed under Luftwaffe, rather than naval, control. Coeler himself was decorated with the Knights Cross and promoted to lieutenant general in the massive promotions of July 19, 1940.[2]

Meanwhile, Hans Geisler was in charge of direct bomber attacks against British naval forces. Geisler, who was also headquartered at Kiel, had joined the navy in 1909 and had served as an aerial observer and reconnaissance pilot in World War I. Later a flotilla commander and a frigate captain, he had joined the Luftwaffe as a lieutenant colonel in September, 1933, and had become commander of the Luftwaffe's naval air units as a colonel in 1935. Because the war started three years ahead of schedule, Geisler's forces, which had been designated 10th Air Division in the autumn of 1939, had only two understrength bomber wings. His operations against the Royal Navy were generally unsuccessful, so Geisler turned his attention to British shipping and sent several merchant vessels to the bottom. Not as successful as Coeler, he was nevertheless promoted to general of flyers on May 7, 1940. His command was upgraded to X Air Corps on February 1, 1940.[3]

The combined efforts of the 9th Air Division and X Air Corps constituted a considerable nuisance to the British navy but were nothing compared to the body blow the R.A.F. suffered in the Battle of France in 1940. During this campaign, most of the British air units sent to the Continent lost more than half of their aircraft, and several were completely wiped out.

Early on the morning of June 5, 1940, the day after the evacuation of Dunkirk ended, Erhard Milch walked along the beach near the city with Maj. Gen. Otto Hoffmann von Waldau, the caustic but extremely capable chief of the Operations Branch of the General Staff of the Luftwaffe. Waldau was in an expansive mood. Waving his arm across the horizon, Waldau exclaimed: "Here is the grave of the British hopes in this war!" Then, prodding a bottle with the toe of his boot, he contemptuously added: "And these are the grave stones!"

General Milch was more thoughtful. "They are not buried yet," he muttered. He was hatching a plan in his mind. "We have no time to waste!" he said suddenly. Later that day the state secretary showed up at a command conference held aboard Goering's armored train *Asia*, his temporary command post. The jubilant Goering told Milch, Kesselring, Sperrle, Stumpff, and Jeschonnek that the British army had been "wiped out" at Dunkirk. Milch corrected him. He had been to Dunkirk and had not seen more than twenty or thirty dead British soldiers. He strongly advised that the Luftwaffe launch the invasion of Britain "*without delay.*" "I warn you, Herr Field Marshal," the deputy commander of the Luftwaffe concluded, "if you give the English three or four weeks to recoup, it will be too late."

Momentarily crestfallen, Goering's initial reaction was negative. "It can't be done," he said, tersely.[4] But, as the conversation continued, he was won over to Milch's point of view. The state secretary presented a compelling argument. He proposed an immediate invasion of Great Britain, supported by the 2nd and 3rd Air Fleets, even before France was finished off. The paratroopers could seize a few critical airfields in southern England, and then army units could be ferried over by the air transports. At the moment the R.A.F. and British army—which had lost all of its heavy equipment at Dunkirk—were too weak to intervene successfully.[5] As the conversation continued, Goering became convinced that Milch was right. The next day, the "Iron One" went to the village of Bruly-le-Peche, Belgium, and presented a plan to the Fuehrer for the invasion of Britain.[6]

The plan was a good one: even Adolf Hitler appreciated its merits. However, he did not think it was necessary. Surely, the Fuehrer had decided, even the stubborn British prime minister Churchill would recognize that the war was lost and would conclude a negotiated peace, rather than subject his homeland to the ravages of a hopeless war. His orders to Goering were simple: "Do nothing."[7] When Milch heard the order, he was furious. Couldn't the Fuehrer see that this plan might be the only chance Germany would have to defeat Britain and win the war?

Hitler was not the only one blinded by the intoxicating conquest of France. Hans Jeschonnek, the chief of the General Staff, shared the optimism. Three weeks later, after the French surrendered, he was sitting in the dining car of Goering's special train with the Reichsmarschall and Dr. Christian von Hammerstein, the senior legal officer of the Luftwaffe, and other officers. They were discussing the forthcoming air attacks against England. Goering turned to his chief of staff and asked him if he believed these attacks would be successful.

"Yes, of course I do," Jeschonnek replied. Later he affirmed to Goering: "I don't think it will take over six weeks at the most!" Goering doubted this and pointed out that the British ought not be considered softer than the Germans. If it was assumed that the Germans would continue to fight even

if Berlin were destroyed, then they should not assume that the British would
stop fighting just because London was destroyed.[8]

As the summer of 1940 wore on, British diplomats stalled, and Hitler, still
hopeful of a negotiated settlement, refused to unleash the Wehrmacht. The
men of the Luftwaffe played cards, drank wine, sunbathed, visited the cafés,
and generally enjoyed the delights of France. (The French resistance to the
Nazi occupation had not yet begun.) While Goering's men idled away their
time, England feverishly tried to rebuild her shattered war machine. Factories worked night and day to produce every conceivable type of war material—especially fighter planes. Under the dynamic leadership of the highly
efficient Lord Beaverbrook, a Canadian-born newspaper publisher, British
aircraft factories worked without stopping. In the month after Dunkirk they
turned out 446 new fighters—about one hundred more than the Germans
produced. The Luftwaffe was well on its way to losing the quantitative lead it
had established over the R.A.F. prior to the start of the war. They had already
been surpassed qualitatively, although they did not yet realize it. The British
Spitfire was faster and more maneuverable than the Me-109 (although it
could not outclimb it), and the British Hurricane was nearly the equal of the
best German fighter. Both had a much greater range than the Me-109—a
decisive factor in the battle ahead. As the Battle of Britain progressed, the
R.A.F. developed the tactic of sending the heavily armed Hurricanes against
the German bombers, while the Spitfires dealt with the more formidable Me-
109s. As a result, Hurricane pilots scored more "kills" than any other group
in the Battle of Britain.[9]

Although Hitler still hesitated to allow an all-out aerial offensive, he did
allow the Luftwaffe to attack British shipping in the English Channel, beginning in early July. In these encounters, the R.A.F. definitely came out second-
best. Despite their technological inferiority, the more experienced German
fighter pilots were still tactically superior to their R.A.F. counterparts. They
flew loose formations at different altitudes, while British fighters flew tight,
wingtip to wingtip formations. Consequently, British pilots were too busy trying to maintain formations to keep a proper lookout for Messerschmitts,
which usually spotted them and attacked first: a major and usually decisive
advantage in aerial combat. From early July to August 12, in the so-called
"Battle of the Channel," Luftwaffe bombers flew about 7,000 sorties and

dropped nearly 2,000 tons of bombs, sinking 70,000 tons of British shipping. True, the R.A.F. shot down 279 German aircraft, but they lost 142 of their precious fighters. Only eighty-five Me-109s were shot down.[10]

Meanwhile, Hitler finally ordered the OKW to prepare for a seaborne invasion of Great Britain, should it prove necessary. The German Army was generally against such an operation, as were Grand Admiral Raeder and the German Navy. Only Goering and the Luftwaffe greeted the idea with enthusiasm. At the end of July, Jeschonnek told Rear Adm. Wilhelm Moessel, the naval liaison officer to OKL, that the navy would not be needed for the defeat of Britain. "The Luftwaffe [alone] will conquer England in a matter of months!" he said.[11]

The Luftwaffe's plan of operations for the Battle of Britain called for an operation of two phases. First, British fighter and other antiaircraft defenses in southeastern England would be annihilated. Then, daylight operations would continue to roll northward until complete air superiority was established. Simultaneously, the British aircraft industry would be annihilated by the *Kampfgeschwadern*.

Three air fleets were to participate in the Battle of Britain. From north to south, they were Stumpff's 5th, Kesselring's 2nd, and Sperrle's 3rd. Stumpff's fleet in Norway had only Geisler's X Air Corps, which had only four wings. One of these was equipped with Me-109s, whose range was insufficient to reach the British coast, so it could be used for defensive purposes only. In all, Stumpff had only 138 He-111 and Ju-88 bombers (124 serviceable) and 37 twin-engine fighters (34 serviceable) to send against Scotland and northern England.[12]

The bulk of the Luftwaffe's combat strength was concentrated in France and Belgium. Hugo Sperrle's 3d Air Fleet, headquartered in Paris, included four Stuka wings, five bomber wings, three Me-109 fighter wings, and a "destroyer" wing equipped with twin-engine Me-110s. Most of his fighters were placed under the direction of Col. Werner Junck's 3rd Fighter Command (*Jagdfliegerfuehrer 3*), a temporary formation designed to close with and destroy the Spitfires and Hurricanes as they tried to intercept the German bombers. Sperrle's remaining aircraft came under the control of Richthofen's VIII, Greim's V, and Kurt Pflugbeil's IV Air Corps.

The strongest of the Luftwaffe's air fleets was Albert Kesselring's 2nd. Headquartered in Brussels, it controlled Ulrich Grauert's I Air Corps, Loerzer's II Air Corps, Coeler's 9th Air Division, and the weak and recently formed 1st Night Fighter Division, commanded by Col. Joseph Kammhuber. Most of Kesselring's fighters were under the 2nd Fighter Command, which was led by Col. Kurt von Doering, a veteran of the Richthofen wing who had scored eleven kills in World War I.[13] Between them, Sperrle and Kesselring controlled 1,232 He-111, Ju-88, and Do-17 bombers; 406 Stuka dive-bombers; 282 Me-110 twin-engine fighters; and 813 Me-109 single-engine fighters. Of these, 875 bombers, 316 Stukas, 227 Me-110s, and 702 Me-109s were operational on August 13, 1940. Table 8 shows the Luftwaffe's order of battle on August 13.

Goering set "Eagle Day" (*Adler Tag*), the start of the Battle of Britain, for August 10. His plan called for German bombers to attack British shipping, radar sites, the R.A.F. ground organization, aircraft factories, plus a number of other targets. The bombers were thus to serve as bait for the R.A.F. fighters, which would be destroyed by the escorting Me-109s and Me-110s as they attacked the German bombers. Both Kesselring and Sperrle opposed these tactics. They wanted to first destroy the R.A.F. ground organization (airfields, supply depots, radar stations, etc.) by continuous nighttime bombing.[14] Goering refused to modify the plan, however. Because of the lateness of the season, September 15 had been set as the last possible date to begin Operation "Sealion," the code name for the invasion of Britain. The Luftwaffe had to achieve air superiority by that date. Even as it was, Eagle Day had to be postponed until August 13 because of bad weather.

The German tactics placed the Me-109 pilots at a severe disadvantage. Already they were limited to ninety minutes' flying time by their fuel tanks. This would give them only a maximum of thirty minutes' flight time over Great Britain. Now, under Goering's plan, they would have to fly zigzag patterns to keep up with the slower speeds of their bombers. Also, tied to the bombers, they could not dictate the timing of the fighter battles, nor take advantage of altitude or of the sun. The mistakes of the Spanish civil war were now becoming apparent. The bombers could not protect themselves against enemy fighters, as the Luftwaffe High Command had assumed. There had been no training in cooperation between fighters and bombers, and there would be no time for it now. Meanwhile, R.A.F. Fighter Command, led by Air Chief Marshal Sir Hugh C. T. Dowding, had assembled 749 fighters (mainly Hurricanes and Spitfires, plus a few obsolete Bleinheims, Defiants, and Gladiators) to meet the onslaught.[15] Dowding divided his fifty-nine squadrons among four fighter groups, the most important of which was Air Vice Marshal Keith Park's 11th Group in southeastern England. Park had 40 percent of Fighter Command's operational aircraft on August 13.

In addition to the initially poor fighter tactics used by the Luftwaffe, the R.A.F. possessed a number of other advantages. First, they were operating over their own territory. This minimized losses of damaged aircraft and maximized their flight time over combat areas. Also, it minimized aircrew losses, as pilots who bailed out were quickly returned to their units, while downed Luftwaffe airmen were promptly captured and spent the rest of the war in POW camps. Second, the R.A.F. had a chain of twenty-nine radar stations

TABLE 8: LUFTWAFFE ORDER OF BATTLE, "EAGLE DAY," AUGUST 13, 1940

5th Air Fleet (Stumpff)
  X Air Corps (Geisler)
    KG 26 (He-111s)
    KG 30 (Ju-88s)
    I/ZG (Me-110s)
3rd Air Fleet (Sperrle)
  VIII Air Corps (Richthofen)
    StG 1 (-) (Ju-87s)
    StG 2 (Ju-87s)
    StG 77 (Ju-87s)
    JG 27 (Me-109s)
  V Air Corps (Greim)
    KG 51 (Ju-88s)
    KG 54 (Ju-88s)
    KG 55 (He-111s)
  IV Air Corps (Pflugbeil)
    LG 1 (Ju-88s)
    KG 27 (He-111s)
    StG 3 (Ju-87s)
  3rd Fighter Command (Junck)
    JG 2 (Me-109s)
    JG 53 (Me-109s)
    ZG 2 (Me-110s)
2nd Air Fleet (Kesselring)
  I Air Corps (Grauert)
    KG 1 (He-111s)
    KG 76 (Do-17s and Ju-88s)
    KG 77 (Ju-88s)
  II Air Corps (Loerzer)
    KG 2 (Do-17s)
    KG 3 (Do-17s)
    KG 53 (He-111s)
    II/StG 1 (Ju-87s)
    IV/LG 1 (Ju-87s)
    Gruppe 210 (Me-109s and Me-110s)
  9th Air Division (Coeler)
    KG 4 (He-111s and Ju-88s)
    I/KG 40 (Ju-88s and FW-200s)
    KG 100 (He-111 "Pathfinders")

TABLE 8: LUFTWAFFE ORDER OF BATTLE, "EAGLE DAY," AUGUST 13, 1940
(*continued*)

1st Night Fighter Division (Kammhuber)
   NJG 1 (Me-110s)
2nd Fighter Command (Doering)
   JG 3 (Me-109s)
   JG 26 (Me-109s)
   JG 51 (Me-109s)
   JG 52 (Me-109s)
   JG 54 (Me-109s)
   ZG 26 (Me-110s)
   ZG 76 (=) (Me-110s)

Source: Bekker, p. 545.

(known as Radio Direction Finders, or RDFs), posted along the southern and eastern coasts of England. Since they knew where the Germans were heading, the R.A.F. pilots did not have to fly standing fighter patrols, and they were thus able to extend their resources to the limit. Since it had yet to develop a truly effective radar, the Luftwaffe had to hold fighters in reserve to protect its bases. It also had to keep a fighter wing in Norway (to protect the bases there) and had to keep 300 fighters in Germany, to protect the Reich against possible raids by the R.A.F. Bomber Command.

Eagle Day started badly for the Germans. Because of poor weather, Kesselring had to cancel his part of the morning's operation. To the South, Sperrle committed his air fleet, which included Richthofen's Stukas. The weather improved as the day wore on, and Kesselring committed his forces in the afternoon. Like Sperrle's units, they launched a number of heavy raids against a variety of targets but did not concentrate against Fighter Command—a major German failure through most of the battle.

In all, the Luftwaffe flew 1,485 sorties (most of them by fighters) against 727 by Fighter Command. The Germans lost forty-five aircraft (only nine of which were Me-109s) against thirteen for the R.A.F. The Me-110s and the Stukas, which climbed slowly after diving, had been particularly hard hit. The Me-110, in fact, was a major disappointment. Designed as a bomber escort, it had been unable to protect either the bombers or itself from the Spitfires and Hurricanes. During the early stages of the Battle of Britain it was proven to be technologically inferior to modern enemy aircraft, although Goering refused to withdraw it from the battle. In fact, he ordered that Me-109 units be detached to escort Me-110 units, so the Battle of Britain saw the absurd spectacle of fighters flying escort missions for other fighters![16]

The next three days were just as dismal as Eagle Day had been. The Luftwaffe lost nineteen aircraft on the August 14, seventy-five on the fifteenth, and forty-five on the sixteenth. R.A.F. losses were eight, thirty-four, and twenty-one, respectively. The weather cancelled most operations on the sevnteenth, but on the eighteenth, Fighter Command shot down seventy-one German airplanes and lost only twenty-seven itself. Goering and his intelligence branch now estimated that the British had only 160 fighter aircraft left; they only missed the mark by 590 planes. Still, Goering was far from satisfied with the Luftwaffe's performance. He pulled the slow Stukas out of the battle and, on the 19th, held a meeting at Cape Blanc-Nez. Every leader down to squadron level heard the Reichsmarschall loudly reprimand the Luftwaffe's pilots for a lack of aggressiveness. It was the first time the flyers had felt the rough side of his tongue. Goering also changed his tactics. No longer were naval vessels, radar sites, or military facilities to be the focus of operations. From now on his pilots were to concentrate exclusively against the enemy air forces in southeast England: its aircraft, its oil depots, and its sector stations, the nerve centers of the R.A.F.[17]

There were also personnel changes. Kurt von Doering was replaced as Fighter Commander 2 by *Pour le Merite*–holder Col. Theo Osterkamp, commander of the 51st Fighter Wing, a seasoned veteran who had shot down thirty-two enemy airplanes in World War I and six more in the battles of France and Britain. Osterkamp, who was forty-eight years old in 1940, was eventually promoted to lieutenant general and was fighter commander Italy later in the war.[18] This rare ace of both world wars was replaced as commander of JG 51 by Maj. Werner Moelders, a twenty-eight-year-old group commander in the 53d Fighter Wing. In the succeeding days other wing and group commanders were also replaced by younger men, in whom Goering had greater faith.

The Cape Blanc-Nez meeting ended the first phase of the Battle of Britain. The Reichsmarschall's tough words, plus the changes in tactics, opened the second phase, which came very near to winning the war for the Third Reich. Goering had correctly assumed that the R.A.F. would commit its precious fighters for the defense of their bases.

The second phase of the Battle of Britain began when the weather cleared on August 24 (see Map 5). On the twenty-fifth the Fighter Command airfield and communications center at Warmwell was severely damaged, and the next day the Debden and Southhampton airfields suffered the same fate. The airfields at Rochford and Eastchurch were attacked on the 27th, and the

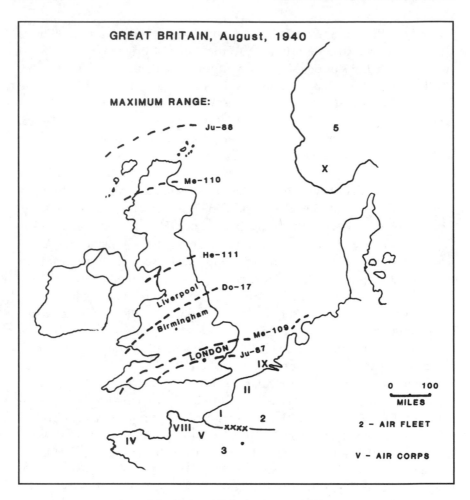

Map 5: Great Britain, August 1940

big airfield at Biggin Hill was raided twice and severely damaged on August 29. On the 31st the Luftwaffe made its biggest effort to date, launching 1,450 daylight sorties against Fighter Command bases at Biggin Hill, Debden, Hornchurch, Croydon, and Eastchurch. Biggin Hill was visited again on September 1, Lympne and Hornchurch on the 2nd, North Weald and West Malling on the 3rd, Lympe and Eastchurch again on the 4th, and Biggin Hill once again on the 5th. As a result the Biggin Hill air base was operating at one-third capacity on September 6, and several others were incapable of functioning normally. As Goering predicted, the R.A.F. committed its fighters to the battle for the airfields of southeastern England. In the period August 24 to September 6, 1940, the R.A.F. lost 273 fighters, against 308 Luftwaffe aircraft. During the first three days of September, the Luftwaffe had destroyed sixty-two vital British fighters, at a cost of only forty-three German airplanes.

In the decisive category of fighter aircraft, however, the Luftwaffe had lost 146 Me-109s, but they had shot down 208 Spitfires and Hurricanes. British factories could no longer make good Fighter Command's losses, because casualties exceeded production. The R.A.F.'s frontline strength remained more or less constant at 650 fighters, but the number in reserve declined from 518 in the first week of June to 292 by September 7.[19] Also, for the first time, Fighter Command was experiencing a shortage of trained pilots. It had lost about 300 trained pilots in France and Flanders, and there had been a continual drain since. In the week of August 24-September 1, it lost 231 pilots killed, wounded, or missing—more than 20 percent of its pilot strength in a single week. By the first week in September, the average British fighter squadron had only sixteen pilots out of a normal complement of twenty-six.[20] The survivors had to take up the slack by flying three or four missions a day—a physical and mental strain that could not be kept up indefinitely.

Fighter Command's junior leaders, so essential to a successful air battle, were also disappearing. In July and August, 24 percent of its squadron leaders and 40 percent of its flight commanders had been killed or seriously wounded.[21] The R.A.F. Fighter Command was clearly nearing its breaking point. Air Chief Marshal Dowding was faced with two choices: lose the entire Fighter Command to attrition, or withdraw it north of London, out of the range of the Me-109s. If he did this, however, Germany would control the Channel and the airspace over southeastern England—including the invasion beaches. Either choice would mean a German victory and the fall of the United Kingdom. "What we need now," Dowding muttered, "is a miracle."[22]

He got one. England's savior was the same unlikely one who halted the panzers near Dunkirk: Adolf Hitler. The R.A.F. Bomber Command, beginning on August 25, made five minor raids on Berlin in eleven days, doing little material damage but infuriating the Fuehrer. On September 4, Hitler publicly announced: "When they declare that they will attack our cities in great strength, then we will erase theirs!"[23] Supported by Jeschonnek, he ordered massive retaliatory daylight bombing attacks on London, diverting the Luftwaffe from what should have been its real objective: air superiority over the invasion beaches.

Goering saw that terror bombing for retribution's sake was a mistake. He asked Jeschonnek why he supported it. The chief of staff replied that it would force the British to sue for peace. The Reichsmarschall then asked him if he thought Germany would surrender if Berlin were bombed into ruins. No, Jeschonnek replied, but British morale was made of more fragile stuff than German morale. "That," Goering responded, "is where you are wrong."[24] However, if Goering expressed any objections to Hitler himself about meddling in his battle plan, that protest could not have been strong and has not come down to us.

Perhaps the most fateful meeting in the history of the Luftwaffe took place between Goering and his two principal air fleet commanders at The Hague on September 3, the day before Hitler made his public pronouncement about erasing British cities. Goering suggested that the current tactical plan of concentrating on smashing the R.A.F. and its bases be abandoned in favor of large-scale bombing of London, the hub of the British war effort. He wanted to know if the R.A.F. had been sufficiently weakened to accomplish this task without undue risk to the bomber force.

Sperrle had always advocated the destruction of the R.A.F., and he correctly stated that it was still a force to be reckoned with. His chief of staff, Lt. Gen. Paul Deichmann, the Cassandra of the Luftwaffe, agreed with him. Kesselring, optimistic as usual, believed Luftwaffe intelligence reports that the British had only a few fighters left and was convinced that massive aerial attacks on London would end the war. "By the time we have killed a few thousand Cockneys, the British will be screaming for peace," he declared.[25] Sperrle, on the other hand, was not an optimistic man. He estimated that the British had about a thousand fighters and strongly urged that the battle continue exactly as it was being fought. The pressure on the R.A.F. was intolerable to them and must not be relieved, he cried. The argument became heated, but Goering—under pressure from Hitler—ruled against Sperrle in the end. The first major attack on London took place two days later.[26] The British capital superseded the R.A.F. as the primary target of the Luftwaffe. The British Fighter Command quickly recovered and was never again threatened with annihilation, as it was in early September, 1940. The decision to suspend the attacks on the R.A.F. Fighter Command was perhaps the decisive turning point of the entire air war.

It should be noted here (as Sperrle did) that Luftwaffe intelligence reports were usually wrong. They reflected the personality of Col. (later Lt. Gen.) Joseph "Beppo" Schmid, whom General Plocher called "a colorful and sometimes controversial character."[27] General Galland was less diplomatic. "Beppo Schmid was a complete wash-out as intelligence officer, the most important job of all," he told his interrogators in 1945.[28] Milch agreed, saying that Schmid "was a man who trimmed his sails to the wind for fear of Goering. Besides which he wasn't an airman and didn't understand the significance of the reports he received."[29] Unlike most intelligence officers, who tend to overstate the strength of their opponents, Schmid consistently underestimated the strength and production capacity of the enemy, especially that of the R.A.F., the Soviet Union, and the United States. His efforts tended to confirm the overly optimistic views of Goering, Jeschonnek, and the Nazis, and, by telling Goering what he wanted to hear, he contributed to the Luftwaffe's defeat in the Battle of Britain. His reports the following year also led the Luftwaffe leadership to believe it faced a much easier task when it invaded Russia than, in fact, was the case.

Joseph Schmid, who was born in Bavaria in 1901, first saw action as a member of Gen. Ritter Franz von Epp's Freikorps. An early Nazi, he took part in Hitler's unsuccessful Beer Hall Putsch of 1923. Schmid joined the Reichsheer as a private and received his commission in the infantry in 1924. He transferred to the Luftwaffe as a captain in 1935 and, as a major, became chief of the Military Intelligence Branch on January 1, 1938, a post he held until November 9, 1942. During his long tenure, Schmid did nothing to upgrade the low quality of the intelligence service. Galland wrote later that the most sophisticated piece of technical equipment the Intelligence Branch used, up to 1944, "was a pair of binoculars. The personnel consisted of some old reservists of the intelligence battalions, pensioned policemen, unfit men, or overaged civil servants from the local authorities, and a horde of female assistants."[30]

In late 1942, as a colonel, Schmid took command of a battlegroup of Goering's Panzer Division in Tunisia. He showed no great talent in commanding ground forces but was nevertheless flown out of the Tunisian pocket at the very last moment on the personal orders of his friend, Hermann Goering. Promoted to major general on February 1, 1943, and lieutenant general on July 1, 1944, he served as commander of I Fighter Corps (September 15, 1943, to November 15, 1944) and was commander-in-chief of Luftwaffe Command West (formerly 3d Air Fleet) from November 15, 1944, until April 28, 1945. Apprehended by the Western Allies on May 15, 1945, he was a prisoner of war until April 1, 1948. Thereafter he lived in Augsburg[31] and contributed to the U.S. Air Force's German Historical Monograph Project in Karlsruhe. He died suddenly on August 30, 1956.[32]

Hugo Sperrle was disgusted after the Hague conference. The Luftwaffe was defeated over the skies of London. In October, Goering seized on the pretext of deteriorating weather conditions to call off daylight operations over the United Kingdom. Great Britain remained in the war, and the Luftwaffe had suffered its first major defeat.

It is clear that Hitler, Goering, and Kesselring were wrong in changing their tactics, but was Sperrle's assessment of the situation correct? It would appear so. After the war, Churchill wrote:

If the enemy had persisted in heavy attacks against the adjacent sectors and damaged their operations rooms or telephone communications, the whole intricate organization of the Fighter Command might have been broken down. This would have meant not merely the maltreatment of London, but the loss to us of the perfected control of our own air in the decisive area . . . It was therefore with a sense of relief that Fighter Command felt the German attack turn on to London on September 7, and concluded that the enemy had changed his plan. Goering should certainly have persevered against the airfields, on whose organization and combination the whole fighting power of our air force at this moment depended . . . he made a foolish mistake.[33]

The third phase of the Battle of Britain began during the late afternoon of September 7, when the Luftwaffe raided the London docks with 650 bombers and more than a thousand fighter sorties. The aerial bombardment continued throughout the night, as 660 tons of high explosive (HE) bombs and thousands of incendiaries rained down on the British capital. The terror raids were soon expanded to Southampton, Portland, Brighton, Eastbourne, Canterbury, Yarmouth, Norwick, and other cities. This delighted Winston Churchill, who realized that the changing focus of the battle had saved the United Kingdom. The Luftwaffe's losses were soon more than doubling those of the R.A.F. During the period September 7 to 15, British fighters lost 174 aircraft but shot down 321 German warplanes. More important, British fighter units were given a much-needed and well-deserved respite, and losses declined from an average of 19.5 aircraft a day in phase two to 14 a day in phase three. British factories could now once again make good R.A.F. losses.[34]

On the other hand, Luftwaffe morale was hurt by these casualties. Typically, the Reichsmarschall put the blame for this defeat on his pilots. "The fighters have let us down," he said on September 16.[35] The next day, Hitler made the decision to postpone Operation Sealion indefinitely—in effect cancelling it altogether. Goering realized that the battle was lost and on October 20 called off all but nighttime harassing operations over England. During the six weeks of the third phase of the Battle of Britain, the Luftwaffe bomber units had lost 30 to 35 percent of their strength and the fighters 20 to 25 percent. According to General Galland, the overall combat strength of the Luftwaffe in the latter part of October was only one-quarter of what it had been when the battle began. Great Britain had been saved and the western front had become what Moelders called a "Verdun of the air."[36]

Goering grew tired of the Battle of Britain even before it reached its climax. On one occasion Goering was caught by his signals officer in the Ritz Hotel in Paris, telling his wife on the telephone that he was at that very moment on the cliffs of Calais, watching his squadrons crossing the Channel for Britain. Now that the battle could not be won, he completely lost interest in the campaign and went back to Berlin. He still found time to interfere with operations at the front, however. Werner Kreipe, then chief of operations of 3rd Air Fleet, recalled later:

> . . . at the highest levels there continued to be constant vacillations in the matters of strategy, and nowhere was this more apparent than at the Air Force High Command. Goering and his staff had by now retired to Berlin . . . Quite frequently, and often at the very last moment, he would order the cancellation of a well-prepared operation, and on the basis of unconfirmed intelligence . . . would order an altogether different operation to be undertaken at once.[37]

At last Goering grew tired of even this. On November 14 he went on an extended leave. Because he could not bear to work with Milch, Hans Jeschonnek also went on leave. His chief of operations, Maj. Gen. Hoffmann von Waldau, became acting chief of staff. The pair did not return to duty until January, 1941. For over a year after that Goering took little interest in the air force and mainly devoted his time to pleasure and collecting art treasures; in fact, Goering will probably go down in history as the greatest art thief of all time.

Goering managed to deceive Hitler for a very long time into believing that he was working tirelessly for the Luftwaffe. He and Gen. Karl Bodenschatz, his liaison officer at Fuehrer Headquarters, developed an excellent arrangement. Bodenschatz would attend Hitler's afternoon situation conference and learn the Fuehrer's views on a particular matter. He would then inform Goering, who would appear at the evening conference and voice Hitler's own ideas as if they were his own. This gave the Fuehrer much pleasure and reinforced Goering's own standing in Hitler's mind.

Hitler continued the nighttime blitz against London because he had publicly committed himself to heavy bombing raids, there was still an outside chance that British morale would collapse, the raids were damaging to the economic framework of the United Kingdom, and they were a safe way to continue the air war against Britain without significant loss to the Luftwaffe. The number of German sorties gradually declined, from 3,884 in December 1940, to 2,465 in January 1941, to only 1,400 in February.[38] The Battle of Britain faded into history with a whimper, not a bang. The last major raids took place on the nights of April 16, April 19, and May 10, 1941.

In the first two of these, well over 1,000 Londoners were killed and about 148,000 buildings (mostly houses) were destroyed. During the raid of May 10, London suffered its worst night of the war. More than 1,400 people were killed and 1,800 wounded. One-third of the city's streets were blocked, and some fires continued to burn for eleven days.[39] It was a prelude to the end, however, as the Luftwaffe was secretly withdrawing most of its units to the east, for its invasion of the Soviet Union. The 1941 attacks on London had, in reality, been only a diversion aimed at fooling the Allies into thinking that Hitler was planning to resume his air war against Britain, when in fact he had set his sights on the Russian Bear. On May 21, as Kesselring moved his headquarters to Posen in occupied Poland, Field Marshal Sperrle became the sole air commander in the West. Of the forty-four bomber groups previously operating against Britain, however, Sperrle retained only four. Of the fighter wings, only Maj. Wilhelm Balthasar's JG 2 "Richthofen" and Col. Adolf Galland's JG 26 "Schlageter" remained in the Channel area. By the end of June 1941, there were only 780 aircraft left in the 3rd and 5th Air Fleets, which became a reservoir of reserves for the eastern front.[40]

Meanwhile, Hugo Sperrle also gradually lost interest in the air war. His decline began in 1940, when he transferred his headquarters to Paris and took up residence at the Palais du Luxembourg, the former palace of Marie de Medici. Prior to this General Veith described him as "very unpretentious," but now "gradually everything went to his head."[41] The brewer's son was corrupted by the debauchery of Paris. He became addicted to laziness, luxurious living, and gambling, Munitions Minister Albert Speer later commented: "The Field Marshal's craving for luxury and public display ran a close second to that of his superior Goering; he was also his match in corpulence."[42]

As early as September 1, 1940, Sperrle was seen in the company of Field Marshal Milch, enjoying life in the gambling casinos of Deauville, where Sperrle had a command post.[43] While Hugo Sperrle enjoyed the life of Riley, training went to seed. On March 1, 1943, the R.A.F. attacked Berlin. When the last bomb fell, 35,000 people in the German capital had lost their homes. Hitler immediately ordered Sperrle to raid London in reprisal. On March 3, Sperrle's men flew across the Channel. They dropped 100 tons of bombs, but only 12 tons fell on London. Hitler was furious. In his conference of March 5 he lambasted 3rd Air Fleet's inability to find London, a target thirty miles wide and only ninety miles from the French coast.[44] The Fuehrer was still criticizing Sperrle on March 9. Propaganda minister Dr. Paul Joseph Goebbels recorded Hitler's views (and his own) in his diary: "Field Marshal Sperrle . . . was not equal to his tasks. Like all air force generals he had withdrawn to a castle and was there leading a sybaritic life. Air warfare against England probably didn't interest him much more than, say, an excellent luncheon or dinner. The Fuehrer wants to recall him."[45]

Hitler's attitude toward Sperrle had mitigated by early July 1943. Perhaps because Sperrle was in debt due to his luxurious lifestyle and gambling, the Fuehrer sent him a gift of 50,000 reichsmarks. The field marshal was not found at his headquarters, however; he was busy vacationing on the Atlantic coast south of Biarritz at the time.[46]

With the command of the air war in the west in such hands, the actual conduct of operations naturally fell to Sperrle's more responsible subordinates. With about 250 largely obsolete aircraft, Joachim Coeler continued to inflict costly casualties on British shipping with his hit-and-run mine-laying operations. His 9th Air Division was upgraded to IX Air Corps in October, 1941, and the dependable Coeler was promoted to general of flyers on January 1, 1942. Later in the war he would be named commander of the XIV Air Corps (on April 30, 1943) and commander of transport aircraft (from October 15, 1944). He was sent into reserve on February 5, 1945.[47] The most important Luftwaffe commander in the West in late 1941, however, was Lt. Col. Martin Harlinghausen, the air commander Atlantic (*Fliegerfuehrer Atlantik*). The main aircraft in his arsenal was the FW-200, better known as the "Condor."

Although Hans Geisler was not successful as an air corps commander (he was replaced as commander of the X Air Corps on August 25, 1942, and was never reemployed), he was good at antishipping operations. In late 1939 or early 1940 he suggested to Jeschonnek that the Focke-Wulf 200, a four-engine civil aircraft, be converted into a military aircraft until the He-177 four-engine bomber could be brought into production. Jeschonnek saw the merits of such a proposal, and the first Condors joined the squadrons as long-range maritime reconnaissance-bombers. The converted civilian airplane had a number of weaknesses. It was too slow (224 mph. maximum), it was vulnerable to antiaircraft fire, and it had a weak structure. Nevertheless it had a radius of action of 1,000 miles with 2,000 pounds of bombs, or 1,400 miles with a single 550-pound bomb. Because of their range, the Condors enjoyed considerable success early in the war, before the Allied convoys developed defenses against them. From August 1, 1940, to February 9, 1941, Naval Air Group West at Lorient, equipped with fifteen He-111s and six to eight Condors, sank eighty-five merchant vessels, totalling 363,000 tons.[48]

In early 1941, with all hope of defeating Britain by direct aerial bombardment gone, the Luftwaffe General Staff turned its attention to helping the navy defeat her via the blockade. To direct the Luftwaffe's part in these operations, OKL established Air Command Atlantic under Harlinghausen, a pioneer in antishipping operations.

Martin Harlinghausen, a native of Rheda, was only thirty-nine years old in 1941. He had entered the navy as a seaman in 1923, serving in torpedo boats. He received his commission in 1929 but remained with the torpedo boats until late 1931, when he began his pilot's training. Transferred to the Luftwaffe in 1933, he trained as an aerial observer until October 1934, when he joined the training section of the Reichs Air Ministry. In late 1937 he earned his first distinction as commander of the sea reconnaissance squadron with the Condor Legion in Spain. Back in Germany, he joined the operations staff of the 2nd Air Fleet in 1938 and attended a brief General Staff course at the Air War Academy in early 1939. Harlinghausen's first General Staff assignment was as operations officer of the 10th Air Division. After a brief period as air commander Trondheim (April 17–May 21, 1940) during the invasion of Norway, he won his Knights Cross and was named chief of staff of the X Air Corps on May 21, 1940. He was promoted to captain (1934), major (1938), and lieutenant colonel (January 1, 1941).[49]

Harlinghausen directed his new command with considerable skill and daring. He had already developed the "Swedish Turnip" system of attack, which was based on the old naval premise that ships present the best target when approached directly from the beam. Harlinghausen also concluded that the lower an aircraft was when it approached its target, the higher and clearer its victim's silhouette stood against the horizon. Using these tactics, Condor pilots alone sank fifteen vessels (63,175 tons) in January, 1941, and twenty-two more (84,515 tons) in February, in what was called "armed reconnaissance" missions. They also guided U-boats to dozens of other targets, at a time when Great Britain was threatened with starvation. Unfortunately for Germany, few Condors were produced (only about five per month in 1941), serviceability was low (seldom above 25 percent), and the British took countermeasures by equipping their merchant ships with light antiaircraft guns, which were very effective against the slow Condors. Aircraft losses were so heavy that Harlinghausen was forced to prohibit the Swedish turnip tactics that he himself had invented. Worse still for Germany, the British antisubmarine tactics were equally successful, forcing Adm. Karl Doenitz to withdraw the U-boats from the sector around Britain and Ireland in mid-July, 1941.[50] The Battle of the Atlantic was lost.

Colonel Harlinghausen continued to patrol the North Atlantic until November, 1941, when his low-flying He-111 was hit by anti-aircraft fire over the Irish Sea. He managed to nurse his badly damaged airplane to the French coast, where he crash-landed and was rescued by French fishermen. He spent the next three months in the hospital. Discharged at the beginning of 1942, he was named commander of the 26th Bomber Wing and inspector of aerial torpedoes.[51] He was replaced by Lt. Gen. Ulrich Kessler, who had commanded the 1st (previously 152nd) Bomber Wing in Poland and was chief of staff of the 1st Air Fleet from December 1939, to April 25, 1940. Although he had little success, this World War I naval observer was a favorite of Goering and remained air commander Atlantic until 1944. Promoted to general of fly- ers in 1944, he was named air attaché to Tokyo and was on his way to Japan when the war ended.[52] As air commander Atlantic, Kessler's post was looked upon as one of little significance, because the focus of the air war had long since shifted elsewhere.

CHAPTER 7

The Balkans Campaign

Axis military involvement in the Balkans began on October 28, 1940, when Italian dictator Benito Mussolini invaded Greece from Italian-held Albania with his Ninth and Eleventh Armies: about 150,000 men.[1] They advanced across the Kalamas (Thiamis) River on November 1, but were halted by a Greek counteroffensive in the Pindus Gorge on November 8, in which 5,000 men of the Italian 3rd Alpine Division were captured. Mussolini sacked his commander, Gen. Sebastiano Visconti-Prasca, and replaced him with Gen. Ubaldo Soddu, but there was little Soddu could do. By November 14 Gen. Alexander Papagos's Greek forces had pushed into Albania. On the 22d they routed the Italian ninth Army at Koritsa (Korce) and overran their principal forward air base. By December 4, when they captured Permet, the Greeks were claiming to have captured 28,000 men. The defeats forced the resignations of Marshal Pietro Badoglio, the chief of staff of the Italian army, and Adm. Domenico Cavagnari, the commander of the Italian navy. They were replaced by Gen. Ugo Cavallero and Adm. Arturo Riccardi, but again it did little good. By December 9 the Greeks had captured Porto Edda and had taken Pogradec On Lake Ohrid, more than forty miles from the Greek border, and Italy was calling for German military intervention in the Greek war.[2]

Hitler was at first reluctant to assist his ally, especially since he had not conquered Britain and he was seriously considering invading the Soviet Union the following year. On January 19–20, 1941, however, following a similar Italian rout in the desert, he met with the Italian dictator at Berchtesgaden and agreed to intervene in Greece in April. He also consented to send two German divisions to Libya (the Deutsche Afrika Korps) and Geisler's X Air Corps to Sicily, to preserve the Italian position in the central Mediterranean.[3] The task of supporting the German invasion of Greece fell to Col. Gen. Alexander Loehr's 4th Air Fleet, which headquartered in Vienna. Loehr was still assembling his forces on March 26, when the political situation changed dramatically.

On March 25, the Yugoslav government of Prince Paul yielded to intensive Nazi diplomatic pressure and agreed to join the Axis, rather than be subjected to German military occupation. The following night Gen. Richard

D. Simovic, the former commander of the Yugoslavian air force, launched a coup d'état and ousted Paul. The new government immediately assured Hitler of its friendship and sent out diplomatic feelers to Moscow. Hitler did not credit the friendship of the new government; instead he expanded Loehr's mission. Fourth Air Fleet was now to support Twelfth Army's invasion of Greece and Second Army's invasion of Yugoslavia. These ground forces were commanded by Field Marshal Siegmund Wilhelm List and Col. Gen. Baron Maximilian von Weichs, respectively.

To fulfill its new mission, 4th Air Fleet was hurriedly reinforced with 576 aircraft, rapidly deployed from Sicily, France, and Germany. Many of these belonged to Geisler's X Air Corps. By April 5, Loehr controlled about one thousand aircraft.[4] The bulk of his strength belonged to Gen. Baron Wolfram von Richthofen's VIII Air Corps.

Baron von Richthofen had a blot to remove from his escutcheon in the spring of 1941. The architect of the close air support doctrines of the Luftwaffe, he had failed miserably during the Battle of Britain. His vaulted Stukas had been shot to pieces on Eagle Day and had done no better on August 15. Three days later, on August 18, the Stukas tried again. Richthofen sent up four Ju-87 groups, which attacked the British airfields at Gosport, Thorney Island, and Ford, as well as the radar station at Poling on the southern coast. Thirty Stukas were lost or critically damaged in the attack. One group, I/StG 77, lost twelve of its twenty-eight aircraft, and six of the survivors were so badly damaged that they only just managed to reach the Continent.[5] Such losses were more than could be tolerated. Eighth Air Corps was withdrawn from the battle. For Richthofen, the Western air offensive was over.

Richthofen's VIII Air Corps had been gradually assembling in Rumania and Bulgaria since November, 1940. By February, 1941, he had 400 aircraft in these two countries. When the Simovic coup was launched, Richthofen had 135 fighter and reconnaissance aircraft in Rumania and 355 bombers and dive-bombers in Bulgaria. In early April he received Archer reinforcements from Germany, France, Sicily, and North Africa. On the morning of April 6, VIII Air Corps had about 600 aircraft. Richthofen stationed his fighter and reconnaissance aircraft at Arad, Deva, and Turnu-Severin in western Rumania, within easy range of Belgrade. The long-range bombers were placed at Wiener Neustadt, Austria, and at Sofia, Bulgaria, northwest and southeast of Belgrade, respectively. Both were within 200 miles of the Yugoslav capital.[6]

The Balkan campaign began with the saturation bombing of Belgrade on April 6. One hundred fifty bombers and dive-bombers (mainly He-111s and Stukas), heavily protected by fighters, bombed the city in relays for an hour and a half. The Yugoslav air force tried to intervene with about 400 inferior aircraft but was overwhelmed and virtually wiped out in the first attack. Two

German fighters were shot down, but twenty Yugoslav fighters were knocked out of the sky and forty-four other Yugoslav aircraft were destroyed on the ground. The German bombers concentrated on the center of the city, where the public buildings were located. Before the raid was over, the Yugoslav government was totally paralyzed. Communications were totally disrupted and the Yugoslav High Command could not even transmit orders to its forces in the field. Some seventeen thousand civilians were killed in the attack.[7]

The Yugoslav air force had been destroyed and all central control of their armed forces was lost at Belgrade in the very first hours of the campaign. Richthofen had accomplished his strategic missions. The VIII Air Corps then switched to its tactical mission: support the German ground forces by attacking Yugoslav troop concentrations and targets of opportunity in the combat zone. Striking almost at will, the corps was quite successful in this mission as well.[8] By April 18 the last organized Yugoslav resistance had ended.

The air battle for Greece proved more difficult for a number of reasons. First, Greece had been at war for some time, so a surprise victory of the magnitude of Belgrade was impossible. Second, Greece is a much more mountainous country, so atmospheric conditions made flying, and especially close air support, much more difficult. Third, the British quickly committed significant ground forces to the battle, in support of the Greeks. These included the I Australian Corps (6th Australian and 2d New Zealand Infantry Divisions) plus the 1st Tank Brigade and the British 2d Armored Division. Royal Air Force units (eighty operational aircraft under Air Vice-Marshal J. H. D'Albiac) flew missions from southern and central Greece from the first day of the campaign,[9] while most of Richthofen's units were committed to Belgrade and the support of Col. Gen. Baron Maximilian von Weichs' second Army and Col. Gen. Ewald von Kleist's 1st Panzer Group, which were responsible for the rapid conquest of Yugoslavia.[10]

Field Marshal Wilhelm von List's Twelfth Army was charged with the task of overrunning Greece. His forces, closely supported by dive-bomber elements of the VIII Air Corps, broke through the Metaxas line in a three-day struggle and captured Salonika on the morning of April 9. That evening the Greek Second Army capitulated to the XVIII Mountain Corps, and Macedonia and western Thrace were in German hands. List continued his offensive the next day by attacking the I Australian Corps north of Kozani with his XLI Panzer Corps. By evening the British forces were withdrawing. The critical Vevi Pass was captured by the 1st SS Motorized Infantry Division the next day.[11] The Allied forces were in full retreat for the rest of the campaign.

By April 19, Air Vice Marshal D'Albiac's R.A.F. contingent had been forced back to the Athens airfields. Richthofen attacked them on the twentieth with a large force of fighters and bombers. D'Albiac sent up his last fifteen Hurricanes to intercept them, but it was an unequal fight. Five of the

Hurricanes were shot down and most of the rest were damaged, against a German loss of eight airplanes. This battle virtually assured air supremacy for the Luftwaffe.[12]

With enemy aerial opposition crushed, Richthofen turned his attention to the Greek navy. On April 21 and 22 his bombers and dive-bombers sank twenty-three Greek ships, including a destroyer and a hospital ship.[13] Meanwhile, the British army retreated rapidly for the Isthmus of Corinth and the evacuation ports, for it was clear that the Allied cause in Greece was a doomed one.

Richthofen had his first experience in parachute operations in Greece, when he was ordered to cut off the British retreat at the Isthmus of Corinth in late April. He assembled more than 400 Ju-52s and many gliders at the former R.A.F. airfield at Larisa, south of Mount Olympus. At 5 A.M. on April 26 the first elements took off, and, taking advantage of the early morning haze, dropped two battalions of the 2nd Parachute Regiment plus a parachute medical company and a parachute engineer platoon at the isthmus at 7 A.M. on April 26. The drop altitude was only 400 feet.[14]

A large number of British troops were cut off when the paratroopers seized the bridge at the isthmus, but the airborne operation at Corinth was not an unqualified success. For one thing, the bulk of the British forces had already escaped. Second, although the bridge was seized intact according to plan, a lucky shot from a British antiaircraft gun detonated the demolition charges, even after the engineers had cut the demo cords. Several paratroopers were killed in the explosion, and the German advance was held up another twenty-four hours. Also, several aircraft and gliders were lost or damaged by antiaircraft and machinegun fire. Total German casualties at Corinth were 63 killed, 158 wounded, and 16 missing. Nine hundred British and 1,450 Greek troops were cut off and captured due to the loss of the isthmus.[15] The main British retreat continued, however, and on May 1 the last Allied units evacuated the Greek mainland. Between April 24 and May 1, the Royal Navy had evacuated 50,732 men, including Yugoslavs and Greeks, from the mainland.[16] This set the stage for the Luftwaffe's next major campaign: the Battle of Crete.

Crete is a Greek island in the Mediterranean, about 180 miles south-southeast of Athens. Approximately 160 miles long and 8 to 35 miles in width, it is barren and mountainous, with little water and limited lines of communication, especially north to south. Today it is little visited and of little importance. In 1941, however, it assumed a special strategic significance. With it, the British could maintain air and naval superiority in the eastern Mediterranean, raid the Balkan coast, and threaten the peninsula with invasion (thus tying down many German troops). More important for Hitler, from Crete the British would be able to launch long-range air raids on the Rumanian oilfields at Ploesti, Nazi Germany's main source of petroleum. Therefore, on April 20, Hitler decided to seize Crete by an airborne attack, in accordance with April 15 plans submitted to Goering by Loehr and Gen. Kurt Student, the ranking paratrooper commander in the Reich.[17]

The Crete operation was to come under the general direction of General Loehr, the commander of the 4th Air Fleet. He had two principal units under his command: Student's XI Air Corps and Richthofen's VIII. Student's corps, the ground attack force, consisted of the reinforced 7th Air Division (three parachute regiments and one glider assault regiment), plus several parachute engineer, parachute antiaircraft, and medical battalions, or about 25,000 men in all. Student also controlled ten air transport groups (Ju-52s) of approximately 500 aircraft and 100 gliders, plus a reconnaissance squadron.[18] The reinforced 6th Mountain Division, elements of the 5th Mountain Division, and two battalions from the 5th Panzer Division (II/31st Panzer Regiment and the 55th Motorcycle Battalion) were temporarily attached to Student's command for this operation.[19] Richthofen controlled 2d Bomber Wing (with three Do-17 groups), 1st Lehr Wing (two Ju-88 groups and one group of He-111s), 2nd Stuka Wing (three groups), 77th Fighter Wing (three groups of Me-109s), 26th Destroyer Wing (two groups of Me-110s), and two reconnaissance groups. In all he had 650 operational aircraft, including 280 bombers, 150 Stukas, 90 Me-109s, 90 Me-110s, and 40 reconnaissance aircraft.[20] In addition, Loehr had II Group, 4th Bomber Wing (for mine-laying operations in the Suez Canal), and the 126th Sea Reconnaissance Group in air fleet reserve.[21] The British opposed this air armada with twenty-four Hurricanes, Gladiators, and Fulmars—only half of which were serviceable.[22] Small wonder that the Allied garrison commander, New Zealand major general Sir Bernard C. Freyberg, had serious misgivings about the feasibility of defending the island. He appealed to the British C-in-C Mediterranean for more aircraft, but Field Marshal Sir Archibald Wavell, who was busy fighting Rommel in the desert, told him that no additional airplanes would be forthcoming.

Goering's final plan for the conquest of Crete was a hybrid of plans submitted by Loehr and Student. It called for the capture of the four main British airfields at Maleme, Canea, Retimo, and Heraklion. To make maximum use of Richthofen's Stukas, the assault was to come in two waves: Maleme and Canea were to be taken in the morning of D-Day, and Retimo and Heraklion were to be seized in the afternoon. Ninth Air Corps was to be divided into three groups for the operation. Group West (Maj. Gen. Eugen Meindl) consisted of the glider assault regiment, three parachute battalions, a parachute machine gun company, and a miscellaneous assault battalion. Group Center (Maj. Gen. Wilheim Suessmann) was to attack Canea with the 3d Parachute Regiment, the 100th Mountain Infantry Regiment, a small gliderborne battalion, a parachute machine gun company, a parachute engineer battalion, and miscellaneous light artillery and antitank detachments. A second force under Suessmann's overall command—the 2nd Parachute Regiment—was to attack Retimo, while Lt. Gen. Julius Ringel's Group East took the airfield at Heraklion. At Crete, Ringel commanded the reinforced 1st Parachute Regiment, the 5th Mountain Division (minus the 100th Mountain Infantry Regiment), the II Battalion, 31st Panzer Regiment, and a light antiaircraft battalion.[23] Meindl and Suessmann, who were paratroopers, were to go in with the initial assaults. Ringel, who was not airborne qualified, left the initial attack to Col. Bruno Brauer (commander of the 1st Parachute Regiment) and was not scheduled to take personal command at Heraklion until the airfield was secured. Map 6 shows the Battle of Crete.

Richthofen had the tasks of providing close air support for all of these attacks, destroying all R.A.F. fighter units before the airborne attacks began, sealing off the battle area to prevent the British from reinforcing the airfields from the south, as well as clearing the sea lanes to Crete so that the German bridgeheads could be reinforced with infantry, artillery, and heavy equipment.

The Allied defenses of the island were much stronger than the Germans estimated. They included 42,640 men, of which 10,258 were Greeks, who were demoralized, ill-equipped, and of little combat value. The troops from the British Empire, however, had much higher morale than the Germans expected, considering the defeat that they had just sustained on the mainland. In addition, they were well positioned. Freyberg was a highly competent field commander and he apparently based his dispositions on the assumption that the Germans might launch an airborne attack, since the British fleet dominated the sea routes to the island. He placed 8,024 men at Heraklion under Brigadier B. H. Chappel's 14th British Infantry Brigade; 6,730 at Retimo under Brigadier G. A. Vasey's 19th Australian Infantry Brigade; 14,822 in the Suda Bay-Canea area under Maj. Gen. E. A. Weston; and 11,859 men at Maleme under Brig. Gen. E. Puttick, the temporary commander of Freyberg's own 2nd New Zealand Division. (Puttick had only two brigades; the third New Zealand brigade had been so badly mauled in Greece that it had to be sent to Egypt to rebuild.) Freyberg also had twenty-two tanks and thirty-two heavy and thirty-six light antiaircraft guns. In addition, the British Mediterranean Fleet guarded the sea approaches to Crete with the bulk of its four battleships, eight cruisers, thirty destroyers, and the aircraft carrier *Formidable*.[24] Adm. Andrew Cunningham's dispositions set the

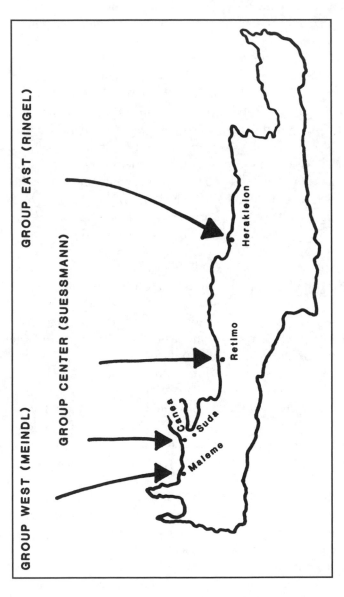

Map 6: Crete, 1941

stage for a major confrontation between his fleet and German air power, represented by Richthofen's VIII Air Corps.

Richthofen's first task, however, was to establish air supremacy over the battlefield from the very first day of operations. Attack-day had to be postponed until the third week in May because of logistical problems. It was necessary, for example, to stockpile 792,000 gallons of aviation fuel for XI Air Corps alone. All of this fuel had to be transported over Balkan roads and/or railroads, which were chaotic enough even in peacetime. Of course VIII Air Corps also had to be supplied, so it was not until May 20 that the assault could begin. Between 5:30 A.M. and 6 A.M. that day, Baron von Richthofen's fighters and dive-bombers struck the British airfields at Maleme, Heraklion, and Canea, completely neutralizing the Allied air defenses. Only seven of the 493 Ju-52s employed that day were lost.[25]

Richthofen's initial air attack was about the only success the Germans experienced on the first morning of the battle. Enemy resistance was much heavier than anticipated. Many paratroopers were killed by enemy infantrymen before they touched the ground or could disengage their parachutes. Many of those who survived were instantly pinned down and unable to reach their weapons containers, which contained their mortars and crew-served machine guns. Col. Richard Heidrich's 3rd Parachute Regiment was cut to ribbons south of Retimo, where it was surrounded by about a brigade of Australians. Heidrich did well to save the remnants of his command; seizing the airfield was totally out of the question.[26]

Elsewhere, Major General Suessmann, the commander of the 7th Air Division and Group Center, was killed instantly when his tow-cable broke and his glider crashed into the Aegean Sea, many miles closer to Athens than to Crete. Shortly afterwards, Major General Meindl was seriously wounded by a burst of machine-gun fire from a New Zealand unit. Eleventh Air Corps had thus lost two of its three group commanders just as the battle was beginning. Confusion reigned for the rest of the day as parachute drops were badly scattered and the German units were unable to form up due to enemy opposition. Individual paratroopers fought on under the ranking officer or NCO available. Surviving officers did not know where their men were and privates often could not find their own squads or commanders and did not even know if they were alive. The fighting evolved into a series of uncoordinated small-unit actions, with the Allies definitely getting the better of it. The paratroopers of Lieutenant General Ringel's Group East were also decimated near Heraklion, and the German naval flotilla, carrying desperately needed reinforcements and heavy weapons from the mainland and the German-held island of Milos, was turned back by the British Mediterranean Fleet. As night fell, not one of the four vital airfields was in German hands. Student's men had, however, scored one important victory: during the afternoon, two detachments of the assault regiment, led by a first lieutenant and the regimental surgeon, had captured Hill 107 overlooking Maleme airfield with pistols and hand grenades. They had no heavy weapons and were almost out of ammunition, but the New Zealanders failed to counterattack. It was the turning point of the battle. That night Student decided to shift the focus of the attack to Maleme. He ordered the Ju-52s carrying elements of the 5th Mountain Division to crashland on the beaches west of Maleme the following day. This, of course, was a very expensive way to ferry in reinforcements and supplies, but it worked. Richthofen's Stukas also played a major role in the Battle of Maleme by fiercely protecting the defenders of Hill 107. Nearby New Zealand assembly areas were bombed and strafed, and Freyberg's troops were completely pinned down by the dive-bombers, while Col. Hermann Ramcke (who had replaced Meindl) tried to secure the airfield. At 4 P.M. a flight of Ju-52s carrying elements of a reinforced mountain battalion landed on the airfield, despite heavy enemy artillery and machine-gun fire. Several aircraft were destroyed, but the town of Maleme was captured by 5 P.M., and the airfield was made safe. Before nightfall, the entire 100th Mountain Infantry Regiment (Col. Willibald Utz) had landed at Maleme. The following day Lieutenant General Ringel was given command of Group West, and three more battalions of his 5th Mountain Division landed at Maleme.[27]

"Maleme was like the gate of hell," General Ringel later reported. Eighty Ju-52s—every third transport to land—were destroyed. The single runway was cleared by pushing the damaged transports off with a captured British tank. Bekker described the sides of the airstrip as a "giant aircraft cemetery."[28] It was nevertheless secured by the morning of the twenty-second. Although the Battle of Crete was not yet decided, the crisis had, for the moment, passed. Richthofen was now in a position to turn his attentions to his other mission: clearing the sea lanes to Crete. This meant engaging the British Mediterranean Fleet in an air-sea battle, something the baron and his pilots were extremely eager to do.

The air-sea battle had actually begun on the twenty-first, when an Italian naval flotilla carrying heavy weapons to Crete was dispersed and ten small vessels sunk by a British task force. Richthofen immediately committed his corps reserve (which he had been withholding for just such an eventuality) against this task force and sank the British destroyer *Juno* and damaged the cruiser *Ajax*. On the twenty-second, however, the battle between Richthofen and Admiral Cunningham became general. At 5:30 A.M. several Stukas, diving from 12,000 feet, bombed the cruisers *Gloucester* and *Fiji* but did not sink them. These vessels then took positions further west, nearer the main fleet (task forces A, B, and D), located about thirty miles west of Crete. Meanwhile,

Rear Admiral King's Task Force C patrolled the waters north of Crete with four cruisers and three destroyers. They located and pursued a German flotilla that was trying to ship heavy weapons to Crete. Just before King could catch the small vessels, however, he was attacked by the Ju-88s and Do-17s from the VIII Air Corps. Two of the cruiser *Naiad*'s gun turrets were knocked out, and her side was ripped open. Her bulkheads held, however, and she managed to limp off at half speed. Meanwhile, the cruiser *Carlisle* suffered a direct hit and her captain was killed, but she also remained afloat.[29]

The air-sea battle continued that afternoon when the battleship *Warspite* suffered serious damage under a direct hit and the destroyer *Greyhound* went to the bottom following a Stuka attack. Admiral King ordered the destroyers *Kandahar* and *Kingston* to pick up survivors from the *Greyhound* and recalled the cruisers *Gloucester* and *Fiji* from the west, to provide them with antiaircraft covering fire. King did not realize that the cruisers had expended virtually their entire supply of antiaircraft ammunition that morning. When he was informed of this fact, he promptly ordered them to retire, but it was already too late. Several schwarms of Ju-87s and Ju-88s spotted the *Gloucester* and attacked her. Soon her entire deck was afire, and her damage control teams were unable to check the blazes. At 4 P.M. the flames must have reached her fuel or her magazine, for she was racked by an internal explosion and sank. Admiral King made the difficult though necessary decision to leave the crew of the *Gloucester* to its fate, because any vessels attempting a rescue would only themselves fall victim to the Stukas and Ju-88s. About 500 members of the crew were saved during the night by the small German flotilla and by Luftwaffe sea rescue aircraft.[30]

Escorted by destroyers, the *Fiji* attempted to escape to the main British naval base at Alexandria, Egypt. At 5:45 P.M. she was spotted by a lone Me-109 fighter-bomber carrying a single 500-pound bomb. As fate would have it, the bomb struck the *Fiji* on the side, below the water line, and exploded, fracturing the hull. It was listing heavily and was almost defenseless when a second Me-109 (summoned by the first pilot), attacked and scored a direct hit. The *Fiji* capsized at 7:15 P.M.[31]

During the night of May 22–23, the destroyers *Kelly* and *Kashmir* shelled the German airfield at Maleme and, when dawn broke, were off the northern coast of Crete, in a position to block any German-Italian seaborne attempt to bring heavy weapons to the parachute and mountain troops on Crete. The sun did not bring to light Axis ships, however, but rather twenty-four Ju-87s from I Group, 2nd Stuka Wing. Both destroyers were soon sunk by direct hits. Despite exhortations from Prime Minister Winston Churchill, Admiral Cunningham signaled London that they would have to accept defeat: the losses involved were simply too heavy for the Royal Navy to continue trying to

TABLE 9: THE BRITISH MEDITERRANEAN FLEET, MAY 1941

Battleships

Barham	Damaged, May 27
Queen Elizabeth	
Valiant	Damaged, May 22
Warspite	Severely damaged, May 22

Cruisers

Gloucester	Sunk, May 22
Fiji	Sunk, May 22
Orion	Severely damaged, May 29
Ajax	Damaged, May 22 and 28
Perth	Severely damaged, May 30
Dido	Damaged, May 29
Naiad	Severely damaged, May 22
Phoebe	
Coventry	
Calcutta	Sunk, June 2
Carlisle	Damaged, May 22

Destroyers

Napier	Damaged, May 30
Nizam	
Kandahar	
Kingston	
Kimberly	
Kelly	Sunk, May 23
Kashmir	Sunk, May 23
Kipling	
Kelvin	Damaged, May 30
Juno	Sunk, May 21
Janus	
Jervis	
Jackal	
Jaguar	
Nubian	Damaged, May 26
Isis	
Imperial	Sunk, May 29
Ilex	
Hero	
Hotspur	

TABLE 9: THE BRITISH MEDITERRANEAN FLEET, MAY 1941
(*continued*)

Hereward	Sunk, May 29
Hasty	
Havock	
Griffin	
Greyhound	Sunk, May 22
Decoy	Damaged, May 29
Defender	
Stuart	
Voyager	
Vendetta	

Totals: 3 cruisers and 6 destroyers sunk; 3 battleships, 1 carrier, 7 cruisers, and 4 destroyers damaged.

Sources: Gundenlach: 115; Bekker: 548.

prevent seaborne landings at Crete. The British had at last learned the lesson that Gen. Billy Mitchell had tried to teach the Americans in the early 1930s: ships without air cover could not survive against an enemy with air superiority. Richthofen's air-sea victory had opened the German supply lines. The Battle of Crete was now decided, although Churchill was not yet ready to recognize the fact. New German ground units with heavy weapons and artillery now arrived and, by nightfall on the twenty-third, had linked up with Group Center west of Canea.[32] The British Mediterranean Fleet had not yet seen the last of the Luftwaffe at Crete, however, for it was ordered to reinforce and resupply Freyberg's corps. The aircraft carrier *Formidable* was committed to a battle to provide air support for the fleet, but it suffered two direct hits from German bombers on the twenty-sixth and had to be withdrawn. By the next day the first panzers were landed on the northern coast of Crete and Gen. Sir Archibald Wavell, the commander-in-chief, Mediterranean, signaled London that the island was untenable. The battered Mediterranean Fleet now conducted the evacuation of Crete, under continuous harassment from VIII Air Corps, and suffered further damage. The Battle of Crete ended on June 1, when the last Allied troops on the island surrendered. Table 9 shows the losses suffered by the British fleet during the battle.

Richthofen apparently did not report his losses in this campaign separately, but they were relatively light. Some 350 German aircraft of the 4th Air Fleet were destroyed during the campaign,[33] but 271 of these were Ju-52 transports from Student's corps.[34] The British army lost 15,743 men killed, wounded, and captured (mostly captured),[35] excluding 14,000 Greek soldiers who were left on Crete.[36] The Royal Navy also lost 2,011 men. The big loser in the campaign, however, was the German Parachute corps. It suffered a total of 6,580 casualties, which Hitler considered appalling. Indeed, it did exceed the entire casualties suffered during the whole Balkan campaign (5,650) by almost one thousand men. Hitler resolved never to employ parachute units on a massive scale again and he never did.[37]

Richthofen emerged from the Cretan campaign with new laurels. His close air support tactics had proven the difference between victory and defeat at Crete, and he had even administered a serious defeat on the Royal Navy, Germany's arch-foe. Shortly afterward he was awarded the Oak Leaves to his Knights Cross by Adolf Hitler himself.[38] He had no time to enjoy his new glory, however. His corps was immediately sent to Poland and only three weeks after the fall of Crete was engaged in the bloodiest and probably most difficult military campaign that the world has ever known.

CHAPTER 8

Russia, 1941: The Last Blitzkrieg

Germany's invasion of Poland (and the start of the war) was made possible by an August 23, 1939, nonaggression treaty between Hitler and Stalin, which had the effect of securing Germany's rear while Hitler dealt with the West, in exchange for the eastern half of Poland. Stalin was not idle while the Wehrmacht overran Poland, Denmark, Norway, Holland, Belgium, and France. With Hitler busy elsewhere and unable to intervene, Stalin incorporated the Baltic States of Latvia, Estonia, and Lithuania into the Soviet Union—including a strip of Lithuania that was specifically reserved for Germany under the terms of the treaty. Instead of merely exerting influence over Finland, as the treaty called for, Stalin invaded that country in 1939. When Helsinki sued for peace in May 1940, Stalin annexed large chunks of territory, including Finland's second-largest city. In June 1940, he took Bessarabia away from Rumania (as was agreed upon in the treaty) and Northern Bukovina as well—a seizure not authorized by the Treaty of Moscow. In less than a year Stalin had added 175,000 square miles of territory and twenty million people to his empire—and he wanted more.[1] He made territorial demands on Turkey (which were ignored) and was even speaking about guaranteeing Rumania's security—a euphemism for Soviet annexation. The Soviet dictator was not at all happy when France surrendered to Germany on June 21, 1940.

Adolf Hitler was thoroughly alarmed, for he depended on Rumanian oil to fuel his war machine. The Rumanians were also frightened, because they had already lost 17 percent of their territory (19,300 square miles) and three million five hundred thousand people. On July 2, Rumania announced a "new orientation," and on July 4 King Carol appointed a pro-Nazi government in Bucharest. Five days later Rumania was declared to be under the military protection of Germany, and Hitler sent troops to that country,[2] effectively blocking further Soviet expansion to the west.

The developments of 1939–40 confirmed Hitler's belief that Russia intended to stab Germany in the back as soon as a favorable opportunity presented itself. He had already gone on record as early as 1924 as favoring "the acquisition and penetration of the territory east of the Elbe" at the expense of the Soviet Union.[3] After unsuccessful negotiations with Soviet Foreign Secretary Vyacheslav Molotov in Berlin on November 12 and 13 (during which the tactless Russian demanded that Hitler recognize that Finland, the Balkans, and the Dardanelles all lay within the Soviet sphere of interest),[4] Hitler decided to invade the Soviet Union in 1941. On December 18 he signed and issued Directive Number 21, in which he ordered the German armed forces to make preparations to "crush Soviet Russia in a lightning campaign, even before the termination of hostilities with Great Britain ["Operation Barbarossa"]."[5]

The Luftwaffe High Command was divided on the issue of invading the Soviet Union. When Jeschonnek heard of the plan, General Schmid said later, he exclaimed: "At last a proper war!"[6] On the other hand Maj. Gen. Otto Hoffmann von Waldau, the chief of operations of the General Staff, opposed the invasion as a dangerous and irresponsible dissipation of strength.[7] Kesselring, the incurable optimist, was also in favor of invasion. Even after the war he wrote that "Hitler's contention that Russia would seize the first favorable moment to attack us seemed to me indisputably right."[8] Beppo Schmid, the chief of the 5th (Military Intelligence) Branch of the Luftwaffe General Staff, was also opposed to the invasion, but then, as usual, submitted intelligence reports underestimating the strength of the enemy. When Erhard Milch returned from leave in February, 1941, he was told of the new campaign by Gen. Otto Ruedel, the chief of Air Defense. The state secretary, a veteran of the eastern front in World War I, was momentarily overcome with surprise and then told Ruedel that the campaign could not be finished before winter, as Hitler claimed. He predicted that it would take four winters. When the plans for the campaign went ahead despite his objections, Milch and Lt. Gen. Hans-Georg von Seidel, the chief of supply and administration for the Luftwaffe, saw to it that extra woollen underwear, big fur boots, and other winter clothing were manufactured for all 800,000 Luftwaffe personnel on the eastern front. Unlike the army, the airmen would be provided for during the first Russian winter.[9] The most vocal opponent of the invasion of the Soviet Union, however, was Hermann Goering, who strongly opposed it from the very beginning. He felt that Germany should adopt a Mediterranean policy, and the specter of a two-front war was so terrifying to him that, for one of the few times in his life, he stood up in plain-spoken opposition to the Fuehrer's plans. He told Hitler: ". . . the Luftwaffe is the only Wehrmacht branch which has not had a breathing space since the war began. I told you when we first went to war that I was going into battle with my training squadrons, and now they're all gone. I'm not at all sure that you can beat Russia in six weeks. There's nothing I'd like better than to have you proven right, but, frankly, I doubt that you will be."[10]

The Reichsmarschall tried on several other occasions to sway Hitler from his course. Finally the Fuehrer had enough. "Goering!" he snapped, "why don't you stop trying to persuade me to drop my plans for Russia? I've made up my mind!"[11] Thus rebuffed, Goering washed his hands of the whole affair and went on another month's leave, this time to his tenth-century castle near Nuremberg. He did not return to duty until less than three weeks before the panzers crossed the Soviet border.[12]

Goering had compelling reasons for not wanting to go to war with Russia in 1941. First, the Luftwaffe was deeply committed in the Mediterranean, in the Balkans, and against England. Second, there were serious problems in the air armaments industry, and the appearance of the newest models of aircraft was far behind schedule (see below). In fact, the Luftwaffe had only about 100 more airplanes in June 1941, than when it invaded France a year before (see Table 10). Finally, if Hitler's calculations were wrong and Russia could not be defeated in six to eight weeks, Germany would be enmeshed in a war she could not win. The invasion, initially scheduled to begin in May, was postponed four to six weeks due to the Balkans campaign—a fatal delay. On April 30, 1941, Hitler set the new D-Day as June 22.[13]

For the fateful invasion of the Soviet Union, the Luftwaffe concentrated most of its combat aircraft, its veteran pilots, and its best commanders. As in Poland, France, Scandinavia, and the Balkans, it had two primary missions:

TABLE 10: THE STRENGTH OF THE LUFTWAFFE BY AIRCRAFT TYPE, MAY 10, 1940, AND JUNE 21, 1941

Aircraft Type	10 May 40	21 Jun 41
Short-Range Recon	335	440
Long-Range Recon	322	393
Single-Engine Fighter	1,356	1,440
Night-Fighters	—	263
Twin-Engine Fighters	354	188
Bombers	1,711	1,511
Dive-Bombers	414	424
Ground-Attack	50	
Coastal	240	223
Total	4,782	4,882

Source: Murray, Strategy for Defeat, p. 80.

1) destroy the enemy air force, and 2) give direct and indirect support to the army. There were no provisions for strategic air warfare, because the plan called for a rapid and decisive victory; besides, without a four-engine bomber, the Luftwaffe was not equipped for a long-range strategic bombing campaign. In fact, the entire Luftwaffe in Russia was little more than flying, long-range artillery for the army.

For the invasion of Russia, the army was divided into three major commands: Army Groups North, Center, and South. The Luftwaffe committed three full air fleets to the campaign: 1st Air Fleet to support Army Group North, 2nd Air Fleet to support Army Group Center, and 4th Air Fleet to support Army Group South. In the far north, the army sent the Army of Norway (later replaced by HQ twentieth Mountain Army) to seize the Russian arctic ports. The Luftwaffe committed Luftwaffe Command Kirkenes to support it. Table 11 shows the Army's Order of Battle for Operation "Barbarossa."

Although outnumbered and without strategic equipment or tactical depth, the Luftwaffe faced into Russia with a capable roster of commanders. These men, in fact, were much better than most of the men they opposed and, indeed, were generally superior to those in their own High Command.

TABLE 11: GERMAN ARMY ORDER OF BATTLE, JUNE 22, 1941 (NORTH TO SOUTH)*

Army Group North	Field Marshal Ritter Wilhelm von Leeb
Eighteen Army	Col. Gen. Georg von Kuechler
4th Panzer Group	Col. Gen. Erich Hoepner
Sixteenth Army	Col. Gen. Ernst Busch
Army Group Center	Field Marshal Fedor von Bock
3rd Panzer Group	Col. Gen. Hermann Hoth
Ninth Army	Col. Gen. Adolf Strauss
Fourth Army	Field Marshal Guenther von Kluge
2nd Panzer Group	Col. Gen. Heinz Guderian
Army Group South	Field Marshal Gerd von Rundstedt
Sixth Army	Field Marshal Walter von Reichenau
1st Panzer Group	Col. Gen. Ewald von Kleist
Seventeenth Army	Col. Gen. Heinrich von Stuelpnagel
Third Rumanian Army	General Dumitrescu
Fourth Rumanian Army	General Ciuperca
Eleventh Army	Col. Gen. Ritter Eugen von Schobert

*Excluding the Far North sector

Because of them and their pilots, Germany did not lose control of the air over the eastern front until 1944.

First Air Fleet, the weakest of the three, was commanded by Col. Gen. Alfred Keller, who was also the poorest of the air fleet commanders. A bomber specialist and an ardent Nazi, he was a member of the "Little General Staff" and largely owed his promotion to his influence with Goering. Born in 1882, he was considered an "old eagle," having joined the Flying Corps before World War I. During the Great War, he commanded the 1st Bomber Wing, where he won the highest decorations and earned the nickname "Bomben-Keller." After the war he worked in civil aviation and became head of training at the Transport Aviation School at Braunschweig, before returning to the service as a major in the army. He transferred to the Luftwaffe and held several administrative commands (including Luftkreis IV) before being promoted to general of flyers and commander of the 4th Air Division (later IV Air Corps) on March 1, 1939. He served on the western front in 1939 and 1940, and at the advanced age of fifty-eight personally led his squadrons into action against the R.A.F. at Dunkirk. (Keller's ability may be open to question, but not his courage.) He had taken over 1st Air Fleet in the summer of 1940, after Stumpff went to Norway, but had spent the entire time since then on occupational duty in Poland. He would command 1st Air Fleet until July 28, 1943, when he retired from the service and became leader of the National Socialist Flying Corps (NSFK), which was responsible for giving primary flight instruction to future Luftwaffe pilots. He survived the war.[14]

Both of Keller's principal subordinates—General of Flyers Helmuth Foerster (CG, I Air Corps) and Col. Wolfgang von Wild (air commander Baltic)—were also new to their posts. Foerster was not originally slated to command I Air Corps at all. Its commander in France and the Battle of Britain was the highly competent Col. Gen. Ulrich Grauert, a World War I flyer who had directed the 1st Air Division in Poland with considerable success.[15] Unfortunately for the Luftwaffe, Grauert had been shot down and killed over the Channel coast by the R.A.F. in May, 1941. His successor, Foerster, was a highly decorated World War I aviator. Returning to the service in 1934 as a lieutenant colonel in the Luftwaffe, Foerster was promoted to colonel in March, 1936, and assumed command of the 4th Bomber Wing "General Wever." He had commanded the Lehr-division in the Polish campaign with great success, as we have seen. Thereafter he had been chief of staff of the 5th Air Fleet (April 15–June 22, 1940) and a member of the German-French Peace Commission and Wehrmacht commander in Serbia. He would lead I Air Corps until October 1, 1942, when he became chief of administration at RLM, a post he held until the end of the war. Foerster was pensioned by the West German government as a lieutenant colonel in 1952.[16]

Wolfgang von Wild had served as a naval cadet in World War I and fought with irregular units in the Baltic States and with the right-wing Ehrhardt Naval Brigade in Upper Silesia and Berlin during the civil unrest of 1919 and 1920. He received his commission in the Reichsmarine in 1923 and transferred to the secret air force in the mid-1920s. A major when the war broke out, he served in coastal air units in Poland. He was named air commander Baltic on April 21, 1941. Later he served under the air commander Atlantic (October 30, 1941, to November 1, 1942) and then became air transport commander I (Southeast), headquartered in Athens. Finally promoted to major general on March 1, 1945, he ended his career as air attaché to Tokyo.[17]

The principal commanders in the 2d Air Fleet, the strongest of the three, had greater experience at their posts. Kesselring, the former chief of the General Staff, had been an air fleet commander since before the war. Richthofen, the leader of VIII Air Corps, had more experience at modern aerial warfare than any other combat commander in the Luftwaffe; and Bruno Loerzer, CG of II Air Corps, was a World War I ace and a veteran corps commander.

Col. Gen. Alexander Loehr, a native of Croatia, had seen extensive service as a pilot and as a member of the Austro-Hungarian General Staff during World War I. The commander-in-chief of the Austrian air force at the time of the Anschluss, he had led 4th Air Fleet since 1938. Loehr was not promoted to field marshal only because of Hitler's prejudice against Austrians, although he held high command throughout the war.

Loehr's two corps commanders were Gen. Ritter Robert von Greim (V Air) and Gen. Kurt Pflugbeil. Greim, who we shall meet later, had considerable experience as an air division and corps commander. Kurt Pflugbeil, a World War I flyer, had fought the Poles as a member of the border police in 1919. He returned to the army in 1920 and underwent secret aerial bombing training in Russia in 1928. Joining the Luftwaffe in 1935, he became a major general and commander of the VIII Air Corps in 1939. After directing air administrative commands (support units) in Belgium and France, he was named commanding general of IV Air Corps. Extremely capable, he led his corps until September 4, 1943, when he assumed command of 1st Air Fleet, which he led on the northern sector of the Russian front until the end of the war.[18]

The leader of the squadrons in the Far North, Col. Andreas Nielsen, was simultaneously chief of staff of the 5th Air Fleet. Born in Flensburg on December 23, 1899, he joined the army and served in the last days of World War I. An early Nazi, he took part in the Beer Hall Putsch in Munich in 1923. Nielsen served in the Reichswehr between the wars and underwent flight training in Russia in 1928. He attended the army's prestigious War Academy

from 1933 to 1935, joined the air force in 1935, and served under Stumpff in
the Personnel Office from then until 1937. He commanded a bomber group
in the Condor Legion in the last five months of the Spanish civil war, led III
Group, 27th Bomber Wing, in the Polish campaign, and was chief of staff of
Loerzer's II Air Corps in France. After serving briefly as chief of staff of the
4th Air Fleet, Nielsen was chief of staff of Stumpff's 5th Air Fleet from October 20, 1940, to December 31, 1943, when he became Luftwaffe commander
Denmark (January–May, 1944). From May 12, 1944, until the end of the war,
he again worked for Stumpff as chief of staff of Air Fleet Reich. A lieutenant
general at the time of the surrender, this highly capable staff officer authored
a study on the Luftwaffe General Staff for the United States Air Force (see
bibliography). He died in April 1957.[19]

All in all, the Luftwaffe forces opposing the Soviet Union included 2,840
aircraft, of which about 1,910 were combat aircraft. This amounted to 59
percent of all combat aircraft in the Luftwaffe. Table 12 shows the dispositions by air fleet and aircraft type. The other 1,340 combat aircraft were

TABLE 12: DISPOSITIONS BY AIRCRAFT TYPE BY AIR FLEET, JUNE 22, 1941

Aircraft Type	1st Air Fleet	2nd Air Fleet	4th Air Fleet	5th Air Fleet
Bombers	270	240	360	10
Dive-Bombers	—	250	—	30
Single-Engine Fighters	110	270	210	10
Twin-Engine Fighters	—	60	—	—
Liaison Aircraft	20 (30)	30 (30)	30 (50)	—
Long-Range Recon	50 (40)	30 (40)	30 (50)	10
Short-Range Recon	— (110)	— (110)	— (140)	— (10)
Transport	30	60	60	—
Ground Attack	—	60	—	—
Total:*	660	1,180	930	70
Grand Total:	2,840 (610 attached to the army).			

*Excluding coastal aircraft.

Note: Aircraft in parentheses were attached directly to the army.

Source: Plocher MS 1941.

divided among the 3rd Air Fleet in the West (660), 5th Air Fleet in Norway (120), X Air Corps and Air Command Afrika in the Mediterranean sector (370 airplanes), and in various air defense units in Germany (only 190 aircraft). Clearly the Luftwaffe, like the army, was gambling on a quick and decisive victory over the Soviet Union.

Two antiaircraft corps also took part in the advance. Maj. Gen. Walter von Axthelm's I Flak Corps was assigned to the 2nd Air Fleet. His 101st and 104th Motorized Flak Regiments particularly distinguished themselves in support of second Panzer Army. The II Flak Corps (Lt. Gen. Otto Dessloch) was assigned to 4th Air Fleet. Three independent flak regiments were assigned to Keller in the north. Since there was little Soviet air activity, these units were used primarily to support the ground forces, so their operations will not be covered here in detail. Suffice it to say that the AA guns, with their flat trajectory and high rate of fire, were extremely effective against Soviet bunkers, border fortifications, and entrenched tanks. The 88mm guns were particularly effective in an antitank role. Second Flak Corps, for example, destroyed 250 tanks and 51 bunkers between June 22 and July 15 and also brought down 92 Soviet aircraft. Almost all the tanks were destroyed by the 88s. The best German tanks at that time (the PzKw IIIs and IVs) were armed with only 75mm guns. Later in the war the famous PzKw VI "Tiger" tanks were armed with the 88s and became one of the most feared weapons in the German arsenal.

Besides its aviation and flak units, each air fleet controlled one or more air administrative command headquarters, which were responsible for supplying the air fleet, plus one or more air administrative command staffs, which were charged with building up ground organizations in newly occupied territory. Finally, Lt. Gen. Wilhelm Speidel's Luftwaffe Mission in Rumania was attached to the 4th Air Fleet and had responsibility for defending the Rumanian oil fields against Soviet air attack. The mission was, in effect, a defensive tactical unit, since it had numerous flak batteries and a wing of Me-109s attached to it. The Russians did, in fact, launch several ill-coordinated attacks against the oilfields, but they inflicted only minor damage. Units of Speidel's command shot down 143 Soviet aircraft in these attacks—73 of them by fighters.[20]

Schmid's Intelligence Branch placed the strength of the Red Air Force at 8,000 airplanes, of which 6,000 were in European Russia.[21] As usual, the report was terribly wrong. The Russians had about 10,000 aircraft in the western areas alone, supported by an average production of 1,131 per month,[22] plus at least 3,000 in the East, available as a reserve.[23] Although most of the airplanes on its western frontier were obsolete, the Red Air Force was in the process of converting to new fighters (Yak-1s, MiG-3s, and LaGG-3s), and some 3,700 of these were already with the units or on their way.[24] A few experts from the Luftwaffe had been allowed to visit Russia in the spring of 1941 and, after visiting six factories in the Urals, reported that a large-scale aircraft production program was underway. Luftwaffe intelligence ignored the reports.[25] Although their leaders did not know it, the Luftwaffe pilots were attacking a foe that outnumbered them seven to one.[26]

✠

The German air offensive began at 3:30 A.M. on June 22. All available airplanes were in the air at first light. German bomber units flew up to six missions a day in the first few days, while dive-bombers and fighters flew five to eight missions daily, depending on the distance from their forward airfields to their targets. It was essential that they establish air superiority from the outset, so they could turn their attention to the Russian armies. It was absolutely vital that the Red colossus be destroyed by winter.

The German airmen achieved surprise all along the front. Soviet airfields were pulverized, their aircraft destroyed on the ground. Foerster's I Air Corps alone attacked 77 Russian airfields in 1,600 sorties during the first three days of operations.[27] It shot down 400 enemy airplanes and destroyed another 1,100 on the ground. By August 23 it had shot down 920 enemy aircraft and destroyed 1,594 more on the ground, for a total of 2,514 aircraft destroyed—more than three times the number of aircraft in the entire 1st Air Fleet. To the north, Wild's Luftwaffe Command Baltic sank 66,000 tons of shipping, including five destroyers. It also destroyed fifty-eight Soviet airplanes, while losing only twenty itself. Most important, it forced the Soviet Baltic Fleet back towards Leningrad, where it could not hinder the advance of the left flank of the Eighteenth Army. Having accomplished its mission with its limited sources, it was transferred to the Crimea and redesignated Luftwaffe Command South in October.[28]

The success of I Air Corps was matched all along the front. During the first two days of the invasion, Kesselring's 2nd Air Fleet attacked every Soviet airfield within a 185-mile radius of the front line. The Red Air Force in the central combat zone was virtually wiped out within the first forty-eight hours. Kesselring claimed to have destroyed 2,500 Russian airplanes in the first week. This success was of such magnitude that Goering did not believe it. He ordered an investigation to determine if Kesselring had inflated the size of his triumph. The investigators reported that Kesselring had underestimated the number of airplanes destroyed by his pilots by 200 to 300 aircraft.[29]

Meanwhile, Baron von Richthofen was distinguishing himself again. For Operation Barbarossa, his VIII Air Corps was part of Kesselring's 2nd Air Fleet and was initially given the mission of supporting Col. Gen. Hermann Hoth's 3rd Panzer Group's deep armored thrust into the Soviet Union. He also supported Col. Gen. Adolf Strauss' Ninth Army. His forces included StG 1, StG 2 (Ju-87s), KG 2 (Do-17s), II/KG 11 (Do-17s), JG 27 (Me-109s), and ZG 26 (Me-110s). He also had a group of Ju-52s from a special employment transport wing, which he used to resupply the other air units and the fast-moving motorized columns.[30] His was one of the strongest corps in the Luftwaffe at the time.

Baron von Richthofen set up his command post on the north shore of Lake Wigry on the old East Prussian-Polish border as soon as he left Crete and worked feverishly to assemble his units before attack day, which was set for June 22. By the twentieth he was ready. Initially, VIII Air Corps only had to cover a frontage of 186 miles.[31] As the armies advanced from west to east, however, the Eurasian continent expanded both north and south. The frontage would grow larger and larger with each advance.

The Russo-German war was scheduled to begin at 3:30 A.M., a very unfavorable time for the 2nd Air Fleet because, according to Richthofen, the German dive-bombers and single-engine fighter pilots had not yet learned to fly in formation at night. If he waited until dawn to attack, the Soviet air force would have forty minutes' warning before the Stukas and fighters struck. This delay might well prevent the Germans from establishing air superiority by destroying the enemy air force on the ground, as it had done in Poland, France, and Yugoslavia. Richthofen therefore adopted what General Plocher later called a "dangerous plan of operations." He sent three aircraft, each manned with crews experienced in night flying, to each Soviet airfield on which fighter aircraft were based. The plan worked perfectly. On only one airfield did the Germans meet a Russian formation, and it was preparing to take off. The German unit dropped its bombs into the midst of the taxiing Soviet unit, smashing all of its aircraft. The other fields were knocked out before the Russian pilots could scramble. Eighth Air Corps destroyed well over 1,000 Russian airplanes in the first week of the campaign—almost all of them on the ground.[32] To the south, II, V, and IV Air Corps experienced similar successes. In the first four days of operations, Greim's relatively weak V Air Corps flew 1,600 sorties against seventy-seven Soviet airfields, destroying 774 Soviet aircraft on the ground and 136 in the air. By July 3, Greim was able to report that his units had destroyed their 1,000th Soviet airplane on the ground.[33] Goralski wrote that on June 24, "About 2,000 Soviet planes had now been destroyed. In just seventy-two hours the largest air force in the world had been reduced to an ineffectual remnant."[34]

If anything, Goralski understated the case. An estimated 1,800 Soviet aircraft were destroyed on the ground during the first day of operations. On June 29, at the end of the first week of the campaign, OKW reported the destruction of 4,017 enemy aircraft at the cost of 150 German airplanes destroyed or heavily damaged—a ratio of 27 to 1.[35]

By June 24, with most of the Red Air Force destroyed, the primary mission of VIII Air Corps became direct and indirect support of the army. On the afternoon of the 24th, the VIII and XX Army Corps of the Ninth Army came under heavy Soviet tank and cavalry attack near Bialystok and Lunna. Richthofen committed his entire corps to these sectors and destroyed 105 Russian tanks by evening. The next day it also destroyed a large number of Russian tanks in the Kuznica-Odelsk-Grodno-Dabrowa area. The Russian ground forces, under the overall command of Marshal Semen Konstantinovich Timoshenko, tried to turn the tables on Richthofen on June 26 by launching a counterattack toward the main VIII Air Corps base at Lida. The Russians established bridgeheads over the Neman River at three points and headed for Lida, opposed only by weak security forces. Their overall objective was obviously to force Ninth Army to divert units to the threatened sector, weakening or possibly even preventing the encirclement of Bialystok. Richthofen's corps was forced to defend its own bases. The Stukas attacked the forward Soviet positions north of the Neman, concentrating against Mosty, Orlya, Bolitsa, and Ruda. They delayed the Reds long enough for the infantry of the V Army Corps to come up and beat back the Russians. Meanwhile, Col. Gen. Adolf Strauss's Ninth and Field Marshal Guenther von Kluge's fourth Armies encircled Bialystok without having to divert their main forces.[36]

No sooner was the Soviet Tenth Army encircled at Bialystok than a larger encirclement developed to the east. Hoth's 3rd Panzer Group on the northern wing was deep in the Soviet rear, driving on Minsk from the northwest. Col. Gen. Heinz Guderian's 2nd Panzer Group was also advancing on the White Russian capital from the southwest. Richthofen gave close air support to the 3rd Panzer Group, while Gen. Bruno Loerzer's II Air Corps supported Guderian (who was less than pleased with its performance).[37] Richthofen's units attacked road and railroad junctions at and near Minsk, slowing down the Soviet retreat and cutting off their resupply efforts. Meanwhile, other elements of the VIII Air bombed and dive-bombed the remnants of the Soviet Tenth Army, which still held out at Bialystok.[38]

In late June, Richthofen had to modify his tactics for dealing with Russian withdrawals and with Soviet units trying to escape German air and ground forces. The Russians withdrew mainly at night, but during the day they broke into very small units and proceeded cross-country, away from the roads. Luftwaffe attacks on these small units usually came too late, because the Russians were warned of the bombers' approach by the appearance of German reconnaissance aircraft. Richthofen's solution was simple: he developed a policy of armed reconnaissance. Bombers and dive-bombers roamed the skies above

the battlefield in formations of three to six aircraft and did their own reconnaissance. Relatively few Soviet troops survived attacks by such formations.[39]

Meanwhile, a new command was formed in the zone of II Air Corps: the
Nahkampffuehrer, or Close Air Support Command. The VIII Air Corps, it will
be recalled, was especially designed for close air support, but the II Air
Corps was not. As a result, Guderian's panzer spearheads were not getting
the kind of immediate aerial support they had come to expect. To solve this
problem, Loerzer set up the temporary headquarters, 2nd Close Air Support
Command, under Col. Martin Fiebig, a close air support specialist who had
first learned his trade at the clandestine German aviation school in the
Soviet Union in the 1920s.[40] He had led the 4th Bomber Wing "General
Wever" (He-111s) in Poland, France, and the Low Countries, where his
pilots had bombed Rotterdam.[41] Under Richthofen, Fiebig had played a
major role in the bombing of Belgrade, for which he would later pay with
his life. (He was executed by the Yugoslavs in 1946.)[42] Now, however, Fiebig
put his expertise to good use, guiding the light forces of II Air Corps to targets in front of the 2nd Panzer Group and smashing Soviet resistance to the
spearheads. As a result, Guderian was able to move rapidly toward Minsk.
Meanwhile, Loerzer continued to direct the heavier bomber wings of his air
corps against Soviet supply installations, airfields, and railroads, especially
the Minsk-Borisov-Orsha and Minsk-Molodechno routes, and against the
Orsha, Zhlobin, and Osipovichi rail junctions. In doing so, he disrupted
Soviet troop movements, and the Red Army was not able to launch a coordinated relief attack to rescue its forces surrounded at Bialystok.

The close air support command arrangement worked out so well in the II
Air Corps zone that Colonel General Loehr copied it. He established Close
Air Support Command South (Lieutenant Colonel Count Schoenborn) to
support the First Panzer Army and Close Air Support Command North (Maj.
Guenther Luetzow) to support Sixth Army. Both controlled three groups of
fighters and dive-bombers. Luetzow, who was simultaneously commander of
the 3rd Fighter Wing, was particularly successful in his relentless support of
German ground forces.[43]

The last Russian units in the Bialystok Pocket surrendered or were
destroyed on July 1, but another huge pocket had been created in the Minsk
sector on June 27, when Hoth and Guderian linked up east of the city. Crushing the pocket was, of course, another task, as the Soviets tried desperately to
break the encirclement. Several units did manage to escape to the east, and
Richthofen's headquarters was besieged by requests from ground commanders for air support against this or that Soviet formation, which was either
counterattacking or trying to escape the pocket. On July 5 Richthofen complained in his diary that the army refused to realize that the Luftwaffe could

not be committed everywhere in dribbles, but rather must be concentrated at major points.[44] General Plocher later wrote: "Everyone in the Army wanted to take over the Luftwaffe, but the Army was completely unaware of the potentialities of air power."[45] In fact, many unit commanders in the army demanded close air support for their units and were unable to see the larger framework in which air power must be employed. This was an understandable and very human failing on their part, but the Luftwaffe commanders found it frustrating nevertheless. Many calls for air support had to go unanswered.

Minsk fell on July 9. Two days later the OKW reported that 328,898 prisoners had been taken in the double battle of Minsk-Bialystok, and that 3,332 tanks, 1,809 guns, and large quantities of other war material had been captured or destroyed.[46] Meanwhile, Hoth and Guderian had diverged once more, only to join hands again near Smolensk on July 16, forming another huge pocket, which was not cleared until August 5. Operating under the general direction of Kesselring's 2nd Air Fleet, VIII Air and II Air Corps flew devastating sorties against the Russian units, prompting a desperate counterattack by the trapped Russians. Richthofen had moved his command post and his close air support aircraft (mainly Stukas) to the Dukhovshchina area, near the edge of the pocket. This base was the objective of a heavy Soviet armored attack on July 23. Once again the Stukas flew in defense of their own airfields. Richthofen committed the 99th Antiaircraft Regiment—which had been attached to VIII Air Corps for airfield defense—to the fighting. Many Soviet tanks were knocked out by the 88mm antiaircraft guns, but the Russians kept advancing. The Stukas and 88s delayed the Russians just long enough for the army to rush ground forces to the sector. These units counterattacked and pushed the Russians back, just in time to save the Dukhovshchina airfields.[47] It appears that, on this occasion, Richthofen's desire to provide close air support led him to select a base a little too close to the front.

The fighting at Smolensk ended on August 5. The Germans took another 310,000 prisoners, as well as 3,205 tanks and 3,120 guns.[48]

✠

Meanwhile, to the south, Loehr, Greim, and Pflugbeil were also heavily engaged in what was now their primary mission: close air support of the ground forces.

Field Marshal Gerd von Rundstedt's Army Group South struggled forward against difficulties Field Marshal von Bock did not face to the north. The wooded and swampy terrain of Soviet Galicia and the western Ukraine did not lend itself to rapid mobile operations, as did the terrain to the north.

Also, Rundstedt had only one panzer group (Col. Gen. Ewald von Kleist's 1st), as opposed to Army Group Center's two. In addition, Rundstedt faced the bulk of the Soviet army and most of its armored and mechanized forces. Indeed, Stalin's forces in June, 1941, had not been disposed in a defensive arrangement at all. Concentrated in the south, they were better positioned for an attack against Rumania (and the vital oilfields), leading one to believe that Stalin planned just such a move sometime in the future, possibly when the Germans were decisively engaged on the western front. Hitler, however, had forestalled him.

The first crisis in the south came on June 26, when the Soviets mounted a massive tank attack along the Kholoyuv-Brody line against Kleist's rapidly advancing flank. Greim's V Air Corps was committed immediately. It launched continuous, low-level attacks on the Soviet spearheads and troop concentrations, disrupting the Russian offensive and allowing Kleist to continue his advance. A similar crisis took place near Dubno, where V Air's Ju-88 and He-111 bombers destroyed 40 tanks and 180 other vehicles and damaged hundreds more. Many of these tanks were the superheavy fifty-two-ton models, superior to anything Germany had in 1941 (the Tigers and Panthers did not appear until 1943). "The equipment of the Red Army amazes us again and again," the chief of staff of the V Air Corps wrote.[49]

Meanwhile, the Red Army began to withdraw. Ranging far to the rear, the fighters of V and IV Air Corps strafed retreating Soviet troop columns while the Kampfgeschwadern bombed important road junctions. Interdiction of railroad traffic was also an important bomber mission, as it prevented the Russians from regrouping and, at the same time, allowed rapidly advancing ground forces to capture important rolling stock, which was needed to resupply both ground and air units.[50] On July 13, 1941, Col. Gen. Franz Halder, the chief of the General Staff of the army, noted in his diary that thirty-four isolated trains had been captured in the Cherkassy sector alone. In the Gusyatin area, the 5th SS Panzer Grenadier Division "Viking" captured another thirty undamaged, loaded trains.[51]

Unfortunately for the Germans, the Luftwaffe bombers had neither the numbers nor the range to disrupt rail traffic east of the Dnieper. Because Germany had no strategic air force, Soviet engineers were able to hastily dismantle every possible piece of industrial machinery and send it east, where it would be reassembled in the Urals or beyond. Although badly hurt, the industrial potential of the Soviet Union had not been destroyed. If the blitzkrieg failed to conquer Russia before the onset of winter, the war machine of the Soviet Union—with almost three times the population of Germany—would be able to recover.

Meanwhile, the Soviet armies made a stand at the Stalin line, the heavily fortified pre-1939 frontier of Soviet Russia. Attacking gun emplacements, bunkers, artillery positions, troop concentrations, and strongpoints, the combat units of the 4th Air Fleet paved the way for the breaching of the fortified line in the second week of July. The Soviet retreat continued towards the Dnieper.

General von Greim attempted to cut off the Soviet retreat by destroying the six Dnieper bridges at Cherkassy, Kanex, Kiev, and Gornostaypol. He was not successful, partially because he used bombs that were too light, but mainly because the Russians were demonstrating great ingenuity. Despite forty-two hits on the bridges, the Soviet engineers repaired them all almost instantly. Using in some cases 1,000 workers per bridge, they were able to fix even the heaviest damage within thirty-six hours.[52]

Not all of the Soviet forces escaped across the Dnieper, because Kleist was too quick for them. Leaving weak forces to screen his northern flank, the Prussian panzer group commander advanced rapidly to the southeast and then due south, enveloping a large Soviet force at Uman, in front of the seventeenth Army. Greim's air corps quickly established aerial supremacy over the pocket, shooting down at least 157 Soviet aircraft in the process. It then turned its attention to the pocket itself, frustrating Soviet breakout attempts and destroying 58 enemy tanks, 420 motor vehicles, and knocking out 22 batteries in the process. When the Uman Pocket was finally wiped out on August 9, 103,000 Soviet troops, 317 tanks, and 1,100 guns had been captured.[53] Soviet power west of the Dnieper had been broken.

Meanwhile, Adolf Hitler was engaged in a great strategic debate with Field Marshal Walter von Brauchitsch, the commander-in-chief of the army. Brauchitsch saw Moscow as the primary strategic objective of the campaign and wanted to drive straight for it with Army Group Center and all of the air power of the 2nd Air Fleet. The Fuehrer saw things differently. He commanded that the right wing of Army Group Center (Guderian's 2nd Panzer Group, supported by Weichs's Second Army) attack south, behind Kiev. Meanwhile, Kleist was to drive north to link up with Guderian and pinch off the huge salient forming around Kiev, the third-largest city in Russia and the key to the Ukraine, the breadbasket of the Soviet Union. Meanwhile, he detached 3rd Panzer Group (Col. Gen. Hermann Hoth) from Army Group Center and transferred it to Army Group North, for an attack on Leningrad. Richthofen's VIII Air Corps was assigned to 1st Air Fleet for the Leningrad attack, while Loerzer's II Air Corps was given the task of supporting Guderian. Army Group Center thus lost all but one of its panzer corps and was virtually denuded of air cover at a time when the road to Moscow was held only by weak Soviet forces that had been mauled in the battles of encirclement at

Bialystok, Minsk, and Smolensk. The capital of the Soviet Union was his for the taking, but Hitler let the opportunity pass. He had made a great strategic mistake, but it led to the greatest tactical victory of the war.

✠

The Battle of Kiev began on August 25, 1941, when 2nd Panzer Group launched its drive to the south. Marshal Budenny, the Soviet commander, saw that he was facing envelopment, but Stalin denied him permission to retreat; he therefore tried to concentrate against Guderian's spearheads. The fighting was bitter, but Budenny's plans were disrupted time and time again. While Fiebig directed dive-bomber and ground attack units against Soviet resistance at the front, Loerzer employed his bombers en masse against the Russian railroads and troop concentrations, disrupting troop movements and resupply efforts and causing widespread confusion and disorganization. The 3rd and 53rd Bomber Wings were specifically commended by OKL. Between June 22 and September 9, for example, KG 3 alone destroyed 471 Soviet planes (450 of them on the ground), 30 tanks, 488 other vehicles, and 355 railroad trains; interrupted rail traffic 332 times; flew 290 sorties against troop concentrations, columns, and barracks; and attacked 21 supply depots. In a similar period, the 210th Ground Attack Wing of the 2nd Close Air Support Command shot down 96 Soviet aircraft; destroyed 741 aircraft on the ground; destroyed 148 tanks, 3,280 other vehicles, 166 artillery pieces, and 50 trains; cut railroad lines repeatedly; and carried out numerous successful attacks against troop concentrations, strongpoints, and other positions.[54]

Second Air Corps could not have achieved these successes had it not been for the efforts of Col. Werner Moelders, the commander of the 51st Fighter Wing and one of the greatest genuine heroes in the history of aerial warfare. "Wherever he showed himself," Guderian wrote later. "The air was soon clear."[55] On September 8, JG 51 reported its 2,001st aerial "kill" of the war. On the eastern front alone its pilots had shot down 1,357 Soviet aircraft and destroyed 298 more on the ground. It had also destroyed 142 tanks and armored cars, 16 guns, 35 trains. and 432 trucks.[56]

Young Moelders was nearing the zenith of his remarkable career. He had been born in Gelsenkirchen on March 18, 1913. His father, a school teacher, had been killed in the Argonne in World War I. Despite this fact (or perhaps because of it), Werner was set on a military career from childhood. He entered the Dresden Cadet Academy in 1932 and was commissioned second lieutenant in the 2nd Infantry Regiment in 1934. Later that year he applied for duty in the clandestine Luftwaffe. He initially failed his flight physical because he got sick and threw up during the spin-chair test. The determined and intense Moelders practiced the test continuously until he mastered it, but he continued to suffer from air sickness until months after he graduated from Alfred Keller's bomber school at Brunswick. In the meanwhile he was posted to the Immelmann Wing (later StG 2) in Schwerin, where he became a Stuka pilot. After participating in the occupation of the Rhineland in 1936, he transferred to Osterkamp's 1st Fighter Wing as a squadron leader. In April, 1938, he assumed command of a fighter squadron in the Condor Legion in Spain.

Mild-mannered and sensitive, this devout Catholic did not seem like the kind of man who would revolutionize fighter tactics forever, but he did (see Chapter 3). In the process he became the leading ace in the Spanish Civil War and the model all fighter pilots looked up to. Promoted to captain during the Iberian conflict, he became an inspector of fighter units at RLM and became commander of III Group, 53rd Fighter Wing, on the western front in 1939.

Moelders shot down his first Allied airplane on September 20, 1939, and soon distinguished himself both as a leader and an aviator. He was the first pilot of World War II to score twenty victories and the first pilot in history to score 100 victories. During his career he was shot down and captured by the French. He was wounded in the knee during the Battle of Britain and forced to crash-land in France as a result.

Promoted to major on July 19, 1940, and lieutenant colonel on October 27, 1940, he led the 51st Fighter Wing in the latter part of the Battle of Britain. He had sixty-eight kills when he led his Geschwader across the Soviet frontier on June 22, 1941.

Werner Moelders was a great wing commander. Because he had had problems in his early flying career, he understood the problems of his younger pilots and helped them master their airplanes and bring out the best of their abilities. In return, they idolized him and nicknamed him "Father," despite his youth. Hitler, Goering, and the entire Luftwaffe hierarchy held him in the highest esteem. Everyone respected him—even the enemy. He was promoted to colonel in 1941 and was awarded the Knights Cross with Oak Leaves, Swords, and Diamonds, a decoration roughly equivalent to the Congressional Medal of Honor.

Shortly after Moelders scored his 115th victory, Goering made him the first *General der Jagdwaffe*—general of fighter forces. He had become the youngest general in the Wehrmacht, but his Berlin desk was seldom occupied. Moelders was busy on the eastern front, directing fighters and Stukas in the Crimea. In November 1941, he was summoned back to the capital to join the Honor Guard at Ernst Udet's funeral.

General Moelders was in a hurry to get back to Berlin, not only to attend the funeral but also to obtain more fuel, ammunition, and repair parts for his depleted squadrons. On November 11, 1941, he boarded a He-111 bomber and, despite bad weather and the objections of his pilot, Moelders insisted that they proceed at once to Berlin. Near Breslau, one of their engines failed. Moelders then ordered the pilot to land at Schmeidefeld on the edge of the city. As the plane made its final approach, the second engine quit and the He-111 smashed into the ground. Moelders, who was sitting in the copilot's seat, died instantly of a broken neck. The pilot, Lieutenant Knobe, a veteran of the Condor Legion, died on the way to the hospital, and the head mechanic was also killed. Moelders' aide and the radio operator survived.[57]

Werner Moelders was described by a colleague as being a man whose "happy disposition, an incomparable charm, and the urge to get the best out of life made it impossible to dislike him. He was a real person with a warm heart, talented, and with a natural sense of humor."[58] He was also known for standing up to the Nazi party, especially when it attacked the Catholic Church and her institutions.

The entire nation mourned the dashing young aviator and his old wing was designated JG 51 "Moelders" in his honor. Even after the war the Germans fondly remembered their hero. In 1969 the West German Air Force named a missile-firing destroyer in his honor.[59] He was succeeded as general of fighter forces by Adolf Galland, the commander of JG 26.

✠

Meanwhile, on September 10, Ewald von Kleist began his advance east of Kiev, in an attempt to encircle the city. He experienced considerably less resistance than did Guderian. The two linked up at Romny, 124 miles east of Kiev, on September 14. Kiev fell to Field Marshal von Reichenau's Sixth Army on the 18th, and by September 26 the greatest battle of annihilation of the war was over. Stalin had lost 665,000 men, 3,718 guns, and 884 tanks captured.

✠

Elsewhere on the eastern front, Keller's reinforced 1st Air Fleet supported Army Group North's drive on Leningrad. The Red Air Force was already beginning to recover and continued to commit fresh units to the battle. By August 23, Foerster's I Air Corps alone had shot down 920 Soviet aircraft.

Meanwhile, two days before the mopping up operations at Minsk were completed, VIII Air Corps left the central sector of the Russian front and flew north, where it joined 1st Air Fleet. While it was in the northern sector, VIII Air Corps spent most of its time supporting Col. Gen. Erich Hoepner's 4th Panzer Group, which cut its way to the outskirts of Leningrad despite heavy resistance.[60] Richthofen bombed Leningrad and set it on fire "from one end to the other."[61] In mid-September he attacked the Soviet Baltic Fleet, at anchor at Leningrad, and the nearby ports at Oranienbaum and Kronstadt. Kronstadt, an island in the Gulf of Finland twelve and a half miles from Leningrad, was the largest war harbor in the Soviet Union.[62] The Baltic Fleet included two battleships, two cruisers, thirteen destroyers, forty-two submarines, and more than two hundred auxiliary vessels.[63] It was subjected to attack after attack by the Ju-87s. Unlike the British Mediterranean Fleet in Cretan waters, however, the Baltic Fleet was closely guarded by hundreds of antiaircraft guns and protected by numerous squadrons of Red Air Force fighters (Rata and Curtiss aircraft). The Stukas, therefore, had to be closely protected by the Messerschmitt fighters, as indeed they were.

On September 16, 1st Lt. Hans Ulrich Rudel of StG 2 flew his dive-bomber through heavy weather, dove through the clouds to an altitude of 2,400 feet, and dropped a 1,000-pound bomb on the deck of the battleship *Marat*, the pride of the Baltic Fleet. Flak was very heavy, of course, so Rudel ducked back into the clouds as quickly as he could. The *Marat* was severely damaged, but a 1,000-pound bomb could not sink it. Later that week, however, Rudel had another opportunity to attack the *Marat*, this time with a 2,000-pound bomb. He dove straight down from 9,000 feet and released his bomb at the dangerously low altitude of 900 feet. It hit the battleship's ammunition magazine. The *Marat* exploded and split in two. Rudel managed to pull up from his dive just above the surface of the Gulf of Finland, where he was instantly attacked by a Rata, but a protecting Messerschmitt shot it down, and the lieutenant made good his escape. Richthofen personally decorated Rudel with the Knight's Cross for this feat.[64]

The sinking of this 23,500-ton battleship was the first major success for the twenty-four-year-old Rudel, who became the most highly decorated pilot of the war. The son of a Lutheran pastor in Silesia, Rudel was a delicate youth who had been afraid of his own shadow. His mother had to hold his hand in thunderstorms until he was twelve and his older sister once said, "Uli will never be any good in life; he is afraid of going into the cellar by himself." This frightened child grew up to terrorize the Soviet army and be the most successful pilot in the history of the Luftwaffe. He was commissioned on April 20, 1938, and served as a long-range reconnaissance pilot in Poland. Assigned to a Stuka wing during the Balkans campaign, he was not allowed to fly combat missions in Yugoslavia, Greece, or Crete because of his alleged inability to manage his aircraft. Given his chance in Russia, he flew 2,530 combat missions on the eastern front and destroyed 519 enemy tanks—enough to equip an entire armored corps. Wounded five times, Rudel continued to fly despite the loss of his right leg below the knee. He was promoted very rapidly and became a colonel on January 1, 1945, at the age of twenty-eight. Near the end of the war, Adolf Hitler decorated Rudel with the Golden Oak Leaves, Swords, and Diamonds—a medal the Fuehrer created just for him. After the war Rudel emigrated to Argentina, where he worked for an aircraft firm.[65]

✠

Besides sinking the *Marat*, Richthofen's dive-bombers also sank the heavy cruiser *Kirov* and several other vessels and generally wrecked the Russian Baltic Fleet in September, 1941.[66] On the ground, VIII Air Corps helped Eighteenth Army breach the fortifications at Luga and supported its advance on Novgorod. As the Germans came closer and closer to Leningrad, Soviet resistance intensified, and progress became slower. The VIII Air Corps very effectively supported 4th Panzer Group's breakthrough past the outer fortifications of Leningrad on August 11 and its subsequent advance to seal off the city.[67] On September 8, XLI Panzer Corps of the 4th Panzer Group, supported by Richthofen's divebombers, began its drive through the Duderhof Hills near Leningrad against fierce resistance. The panzer corps' right flank was exposed to strong Russian counterattacks that inflicted heavy losses on the 6th Panzer Division, despite constant interdiction sorties by VIII Air Corps. Finally. however, the XLI Panzer battered its way to Hill 167, the "Generals Hill" of the Czars. It fell on September 11. At 11:30 A.M. that day, Second Lieutenant Darius, the commander of the spearhead, signaled: "can see St. Petersburg and the sea!" Leningrad was only six miles away and had been cut off from the east.[68] Hitler, however, commanded that the city not be taken. He ordered it be surrounded and starved into submission that winter. This was a fatal mistake on his part, because the Russians managed to supply it over the ice of Lake Lagoda. As a result of this order, Leningrad never did fall, although it remained under siege until January 1944, tying down two German armies and the entire 1st Air Fleet in the process. On September 17, 1941, 4th Panzer Group and VIII Air Corps were withdrawn from Army Group North and sent southeast, toward Moscow.

✠

Hitler considered going into winter quarters after his victory at Kiev, but Bock, Brauchitsch, and the ever-optimistic Kesselring convinced him to launch a drive on Moscow. There would be other victories, to be sure, and the Luftwaffe continued to support the army well, but the momentum of the blitzkrieg was ebbing. So was the Luftwaffe's combat strength. The continuous operations, losses, damage to aircraft due to combat action and poor

TABLE 13: THE DECLINE IN OPERATIONAL READINESS, EASTERN FRONT, JUNE–DECEMBER, 1941

Type of Unit	Date	Total Aircraft Strength Actual	Operational	Operational Percentage
Bombers	28 Jun 41	1,310	754	57.6
	27 Dec 41	1,332	458	34.4
Fighters	28 Jun 41	1,266	885	69.9
	27 Dec 41	1,472	670	45.6
Dive-Bombers	28 Jun 41	410	278	67.8
	27 Dec 41	326	163	50.0

Source: Plocher MS 1942.

landings by exhausted pilots, primitive Russian airfields, and long supply lines made it harder and harder for German ground crews to keep the planes in the air. Already fewer than half of the aircraft in some units were serviceable. Things became even worse in November, when the problems of icy runways and a lack of heating equipment led to a further decline in serviceability. Long hours of flying, primitive airfields, and inadequate maintenance time had taken their toll. Operational readiness in the Stuka groups was down to 50 percent and was even lower in the fighter units. Bomber units were down to an operational readiness of 34 percent by December 27 (see Table 13), which meant that only one out of every three aircraft was battleworthy. Despite losses of 1,400,000 killed and 3,600,000 captured,[69] the Soviets used their seemingly limitless manpower reserves to strengthen their Moscow defenses, which Army Group Center proved unable to penetrate. The German offensive ground to a halt within fifteen miles of the Kremlin. The blitzkrieg had failed. As Milch had predicted, the war against Russia would be a long one.

✠

The Luftwaffe had performed magnificently during Operation Barbarossa. By the end of the campaign it had destroyed 15,500 Soviet airplanes,[70] 3,200 tanks, 57,600 vehicles, 2,450 guns, 650 trains, and 1,200 locomotives, and had cut Soviet rail lines in 7,000 places. In addition, it had prevented the Red Air Force from launching any significant aerial bombardments on German troops. It had lost 2,093 airplanes (largely to bad landings; only 900 were lost in combat), including 758 bombers and 568 fighters, with another

1,361 airplanes damaged. Replacements were not slow in coming, however, so the overall strength of the eastern front air fleets never fell below 1,700 aircraft.[71] On the other hand, the Luftwaffe had served almost exclusively as an appendage of the army. It had dealt effectively with the Soviet air and ground forces at and near the front, true enough, but it had never attempted to bomb the Soviet industrial complexes—and would never do so. The Luftwaffe must therefore be rated a strategic failure. By the end of 1941, 80 percent of the Soviet war industry was in the East. Russian tanks, guns, and airplanes would continue to be destroyed en masse at the front, but the undisturbed factories continued to grind them out until the Wehrmacht—and Nazi Germany—was destroyed. From July to December alone Russian factories had turned out 5,173 of the new Soviet fighters. In the same period, Great Britain manufactured 4,408 fighters, but German factories only produced 1,619 fighters for the Luftwaffe.[72]

The Russian campaign of 1941 ended the predominantly tactical phase of the air war. From this point on, the Luftwaffe would be engaged in a conflict that was more and more strategic in character, a type of war that the German Air Force proved singularly unable to fight or adapt to. The question must now be asked: Why was the Luftwaffe such a mammoth strategic failure? Part of the responsibility, of course, can laid at the door of Adolf Hitler, who pursued a multifront war, but most of the blame lies with the Luftwaffe itself, and especially with two men—Hermann Goering and Ernst Udet.

CHAPTER 9

The Fall of Ernst Udet

It would be hard to envision a man less suited to the post of chief of the Technical Office than Ernst Udet was in 1936. He had had no long-term responsibility for seventeen years, had a happy-go-lucky attitude, trusted the wrong people (especially industrialists), disliked regular hours, and hated to be tied to a desk. He also had a talent for appointing the wrong subordinates. His chief of staff, Maj. Gen. August Ploch, was incompetent. His chief engineer, *Generalstabsingenieur* (lieutenant general of engineers) Rulof Lucht, a thirty-four-year-old former naval aviator, was inexperienced and incapable of properly evaluating an aircraft technologically ("even Udet's understanding was regarded as more profound," Cooper wrote later).[1] The head of technical planning, *Generalingenieur* (major general of engineers) Guenther Tscherich, who managed to acquire a great deal of influence over Udet, was far more interested in aircraft development than production and procurement, which he neglected.[2]

Because of Udet's lack of management and supervisory abilities, the Technical Office was already out of control by early 1939. However, since it took four years for an aircraft to go from the drafting board to the flight lines, this fact was not yet apparent. Hermann Goering, who was not interested in the day-to-day activities of the Air Ministry, certainly did not see the warning signs that Germany was beginning to lose its edge in military aircraft technology. His "conferences" with Udet (as Goering himself later admitted) were little more than "bull sessions" about the days when they flew together as part of the old Richthofen Fighter Wing in World War I.

On February 1, 1939, partially to further reduce Milch's power, Goering appointed Udet *Generalluftzeugmeister*—a post roughly translatable as chief air armament officer of the Luftwaffe. The new office included not only the thirteen departments of the Technical Office, but also the five aircraft testing stations, an industrial section, and the Supply office, which was taken from the Air Defense Office. There were now twenty-six department chiefs directly responsible to Udet—more than any one man could hope to manage. "The Technical Office soon became a department in which the Engineer Generals did pretty much what they liked," Col. Werner Baumbach, the famous bomber pilot, wrote later.[3]

Udet's new appointment also earned him a bitter enemy in Erhard Milch. The two men had had a father and son relationship prior to 1933. Udet even taught Milch how to fly. This relationship continued during the 1933–36 period. Udet still asked Milch for advice, and Milch was pleased to give it, for he was happy that he was still able to exercise his influence in the field of air armament. The relationship cooled in late 1936, when Udet submitted a major production plan to Goering without consulting Milch, who felt slighted and offended. After Udet became Generalluftzeugmeister, however, Milch was largely excluded from aircraft design, production, and procurement, and the two men became enemies.

Other than accepting the post in the first place, Udet's major mistake was in his selection of aircraft to succeed current models. He decided to base the Luftwaffe's offensive capability on four main combat types by early 1940—the Me-109, Ju-88, Me-210, and He-177. The Me-109, as we have seen, was fairly successful, but the Ju-88 had a great many problems, and the Me-210 and He-177 were total failures, thus considerably inhibiting the Luftwaffe's ability to wage war from 1940 on.[4]

The Ju-88 was developed by Dr. Heinrich Koppenburg, the managing director of Junkers. Originally designed as a superspeed, unarmed, six-ton bomber, it was first successfully test-flown in March, 1938. Dubbed the "Wonder Bomber," it never lived up to expectations, largely because the Technical Office kept adding requirements for it and modifications to it. "Probably no other aircraft in history has been developed in so many quite different forms," Wood and Gunston wrote.[5] The Technical Office ordered that it be equipped with guns and defensive armament, greatly increasing its weight, reducing its speed, and retarding its performance. Even its basic structure had to be changed, as now it needed an extra crewman to operate the guns. The worst added requirement, however, was that it be able to dive. Both Udet and Jeschonnek were firm believers that an effective bomber had to be able to dive, to increase the accuracy of its attack. This requirement meant that the structure had to be strengthened again—further reducing its speed. Essentially they had tried to convert it into a twin-engine Stuka. Eventually some 25,000 changes were required and the weight of some models exceeded thirteen tons. Performance was, of course, greatly reduced and, since it weighed three times as much as the Ju-87 (4.2 tons), it never did dive well. One of the most distinguished pilots of the Luftwaffe, Capt. Baron Rudolf von Moreau, was killed trying to test-dive a Ju-88 at Rechlin. Engineer-General Marquardt later wrote—with considerable justification—that the dive-bomber concept ruined the Luftwaffe.[6] It certainly ruined the Ju-88. The maximum speed of the original prototypes exceeded 400 miles per hour, but the Ju-88A-4 could not even reach 280 miles per hour. Its climbing rate and handling character-istics were also reduced to the point that Milch referred to it as a "flying barn door" in 1939.[7]

On September 30, 1938, during the Czech crisis, Goering ordered the Ju-88 into mass production, despite the fact that testing had not yet been completed. Mass production began at a half-dozen factories, but by the time the war broke out not one had reached the squadrons. When the first model (the Ju-88A-1) did enter service in September, 1939, it was slower than the He-111s it had been designed to replace. It also had difficulties taking off with full tanks, was difficult to fly, and some of the Ju-88A-1s caught fire in mid-air from no apparent cause. Its range was limited to 250 miles when fully loaded with two tons of bombs. This version was plagued with technical problems until it was taken out of service. Other models were better, but all caused early pilot fatigue, and none really lived up to expectations. Never-theless more than 15,000 were manufactured during the war (because the Technical Office could develop nothing better), and they were used in a variety of roles, including horizontal and dive-bombing, long-range recon-naissance, torpedo bombing, and night-fighting. They were effective in some roles, but this did not make up for the fact that Germany had no mod-ern bomber by 1942.

If the Ju-88 was a disappointment, the He-177 was a disaster. In early 1938 Udet apparently decided that the Luftwaffe might need a long-range bomber after all (for a possible war against Russia), and he issued specifica-tions for such an aircraft. It would have to carry two tons of bombs and have a range of action of more than 1,000 miles. In the early spring, Ernst Heinkel submitted a proposal, and a few weeks later Udet and Jeschonnek saw a mock-up of the He-177. It featured four engines joined to two propellers by a coupling arrangement. Both Udet and Jeschonnek had requested a four-engine, four-propeller construction, only to defer to Heinkel's enthusiasm for the tandem-engine arrangement.[8]

A few months later Udet, with the agreement of Lucht, Reidenbach, and Jeschonnek, issued the requirement that the He-177 be capable of div-ing at a 60-degree angle. Udet told Heinkel: "The He-177 must be capable of diving at all costs."

"You can't make a dive-bomber out of an aircraft that size!" Heinkel responded. The He-177 weighed 30,000 pounds at that time.

"For all practical purposes it's a twin-engine aircraft," Udet replied. "If the twin-engined Ju-88 can dive, why shouldn't the He-177?"[9] The new requirement forced Heinkel to increase the weight of the He-177 to thirty-two tons, at a sacrifice of speed and maneuverability.[10] On November 19,

1938, it was test-flown at Rechlin. The results were unsatisfactory, due to high engine oil temperatures. Udet nevertheless authorized the production of the He-177, but at a very low rate and priority. In June, 1940, only three of these bombers were being produced per month.[11]

The weaknesses of the He-111 and Ju-88 had been amply demonstrated in the Battle of Britain. Udet's failures were also made public for the entire world to see. Clearly Germany had lost its lead in military aviation technology. To regain it quickly, Udet gambled. In October, 1940, he ordered the He-177 into mass production, despite its negative test results. This order demanded a time-consuming reorganization of the aircraft industry. The He-111 was taken out of production, the factories were retooled, and the mass production began. All of this took months. Only when it came off the production lines were the defects of the parallel-coupled engines discovered. Most serious was its tendency to explode in mid-air for no apparent reason (apparently the fuel lines dripped on the hot manifolds) or to break apart during dives. Its connecting rods were also prone to breaking, penetrating the crankcase and letting hot oil fly everywhere. Even if fire was avoided, the valves fouled after a maximum of six hours' flying time. Everything was so jammed together that it was almost impossible to install fire walls.[12] Wood and Gunston described it as "possibly the most troublesome and unsatisfactory aircraft in military history . . . no engines in bomber history have caught fire so often in normal cruising flight."[13] The He-177 became known as the *Luftwaffenfeuerzeug*—"the Luftwaffe's lighter." More than fifty prototypes broke up during dives or turned into giant Roman candles in level flight. Despite the fact that 1,446 were manufactured during the war,[14] only 33 had been accepted for service by late 1942. Of these, only two were still operational a few weeks later.[15]

Because so many prototypes went down in flames, crews and all, the He-177 had to be withdrawn from the production lines. The aircraft industry had to reorganize and retool again, at the cost of tens of thousands of hours, so it could resume the production of bomber models that were already obsolete. The waste of raw materials was tremendous.

The Me-210 was another of Udet's failures. It was designed by Willi Messerschmitt as a multipurpose replacement for the Me-110, the Ju-87, and the Hs-123. The plans for this aircraft were submitted to RLM and approved in the summer of 1938. Jeschonnek had such confidence in the designer's abilities that he requested 1,000 airplanes, even before the first prototype was completed. Udet was also taken in. Udet was "no match for the tricks of the industrialists," his adjutant, Col. Max Pendele, noted later.[16] The Air Ministry's order was based solely upon performance forecasts and Messerschmitt's effective sales pitch.[17]

Delivery of the Me-210 was scheduled for mid-1941. The first prototype flew on September 5, 1939. It was unstable and unpredictable and whipped into spins at high angles of attack. Nevertheless, the airframes of the Me-210s were being assembled in mid-1940, even though no solutions to its shortcomings had been found. The progressive phasing out of the Me-110 had already been ordered; reliance on the Me-210 was total.[18]

Finally brought into production in 1941, the Me-210 proved to be a total failure. Airplane after airplane crashed, and pilots looked upon it as a death-trap. Milch finally cancelled the program altogether and called for Messerschmitt's resignation (which he did not get). Milch estimated that the Me-210 program cost the Luftwaffe 600 aircraft.[19]

✠

It was conceded even by his enemies that Ernst Udet was a charming man. He was also a good actor and deceiver. When French Air Marshal Joseph Vuillemin visited Germany, Udet led him around "by the nose."[20] He convinced the French air force commander-in-chief that the Luftwaffe was much stronger than it really was. Later he did the same thing to Goering and Hitler.

On July 3, 1939, Hitler visited the Luftwaffe's experimental testing station at Rechlin. The purpose of the display was to win Hitler's support for the allocation of the economic resources necessary to fulfill the Hitler Program. Hitler saw the new Ju-88, the Me-110, the Me-209, the He-100, an air-to-ground missile, an early warning radar, a 30mm cannon, rocket-assisted take-offs, and other miracle weapons (by 1939 standards). Most of this equipment still required further testing and some of it was never developed, but Adolf Hitler did not know that, and Hermann Goering did not know it either. Udet, in fact, made very uncautious predictions about when this equipment would be ready. This time, however, Udet's showmanship backfired on him. To deceive one's enemies can be a service to one's country; to deceive one's own leaders is the height of irresponsibility. Later, in May 1942, Reichsmarschall Goering moaned that Hitler made the most serious decisions on the basis of this visit, implying that the decision to invade Poland and risk a second world war was predicated on the assumption that the Luftwaffe was much stronger than it actually was.

Ernst Udet was still a complacent, happy-go-lucky man in the summer of 1939. He had the good will and respect of the Fuehrer and his old buddy Goering, and his life was a happy one. He ate at the best restaurants, drank the best liquor, and had all the women he wanted. The Luftwaffe's technical situation could have been better, of course, but in the summer of 1939 it didn't look too bad. To maintain its technological superiority, the Luftwaffe was depending on the arrival of the "next generation" of aircraft: the Ju-88, the He-177, and the Me-210. The Ju-88 was a year behind schedule, the delivery date of the He-177 was set for late 1940, and the Me-210 was to appear on the flight lines in mid-1941. There were problems in the He-177, to be sure, but Heinkel was reporting steady progress, and Junkers was already working on an updated Ju-88 (designated the Ju-188) and a new transport aircraft, the Ju-288. There was no reason to believe that war would break out before 1942; indeed, all of the Luftwaffe's plans were predicated on this assumption.

The assumption was all wrong. The outbreak of hostilities took Ernst Udet totally by surprise. He was very uneasy after Great Britain declared war against Germany on September 3, 1939. Udet had never counted on this possibility. Still, he did not call for a total war effort. German industry continued to produce on a peacetime basis, while British industry was accelerating its production of war goods as rapidly as it could. Udet, the "Old Eagle," was exuberant over the Luftwaffe's victory over France in June, 1940. "The war is over!" he exclaimed. "All our plans can be tossed into the waste basket! We don't need them any longer!"[21] Some of his former cheerfulness returned to him, especially after his own promotion to colonel general on July 19, 1940, but his optimism soon faded. When Heinkel met Udet in the Hotel Bristol in Berlin in late October, 1940, he hardly recognized him: "He looked bloated and sallow . . . as if he were heading for a nervous breakdown. He was suffering from irremedial buzzing in his ears and bleeding from his lungs and gums." Udet told Heinkel that Goering wanted to send him off to Buehlerhoene, a sanatorium in the Black Forest, but he refused to go.[22]

A week or two later Udet actually did go to Buehlerhoene, but he only stayed a few days, apparently because he felt Milch would try to undercut him if he stayed longer. Udet knew the ambitious and ruthless state secretary was aware that all was not well in the Technical Office. Even so, Udet could not bring himself to deal firmly with the industrialists. He wrote harsh letters to Heinkel, Dornier, Messerschmitt, and others, but never mailed them. He just didn't have the heart to send them.[23]

Meanwhile, technical problems mounted. The He-177 and Me-210 projects floundered, the Ju-88 was not what it was supposed to be, and the deliveries of the new BMW-801 air-cooled engine, which was supposed to power the new Focke-Wulf 190 fighter and Do-217 bomber, were far behind schedule, resulting in further production delays. In February, 1941, Hitler sharply criticized Goering and demanded to know why the German Air Force was so far behind its production schedules. In keeping with his character, Goering turned on Udet—their first argument.[24]

Udet, of course, saw disaster coming—and he knew why. Without a single strong and competent subordinate behind him, he took to the bottle for support. He also chain-smoked, took pills with depressing side effects, and ate only meat. Cajus Bekker later wrote: "After spring, 1941, Ernst Udet became a mere shadow of his former self. Though he drove himself to the limit, as chief of supply, he became the scapegoat for every failure, and the weight of responsibility broke him."[25]

On June 20, 1941, Goering turned to the man who had plotted to replace him: Erhard Milch. He ordered the state secretary to effect a quadrupling of production levels in all sectors of armament in the shortest possible period of time. Milch was given full powers to shut down and requisition factories, seize and expropriate construction materials, requisition workers, confiscate raw materials, and remove from office or transfer key personnel within the entire air armaments industry, regardless of existing contracts. He was given permission to ignore any existing regulations that might interfere with the attainment of the highest possible increase in production. Goering stopped short, however, of giving Milch permission to replace Udet or making Udet directly subordinate to Milch.

The result of this order was a division of authority and inevitable friction. Indeed, the Reichsmarschall refused to delineate their authorities. Now, however, Udet's huge agency had to have Milch's cooperation to function. Friction increased, and so did the pressure on Udet.

Hermann Goering still cared for his old friend, however, and in August, 1941, advised him to go on a vacation. He even invited Udet to spend some time at his luxurious hunting lodge, Rominten. Udet, however, had lost interest in hunting and on August 25 checked back in to Buehlerhoene. He did not return from leave until September 26.[26]

While Udet was gone, Milch continued his relentless drive to gain power at Udet's expense. On September 7, he gained the authority to reorganize the Technical Office and the Office of the Chief of Supply and Procurement. Two days later, Milch fired *Generalingenieur* Tschersich. Later that month he dismissed Reidenbach and relieved Ploch, who was sent to direct Air Administrative Command II in Russia. Ploch left for the eastern front on October 1, 1941.

Meanwhile, Milch took energetic measures to put the air industry back on a firm footing. He ordered Albert Speer, the Fuehrer's architect, to construct three aircraft factories at Bruenn, Graz, and Vienna. They were to be as large as the Volkswagen Works. He gave Speer eight months to complete them. Milch also reorganized the aircraft industry, put an end to trade secrets, reorganized Udet's office, and, to reassure himself of the Reichsmarschall's support, christened the whole project "the Goering Program."

On October 4, 1941, a week after he returned from leave, Udet was forced to officially approve the new organization of his agency. There were to be four office chiefs: Col. Wolfgang Vorwald for the Technical Office, Maj. Gen. of Reserves Baron Karl-August von Gablenz for the Air Force Equipment Office, Ministerial Director Hugo Geyer for the Supply Office, and Ministerial Director Alois Czeijka for the Industrial Office. "By this time it was all over for Udet," Colonel Pendele remarked later.[27]

On November 15 General Ploch, on leave from the eastern front, visited his old chief. He told Udet about the mass murder of Jews in the East. Udet was terribly upset.[28] Whatever else he was, he was no monster.

Two days later Udet drank two bottles of cognac and telephoned his mistress, Mrs. Inge Bleyle. "Inge," he said, "I can't stand it any longer. I'm going to shoot myself. I wanted to say goodbye to you. They're after me!"[29] She was still trying to talk him out of it when he pulled the trigger. He left behind a suicide note to Goering, asking him why he had surrendered to "those Jews," Milch and von Gablenz.[30] Over the wall of his bed he had scrawled in red crayon a note to Goering: "Iron Man, you deserted me."

Udet was officially reported as having been killed in a crash while testing a new airplane. Goering wept openly at his funeral, but later (on October 9, 1943) he said: "If I could only figure out what Udet was thinking of! He made a complete chaos out of our entire Luftwaffe program. If he were alive today, I would have no choice but to say to him: 'You are responsible for the destruction of the German Luftwaffe!'"[31]

Goering blamed Udet for the technological failure of the Luftwaffe, but he must share much of the blame himself, as his own people told him. In February, 1942, an investigation was launched against Ploch, Lucht, Tschersich, and Reidenbach—Udet's chief of staff and his leading engineers. The investigation was headed by Generalrichter Dr. Kraell and Col. Dr. Manfred Roeder, both of the Judge Advocate's Branch. It was stopped in the summer of 1942, twice resumed, and twice halted again. There were no indictments and no trials for four major reasons: first, the Luftwaffe General Staff could not be absolved of responsibility, because it had neglected to see the problem, apparently due to a lack of interest; second, there was no way to avoid implicating leading aircraft designers and industrialists; third, there was no evidence of criminal intent; and fourth, Goering himself would be implicated for having neglected his supervisory responsibilities.[32] The investigation was quietly dropped.

Milch succeeded Udet in all of his offices. He cut Udet's 4,000-man staff by 2,000 men, removed the inefficient, cut out numerous useless projects (including the Me-210), streamlined the bureaucracy, cut paperwork in half, and improved production remarkably. Realizing that, despite the assurances of Dr. Koppenberg, the Ju-288 (or "B Bomber," on which the General Staff placed great hopes) could not possibly be ready before 1944, he prevailed on Goering to cancel it, which he did in late 1941. Shortly thereafter, Milch sacked Koppenberg altogether. Because he realized that obsolete airplanes were better than no airplanes, the state secretary further decreed that existing aircraft be continued in production until their replacements were ready. He also called for the adoption of total war measures, but this recommendation was rejected by Hitler. Under Milch's capable and ruthless leadership, aircraft production began to rise again in 1942.[33] Nevertheless, Milch was not able to make good five years lost to incompetence and neglect overnight. He faced the same problems Udet had, plus he had to straighten out Udet's mess. He had to deal with a shortage of raw materials and the manpower drain to the eastern front, which made it impossible to demobilize workers for the aircraft industry, as Hitler had planned. He also had to compete with the other services—the navy, SS, and army—for resources and money, at a time when the fighting (and the manpower and equipment losses) on the eastern front was near its peak. Due to the needs of the armies in the East, the Luftwaffe lost its number one priority in raw material allocation. After he was captured in 1945, Gen. Karl Koller complained: "Air armament was placed way down the list; first were submarines, then tanks, then assault guns, then howitzers, and Lord knows what, and then came the Luftwaffe. We were smothered by the enormous superiority of Allied material, because the German High Command undertook too much on the ground in the East, and because it did not direct the main weight of armament right from the start toward air supremacy."[34]

As a result of the chaos in the Technical Office and of the shortage of raw materials, aircraft production in 1942 was only 32 percent above that of 1941,[35] and many of these were obsolete models. Britain had surpassed Germany in aircraft production in 1940, and Russia had done the same in 1941, if not before. On December 11, 1941, at the request of the Japanese government, Hitler declared war on the United States—the nation with the greatest industrial potential in the world. It did not take a genius to see that the handwriting was on the wall for Germany and the Luftwaffe.

An aerial photograph of Stalingrad after it had been pounded by the Luftwaffe, 1942.

Bruno Loerzer, World War I flying ace and close friend of Hermann Goering. During World War II, he served as the Luftwaffe's chief personnel officer, commander of the II Air Corps, and chief of personnel armament.

Erich Hartmann as a *Fahnenjunker*.

Lt. Hermann Goering, commander of the 1st (Richthofen) Fighter Wing, during World War I.

A Luftwaffe light mortar crew.

Hermann Goering as president of the
Reichstag, circa 1932.

Adolf Galland, general of fighter pilots.
UNITED STATES NAVAL ACADEMY

Field Marshal Baron Wolfram von
Richthofen and Col. Gen. Hans
Jeschonnek, the fourth chief of the Gen-
eral Staff of the Luftwaffe. UNITED STATES
NAVAL ACADEMY

Two innovators: Col. Gen. Kurt Student, a World War I ace on the Eastern Front and father of the German parachute branch, and Field Marshal Richthofen outside Fuehrer headquarters, 1943. UNITED STATES NAVAL ACADEMY

A pair of Heinkel He-111 bombers returning to base in France after a daylight raid on Britain, 1940. Although obsolete by 1940, the He-111 remained the standard Luftwaffe bomber throughout the war. UNITED STATES NAVAL ACADEMY

General of Flyers Karl Korten, Col. Klaus Uebe, and Col. Gen. Kurt Pflugbeil on the Eastern Front, circa 1944. Korten was the fifth chief of the General Staff of the Luftwaffe. Uebe served as the chief of staff of the 1st Air Fleet in 1944–45. Pflugbeil commanded VIII Air Corps, IV Air Corps, and 1st Air Fleet. UNITED STATES NAVAL ACADEMY

Gen. Walter Wever, the first chief of the General Staff of the Luftwaffe. He was killed in an air accident in 1935. COURTESY OF JOHN ANGOLIA

Erhard Milch, the secretary of state for the Aviation Ministry and the chairman of the board of Lufthansa. UNITED STATES NAVAL ACADEMY

A flight of Dornier Do-17s on a raid during the Battle of Britain, 1949. UNITED STATES NAVAL ACADEMY

German soldiers bury a British pilot with full military honors in France, 1940. UNITED STATES NAVAL ACADEMY

Hitler speaks with Field Marshal von Richthofen while Kurt Student and Hans Jeschonnek look on, 1943. UNITED STATES NAVAL ACADEMY

The Wanne-Eickel Synthetic Oil Plant under attack by U.S. forces, November 1944. The destuction of the synthetic oil industry was a decisive blow to the ability of the Luftwaffe to wage war in the last year of the conflict. UNITED STATES NAVAL ACADEMY

A German gunner from a rocket launcher battery scans the sky for Allied fighter bombers in Normandy, 1944.

Hermann Goering as Reichsmarschall.

UNITED STATES NAVAL ACADEMY

Another look at the Ju-88. UNITED STATES NAVAL ACADEMY

A pair of "Stuka" dive bombers

A British fighter roars past a Do-17 bomber during the Battle of Britain, 1940.
UNITED STATES NAVAL ACADEMY

A Do-17. UNITED STATES NAVAL ACADEMY

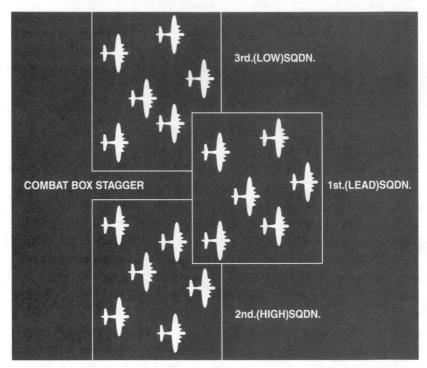

A diagram of the American "box" (or combat box stagger) formation that was so effective in defeating the Luftwaffe in the skies above Germany.

An Allied ship sunk by Stukas at Dunkirk, 1940.

Field Marshals Walter von Reichenau and Erhard Milch. UNITED STATES NAVAL ACADEMY

Gen. Ernst Udet, 1936.

Col. Gen. Alexander Loehr. Commander of the Austrian Air Force when the Third Reich annexed the country in 1938, Loehr later commanded the 4th Air Fleet on the Eatern Front and Army Group F in the Balkans.

Col. Hans-Ulrich Rudel, the leading ground-support and dive-bomber ace of World War II. He personally destroyed more than 700 Soviet tanks and armored vehicles.

CHAPTER 10

The Russian Front, 1942–43

While Milch struggled with the mammoth problems of the air armaments industry, the men on the eastern front struggled just to stay alive. On December 6, 1941, Stalin launched a major offensive all along the eastern front. The situation was especially critical in the zone of Army Group Center, which was supported now by only the VIII Air Corps of General Baron von Richthofen. (Kesselring's HQ, 2nd Air Fleet, and Loerzer's II Air Corps had both been sent to the Mediterranean to fight the British on December 1.) The situation of Richthofen's units was typical of those on the Russian front in the winter of 1941–42, if not worse. The Red Air Force now had major advantages over the VIII Air Corps. Not only were they more experienced at flying in extremely cold weather, but they had shorter supply lines and were using the paved airports in the vicinity of Moscow. All Richthofen had was dirt strips.[1] It was very difficult for his airplanes to even take off in the terrible Russian winter. Under heavy pressure, Army Group Center began to give ground in the second week of December. Then, on December 16, Hitler issued his first "hold at all costs" order. He also directed that VIII Air Corps was to be reinforced with a full bomber wing from the West, as well as three newly activated bomber wings, a twin-engine fighter wing from the night-fighter forces (to replenish the two fighter wings that Richthofen already had), a transport wing from the 4th Air Fleet in southern Russia, and four air transport wings from Germany, equipped with the last Ju-52s of the chief of training of the Luftwaffe. This short-sighted order completely disrupted air transport training and would have serious consequences in the days ahead.[2]

The German armies in the East did not hold, despite Hitler's orders. They were gradually pushed back 100 to 200 miles all along the front and lost 30 percent of their strength in the process. Naturally, casualties were heaviest in infantry and panzer units. Eighth Air Corps acted as a fire brigade for Army Group Center during the winter of 1941–42, when weather permitted. It opposed at least eight Soviet fighter regiments in the Moscow sector alone and suffered heavy casualties in both men and equipment due to the weather and enemy action. It nevertheless provided close air support to hard-pressed ground units and airlifted or airdropped vital supplies for troops that had been cut off or encircled. It conducted medical evacuations and reconnaissance and aerial interdiction missions and bombed several partisan concentrations out of existence. The hard-working pilots air-transported fresh combat battalions to threatened sectors, sometimes almost to the front lines. It accomplished all of these tasks despite the Russian winter, in cold so intense that rubber items—especially tires—froze and ruptured easily on takeoffs and landings. In early 1942 VIII Air Corps played a major part in slowing the major Russian breakthrough toward Rzhev (between Ostashkov and Kalinin), as well as in stopping the Russian offensive on the boundary between the Fourth Army and the Fourth Panzer Army.[3] By the time the Red Army was finally halted in March 1942, VIII Corps was exhausted. General Plocher observed:

> The air forces, being more complex in character and staffed by technically trained personnel who were more difficult to replace, suffered more immediately from the war than did the German Army, with its sounder and more robust organizational structure.[4]

Plocher also noted another shortcoming of the Luftwaffe in Russia in 1941, and that was the failure to apply the principle of mass. He wrote:

> The principle of concentration of forces was not uniformly observed among Luftwaffe units in the Soviet Union. Real concentrations of air power were observed on only two occasions in 1941, once in the general advance upon Leningrad and again during the offensive against Moscow. At all other places the German Air Force was employed in a piecemeal fashion, usually in accordance with the demands of front line ground units. Unfortunately for the Luftwaffe, German ground forces found themselves in a series of crises at the very time when Air Force reserves were least able to give support. By the winter of 1941–42, the effects of the war were beginning to tell heavily upon the Luftwaffe organizations in Russia and in other theaters as well. It was the beginning of the death of the German Air Force.[5]

The strategic failure of the Luftwaffe during this period has already been noted. It lacked the four-engine bomber, which might have been used to disable the Soviet aircraft industry or destroy the massive tank factories at Gorky, east of Moscow. The tactical doctrine of the Luftwaffe also contributed to this failure, however, because the air units were used almost exclusively in support of the army. Not even the Soviet tank and aircraft factories within easy range of the twin-engine bombers were attacked. Wolfram von Richthofen must bear partial responsibility for this failure, since he was a major motivating force behind the development of the close air support doctrines of the Luftwaffe, and because he was the principal air force commander on the central sector for five months in 1941–42, when the distance to the main Soviet factories (in the Moscow area) was shorter than it would ever be again. Soviet production continued virtually unimpeded throughout the war and soon outpaced German industrial output in several vital categories, including tanks, aircraft, and artillery production. In fact, the failure of the Luftwaffe to "think strategically" was probably its major shortcoming during the entire 1936–45 period. The same could probably be said of Wolfram von Richthofen.

Richthofen's VIII Air Corps was certainly not the only Luftwaffe unit to be engaged in heavy fighting in the winter of 1941–42. In November, 1941, First Panzer Army had captured Rostov. Air support by Greim's V Air Corps had been vigorous, but costly. Its 54th Bomber Wing had to be withdrawn to Germany to rebuild, leaving it with only the 55th Bomber Wing. The operational strength of this Geschwader was only six to nine aircraft per day, on the average.[6] When the Soviets launched massive counterattacks on November 25, air cover for First Panzer (when weather permitted) was provided by Close Support Air Command North, now under Lt. Gen. Otto Dessloch. Between January 6 and March 21, 1942, alone, this small command flew 5,087 sorties in 56 days, destroying 158 enemy aircraft (76 of them on the ground), as well as 838 motor vehicles, 44 tanks, and 73 guns.[7] Elsewhere, the Luftwaffe was even more hard-pressed. At Kholm, in the zone of Army Group North, Maj. Gen. Theodor Scherer (CG, 281st Security Division) was surrounded with about five thousand two hundred men on January 21, 1942, while at Demyansk Gen. of Infantry Count Walter von Brockdorff-Ahlefeldt's II Corps was surrounded on February 8. Count von Brockdorff-Ahlefeldt had six divisions and the remnants of others—about 103,000 men in all, and he was tying down the bulk of five Russian armies. Kholm and Demyansk were the key defensive positions on the northern sector of the Russian front. It was imperative that the Luftwaffe keep these garrisons supplied until relief attacks could be mounted. Thus began the first large-scale airlifts in military history.

Kholm had no airfield, and the pocket was too small to allow construction of one. Against the advice of Col. Fritz Morzik, the chief of air transportation, Colonel General Keller ordered his Ju-52s to land in no-man's-land, drop their supplies while taxiing, and take off again before the Soviet artillery could open fire. This expedient did not work, and five of the seven transports used in this manner were destroyed. After that, supplies were air-dropped by He-111s or delivered by DFS-230 gliders (each with a one-ton capacity). Large items of equipment were delivered by the huge Gotha Go-242 gliders, which carried 2.5-ton payloads. Later, as the pocket contracted, this became impossible, and supplies could only be delivered via air drop. To achieve an accurate drop into such a small drop zone, the He-111s had to descend to an altitude of 1,300 feet over Soviet-held territory. Naturally the Russians quickly concentrated a large number of antiaircraft guns in the area, and KG 4 "General Wever" suffered heavy casualties. Nevertheless the Luftwaffe continued to resupply Kholm until May 5, when it was relieved after a siege of 103 days.[8] Only twelve hundred of Scherer's men were still standing when the rescuers finally arrived. Fifteen hundred wounded were also rescued. Another fifteen hundred soldiers lay buried in the snow.[9]

The resupply operations for Demyansk were even more difficult than those for Kholm because of the numbers involved. Initially, Keller had only one transport unit available, the 172d Special Purpose Bomber Wing (KG 172 z.b.V.). The 100,000 men trapped at Demyansk would require 300 tons of food and material every day. Hitler promised to make available 337 transports for this operation and, for once, was as good as his word. Jeschonnek attached Col. Fritz Morzik to the 1st Air fleet and put him in charge of the resupply effort. He was given sixteen air transport groups, which flew into his base at Pskov Airfield.[10]

Fritz Morzik was an unusual General Staff officer in that he rose through the ranks. Enlisting as a private in 1907, Sergeant Morzik transferred to the 2nd Flying Battalion in 1914, prior to the outbreak of World War I. As an NCO-pilot, he served on both the eastern and western fronts, as well as in Turkey. A warrant officer in 1916, he did not receive his commission until 1919. From then until March, 1921, he was a member of the Silesian Air Police Squadron in Breslau. After leaving the police force, Morzik worked for the Junkers Company and became an expert in commercial aviation, especially in air transport ventures. He was a flight instructor at the German Aviation School from 1928 to 1934, when he entered the Luftwaffe as a captain. After tours of duty as a squadron and group commander and an assignment with the Inspectorate for Flight Safety at RLM, Morzik was the commander of the 1st Air Transport Wing at the outbreak of the war. Later he would be promoted to major general (October 1, 1943) and become chief of air transport of the armed forces.[11]

Morzik did an absolutely brilliant job in resupplying II Corps. His pilots flew an average of ten to fifteen transports per hour into the pocket, day after day, regardless of blizzards, fog, or heavy antiaircraft fire. The two airstrips inside the pocket were very primitive and could be used only during daylight hours. Perhaps offended by the presence of a special transport command in his zone of operations, General Keller was of little help to Colonel Morzik. He did not provide him with regular fighter escorts and since a fully loaded Ju-52 flew at less than 180 miles per hour and had little in the way of defensive weapons (some had three light machine guns, while others had none at all), they were particularly vulnerable to fighter attack. Fortunately the Red Air Force pilots in this sector were not very aggressive. Morzik soon learned that they only attacked single, unescorted transports, so he flew them into Demyansk in flights of twenty to forty. The air base at Pskov was also vulnerable, but the Soviet fighter and bomber units never even tried to launch a major raid against it, although they did occasionally attack the airfields within the pocket and destroy a number of Ju-52s. Unfortunately for the Germans, the Soviet antiaircraft units were much more active and transport losses were often high.[12]

General Keller also failed to keep Morzik informed of the German and Russian air situation. Once, Soviet paratroopers landed within the pocket. Morzik only found out about this when one of his flights over the pocket sustained several hits from Russian ground fire.[13]

German relief forces from the X Corps made contact with the 3d SS Panzer Grenadier Division "Totenkopf" on the western edge of the Demyansk perimeter on April 20, but it was May 2 before supplies could be moved into Demyansk. Unfortunately this road could accommodate only a limited amount of traffic, and a reduced-scale airlift had to be maintained until Hitler finally allowed the army to abandon the Demyansk salient in early 1943.

During the Demyansk operation, the Luftwaffe air transport units flew 659 missions. They brought in 64,844 tons of supplies and 30,500 replacements and evacuated 35,400 men, almost all of them wounded. During the critical period from February 18 to May 19, 1942, they flew in an average of 302 tons of supplies per day,[14] but they lost 262 Ju-52s in the process, adding to the 271 lost at Crete, along with irreplaceable training crews.[15] After Demyansk, the Air Transport Branch was decimated.

Meanwhile, to the south, the Soviet winter offensive had been halted, and the Wehrmacht was preparing to go over to the attack once more. The first phase of the offensive would be in the Crimean peninsula. Typically, Baron Wolfram von Richthofen was named to command the air forces supporting the main attack.

If he is not mentioned among the top aerial strategists of World War II, Baron von Richthofen is certainly one of the best tacticians in the history of air warfare. He received further recognition for his abilities and accomplishments on March 1, 1942, when he was promoted to colonel general.[16] This was a singular honor, for he was only a corps commander, and the rank of *Generaloberst* was normally reserved for air fleet commanders, the very highest staff officers, or the chief of the General Staff of the Luftwaffe.

In late April 1942, VIII Air Corps turned over responsibility for providing air support on the central sector to General Ritter Robert von Greim's V Air Corps (which was redesignated Luftwaffe Command East) and flew south to the Crimea. Here, Col. Gen. Erich von Manstein's Eleventh Army was expecting the Russians to launch a major offensive from the foothold on the Kerch Peninsula. Their objective would be to relieve Sevastopol, the major Soviet Black Sea naval fortress, which Manstein had been besieging since November 16, 1941. Manstein had a surprise for the Russians, however. He intended to break through the strong Parpach line (which the Soviets had been improving for months) and overrun the Kerch Peninsula, destroying the Soviet Forty-fourth, Forty-seventh, and Fifty-first Armies in the process. Then he would turn west again and deal with Sevastopol with all of his forces.

The brilliant Manstein and the gifted Richthofen undoubtedly made an excellent team. Manstein wrote later:

> Baron von Richthofen was certainly the most outstanding Luftwaffe leader we had in World War II. He made immense demands on the units under his command, but always went up himself to supervise any important attack . . . one was constantly meeting him at the front, where he would visit the most forward units to weigh up the possibilities of giving air support to ground operations. We always got on extremely well together. . . . I remember von Richthofen's achievements and those of his Air Corps with the utmost admiration and gratitude.[17]

Richthofen now had eleven bomber, three Stuka, and seven fighter wings: a formidable air armada.[18] Within a week of his corps' arrival in the Crimea, Richthofen attacked all the Russian airfields believed to be operational in the Kerch Peninsula and the nearby Caucasus area. The VIII Air Corps also subjected the ports of Kerch, Kamysh, Burun, and Novorossiysk to repeated bombings.[19]

Manstein unleashed his attack on the Parpach line on May 8, using only six German divisions and some marginally effective Rumanian formations against three Russian armies. The bombers and dive-bombers of VIII Air Corps never provided better close air support, as they smashed Soviet fortifications and assembly areas and paved the way for Eleventh Army's mobile forces. Overhead, Richthofen's Messerschmitt fighters completely defeated the Red Air Force, establishing absolute air supremacy from the first day. Eighth Air Corps flew more than two thousand sorties on the first day alone, enabling the infantry to make several major penetrations of the Parpach line. On the second day of the offensive, Manstein broke through on a three-mile front. By May 11, the Soviet Fifty-first Army was encircled against the Sea of Azov.[20] Kerch fell on May 15, and by the 18th the battle was over. Manstein's units captured 170,000 men, 1,133 guns, and 258 tanks, as well as 3,800 motor vehicles and almost 300 aircraft.[21] Only minor Soviet elements managed to escape across the Kerch Strait to the Kuban.

Manstein's next target was Sevastopol, then considered to be the strongest land and naval fortress in the world. An outer perimeter encircled the city at a distance of nine to twelve miles, and an inner belt three miles out was also very strong. "Virtually no part of the terrain was without its fortifications," a German general later commented.[22] The city was defended by two Soviet armies controlling 101,238 men, 600 guns, and 2,000 mortars, but only 40 tanks.[23] Sevastopol's air forces were also extremely weak. Its few airfields were within German flak and heavy artillery range, so its good air units had been evacuated in 1941. The Red Air Force at Sevastopol had only sixty obsolete aircraft plus a few seaplanes.[24]

To attack this massive fortress, Manstein had only seven German and two Rumanian divisions. He did have strong support, however: 1,300 pieces of artillery, as well as the VIII Air Corps, with seven bomber, three Stuka, and four fighter wings—600 aircraft in all—plus seventeen antiaircraft batteries (under Headquarters, 18th Flak Regiment) in corps reserve. During the Battle of Sevastopol, the 18th Flak alone fired over 18,700 rounds of 88mm ammunition. Most of the flak units were employed in direct support of the infantry, but several were used to guard Manstein's superheavy guns, one of which could hurl a seven-ton shell more than twenty-three miles.[25]

Several other aviation elements of VIII Air Corps were not used at Sevastopol, but stood by in the Kerch sector, ready to interdict in case the Red Air Force, the Black Sea Fleet, or elite marine amphibious units tried to interfere with Manstein's main operations by landing in the eastern Crimea.

Richthofen believed that the Luftwaffe could best aid the ground forces by breaking Soviet morale, so he adopted "conveyor belt" tactics. Flight units were kept constantly in the air, landing only long enough to refuel or replenish their ammunition, and they kept Soviet positions under more or less continuous attack. Wave after wave of fighters and dive-bombers pounded Russian positions, almost without letup. Richthofen was right: Soviet morale was affected by his unrelenting aerial bombardment.

The battle began on June 2. The few Russian fighters that tried to intervene from the east were promptly shot down. General von Richthofen personally directed aerial operations from a tower, from which he could see most of the battlefield, including the enemy airstrips. The summer sky was cloudless—typical for the Mediterranean climate of the Crimea—and the Russian aircraft threw up dust clouds when they revved up their engines prior to takeoff. When he saw these dust clouds, Richthofen immediately directed the flak artillery to fire on the airfields, which had no doubt been previously registered. The shells landed on target within thirty seconds of his call for fire, smashing most of the garrison's few airplanes before they could even take off. His complete control of the air also allowed Richthofen to station his units at airstrips extremely close to the front, so very little time was lost en route to targets. Ju-87s, in fact, barely had time to climb to their attack altitudes before it was time for them to dive on their targets.[26]

The VIII Air Corps committed 723 aircraft to the battle on the first day and flew up to 2,000 sorties a day. On June 3 it used 643 aircraft, and on June 4, 5, and 6 it flew 585, 555, and 563, respectively. In these five days it dropped 2,264 tons of high explosives and 23,800 incendiary bombs on Sevastopol and its defenders. To the east, other VIII Air units operating from the Kerch Peninsula attacked Russian airfields in the Kuban and the western Caucasus and kept the Soviet Black Sea ports under more or less constant attack. No Soviet naval or amphibious attempts to relieve Sevastopol could be made under such pressure.[27]

Despite magnificent air support, ground progress was slow at Sevastopol. The terrain was difficult, and fortifications were abundant. Led by fanatical political commissars, Soviet infantrymen and marines held their pillboxes and resisted to the end, frequently fighting to the last man. Every machine-gun nest, fort, minefield, cave, and trench had to be cleared individually in bitter fighting. The outer defensive ring was not cleared until June 26. The attack on the inner ring began on the 29th, but by then the effects of the battle began to tell on the defenders. On the night of June 28-29, elements of the 22nd Air Landing and 24th Infantry divisions crossed the wide North Bay in rubber boats and landed in the Soviet rear east of Sevastopol, but there was no counterattack. Russian morale suddenly collapsed, and the fortress fell quickly. Pockets of fanatical resistance continued to exist in the city of Sevastopol, but Manstein refused to add to his already long casualty lists. He asked Richthofen to annihilate the diehards with his Stukas, which the baron did, running the civilian death toll even higher in the process. There were incidents of commissars blowing themselves up, along with women and children, rather than surrendering.[28] When the battle ended on July 4, some 90,000 prisoners had been taken. More than 460 artillery pieces, 758 mortars, and 155 antitank and antiaircraft guns were captured or destroyed.[29] During this battle, VIII Air Corps flew 23,751 sorties, dropped more than 20,500 tons of bombs, destroyed 141 enemy aircraft in the air and on the ground, and destroyed 611 motorized vehicles, 10 tanks, and 20 bunkers. It also silenced forty-eight artillery batteries and heavily damaged two destroyers. There was no rest for Richthofen and his men following this victory, however; they quickly flew 120 miles to the north, to the Rossosh area, where the German summer offensive of 1942 was about to begin.[30] It would end in the Battle of Stalingrad.

While Sevastopol was rocking under the weight of Richthofen's bombs, another battle of great importance was being fought north of the Arctic Circle, off the coast of Norway, Finland, and Russia. Since 1941, the Americans and British had been supplying Stalin with arms, clothing, and equipment. Most of it had come through the White Sea ports of Murmansk and Archangel. By March, 1942, it was obvious that Russia would not be knocked out of the war anytime soon, so Goering ordered Stumpff to cooperate with the U-boats to destroy the convoys. Long-range reconnaissance was to be undertaken by the Condors of I Group, 40th Bomber Wing, based at Trondheim and the recently constructed airfields in the far north. When the convoys were spotted, Stumpff's units were to cease supporting the Army of Norway and attack the convoys. Unfortunately for Stumpff, he had very little to attack them with. In February, 1942, he had only sixty Ju-88 antishipping bombers (of the 30th Bomber Wing), thirty Stukas, thirty Me-109s, and fifteen He-115 seaplane torpedo-carriers.[31] Because of the arctic weather, the length of the arctic nights, and the shortage of aircraft, the PQ 12 convoy passed through in early March without loss. PQ 13, which was split up by bad weather, lost two freighters to Ju-88s and three more to U-boats. PQ 14 ran into a dense ice floe in the fog. Sixteen of its twenty-four vessels were damaged and had to return to Iceland; another was sunk by a U-boat.[32]

By the time PQ 15 came within range, Stumpff had been reinforced with I Group, 26th Bomber Wing (an He-111 unit), but many of his Ju-88 torpedo bombers were back in Germany for refitting, so the convoy lost only three ships (to torpedo vessels). However by late May, when PQ 16 was spotted by the Condors, Stumpff had more than one hundred aircraft ready for the attack. The torpedo bombers scored several hits and damaged a number of vessels, but only seven of the thirty-five ships in the convoy were sunk—a disappointing performance by 5th Air Fleet. The convoy delivered 2,507 vehicles, 321 tanks, and 124 aircraft to Stalin. There were 770 vehicles, 147 tanks, and 77 aircraft aboard the ships that went to the bottom of the Arctic Ocean.[33]

PQ 17, the largest convoy to date (thirty-five freighters and a few escort vessels), began assembling off the southwestern coast of Iceland in early June. Its presence was promptly reported to Stumpff by the Condors. By now, 5th Air Fleet had been reinforced, and Stumpff was able to assemble 103 Ju-88 bombers, 42 He-111 torpedo bombers, 15 He-115 floatplanes/torpedo bombers, 30 Stukas, 8 Condors, 22 Ju-88 reconnaissance aircraft, and 44 Blohm and Voss 138 (BV-138) reconnaissance seaplanes. The convoy left Iceland on June 27. Now Stumpff had the advantage because of the long days of the arctic summer. His reconnaissance aircraft maintained visual contact twenty-four hours a day.[34]

The first attack took place on July 4 and scattered the convoy. The dive-bombers, torpedo bombers, and U-boats then began hunting down the cargo ships one by one. Eight of them were sunk by aircraft, nine by U-boats, and there were seven shared kills. The eleven survivors hid along the coast and finally reached Archangel several weeks later. They delivered 896 vehicles, 164 tanks, and 87 aircraft. PQ 17 had lost 3,350 vehicles, 430 tanks, 100,000 tons of other cargo, 210 aircraft, and 24 ships—a total of 143,977 tons. The loss of material was roughly equal to that the Soviets suffered in the Battle of Uman.[35] It was a disaster for the Allies and the greatest victory 5th Air Fleet had scored since the conquest of Norway—and its last.

The Allies learned a great deal from the PQ 17 catastrophe. They did not send out another convoy (PQ 18) until October, and then they sent an aircraft carrier with it. The Luftwaffe suffered heavy losses and sank only thirteen of the forty cargo ships. The twenty-seven survivors delivered enough war material to equip an entire Soviet tank army.[36]

PQ 18 was the last convoy to come under heavy Luftwaffe attack. The Allies invaded North Africa on November 8, and the Ju-88 and He-111 torpedo bombers were withdrawn to the Mediterranean, where they were based in Sardinia. The Allies had learned the lesson of PQ 17 well. Never again did they send out a convoy without major naval units and aircraft carriers. As a result, Germany lost the Battle of the Northern Approaches. Fifteen million tons of the 16.5 million tons of American supplies dispatched to the Soviet Union reached their destination—most of them via Murmansk. These supplies included 13,000 tanks, 135,000 machine guns, tens of thousands of vehicles, and thousands of modern aircraft equal or superior to those of the Luftwaffe. Their impact would soon be felt at the front, both in the air and on the ground.[37]

In mid-1942, as it prepared for the summer offensive, the Luftwaffe had four major commands (north to south): 5th Air Fleet (Stumpff), 1st Air

Fleet (Keller), Luftwaffe Command East (Greim), and 4th Air Fleet (Loehr). To support Army Group South, the main thrust, Loehr had 1,593 aircraft (1,155 serviceable)—as many as the other three commands combined. In the Far North (including northern Russia, Finland, and Norway), Stumpff had only 182 frontline aircraft, while Keller had only 375 with which to support Army Group North. In the central sector, Greim had 600 frontline aircraft. All totalled, including aircraft not assigned to the four major commands, the Luftwaffe's strength in the East was 2,750 combat airplanes—out of a total of 4,262 in the entire air force. More than 64 percent of the Luftwaffe's combat aircraft were on the eastern front. The Red Air Force still outnumbered it three to one.[38]

To reach even this strength, Jeschonnek had to dip into the training establishment once more. This time he sent fighter training units and their instructor pilots to the front. Adolf Galland, the general of fighter forces, protested and called upon him to increase the number of fighter training units, not to decrease them. "If you reduce them now instead of forcing them up, you are sawing off the branch on which you are sitting," Galland told him.

Jeschonnek listened quietly, without interrupting. He did not try to dispute the validity of Galland's arguments. When Galland was finished, he spoke "without vehemence, presumption or demagogy." He told the general of fighters that he understood the seriousness of his decision, but the rapid annihilation of the Soviet Union was an essential prerequisite for the continuation of the war. This was the Fuehrer's goal in the summer offensive of 1942, and all forces, including the Luftwaffe, now had to be concentrated for this decisive blow. "He was fully aware of the deathly crisis in which the Luftwaffe stood because of the war in the east," Galland recalled.[39]

Operation "Blue"—the German summer offensive on the eastern front in 1942—was to be directed by Army Group South (Field Marshal Fedor von Bock) and essentially consisted of three phases. In the first phase, Col. Gen. Baron Maximilian von Weichs' Second Army, on the left wing, was to drive southeast from the Livny sector toward Voronezh. Hoth's Fourth Panzer Army, the center formation of Army Group South, advancing from Kurst, was to execute a wide sweep to the south, and was then to turn east and north, linking up with Weichs at Voronezh, trapping several Soviet armies in a huge pocket east of Voronezh. To the south (on the army group's right wing), Col. Gen. Friedrich Paulus' Sixth Army was to launch attacks in support of Fourth Panzer Army. Phase two would begin after the Voronezh Pocket had been cleared. Fourth Panzer and Second armies were to execute a bold dash along the western side of the Don River, while Sixth Army drove northeast to meet them, forming another large pocket west of the Don. Finally, in the third phase, Army Group South was to be divided into Army Groups A and B.

Army Group B (Bock) was to mop up the Soviet forces in the bend of the Don, while Army Group A (Field Marshal Siegmund Wilhelm List) was to attack southeast, taking the Caucasus oil regions and even seizing Baku, the oil city on the western shore of the Caspian Sea. In phases one and two, Army Group South was to be supported by Col. Gen. Alexander Loehr's 4th Air Fleet, which included the IV and VIII Air Corps and I Flak Corps. Loehr's first mission in the campaign was to support Fourth Panzer Army's drive to Voronezh.[40] The operation was scheduled to begin on June 27.

Misfortune dogged the steps of Operation Blue even before it began. On June 19, a Fieseler "Storch" (Fi-156) strayed over Russian lines and was shot down. In it was Maj. Joachim Reichel, the operations officer of the 23rd Panzer Division, who was carrying a copy of the plans for phase one of Blue. No one knew if Reichel had been taken alive or how much the Russians had learned from him. Was he tortured into revealing everything? Did the Soviets capture the plans, or were they burned in the crash? To this day we do not know. What is known is that when Operation Blue began on June 28 (it was delayed twenty-four hours by rain), the Soviets retreated rapidly. There was no large bag of prisoners at Voronezh or on the Don. The Germans gained a great deal of ground during the first two phases of Blue, but fell well short of accomplishing their objectives.

These were the last operations Richthofen supported as a corps commander. On July 4 Alexander von Loehr was named commander-in-chief, Southeast, and left for the Balkans and his fate. Born in Croatia, he was successful in recruiting Croatian units to serve in the German Army. This, his anti-guerrilla operations in the Balkans, and his efforts to protect pro-German Croatians at the end of the war, earned him the hatred of Tito's Communists. On February 16, 1947, they executed him after what General Plocher called "a flimsy trial."[41] Meanwhile, he was replaced by Wolfram von Richthofen. The air fleet was the highest command in the Luftwaffe, so in a sense the Silesian baron had reached the pinnacle. He was only forty-seven years old.[42]

Richthofen's new command included his old VIII Air Corps, now commanded by Lt. Gen. Martin Fiebig, the close air support specialist who had formerly commanded the 4th Bomber Wing, 1st Air Division, and 2nd Close Support Air Command. Richthofen also controlled IV Air Corps (Gen. Kurt Pflugbeil) and the I Flak Corps (9th and 10th Flak Divisions plus a few aviation units) under Otto Dessloch, now a general of flyers. Richthofen also inherited Luftwaffe Command North, a temporary organization under Col. Albert Buelowius, charged with supporting Second Army on the northern wing of Army Group B, as well as Col. Gen. Rudolf Schmidt's Second Panzer Army, on the southern flank of Army Group Center.[43]

Richthofen briefly retained Loehr's chief of staff, Maj. Gen. Guenther Korten, but he was promoted soon afterwards and assumed command of I Air Corps (later Air Command Don). He was succeeded by Col. Hans-Detlef Herhudt von Rohden.[44]

Richthofen's first task was to provide air support for the next phase of the summer offensive. Throwing logic aside, Hitler decided to take both Stalingrad *and* the Caucasus at the same time. He sacked Fedor von Bock, a capable and experienced field marshal, replaced him with Col. Gen. Baron Maximilian von Weichs, and gave von Weichs the mission of advancing to the east to seize Stalingrad, while Army Group A was advancing southward on the Caucasus. The two army groups were sent off in divergent directions in the very face of an undefeated enemy. Hitler planned to cover the gaps that would develop between Army Groups Center, B, and A with his allied armies: Hungarians, Italians, and Rumanians.

Richthofen initially left Luftwaffe Command North with the responsibility for providing air cover for Second Panzer and Second armies, although he assigned it the task of supporting the Hungarian Second and Italian Eighth armies south of Stalingrad later in the campaign. He ordered VIII Air Corps to support the Fourth Panzer and Sixth armies in the main drive toward the Volga, while IV Air Corps supported Army Group A (First Panzer and Seventeenth armies) in their drive on the Caucasus oil region.[45] Richthofen then began to come to grips with the huge logistical problems facing an air fleet commander in the immense spaces of the eastern front.

As the Soviets retreated without becoming decisively engaged, the German armies followed them rapidly. The air units had to move frequently to airfields further and further to the east and south. Of course they had to be resupplied with fuel, lubricants, ammunition, bombs, and spare parts. This task grew more and more difficult each day, as supply lines became longer. The Russian road and railroad systems were in terrible condition, and the supply and transportation units of the Wehrmacht were inadequate for the demands made upon them. Not only did Richthofen have to resupply 4th Air Fleet, but he had to help resupply the ground forces as well, because of the difficulties caused by the primitive Soviet road and railroad network. His problems increased with every step the army groups took. In compliance with Hitler's orders, they were advancing in divergent directions. By August the spearheads of Army Groups A and B were 700 miles apart. Fourth Air Fleet now had to cover more than 2,700 miles, instead of the 1,000 it would have had to cover if Hitler had settled on Stalingrad as the primary objective.[46]

To lessen Richthofen's administrative problems, Luftwaffe Command North (Korten) was made an independent command, responsible for supporting the northern wing of Army Group B and covering the area between

Luftwaffe Command East and 4th Air Fleet. General Korten had only sixty airplanes to do this with, however.

Richthofen soon transferred all of his multiengine aircraft to IV Air Corps in an attempt to support the southern push, to which Hitler initially gave priority. Luftwaffe transport units carried more and more material and supplies for the ground units, and less space was available for such things as aviation gas, bombs, and critical spare parts. These efforts in support of the ground forces strained Richthofen's own logistical network and soon had their effect at the front. By mid-July the number of sorties the combat units could fly each day was being severely limited by logistical considerations, and the distances were growing still greater. Nevertheless there were successes. On July 13, for example, fighter pilots destroyed twenty Russian aircraft in a single raid on the Kamensk airfield, and twelve Soviet bombers were shot down by another fighter unit as they tried to take off from an airfield east of the Don.[47] Fourth Air Fleet, which now contained 54 percent of the total Luftwaffe aircraft on the eastern front, continued to dominate the air space over the combat zone. Stukas and bombers blasted Russian troop concentrations and supply installations, although they were unable to prevent the main Red armies from escaping across the Don. The fundamental weakness of the Luftwaffe was again demonstrated: for all of its tactical success, it was essentially a ground support arm, incapable of influencing events at the strategic level.[48]

As the ground units became increasingly spread out, Richthofen came to depend more and more heavily on the flak arm to provide them with anti-tank and antiaircraft protection. First Flak Corps did indeed distinguish itself during the drive on Stalingrad. On July 19, for example, a single battery from the 19th Flak Regiment destroyed eighteen heavy Soviet tanks near Voronezh. A week later, in the same sector, the 153rd Flak Regiment knocked out 130 Russian tanks and halted an enemy counterattack in close combat. On July 29 a single 88mm gun crew attached to the 168th Infantry Division destroyed eleven enemy tanks. All of these engagements occurred within two weeks in the Second Army's sector, but many other examples could be cited. In fact, Richthofen credited the flak artillery with making the rapid German advance of July, 1942, possible.[49]

The aviation units were also heavily engaged. In early August, VIII Air Corps supported Sixth Army's assault across the Don and the double envelopment of Timoshenko's forces at Kalach, where the Soviet First Tank and Sixty-second armies were annihilated. Some 35,000 Russian soldiers, 270 tanks, and 600 guns were captured.[50] Later that month, VIII Air Corps flew 1,600 sorties and dropped 1,000 tons of bombs in support of XIV Panzer Corps' drive to the Volga. It shot down ninety-one Soviet aircraft against a loss of three German planes.[51] Under this air umbrella, General Gustav von Wietersheim and his panzer troops reached the Volga north of Stalingrad on August 22.[52]

Fourth Air Fleet launched its first heavy air attack on Stalingrad on September 3. Bombs from Ju-88s and He-111s hit the city day and night, causing massive fires. The main targets were the Red October, Red Barricade, and Dzerzinsky tractor (and tank) factories, but residential areas were also pulverized. Later that month, as Sixth Army closed in on the city, Luftwaffe units resumed their close air support role, destroying Soviet heavy weapons and artillery positions. They were unable to seal off the battlefield, however. The Russian Sixty-second Army in Stalingrad continued to receive supplies, reinforcements, and replacements from across the Volga by night. As Stalingrad became a battle of attrition, the 9th Flak Division and the 91st Flak Regiment were committed to the ground fighting, where they both inflicted and sustained heavy casualties. They were most effective against Russian tanks.[53]

Richthofen ascribed the German failure to take Stalingrad to poor leadership on the part of the ground commanders, especially to Colonel General Paulus. "It is an actual fact that the efforts to liquidate strongpoints in Stalingrad were nothing but combat patrol operations on a somewhat larger scale," he confided to his diary. He frequently tried to get Paulus to launch an all-out attack, but the cautious Hessian never did.[54] As a result, Sixth Army was slowly bled white in the house-to-house fighting for Stalin's city.

Richthofen became more and more disgusted with Paulus' leadership as the casualty lists grew. He even went so far as to suggest to Col. Gen. Kurt Zeitzler, the chief of the General Staff of the army, that Paulus and some of his senior commanders be temporarily replaced by more aggressive men, but the suggestion got nowhere.[55]

As early as October 1942, aerial photographs by 4th Air Fleet observers convinced Richthofen that the Russians were massing for a major attack against the Rumanians, who were covering Sixth Army's northwestern flank. Richthofen even dispatched a motorized flak battalion to support them, because they had little in the way of antitank guns. Towards the end of October, Richthofen began to attack Russian troop concentrations opposite the Rumanians. The Russians, however, were past masters at the art of camouflage, and nobody really knew how large their concentrations were. It was clear, however, that the Soviet buildup opposite the Rumanian Third Army had not been detected in its early stages. Increasingly worried, Richthofen ordered General Dessloch to be prepared to launch tactical air sorties in support of the Rumanians on short notice.[56] By early November, Richthofen was openly expressing fear of a massive Soviet counterattack. This fear was shared by Zeitzler, and even Hitler became nervous. On November 12, reconnaissance reports indicated that the Russians were bringing up their heavy artillery opposite the Rumanians: a sure sign of an impending attack. Two days later, the Red Air Force began heavy attacks against German and Rumanian airfields.[57] The Germans' worst fears were confirmed on November 19, when the Soviet Don and South-West fronts struck the Rumanian Third Army with the Sixty-sixth, Twenty-fourth, Sixty-fifth, 1st Guards, Twenty-first, and Fifth Tank armies, and the 3rd Guards Cavalry and 4th Tank Corps.[58] Except for one brave division, the Rumanians fled in terror. Colonel Rudel, the Stuka pilot, led his group in missions in support of the Rumanians and remembered the scene:

> Masses in brown uniforms—are they Russians? No. Rumanians. Some of them are even throwing away their rifles in order to be able to run the faster: a shocking sight . . . [We reach] our allies' artillery emplacements. The guns are abandoned, not destroyed. We have passed some distance beyond them before we sight the first Soviet troops.
>
> We [the Stuka pilots] find all the Rumanian positions in front of them deserted. We attack with bomb and gun-fire—but how much use is that when there is no resistance on the ground?
>
> We are seized with a blind fury . . . Relentlessly I drop my bombs on the enemy and spray bursts of M.G. fire into these shoreless yellow-green waves of oncoming troops that surge up against us out of Asia and the Mongolian hinterland. I haven't a bullet left . . .
>
> On the return flight we again observe the fleeing Rumanians; it is a good thing for them I have run out of ammunition to stop this cowardly rout.[59]

The only German ground unit in the vicinity was Lt. Gen. Ferdinand Heim's XLVIII Panzer Corps, which consisted of one weak German panzer division and an ill-equipped Rumanian armored division. It, too, was soon in full retreat. Meanwhile, on the southern side of the Sixth Amy, the Stalingrad Front attacked the Rumanian Fourth Army with the Fifty-first, Fifty-seventh, and Sixty-fourth armies, supported by the 4th and 13th Mechanized and 4th Cavalry Corps. The Rumanian Fourth also gave way immediately. Hoth's Fourth Panzer Army, which had been badly weakened to provide cannon fodder for Paulus in Stalingrad, was unable to halt the Russians and was soon cut in half. By November 20 both Soviet pincers were heading for Kalach, west of Stalingrad. If they reached this position, Sixth Army would be the victim of a double envelopment. Map 7 shows the Stalingrad encirclement.

Richthofen did what he could to halt the Red spearheads, but the weather was so poor that VIII Air Corps could only fly 120 sorties on November 20.

Map 7: Eastern Front

After that it was busy evacuating the tactical (dirt surface) airfields between the Don and the Chir. In some cases the last airplanes took off under Russian tank fire. Much of the 2nd Stuka Wing was overrun by Soviet armor and destroyed.[60]

Hermann Goering thought he saw an opportunity here to regain some of his lost glory. His influence and standing with the Fuehrer had been deteriorating since the Battle of Britain was lost. Since then two events had accelerated his decline: the 1942 bombings of Germany and the rise of Martin Bormann.

Martin Bormann had replaced Rudolf Hess as chief of the Nazi party in May 1941, after Hess stole an airplane and flew to England, in a vain attempt to make peace with the British. When Hitler asked Goering to recommend a successor, the Luftwaffe C-in-C replied: "Anyone but Bormann."[61] When Hitler appointed Bormann anyway, Goering was assured of a permanent enemy who would constantly be at the Fuehrer's elbow.

Bormann was one of the most insidious creatures to come out of the Third Reich. He was brutal, uncouth, unintelligent, unfeeling, and immoral, even to the point of forcing his wife to entertain his mistress. Once a dog became involved in a fight with his mistress's poodle. Bormann had the animal doused in gasoline and set on fire, and roared with laughter as the helpless animal ran screaming down the street. Bormann, however, possessed a quality Hitler now demanded more and more: he was unquestioningly subservient to the Fuehrer.

With this enemy constantly whispering derogatory comments in Hitler's ear, Goering's decline at Fuehrer Headquarters was predictable. The only way the Reichsmarschall could redeem himself in the Fuehrer's eyes was to score a spectacular military victory. Stalingrad seemed to be his ticket. He promised Hitler that the Luftwaffe would resupply Stalingrad by air.

"Supply an entire army by air?" General Fiebig cried when he received the order on the evening of November 21. "Impossible!"[62]

Gen. Kurt Zeitzler, the chief of the General Staff of the army since Halder had been sacked in late September, also thought it was impossible and told Hitler so in no uncertain terms. This lead to a rather heated conference between Goering, Hitler, and Zeitzler, which went like this:

HITLER: "Goering, can you keep the Sixth Army supplied by air?"
GOERING (with solemn confidence): "My Fuehrer! I assure you that the Luftwaffe can keep the Sixth Army supplied."
ZEITZLER: "The Luftwaffe certainly cannot."
GOERING (scowling): "You are not in a position to give an opinion on the subject."
ZEITZLER: "My Fuehrer! May I ask the Reichsmarschall a question?"
HITLER: "Yes, you may."
ZEITZLER: "Herr Reichsmarschall, do you know what tonnage has to be flown in every day?"

GOERING (embarrassed): "I don't, but my staff officers do." Zeitzler stated that the minimum was 300 tons per day. Allowing for bad weather, that meant 500 tons per day was the "irreducible minimum average."

GOERING: "I can do that."

ZEITZLER (losing his temper): "My Fuehrer! That is a lie!" An icy silence descended. Zeitzler recalled that Goering was "white with fury."

HITLER: "The Reichsmarschall has made his report to me, which I have no choice but to believe. I therefore abide by my original decision [not to withdraw from Stalingrad]."[63]

Lt. Gen. Hermann Plocher later wrote: ". . . the second man in the nation, whose prestige in the eyes of the Fuehrer had been steadily declining, might have wished to reestablish himself with Hitler by making him an unqualified promise."[64]

It was the major turning point of the war.

Goering again mortgaged the future by sending school cadres and training aircraft to the Stalingrad sector and by using He-111 bombers as supply carriers in this emergency, but this time to no avail. On December 21, when the situation at Stalingrad was rapidly deteriorating and disaster seemed inevitable, Field Marshal Kesselring visited Fuehrer Headquarters at Rastenburg, East Prussia, on an unrelated manner. He paid a call on Goering, but was met at the door by General Bodenschatz, who asked him what he wanted. Kesselring looked over Bodenschatz' shoulder and could see Goering, who was sobbing aloud, his head on his writing desk.

Richthofen, whose 4th Air Fleet would be responsible for the airlift, considered the prospect of resupplying Sixth Army from the air to be impossible from the first. On November 21, two days before the encirclement was completed, he told Manstein that it was an impossible task. He sent similar messages to Goering and Zeitzler. He telephoned Jeschonnek and screamed at him: "You've got to stop it [the airlift]! In this miserable weather there's no way to supply an army of 250,000 men from the air. It's madness!"[65] His assessment of the situation, however, was ignored at both Luftwaffe and Fuehrer Headquarters, except by Colonel General Jeschonnek.[66] The chief of the General Staff of the Luftwaffe always listened to Richthofen—indeed was too much under his influence, according to some critics—and on the twenty-second reversed his original stand and called for Sixth Army to break out.[67] Like Richthofen and Zeitzler, he was ignored by Goering and Hitler.

On the morning of November 24, Hitler dispatched his famous order commanding Sixth Army to stay where it was. No breakout would be allowed.

The next day, Richthofen telephoned Goering (then in Paris) and urged him to use his influence with Hitler to allow the Sixth Army to break out to the southwest. Goering would do nothing, however, and Hitler refused to reconsider his decision, because he did not believe the Wehrmacht would ever reach Stalingrad again if he withdrew now.[68]

Once the decision to hold Stalingrad was made, General von Richthofen accepted it and did his best to aid the beleaguered garrison. "We have only one chance to cling to," he said. "So far the Fuehrer has always been right, even when none of us could understand his actions and most of us strongly advised against them."[69] He began assembling his units as quickly as the Russian winter would allow, even though he considered the operation futile from the start.

Colonel General Paulus and his strong-willed chief of staff, Maj. Gen. Arthur Schmidt, were demanding 750 tons of supplies per day, a figure that was later reduced to 500 per day. Fourth Air Fleet never came close to reaching this daily goal. Initially, Richthofen had the following forces available for air transport duties:

900th Special Purposes Bomber Wing
172d Special Purposes Bomber Wing
50th Special Purposes Bomber Wing
102d Special Purposes Bomber Wing
5th Special Purposes Bomber Wing
55th Bomber Wing
27th Bomber Wing
HQ, 1st Special Purposes Bomber Wing
III Group, 4th Bomber Wing[70]

These units had all been in more or less continuous action since summer and were worn out. Operational readiness stood at about 40 percent in the *Geschwadern*.[71] In addition, the ground and supply organizations were totally inadequate for a resupply effort of the magnitude Hitler demanded.

Col. Fritz Morzik, the chief of the Luftwaffe Air Transport Branch, calculated that it would take 1,050 Ju-52s to meet Sixth Army's demands, based on an operational readiness of 30 percent to 35 percent and a two-ton payload per aircraft. At that time there were only about 750 Ju-52s in the entire Luftwaffe, which was also engaged in a desperate effort to resupply the XC Army Corps in Tunisia and Field Marshal Erwin Rommel's Panzer Army Afrika, then retreating across Libya after its decisive defeat at El Alamein. Goering reacted to the situation in his typical manner: he stripped the Training Command of 600 aircraft, plus its best instructor pilots and crewmen. He-111 bombers, which could deliver one and a half tons of supplies, were converted into emergency air transporters and were rushed to southern Russia. Ju-90, Ju290, and FW-200 "Condor" long-range reconnaissance aircraft, Ju-86 trainers, and even untried and experimental He-177 long-range bombers were forced into emergency transport duties.[72] All totalled, Richthofen had 500 transports (including converted bombers) by early December, when his operational strength was approximately at its highest. General Fiebig was named chief air supply officer, Stalingrad, and Col. Hans Foerster, the commander of the 1st Special Purposes Bomber Wing, took command of the air transport units. (Foerster was later replaced by Colonel Morzik.) After several days' delay due to bad weather, Foerster assembled the bulk of his units at Tatsinskaya Airfield, and the airlift began. Meanwhile, Sixth Army was already eating its horses, which meant that most of the divisions could not move their artillery and divisional trains, even if the breakout order came. Table 14 shows

TABLE 14: ORDER OF BATTLE, AIR TRANSPORT COMMAND STALINGRAD, 4TH AIR FLEET, EARLY DECEMBER, 1942

Unit	Aircraft Type
5th Special Duty Bomber Wing	He-111
9th Special Duty Bomber Wing	Ju-52*
20th Special Duty Bomber Wing	He-111*
21st Special Duty Bomber Wing	Ju-86*
22nd Special Duty Bomber Wing	Ju-86*
50th Special Duty Bomber Wing	Ju-52
102nd Special Duty Bomber Wing	Ju-52
105th Special Duty Bomber Wing	Ju-52*
172nd Special Duty Bomber Wing	Ju-52
200th Special Duty Bomber Wing (Long-Range)	Ju-90, Ju-290, FW-200*
500th Special Duty Bomber Wing	Ju-52*
700th Special Duty Bomber Wing	Ju-52*
900th Special Duty Bomber Wing	Ju-52
I Group, 1st Special Duty Bomber Wing	Ju-52*
II Group, 1st Special Duty Bomber Wing	Ju-52*
III Group, 4th Bomber Wing	He-111
27th Bomber Wing	He-111
50th Bomber Wing	He-177*
55th Bomber Wing	He-111
I Group, 100th Bomber Wing	He-111*

*Arrived after the encirclement of Stalingrad.

Source: Morzik MS.

the order of battle of the air transport command, 4th Air Fleet, in early December 1942, and indicates the units which arrived after the encirclement of Stalingrad. Many of these units had been recently formed, and their pilots and crews were inexperienced at operating in the Russian winter.[73]

Richthofen initially named Maj. Gen. Victor Carganico, the commander of Airfield Area Tatsinskaya, as air supply chief. Carganico's staff, however, proved too inexperienced in air supply operations, so on November 29 Richthofen relieved Fiebig's VIII Air Corps of all its other missions and gave it full responsibility for the entire airlift.[74] The tactical air support units formerly belonging to VIII Air Corps were placed under a new headquarters, Lt. Gen. Alfred Malinke's Air Division Donets. Richthofen also withdrew General Pflugbeil's IV Air Corps from Army Group A's zone of operations and brought it north, sending Headquarters I Flak Corps (now redesignated Luftwaffe Command Caucasus), south to direct the few antiaircraft and aviation units supporting the First Panzer and Seventeenth armies.[75] Richthofen and Fiebig shifted all the He-111 bomber units to Morozovsk and placed them under a single leader, Col. Berhard Kuehl (former C.O., 55th Bomber Wing). Colonel Foerster at Tatsinskaya was placed in charge of all the Ju-52 units, while Major Willers, the air transport chief at Stalino, assumed command of the long-range bomber and reconnaissance units that had been pressed into air transport service. By concentrating specific types of units at centralized locations, Richthofen was able to at least simplify some of his maintenance problems. He further simplified matters by assigning the 25th Air Administrative Command at Rostov the mission of providing ground support services outside of the pocket, while Maj. Gen. Wolfgang Pickert's 9th Flak Division provided them inside the fortress.[76]

The Stalingrad airlift began on November 29, with thirty-eight Ju52s and twenty-one He-111s taking off for the pocket. Due to poor weather conditions, heavy flak, and enemy fighters, only twelve Ju-52s and thirteen He-111s managed to land in the fortress. The next day seventy-seven aircraft took off, and sixty-six delivered supplies to the garrison. This was totally inadequate for Stalingrad's needs. Losses in men and airplanes were high. Only on December 7 was 4th Air Fleet able to deliver 300 tons of supplies to the Sixth Army. For December, the average daily total was about 90 tons; for the first three weeks in January, it was 120—about 16 percent of the garrison's requirements.[77]

Meanwhile, Richthofen's old comrade Erich von Manstein took charge of the newly formed Army Group Don. He attempted to relieve Sixth Army by attacking the Soviet southern flank with the Fourth Panzer Army, while holding up the Russian advance in the Chir sector with the ad hoc Army Detachment Hollidt (formerly HQ, XVII Corps), the reinforced XLVIII Panzer Corps, the Italian Eighth Army, and a few disintegrating Rumanian units. Despite the impossible demands already placed on it, 4th Air Fleet had to provide support for these forces also. Richthofen assigned this task to General Malinke's Air Division Donets. Army Group A, whose advance had been stalled in the foothills of the Caucasus since September, was virtually stripped of all air support.[78]

The Stalingrad relief attack began on December 12. In the dead of the Russian winter, 4th Air Fleet now had three major, simultaneous missions: 1) resupply Stalingrad; 2) support Manstein's counteroffensive; and 3) provide close air support for Hollidt's men, who were fighting desperately against almost overwhelming odds on the Chir. Like the ground forces, 4th Air Fleet was simply spread too thin. Nevertheless, on December 18, VIII Air Corps flew 270 tons of supplies into Stalingrad-more than twice the daily average so far. Paulus, however, was demanding no less than 1,800 tons of food and 4,000 tons of fuel before attempting a breakout: a requirement that was absolutely impossible and totally unrealistic.[79]

On December 19, the spearheads of Hoth's Fourth Panzer Army were halted in the Myshkova Valley, just thirty miles south of Stalingrad. Manstein again appealed to Hitler to allow Sixth Army to break out. Again Hitler refused. Paulus would not disobey orders and break out on his own. He continued to demand the impossible from the Luftwaffe, but did nothing himself. The last chance for Sixth Army to escape slipped away as the Fourth Panzer was brought to a halt thirty miles from the perimeter of the fortress.

Because of his incessant pleas in favor of a breakout, Hitler's relationship with Manstein deteriorated to the point where he would no longer speak to his brilliant field marshal. On December 26, Richthofen telephoned Hitler on Manstein's behalf. He asked the Fuehrer for a conference and even begged Hitler to come to Russia to see the situation for himself. Again the answer was no.[80]

The initial Soviet counterattacks against Fourth Panzer Army were repulsed, but on December 28 its forward unit, LVII Panzer Corps, had to withdraw from Mishkova to prevent being surrounded. Soon the entire panzer army was in retreat. The 270,000-man garrison at Stalingrad was doomed.

Meanwhile, the Chir front collapsed.

Richthofen never had any faith in the Italians. On November 28 he confided to his diary: "It seems the Russians are going to attack the Italians too—a bad thing, as they will probably run faster than the Rumanians."[81] The blow fell on the morning of December 16. Three days later the Reds had advanced forty miles and captured the major supply base at Kantemirovka. Manstein diverted a badly needed division from Fourth Panzer Army to help them, but it did no good. On the twenty-fourth, after an advance of 150 miles, a Soviet tank corps attacked Richthofen's main airfield at Tatsinskaya and destroyed at least seventy-two Ju-52s—a major catastrophe for 4th Air Fleet. The main He-111 air base at Morozovsk was also threatened by the Soviet 25th Tank and 1st Guards Mechanized Corps.[82]

Richthofen committed a major tactical error at Tatsinskaya and must be held primarily responsible for the loss of the irreplaceable transports. General Fiebig had requested permission to evacuate the base the day before the Russians overran it, but Air Fleet Headquarters insisted that Hitler's orders not to abandon the field until it was under Soviet artillery fire be interpreted literally. As a result, only 108 transports escaped, most of the available spare parts supply was lost, and all of the ground equipment, including the critical engine-warmer wagons, was lost. The lack of this equipment, in turn, led to a further decline in operational aircraft availability due to icing and maintenance-related failures. Operational readiness dropped to 25 percent, even as aircraft losses mounted.[83]

The Ju-52s that escaped the debacle at Tatsinskaya landed at Salsk, a base 250 miles from Stalingrad. The transports were now operating at near their maximum range and were using up the precious reserves of aviation fuel and oil. Also, the further a transport traveled the more fuel it had to carry, with a corresponding loss in payload capacity. Soon even the poor airfield at Salsk was threatened by the Red advance.

In the meantime, Richthofen desperately sought a means to salvage the deteriorating situation. On December 23 he telephoned Jeschonnek with a radical suggestion. He proposed that Col. Gen. Ewald von Kleist's Army Group A (First Panzer and Seventeenth armies) be withdrawn from the Caucasus and sent to reinforce Fourth Panzer Army. Perhaps then the tide could be turned in Germany's favor. The chief of the General Staff of the Luftwaffe made some halfhearted promises, but it was clear to the baron that he would do nothing substantive. Richthofen made similar suggestions to Zeitzler, again without result.[84] Neither man could really do anything to help. As long as Hitler clung to his policy of "not one step back," the tragedy on the Volga would continue to develop to its logical conclusion.

Erhard Milch got into the act in mid-January, when Hitler summoned him to Fuehrer Headquarters for another special assignment. He placed Milch in charge of the Stalingrad airlift and sent him to the Russian front, with special powers to issue orders to all military commands to ensure the resupply of the doomed Sixth Army. Milch took off for the Black Sea town of Taganrog immediately. His arrival on January 16 was greeted with consternation everywhere. General Fiebig commented that there was little left to organize, especially since Pitomnik, the last good airfield within transport range of Stalingrad, had just been captured by the Russians. Richthofen privately informed Milch that the airlift had been impossible to begin with, and it was now madness to continue it. Of the 140 available Ju-52s and 140 He-III bombers being used as transports, only fifteen transports and forty-one bombers were operational, due to the cold weather. Milch, still optimistic, decided to personally fly to Stalingrad the next day to see the situation for himself. En route to the airfield, however, his car was hit by a train, which was traveling at forty miles an hour. An unconscious Milch was taken to a field hospital, where he was treated for a concussion, a severe head injury, and several broken ribs. A few hours later, however, he was back at 4th Air Fleet's command train, from which he commanded the rest of the airlift operation. He could not leave the train again, however, because his back and ribs were encased in plaster.[85]

The next day, January 18, Milch concluded (or at least professed to conclude) that 4th Air Fleet had let Sixth Army down. He instructed Richthofen to sack his chief of staff, Colonel von Rohden. He then instituted new cold-start procedures and sent for cold-start experts from the Luftwaffe's testing and development base at Rechlin. These innovations resulted in an increase in aircraft availability (and therefore losses) at a time when the fortress was already in its death throes. Even if the cold-start experts had been available since November 23, 1942, when the siege began, it would have made little difference. However Gen. Hans Hube, the one-armed tank leader who had commanded XIV Panzer Corps in Stalingrad during most of the battle, was impressed by Milch's efforts. After the fortress fell, Hube and Milch reported to Hitler in East Prussia. Hube informed the Fuehrer that, if he had appointed Milch just fourteen days earlier, Stalingrad would not have fallen.[86] Hube, of course, was a tank general—hardly qualified to judge such technical aviation matters. Hitler, however, accepted Hube's remarks at face value and was very deeply impressed. What is more, Milch saw that he was impressed. This would have very far-reaching implications, as we shall see.

Meanwhile, Sixth Army was dying. Its demise was hastened on January 16, 1943, when it lost Pitomnik, the last usable airstrip in the pocket. Utterly unsuitable and dangerous strips at Gumrak and Stalingradskiy were used for the next few days, but Gumrak was lost on the twenty-first. That same day six transports were wrecked during landings at Stalingradskiy, because the deep snow on the runway concealed deep shell craters. The last Ju-52 landed at Stalingradskiy at 12:20 P.M. the next day and was fortunate enough to take off again unharmed with the last load of wounded and a few sacks of mail. From now on supplies would have to be airdropped, which entailed a further loss of supplies, because many supply containers disappeared into snow banks, were lost in the ruins of the city, or were blown off course, to land behind Russian lines.[87] All the while, the pocket continued to shrink.

Salsk was evacuated about the same time Pitomnik fell. The Ju-52s flew to their last "airfield" within range of Stalingrad. It was a cornfield called Zverevo, the most primitive facility imaginable. The runway consisted of packed snow over the naked ground. There were no buildings at all. Ground crews and pilots worked out of snow huts and, later, tents. The He-111 airstrips in the vicinity were evacuated because of the nearness of the Soviet armor, but the Ju-52s had nowhere else to go: one more retreat would carry them beyond the range of Stalingrad.

The Red Air Force attacked Zverevo on January 18. All of the German flak units had long since been committed to ground combat, and the Rumanian antiaircraft unit assigned to protect the field took cover as soon as the Russians appeared. Thirty more transports were knocked out; ten of them were completely destroyed. The survivors nevertheless continued resupply operations.

On January 22, the Russians again called on Paulus to surrender and threatened to massacre the entire garrison if he did not comply. The trapped Hessian radioed for instructions. Both Manstein and Zeitzler believed he should capitulate, but Hitler rejected the idea, saying that the Communists would not abide by any conventions or international agreements and that no prisoners would survive Soviet captivity anyway. He was almost right on this point: only about 7,000 of the 90,000 men who finally surrendered ever lived to see home again.

The final assault on Stalingrad began on January 23. Three days later the pocket was cut in half. Paulus (now a field marshal) surrendered on January 31, and the last pocket of resistance was eliminated on February 2. The German Army had suffered its most decisive defeat.

Wolfram von Richthofen was referred to by Professor Suchenwirth as the only "man of vision and resolution" in the Stalingrad relief effort.[88] During the seventy days of operation, 4th Air Fleet had flown 6,591 tons of supplies and evacuated 24,910 sick and wounded soldiers, according to General Morzik's estimate.[89] Irving's figures are somewhat higher: 8,350 tons delivered in seventy-two days, for an average of 116 tons per day.[90] General Plocher stated that 4th Air Fleet could have flown 200 to 300 tons per day to the garrison had there been good weather, but there was no good weather.[91]

The 4th Air Fleet flew well over 3,400 missions in logistical support of the Sixth Army during the siege.[92] It lost 488 transport aircraft alone: 266 Ju-52s, 165 He-111s, 42 Ju-86s, 9 FW-200s, 5 He-111s, and 1 Ju-290.[93] Of these, 166 were outright losses, 108 were missing, and 214 were so badly damaged that they could not be repaired. This was enough to equip five full wings—a whole air corps, and a large one at that (by 1942 standards).[94] Nazi Germany had lost well over half of its Ju-52 transport fleet, as well as the majority of its experienced crews and many of its instructor pilots—losses it could never replace.[95] The veteran 9th Flak Division was also destroyed when Stalingrad fell. It had destroyed 174 Soviet tanks and shot down 63 Russian aircraft during the siege.[96]

✠

The Stalingrad airlift failed for numerous reasons. Fourth Air Fleet had to support several operations simultaneously. The size of the encircled force was too large, the number of available aircraft was too small, the air bases and technical facilities were inadequate, the distances involved were too great, the forward bases could not be held, the number of fighter-escorts was insufficient, supply lines were too long, the season was wrong, and the weather was awful. The underlying cause for the disaster, however, was that the battle should never have been fought in the first place. Hitler was wrong in rejecting the advice of his generals and insisting that Sixth Army remain where it was, in Stalingrad. Richthofen bluntly told the Fuehrer all of this and more to his face in a conference at the Wolf's Lair on February 11. The supreme commander, he said, should give his army commanders freedom of action and stop "leading them by the scruff of the neck as though they were children." When Hitler tried to justify his behavior by saying that they would be fighting in Germany by now if he had not acted as he did, the baron contradicted him. Hitler, still shaken by the magnitude of his defeat, was impressed by Richthofen's frankness. He decided it was time to make him field marshal.[97] Richthofen's promotion was made effective on February 16, 1943.[98]

The Siege of Stalingrad had cost the Axis 270,000 soldiers, as well as 488 aircraft, most of them with their crews. Goering, as usual, was looking for scapegoats. He announced his intention of court-martialling Jeschonnek and General of Flyers Hans-Georg von Seidel, the chief of supply and administration of the Luftwaffe, because they were responsible for the disaster, but Hitler would not allow it. He knew where the real blame lay. He later told Manstein: "I alone am responsible for Stalingrad. I could perhaps put some of the blame on Goering by saying he gave me an incorrect picture of the Luftwaffe's potentialities. But he has been appointed by me as my successor, and as such I cannot charge him with the responsibility for Stalingrad."[99] Unofficially, however, he held Goering at fault, as in fact he was. "I certainly got the blame," Goering recalled later. "From that time on, the relationship between the Fuehrer and myself steadily deteriorated."[100]

CHAPTER 11

The Bombings Begin, 1942

While the bulk of the Luftwaffe was engaged on the Russian front, the R.A.F. recovered from the Battle of Britain. British industry, which had necessarily concentrated on the production of defensive aircraft (fighters) in 1940 and the first half of 1941, turned its efforts toward offensive aircraft (bombers) in the latter half of the year. In early 1942 the R.A.F. began to bomb Germany in earnest. Prior to then, the British raids were of little more than nuisance value. Certainly Hermann Goering did not take them very seriously. In the fall of 1941, he said to Galland, Kammhuber, and Moelders of the Western defensive measures: "This whole phoney mess won't be necessary any more once I get my squadrons back to the West."[1]

The first major raid came against Luebeck. Air Marshal Sir Arthur Harris, commander-in-chief of the R.A.F. Bomber Command, chose it as the target because it was "built more like a fire-lighter than a human habitation."[2] Its wooden buildings were built close together, especially in the *Altstadt*, the medieval center of the town. Also, the city was known to be lightly defended.

On the night of March 28–29, 1942, Bomber Command dropped about five hundred tons of high-explosive and incendiaries on the town. More than 250 people were killed and some 200 acres of buildings were destroyed— about half of the old city. In the suburbs another 2,000 homes were destroyed or damaged beyond repair.[3] Dr. Goebbels called the damage "enormous."[4]

The raid on Luebeck was followed by raids against the Baltic seaport of Rostock on four consecutive nights, from April 23–27. Also an ancient city and lightly defended, Rostock was devastated. The R.A.F. employed 468 bombers, many of which were new Lancasters (carrying six-ton bombs). Sixty percent of all houses in the center of the town were destroyed, the center of the town was reduced to rubble, and the Heinkel plant was severely damaged.[5] Goebbels called it "terror bombing."[6]

The *Terrorangriffen* ("terror attacks") reached new heights on the night of May 30–31, when the R.A.F. conducted its first thousand-bomber raid of the war. The attacks reached Cologne shortly after midnight and dropped 1,500 tons of bombs on the city—including 8,300 small incendiary ("stick") bombs, plus HE, phosphorus, fire bomb canisters, and heavy mine bombs. Their targets were not the Rhine River port facilities or the armaments factories in the area, nor the military bases nearby. They aimed for the heart of the city. Entire streets were wiped out. Some twelve thousand fires were started. The mixture of bombs was devastating. The explosive bombs blocked streets, so fire engines could not get to many of the burning buildings. Some 18,500 buildings were destroyed, 9,500 heavily damaged, and 31,000 partially damaged. Four hundred eighty-six civilians were killed, 5,000 wounded, and 100,000 left homeless—more than 59,000 of them permanently so.[7] The entire raid had taken only ninety minutes. Fortunately for the inhabitants, Cologne was one of the eighty-two cities Hitler had singled out in his decree of September, 1940, which ordered accelerated construction of air raid shelters. When the bombs struck there were 500 public air raid shelters (enough to protect 75,000 people), 42,000 private air raid shelters, 14 auxiliary hospitals, 27 emergency first-aid stations, and 14 stations for secondary medical assistance in the city, with 29 more medical facilities under construction.[8] Without these measures, the civilian death toll would have been much higher.

As at Luebeck and Rostock, the Luftwaffe's air defense had proven inadequate at Cologne. Of the 1,046 bombers involved, only 40 were shot down: 3.8 percent of the total. Bomber Command did not consider this loss excessive,[9] so the raids continued.

General Bodenschatz, the Reichsmarschall's liaison officer to Fuehrer Headquarters, later testified at Nuremberg that the Cologne raid caused Goering's first serious loss of prestige with Hitler. "From that moment on," he said, "there were differences of opinion between Hitler and Goering which became more serious as time went on. The outward symptoms of this waning influence were as follows: first, the Fuehrer criticized Goering most severely; second, the endless conversations between Adolf Hitler and Hermann Goering became shorter, less frequent, and finally ceased altogether."[10]

Hitler did not react to the bombings by significantly strengthening the defenses of the Reich, but rather by ordering reprisal raids. He brought the He-111 "Pathfinder" bomber wing (KG 100) back from the eastern front and two bomber groups from Sicily (lessening the effort against Malta) and attached them to IX Air Corps, which was ordered to conduct reprisal raids in addition to its regular mine-laying duties. Some thirty-nine reprisal raids were conducted against Britain in the seven months after Rostock, but with little result.[11]

Sperrle's 3d Air Fleet was also instructed to engage in reprisal raids, but the disillusioned and increasingly pleasure-loving field marshal did so only in a most perfunctory manner. Except for a few night bomber raids, he sent over Me-109 "Jabos" (fighter-bombers) armed with single 550-pound bombs. Only one wing of Me-109s was assigned to this mission, and it only had two groups (about thirty aircraft each). They dropped their bombs with few losses and even less effect on the British war effort.[12]

Of all the leaders of the Luftwaffe, only Erhard Milch saw the situation clearly. As early as March, 1942, he became alarmed over American production statistics, which Goering and Hitler refused to believe. He fashioned an ambitious plan for the air defense of the Reich, "an umbrella over Germany," he called it.[13] In late March he presented it to the Reichsmarschall and Jeschonnek.

"Herr Reichsmarschall," he said, "your total demand is for 360 new fighter aircraft per month. I fail to understand. If you were to say 3,600 fighters, then I would be bound to state that against America and Britain combined, even 3,600 are too few! You must produce more . . ."

"I do not know what I should do with more than 360 fighters!" Jeschonnek shouted violently.[14]

David Irving, the British author, blamed Hermann Goering for the Luftwaffe's failure to defend its Fatherland. "By 1942 at the latest," he wrote, "the provision of adequate air defenses for the Reich should have found first priority. The truth was that the Reichsmarschall lacked the courage to represent this to Hitler."[15]

✠

The air defense of the Reich from March 21, 1942, to December 23, 1943, was the responsibility of Luftwaffe Colonel General Hubert Weise, an antiaircraft artillery expert who had commanded a flak corps on the western front in 1940. His Luftwaffe Command Center (later redesignated Air Fleet Reich) included the fighter units stationed in Germany and the flak units in the Luftgaue, except for those in the Weisbaden sector of southwest Germany (which came under 3rd Air Fleet) and East Prussia (which was the responsibility of Keller's 1st Air Fleet).[16] The flak gun (*Fliegerabwehrkanone*, or antiaircraft cannon) was not a particularly effective weapon against aircraft. To hit its target, a flak battery had to know (or correctly guess) the exact altitude, speed, and direction of its target. Since one cubic mile of airspace contains 5,500,000 cubic yards, and the killing zone of a 88mm shell burst covered only a few thousand yards for 1/50th of a second, it took a well-trained and experienced gun crew to bring down an enemy bomber. The vast majority of these crews were heavily engaged on the Russian front. Many of the flak guns in the Reich were manned by fifteen-, sixteen-, and seventeen-year-olds.[17]

The German people generally ridiculed the accuracy of their antiaircraft artillery, as a joke that swept Germany in 1943 illustrates. A soldier, so the story went, was condemned to death and given his choice of the means of his execution. He chose to be killed by antiaircraft fire. A tower was constructed, the soldier tied to the top, and three flak batteries blazed away at him for three weeks, but never hit the tower. When they finally gave up and went to retrieve the soldier, however, they found that he had died of starvation in the meantime.[18]

German antiaircraft fire was, in fact, not very accurate. During the war, it took an average of 3,400 heavy antiaircraft shells to bring down a single enemy airplane.[19] Enemy bomber formations were decimated only when they ran into the heaviest concentrations. General Weise's main weapon against the Allied bombers was Joseph Kammhuber's XII Air Corps: the night fighters.

Germany started the war with only five squadrons of night fighters, equipped with Me-109s. This aircraft was certainly not the best choice, since it could not be flown "blind" (i.e., flown and navigated by instruments only), so it was replaced with the twin-engine Me-110, which had proven so ineffective in the Battle of Britain. The first night fighter division (*Nachtjagddivision*) was formed on July 20, 1940, under the command of Colonel Kammhuber, the former chief of staff of the 2nd Air Fleet, who had been sacked by Goering after the Mechelen incident. Although Ju-88s and Do-17s were added to Kammhuber's command, the Me-110 formed the "backbone" of the night fighter corps throughout the war.[20]

Working closely with Lt. Gen. (later Gen. of Air Signal Troops) Wolfgang Martini,[21] the Luftwaffe signals expert, Kammhuber developed the idea of establishing ground control interception "boxes" across Germany. Known as the Himmelbett system, each box included two Wuerzburg radars and a shorter-range Freya radar, enabling the night fighters to triangulate the location of British night bombers. Each "box" covered a zone thirty miles deep and controlled its own night fighter and searchlight units. By extending this system from the northern tip of Denmark, through northwestern Germany, Holland, Belgium, and eastern France to the Swiss-Italian border, Martini and Kammhuber assured that the R.A.F. could not enter Reich airspace unopposed.[22]

There were two major weaknesses in the Himmelbett system. First, it was designed for defense in breadth, not depth. Once the bombers broke through the line of Himmelbett stations, there was little behind it to oppose them. Second, of course, was the shortage of night fighters. Hitler's strategy was predicated on offensive weapons, and fighters are essentially defensive weapons; therefore, their production was not emphasized, despite the urgings of Milch and Galland. Kammhuber only had 164 aircraft at the end of 1940; nevertheless, 1941 was a successful year for the night fighters. They shot down 442 enemy aircraft and were gradually reinforced. On August 10, 1941, the

Nachtjagddivision was upgraded to XII Air Corps, and Kammhuber became general of night fighters. His new command included two searchlight divisions, three signal regiments, a few day fighter units,[23] and a new Nachtjagddivision (1st Night Fighter Division) under Maj. Gen. Kurt von Doering, the former C.O. of 2nd Fighter Command during the Battle of Britain and most recently inspector of fighter and ground attack aircraft at RLM.[24]

✠

The bombs continued to fall on Germany throughout 1942, although only one more thousand-bomber raid was launched that year. Flown on the night of June 25-26, its target was Bremen, in particular the Focke-Wulf factory there. The plant was hit by a 4,000-pound bomb and almost completely wrecked, but because of an abrupt change in wind direction the cloud cover did not clear as British meteorologists expected, the bombs were scattered, and the raid was not very successful.[25]

Bremen was the last thousand-bomber attack the R.A.F. sent against a single target until 1944.[26] After May 30, however, thirty-two more major raids were launched against nineteen different targets, including Bremen (five raids), Duisburg (four raids), and Essen, Hamburg, and Emden (two raids each).[27] By the end of the year the Allies (mostly the British) had dropped 78,500 tons of bombs on the Reich and 22,500 tons on occupied Europe since the start of the war, as opposed to the 67,000 tons the Luftwaffe had dropped on Great Britain. Although several fighter groups had been transferred from Russia (where they were badly needed) to the Reich, the R.A.F.'s impact on the German war effort had been minimal. Estimates of the total loss of the Reich's economic output to the bombings vary from 0.7 percent to 2.5 percent of the total for 1942. Britain, on the other hand, had committed roughly 33 percent of her war economy to the prosecution of the air offensive. Kammhuber's night fighters continued to expand (by the end of the year he had 477 aircraft in three night fighter divisions) and continued to enjoy success. By the end of 1942, the R.A.F. had lost 2,859 aircraft in night operations and 627 British bombers had been lost in daytime raids over occupied Europe. The Reich's air defenses were generally taken for granted. As late as December, 1942, 150 flak batteries had been transferred to Italy.[28] Jeschonnek went so far as to say: "Every four-engine bomber the Western Allies build makes me happy, for we will bring these . . . down just as we brought down the two-engine ones, and the destruction of a four-engine bomber constitutes a much greater loss to the enemy."[29]

Of the top Nazis, only Milch was worried. He realized that the Allies had dropped twice as many bombs on Germany in 1942 as the previous two years combined. He also realized that the advent of the four-engine bomber was greatly improving the range and efficiency of the enemy bomber force. He also understood that the military and industrial resources of the United States were about to come into full play in the air war and that, when combined with those of the British, they would overwhelm Germany's defenses. He could not get Goering or Hitler to listen to him on this vital issue, however.

Reichsmarschall Goering was especially militant in refusing to believe that the United States was manufacturing a fraction of the aircraft that it was, in fact, producing. In 1942 he forbade his people to even mention the American production figures, which he considered to be a colossal bluff.[30] That same year Walter Schellenberg, the head of the SS Foreign Intelligence Service, presented him with a special (and accurate) report on American war production. "Everything you have written is utter nonsense," Goering told him. "You should have a psychiatrist examine your mental condition."[31]

Meanwhile, a pregnant event occurred. On August 17, 1942, eighteen American Boeing B-17E "Flying Fortresses," personally led by Gen. Ira Eaker, bombed Rouen-Sotteville, France, and returned to England without loss. It was the modest beginning of the United States Air Force's daylight bombing operations in Europe. Convinced that unescorted daylight bombing could be successful if the bombers were sufficiently well armed, the American four-engine bombers "bristled" with .50-caliber heavy machine guns and flew a formation designed for mutual defense and maximum combined firepower.[32] Although the Rouen raid was insignificant in itself, it argued ill for the future of the Luftwaffe in the West.

By the end of 1942, the Luftwaffe was in dire straits. Due largely to Udet's mismanagement, it was short 43 percent of its establishment in combat aircraft, and (unlike the Allies) it had failed to equip its units with aircraft significantly better than those with which they had entered the war. Only three new models had been introduced in appreciable numbers: the disappointing Ju-88, the FW-189 (a good short-range reconnaissance plane), and the FW-190 fighter which, although an excellent fighter at low altitudes, was also a bit of a disappointment. It was sturdier, more maneuverable, and better armed than the Me-109 it was designed to replace, but its performance deteriorated rapidly above 20,000 feet (i.e., the altitudes at which bombers operated). The FW-190 also had teething problems and its air-cooling system problems were never fully solved.[33] It was therefore decided to keep the old Me-109s in production (indeed, more Me-109s would be manufactured than any other aircraft in the Second World War).

In short, the nonarrival of the Me-210, He-177, and other aircraft from the Udet era meant that most of the warplanes of the Luftwaffe were obsolete by the end of 1942, and the combined air armaments industries of the United States, the United Kingdom, and the Soviet Union were vastly outproducing that of Nazi Germany. Most of the Luftwaffe's senior officers did not realize it yet, but they were on the brink of disaster. They were in for an education in 1943 and 1944.

CHAPTER 12

The Tide Turns, 1943

The Luftwaffe was committed to the Mediterranean front in January, 1941, when the X Air Corps (with 330 first-line aircraft) was transferred from Norway to Sicily and Libya to support the Italians. The preparations were directed by Maj. Gen. Otto Hoffmann von Waldau. By February they were mining Tobruk harbor and the Suez Canal, bombing Benghazi, attacking British truck convoys, and supporting Gen. Erwin Rommel's newly formed Afrika Korps,[1] which formed the nucleus of what became Panzer Army Afrika.

Direct support of Rommel's ground forces was the responsibility of Rumanian-born Maj. Gen. Stefan Froehlich, who had served thirty years in the Austrian armed forces before being incorporated into the Luftwaffe as a lieutenant colonel in 1938. He had commanded I Group, 76th Bomber Wing, in Poland, and then the wing itself in the Western campaign and the Battle of Britain. Prior to the war his group had been based at Wiener Neustadt, south of Vienna,[2] where Colonel Rommel commanded the infantry school. There was never any indication of friendship between the two, however.

The role of the Luftwaffe in Rommel's early victories was not as great as might have been expected, because Air Command Afrika was not subordinate to Rommel. The Luftwaffe flew many dive-bomber and air interdiction missions for the Afrika Korps, and it even flew in supplies, but there were no all-out attacks on British lines of retreat, nor were there any major attempts to destroy the R.A.F. units in Cyrenaica. The R.A.F. was very weak at this time because of the reinforcements it had sent to Greece.[3] Rommel was halted at Tobruk in April, and the R.A.F. gradually took command of the air. Operation "Battleaxe," Rommel's brilliant defensive victory in June, was won despite local R.A.F. air superiority.[4]

As the Royal Air Force and British fleet took control of the air and sea lanes from Italy to Africa, the Italian navy proved unable to supply Rommel, and his supply situation reached dangerous levels. Geisler's X Air Corps attempted to subdue Malta, the strategic island and major Royal Navy base between Sicily and Rommel's main supply port at Tripoli, but was unsuccessful. At the end of April 1941, Geisler had called off the battle due to heavy losses and severe maintenance problems. He then proposed that since the natural German supply route to North Africa was via Greece and Crete, it was the eastern half of the Mediterranean that required X Air Corps' attention. Despite the objections of the Italians, who wanted to concentrate against Malta, Geisler's arguments won the day.[5]

The Italians were right. By November, British naval and air units operating out of Malta were sinking 77 percent of Rommel's supplies. Then, on November 23, the British launched a major offensive (Operation "Crusader"), aimed at breaking the Siege of Tobruk. Rommel's men went into this battle with only 15 percent of the fuel they required and suffered their first major defeat in the field. Clearly something had to be done, or Panzer Army Afrika (and with it all of North Africa) would be lost. Hitler responded by sending II Air Corps (Loerzer) to the area, along with HQ, 2nd Air Fleet (Kesselring). Field Marshal Kesselring was simultaneously named commander-in-chief, South (*Oberbefehlshaber Süd*, or OB South). Second Air Fleet assumed control of all Luftwaffe forces in the Mediterranean (II and X Air Corps and Air Command Afrika). By January, 1942, Kesselring had completed his reorganization of the Mediterranean theater. He had 650 frontline aircraft, of which 260 were in Africa, and more reinforcements were on their way. In mid-January he resumed limited air operations against Malta.

Kesselring launched his major aerial onslaught against the island in mid-March. By the end of April, II Air Corps had flown more than 11,000 sorties and dropped 10,000 tons of bombs on the island. All British submarines and warships had been forced to abandon the island, and the Desert Fox was receiving his supplies regularly. This allowed him to launch a major offensive against the Gazala line in May. Meanwhile, Rommel had succeeded in divesting himself of General Froehlich. His friction with Rommel and his lack of success in Libya did Froehlich's career no harm, however, because the Reichsmarschall and the Desert Fox were also at odds. Rommel referred to the commander-in-chief of the Luftwaffe as "my bitterest enemy." Goering thought that there were easy laurels to be won in North Africa, so he was maneuvering to get the Luftwaffe put in charge of the entire African theater. This, of course, meant getting rid of Rommel, whom Goering denounced as a pessimist and a "fair weather commander."[6] Rommel, however, won the battle of intrigue at Fuehrer Headquarters, and Froehlich lost his command. Nevertheless Goering promoted Froehlich and gave him command of the 2nd Air Division on the Russian front. Later Froehlich rose to command the 10th Air Fleet (later redesignated Replacement Air Fleet) in the last weeks of the war.[7]

The new Air Commander Africa was Maj. Gen. Otto Hoffmann von Waldau, the former deputy chief of the General Staff. He was an extremely capable staff officer, but his "forthright manner" and "fresh approach" had alienated both Goering and Jeschonnek.[8] Among other things, he had warned Goering of the military potential of the United States.[9] This, plus his frank opposition to Hitler's strategy and his opposition to the adoption of the Ju-88 and other aircraft, had cost him his job in Berlin.

Waldau worked well with Rommel and directed his units with great skill. As a result, Rommel had better air support in the Battle of the Gazala Line and at Tobruk than at any time in the entire desert war. Luftwaffe casualties, however, had been high, and aircraft serviceability had declined rapidly in the harsh desert environment. By the time Tobruk fell on June 21, 1942, Air Command Africa was at the end of its strength. Rommel nevertheless wanted to immediately invade Egypt and pursue the defeated British Eighth Army all the way to the Suez Canal.

In the meantime, OKL had depleted II Air Corps by sending six fighter and bomber groups to the East for the Stalingrad campaign. Malta had not yet recovered from its pounding, however, and Kesselring wanted to seize it by a parachute attack *before* Rommel pushed into Egypt. It was the greatest strategic decision of the desert war. Hitler ruled in Rommel's favor. He cancelled Operation "Hercules," the airborne invasion of Malta, and Panzer Army Afrika rolled into Egypt. Malta recovered with amazing rapidity and once again strangled Rommel's supply lines. Without effective air support, the Desert Fox was checked in the First Battle of El Alamein and was decisively defeated in the second. From then on, all roads led backwards in the Mediterranean theater.

On November 8, 1942, American and British forces landed in Algeria and Morocco and quickly subdued most of French North Africa, placing Rommel's defeated army between two fires. He called for the immediate evacuation of North Africa but Hitler, supported by the ever-optimistic Kesselring, decided to hold a bridgehead in Tunisia. On November 9 a new command, Air Command Tunis, was formed under Colonel Harlinghausen, the antishipping expert. Of his 140 aircraft, 109 were fighters and dive-bombers.[10] The German ground forces in Tunisia were controlled by XC Corps (Gen. Walter Nehring), which was upgraded to Fifth Panzer Army when Col. Gen. Hans Juergen von Arnim took over on December 5. When Rommel entered the Tunisian bridgehead in February 1943, he assumed command of all ground forces as commander-in-chief, Army Group Afrika. He left Africa on March 9 and was replaced by General von Arnim. By this time there were 130,000 German and Italian soldiers in Tunisia. Kesselring promised Hitler that he could keep them supplied.

There were several command changes in the Mediterranean from August 1942 to March 1943. Gen. Hoffmann von Waldau succeeded Geisler as commander of X Air Corps and was replaced as air commander Africa by Maj. Gen. Hans Seidemann, who had been Kesselring's chief of staff since

October, 1940. When Rommel's army reached Tunisia, this command was abolished and Seidemann became air commander Tunis. Meanwhile, Hermann Goering recalled Bruno Loerzer. Goering's first pilot and World War I comrade had not been an outstanding corps commander (Irving called him "incompetent and corrupt"), and he is said to have sent back trainloads of oranges and silk stockings to Germany.[11] This was no great sin in Goering's eyes, however; he promoted his old friend to colonel general on February 16, 1943, and named him chief of the Personnel Office at RLM. Later his title was expanded to chief of personnel armament and, on June 19, 1944, he became chief of the National Socialist Leadership Branch of the Luftwaffe as well.[12] Harlinghausen (now a major general) became acting commander of II Air Corps.[13]

These command arrangements fit in well with Kesselring's strategy. Air Command Tunis was given the task of defending Tunis against Allied air attacks and flying close support missions for the army. Second Air Corps had the job of protecting friendly shipping and attacking enemy transports and naval vessels. As a former naval officer and veteran antishipping expert, Harlinghausen seemed well qualified for the job.

Seidemann was also well qualified for his post. Educated at the Royal Prussian cadet schools at Potsdam and Lichterfelde, he was seventeen years old when Imperial Germany collapsed. Set on a military career, young Seidemann joined Freikorps Maerker (the best of these outfits) and spent most of 1919 suppressing Communist and Sparticus revolts inside Germany. Seidemann joined the army when Freikorps Maerker was inducted into the Reichsheer *en masse* in 1920. He became a member of the elite Prussian 9th Infantry Regiment at Potsdam, earned his commission in 1922, and underwent General Staff training. Joining the Luftwaffe as a captain in 1935, he served in various General Staff capacities (and briefly commanded a bomber training group) before joining Baron von Richthofen as chief of staff of the Condor Legion. He remained with Richthofen until 1940, as operations officer and later as chief of staff of VIII Air Corps. From October, 1940, until August 1942, he was chief of staff of 2nd Air Fleet. He had seen action in Spain, Poland, France, and Russia and had learned close air support techniques from the master. Seidemann's expertise paid great dividends in the Kasserine Pass offensive, when much of the U.S. II Corps was routed. Although eventually defeated by sheer weight of numbers, Air Command Tunis was still resisting when the German front collapsed. Then Seidemann flew away to Sicily, taking his pilots, airplanes, and ground crews with him. As soon as he arrived back on European soil and his command was dissolved (May 15, 1943), Seidemann was promoted to the command of his old unit— VIII Air Corps—now fighting on the Russian front. He ended the war as a general of flyers, still leading the VIII.[14] For Martin Harlinghausen, however, there would be no more promotions or field commands until almost the end of the war.

The German front collapsed because Kesselring's strategy was a miserable failure. Second Air Corps was unable to either sink the enemy's convoys or to protect its own convoys—or even its air bases. Because of high losses in the bomber arm and a deteriorating level of training at home, the effectiveness of the bomber attacks dropped appreciably. Many inexperienced crews completely failed to locate their targets—a problem their opponents did not seem to have. By March, 41 percent of the supply ships sent to Tunisia were being sunk.[15]

At the end of March, the Allies mounted heavy air attacks against II Air Corps' bases in Sardinia and inflicted heavy casualties on the gruppen. Unable to successfully defend his bases, Harlinghausen had to withdraw to the mainland, in effect conceding defeat. Sorties against Allied shipping in the Mediterranean dropped from eleven per day to two.[16] American and British air wings were now able to pay even more attention to the convoys. From March to May, 1943, American and British air and naval units sank 108 German and Italian vessels—340,438 Gross Registered Tons of shipping. Allied aircraft sank sixty-three of these (forty-three by U.S. air units alone).[17] Under these losses, the Axis supply lines collapsed completely. Near the end, Army Group Afrika was running its tanks on low-grade Tunisian wine. Out of food, fuel, and ammunition, it had no choice but to capitulate. Some 130,000 German soldiers surrendered. The German civilians referred to this battle as "Tunisgrad."

Martin Harlinghausen, who had fallen out with Kesselring, was relieved of command of II Air Corps on June 10, 1943, and was replaced by Lt. Gen. (later General of Flyers) Alfred Buelowius, the former leader of Luftwaffe Command North and 1st Air Division on the eastern front. Harlinghausen was briefly attached to the staff of the Air Commander Atlantic before being placed in reserve on June 26, 1943. He returned to duty in October, 1943, on the staff of the general of bomber forces, and gradually worked his way back into favor. He was named commander of Luftgau XIV on August 21, 1944, and was finally promoted to lieutenant general on December 1, 1944. On April 27, 1945—three days before Adolf Hitler committed suicide—he was named CG of Luftwaffe Command West (formerly 3rd Air Fleet). After the war he joined the West German Air Force and was commander of Air Force North (headquartered at Muenster) from 1957 until he retired as a lieutenant general in 1961.[18]

✠

Meanwhile, the Wehrmacht had rallied in Russia. As we have seen, Manstein and Richthofen made a most effective team. As commander-in-chief of Army Group South, Manstein had the task of halting the Soviet winter offensive on the eastern front. Richthofen was given the familiar job of supporting him. He conducted the operations of his air fleet from his command train at Chortiza, near Zaporozhye. Stalin's forces had not halted after Stalingrad, but pressed their advantage in the direction of Kharkov and Belgorod. Richthofen, now controlling I, IV, and VIII Air Corps, concentrated his Ju-88 bombers and Ju-87 antitank units against Gen. Markian Popov's armored corps and elements of the First Guards Army and smashed them. The Red Air Force tried to intervene and was given what Colonel Seaton described as "a sharp tactical defeat."[19] With the Luftwaffe smashing Red troop concentrations and supply lines and dominating the air, Gen. Eberhard von Mackensen's First Panzer Army encircled and destroyed the Popov Armored Group.[20] Three Soviet infantry divisions and the Soviet 25th Armored Corps were destroyed. The Reds lost 615 tanks in this battle.[21]

Although he could not hold Kharkov or Belgorod, Manstein conducted a skillful retreat, marshalling his resources while the Soviets exhausted theirs. After the annihilation of the Popov Group, he counterattacked toward Kharkov. Leaving the much-reduced VIII Air Corps and the reconstituted 9th Flak Division to support Army Group A (now isolated in the Kuban), Richthofen concentrated I and IV Air Corps—commanded by generals Guenther Korten and Kurt Pflugbeil, respectively—in support of First Panzer and Fourth Panzer armies: Manstein's main effort. The drive began on March 6. Stukas and fighters bombed and strafed Soviet troop concentrations and blasted ground targets, while simultaneously preventing the Red Air Force from interfering with Manstein's operations. By March 10 the Russians were in a disorderly retreat, pounded by the Luftwaffe, which shot up a large number of motorized columns. Both Kharkov and Belgorod were retaken by the Germans before the spring thaw set in and paralyzed operations throughout the region.[22] Even after its catastrophic defeat at Stalingrad, the German Wehrmacht had managed to halt the Soviets and reimpose a stalemate on the eastern front.

Of Richthofen's conduct of operations during the Kharkov battles, General Plocher later wrote:

> Von Richthofen's 4th Air Fleet was thrown into the battle for Kharkov as one integrated whole, with the participating commands supporting each other, thereby insuring the availability of maximum air power at the crucial point. The main factors behind Richthofen's success were extreme flexibility, good coordination, and concentration,

the latter being secured through the creation of ad hoc battle groups to give air support to spearhead units of the ground forces (SS Division "Das Reich"), which led the assault on the city. 'Massive concentration, 'drastic concentration,' 'concentration of all forces to the highest degree,' were phrases which appeared again and again in Fourth Air Fleet battle orders.[23]

Kharkov was Baron von Richthofen's last major battle on the eastern front. To the south, the remnants of Army Group Afrika surrendered in Tunisia on May 12. The entire German southern flank in the Mediterranean was thus exposed to Anglo-American invasion. Hitler named Field Marshal Kesselring to oppose it. He selected Richthofen to lead the German air forces in the endangered sector (over the objections of Manstein, who wanted to keep the baron in southern Russia). Richthofen was succeeded as C-in-C of the 4th Air Fleet by General Dessloch and, on June 12, assumed the post of commander-in-chief of the 2nd Air Fleet in Italy.[24] It was to be his last command.

Albert Kesselring had commanded 2nd Air Fleet since January, 1940, and since December, 1941, had simultaneously been air fleet commander and commander-in-chief, South (OB South). Now, however, he was to direct a ground campaign for the first time, so he needed Richthofen to direct his air forces. The baron had served under Kesselring in France in 1940 and in Russia in 1941, and the two had worked well together.

Richthofen's arrival in the Mediterranean was an indication of the growing importance that sector was taking on in June, 1943. Richthofen carried with him several squadrons from the East and received more from the 3d Air Fleet, which was operating against Great Britain. The number of German fighters in Richthofen's zone of operations (Italy, Sardinia, Corsica, and Sicily) increased from 190 in mid-May to 450 in early July, despite heavy fighting and heavy casualties.[25]

Field Marshal von Richthofen assembled a talented set of subordinates to defend his large area of responsibility. Gen. Alfred Buelowius commanded II Air Corps, the main subordinate unit under the air fleet. Lt. Gen. Alfred Mahnke, the former commander of Air Division Donets, was given tactical command in Sicily (as air commander Sicily), while Gen. Adolf Galland, the inspector general of the fighter arm, was attached to 2d Air Fleet to speed up the arrival of reinforcements and to improve fighter pilot efficiency. Lt. Gen. Dietrich Peltz, former commander of Attack Command England, assumed command of Richthofen's bomber units. By July 3, 2nd Air Fleet had 380 single-engine and 100 twin-engine fighters. At least half of the single-engine fighters were of the newest variety (FW-190s). Overall combat aircraft strength in the fleet increased 56 percent, to 975 airplanes, before Richthofen had been in the area a month.

The main problem the Germans faced was that no one knew where the Anglo-Americans would strike. Unlike in Poland, France, the Balkans, and Russia, Richthofen faced a situation where the initiative in the air had been completely surrendered. He again tried to concentrate his strength at the decisive point, just as he had done in Russia, but he incorrectly picked Sardinia as the Allied target and concentrated there.[26] He actually reduced Luftwaffe strength on Sicily, from 415 aircraft in mid-May to 175 eight weeks later, when the Allies landed on the island.[27]

In preparation for the invasion of Sicily, the United States and Royal air forces provoked a series of twenty-one air battles over the island prior to D-Day. In these actions, 2nd Air Fleet units defending the islands were decisively defeated by an enemy whose pilots were as capable as they were and whose aircraft were better. The Luftwaffe lost 100 aircraft over Sicily in intense aerial combat shortly before the Allies struck.[28] Goering, furious, wrote a special letter of reprimand to the fighter pilots of the 2nd Air Fleet:

> Together with the fighter pilots in France, Norway, and Russia, I can only regard you with contempt. I want an immediate improvement and expect that all pilots will show an improvement in fighting spirit. If this improvement is not forthcoming, flying personnel from the commander down must expect to be remanded to the ranks and transferred to the Eastern Front to serve on the ground.[29]

The letter did no good; rather, it further weakened morale. In the Battle of Sicily, Richthofen's men were not even able to protect their own airfields. In the first three days of fighting, 2nd Air Fleet flew an average of 275 to 300 sorties every twenty-four hours, against 1,500 for the Anglo-Americans. Half of the German sorties were flown at night, when there was less danger of Allied retaliation. After July 12, Richthofen's pilots only averaged 150 sorties per day, and by the sixteenth the Germans' strength had been reduced to only forty operational aircraft. They were unable to significantly interfere with the Allied landings and only sank twelve naval vessels. The Allied plan allowed for the loss of 300 vessels before the situation became critical.[30] They therefore can be said to have won the air battle by a wide margin.

Richthofen reinforced Sicily after the landings, of course, but it was too late. By July 18 he had committed 635 aircraft to the island. Of these, 600 had been destroyed or damaged by the end of the battle, and only 35 aircraft remained operational. By the twenty-second Richthofen had admitted defeat and had withdrawn to the mainland. Here a few fighters continued to fly support for German ground forces on Sicily, but only at extreme range. Second Air Fleet could average only 60 sorties a day, against 1,500 for the Allied air forces. Meanwhile, his Sardinian concentration came under attack, and losses there were also serious. In the Mediterranean sector during the Battle of Sicily (July 10–August 17, 1943), the Luftwaffe lost 1,850 aircraft to fewer than 400 for its opponents.[31] It was the worst defeat of Richthofen's career.

Over the skies of Sicily, the 2nd Air Fleet lost air superiority and even air parity over the western and central Mediterranean for all time. The demands of the home front also began to take priority during this period, for the British Bomber Command razed Hamburg in July and the United States Eighth Air Force's precision daylight bombing of Germany was also becoming a threat, although not yet a decisive one. Second Air Fleet lost its priority for replacements and reinforcements, for more and more fighter aircraft were needed for the defense of the Reich. Richthofen was forced to transfer several squadrons—a total of 210 combat aircraft—to the Fatherland. Only one of these squadrons ever returned to Italy.[32] The air war was lost in the Mediterranean.

Richthofen made one more bid for glory in his career and that was at the Battle of Salerno (September 9-17, 1943), where the Allies firmly established themselves on the Italian peninsula. Here, Col. Gen. Heinrich von Vietinghoff, the commander of the Tenth Army, counterattacked the Allied invasion force and almost succeeded in pushing Gen. Mark Clark's U.S. Fifth Army into the sea. Despite being outnumbered 4,000 to 300 in aircraft, Richthofen attacked with reckless abandon.[33] His fighters fired rockets into Allied ships and sank several of them. Ground targets were attacked in support of the Tenth Army and, at one point, General Clark was making contingency plans to evacuate the beachhead. However, Richthofen was unable to interfere with the advance of the British Eighth Army, driving up the Italian peninsula from the south. On September 17 he was forced to begin the evacuation of his airfields at Foggia, the best air bases on the entire Italian peninsula. The heavy fighting had also depleted his combat formations. Salerno was the last hurrah for the Luftwaffe in the Mediterranean. Thereafter it was strictly a backwater theater of operations, as far as the German Air Force was concerned.[34]

Richthofen's personal prestige also fell after Sicily and Salerno. In August, 1943, after the Hamburg raids, he was looked upon by Goering as a possible successor to Jeschonnek as chief of the General Staff of the Luftwaffe.[35] By 1944, however, Kesselring complained: "air support had practically ceased, even our air reconnaissance being inadequate,"[36] and Richthofen's star was on the wane. Second Air Fleet was of no help to the XIV Panzer Corps in the battles of Cassino, made no impression on the Allied landings at Anzio in

January, 1944, and was of little value in the ensuing German counterattack in February. In early 1944 Richthofen controlled 370 aircraft, but he received little in the way of reinforcements and could not make good his losses. By mid-1944 he had only 125 airplanes and his best unit, II Air Corps, had been transferred to France. "The Luftwaffe had ceased to play any part in the events in the South," Matthew Cooper concluded.[37]

Despite his defeats in Italy, Richthofen was the most successful of the Luftwaffe air commanders in World War II. He might have been transferred from the Mediterranean sideshow in 1944 to a more important assignment, except that he fell ill. It was discovered that he had an inoperable brain tumor. He nevertheless remained at his post long enough to see 2nd Air Fleet downgraded to the status of Luftwaffe Command South on October 28, 1944.[38] This was, in effect, a personal demotion for Richthofen, who was now stripped of his status as an air fleet commander. Exactly one month later he transferred to Fuehrer Reserve for reasons of health, and he was never able to return to active duty.[39] He was succeeded by Gen. Maximilian von Pohl. Although he occasionally raged against Hitler for treating him and other senior officers as "nothing more than highly paid NCOs," Richthofen had maintained his admiration for the Fuehrer throughout his career.[40]

Richthofen was in great pain in the last months of the war. He lived to see the end of the Third Reich, but just barely. Had he been in good health he undoubtedly would have been tried as a war criminal; however, he was near death when he was captured in May 1945, so the Allies took no steps in that direction. He passed away in Austria on July 12, 1945.[41]

Meanwhile, both the air and ground war on the eastern front were entering another decisive phase. By the spring of 1943, the industrial might of the Soviet Union and her allies had begun to tell, and the Red Air Force had a five-to-one superiority in aircraft. The Luftwaffe fighter wings nevertheless continued to extract a terrible toll on the Russians and maintained air parity in the critical sectors, despite tremendous odds. On November 1, 1942, the 51st Fighter Wing "Moelders" passed an incredible milestone when it scored its 4,000th victory. It was followed by the 52nd Fighter Wing, which shot down its 4,000th victim during the Stalingrad campaign (on December 10, 1942), and by the 54th Fighter Wing, which registered its 4,000th kill on February 23, 1943.[42]

On this sector, the highest number of individual victory totals in the history of aerial warfare were run up by the veteran pilots of the fighter branch. The leading killer was Lt. (later Maj.) Erich Hartmann, a Wuerttemberger in

JG 52 whom the Russians nicknamed "the Black Devil of the Ukraine." He would score an incredible 352 victories in his fighter career—seven against American Mustangs in 1945 and the rest against the Russians.[43]

Hartmann was certainly not the only German ace to turn the eastern front into a shooting gallery for the Luftwaffe. Gerhard Barkhorn, for example, had joined JG 52 soon after the start of the war. Not only did he fail to score in the Battle of Britain, he was shot down twice by the R.A.F. and had to be fished out of the English Channel by the German sea rescue service. He shot down his first enemy airplane on the eastern front on July 2, 1941, a victory that was followed by 300 others—all in the East. Like Hartmann, Major Barkhorn survived the war.[44] Other major aces of the eastern front included Maj. Guenther Rall, 275 kills; Lt. Otto Kittel, 267 victories; Maj. Walter Nowotny, 258 victories; Maj. Wilhelm Batz, 237 victories; Col. Hermann Graf, 211 kills; and Anton Hafner, 204 victories. And there were dozens of others with scores of downed Russians to their credit.[45]

Unfortunately for the Luftwaffe, the bulk of its victories were registered by its experienced pilots. As training deteriorated, the younger replacement pilots were unable to keep up the pace. By early 1943, 25 percent of the new pilots did not survive their fourth mission. As a result, Jeschonnek committed more of his *Lehrgeschwadern*—advanced training wings—to action on the eastern front in the spring of 1943.[46] The Luftwaffe in Russia was literally living on its veteran aces and skilled instructor pilots, who were gradually being killed off or burned out in a war of attrition. When they were gone, the end of air parity in the East would be in sight.

Following Manstein's brilliant victory at Kharkov, a lull descended on the eastern front, as both sides prepared for the German summer offensive of 1943. Hitler picked as his target the Russian salient at Kursk, against which he concentrated Col. Gen. Walter Model's Ninth Army (of Field Marshal Guenther von Kluge's Army Group Center) and Fourth Panzer Army (Col. Gen. Hermann Hoth) and Army Detachment Kempf (Gen. Werner Kempf) of Army Group South. The plan was for Model to attack from the north and link up at Kursk with Fourth panzer Army, advancing from the south. If successful, several Russian armies would be encircled and destroyed. Col. Gen. Ritter von Greim's 6th Air Fleet (formerly Luftwaffe Command East) was to support the northern pincer, while Otto Dessloch's 4th Air Fleet supported the advance from the south. The Luftwaffe concentrated about two-thirds of its combat aircraft in the east to support this offensive. They were nevertheless outnumbered three to one.

The Red Air Force—although still inferior to the Germans in tactical skill—was significantly improved from 1941. They were also more aggressive. On April 22, for example, they attacked Orsha airfield and destroyed two of Greim's three long-range reconnaissance squadrons—another ill omen for the Luftwaffe.[47]

As early as the second week in May Greim's reconnaissance and radio intercept units reported that the Soviets were concentrating large units in the Kursk sector and that these were being backed by the First, Second, Third, Fifteenth, and Sixteenth Soviet air armies. Beginning on May 12, 6th Air Fleet began day and night attacks on Russian railroad traffic and installations. It also took temporary control of the bomber forces of 1st Air Fleet (Combat Zone North) and the 4th Air Fleet (Combat Zone South) for anti-industrial operations: the first strategic bombing the Luftwaffe had conducted in the East in months. Among the targets severely damaged were the huge tank factory at Gorky, the rubber processing works at Yaroslavl, and the marshaling yard and supply base at Yelets. Too late the Luftwaffe was attacking strategic targets in the Soviet Union, albeit on a very limited scale. Meanwhile, Greim's fighters continued to concentrate in the Orel vicinity, to protect the crowded airfields at Orel, Bryansk, and Sechinskaya.[48]

The mainstay of Greim's fighter defenses was the 51st Fighter Wing. It shot down forty Russian aircraft in the Orel vicinity on June 5, sixty-seven more on June 10, and sixty-five more two days later. In the same sector, 12th Flak Division shot down 40 aircraft in June, while 18th Flak Division in the Smolensk-Roslavl sector shot down 130 Russian aircraft in daylight operations and 617 at night. Despite the apparent magnitude of these victories, they were really only minor tactical successes. Greim inflicted serious losses on the Russians, but he was unable to seal off the Kursk battle zone or to annihilate the Soviet troop concentrations in that all-important sector.[49] Meanwhile, the Soviets detected the German buildup. They poured reinforcements into the salient and constructed several huge belts of minefields, while Hitler delayed the offensive until the arrival of the new Ferdinand tanks.

During the Battle of Kursk in early July, 1943, 6th Air Fleet controlled Maj. Gen. Paul Deichmann's 1st Air Division (730 operational aircraft) and Lt. Gen. Ernst Buffa's 12th Flak Division, which had twelve motorized and four truck-drawn flak battalions (with three heavy and two light batteries each), seven light flak battalions, three railway flak battalions, and two or three searchlight battalions. Greim also directed a special night fighter wing, a strategic reconnaissance wing, two Luftwaffe signal regiments, and the 3rd Air Command, an ad hoc unit held ready to commit its attached units to the sector northeast of Bryansk, in case the Soviets counterattacked in that thinly held sector. The XXVII Special Air Administrative Command (formerly Air Administrative Command Moscow) under Lt. Gen. Veit Fischer was in charge of the ground service organizations, supplies, and logistical operations, including Reich Labor Services (Reichsarbeitsdienst, or R.A.D.) battalions.[50]

Greim's main headache was fuel. In June, 6th Air Fleet used 8,634 tons of B-4 (blue) fuel (91 octane, used by bombers and general purpose aircraft) but received only 5,722 tons. The same month it received 441 tons of C-3 (green) fuel, against a consumption rate of 1,079 tons. This high octane fuel (97 octane for weak mixture and 110 to 130 for rich mixture) was used almost exclusively by fighter aircraft. Major General Plocher, Greim's chief of staff, wrote later: "Every assignee mission had to be carefully examined to determine whether it was really worth the fuel expenditure."[51]

The 1st Air Division (Deichmann) of 6th Air Fleet was responsible for supporting the northern arm of the Kursk pincer. To the south Dessloch concentrated 1,100 aircraft under the command of VIII Air Corps (Seidemann) to support Manstein's advance. Like Greim, he stripped his other units (I Air and IV Air Corps) to provide support for the main thrusts.[52]

Operation "Citadel," the Battle of Kursk, began on July 5, 1943. For the Luftwaffe, it almost ended before it began. Early that morning the majority of the German bomber and dive-bomber wings were preparing to take off at the Kharkov airfields when the First, Fourth, and Sixteen Soviet air armies took off and, with 500 bombers, fighters, and ground attack aircraft, headed for the mass of bombers. The German He-111s, Ju-87s, and Do-17s seemed doomed, but 140 Me-109G fighters from JG 52 and JG 3 "Udet" quickly took off to meet them. "It developed into the largest and fiercest air battle of all time," Musciano later wrote. The veterans of the 52nd and 3rd Fighter Wings shot down 432 Soviet airplanes and completely neutralized the threat. Lt. Joachim Kirschner alone shot down nine Soviet airplanes. The Luftwaffe only lost twenty-six aircraft in this bitter struggle.[53]

Meanwhile, the Luftwaffe's bombers, dive-bombers, and ground attack aircraft took off and flew dozens of missions in direct support of the army. In all, the pilots under Greim and Seidemann flew 4,570 sorties, mostly in direct support of the ground units.[54] They suffered heavy losses in this dangerous work, and the operational strength of the combat units declined steadily, as replacement services could not keep up with aircraft attrition. The Red Air Force was much stronger than the Luftwaffe and began to attack German supply routes and airfields, although the Germans won almost every head-to-head dogfight. Greim's chief of staff later wrote: "The Russians were quantitatively very strong, but were mediocre in quality and inadequate in development. Yet they . . . had come a long way from their primitive condition of 1941."[55] Still they were generally outclassed by the veterans of the Luftwaffe. On July 7 JG 52 shot down its 6,000th enemy aircraft, and a few days later the Moelders wing reached the same total.[56]

It was not enough. The vaulted Ferdinand tank (a Porsche product) turned out to be a complete failure. Ninth Army's attack bogged down on July 9, and two days later vastly superior Russian forces attacked the thinly manned German line in the Orel salient, north of Ninth Army. Greim immediately rushed all available forces to the aid of the Second Panzer Army in the endangered sector, but the area was too forested to allow for very good air support. Soon the Russians were driving on the Bryansk-Orel Railroad, the lifeline of Ninth Army. They broke through to Khotynets, where no German ground forces were stationed. No reserves were available, so Greim committed the 1st Air Division, which had been reinforced by antitank squadrons from VIII Air Corps. The air-ground battle lasted from morning to nightfall. Hundreds of Soviet tanks were destroyed in low-level attacks, and the Red spearheads were all but wiped out. "For the first time in military history," Model signaled, "the Luftwaffe has succeeded, without support by ground forces, in annihilating a tank brigade which had broken through."[57] The offensive was not over, however, for Stalin poured eighty-two infantry divisions, fourteen tank corps, twelve artillery divisions, and a number of independent tank brigades into the Orel attacks alone. The 12th Flak Division had to be committed to the front lines in an antitank role, leaving German troop concentrations and installations vulnerable to air attack. Soviet fighters took advantage of the situation, roaming Army Group Center's rear at will, blasting supply depots, railroads, and other facilities.[58]

During the Battle of Orel, 1st Air Division's aircraft averaged five to six missions per day. The division flew 37,421 sorties and shot down 1,733 Russian aircraft, against a loss of only sixty-four German planes. It destroyed or put out of action more than 1,100 Soviet tanks and 1,300 trucks and dropped more than 20,000 tons of bombs on Russian targets. The 12th Flak Division also shot down 383 Russian aircraft and destroyed 229 Soviet tanks and inflicted heavy losses on advancing infantry units.[59] The Communists, however, took full advantage of their vast manpower reserves and threw unit after unit into the fighting. It was a battle of attrition, and in the end Germany could not win. On the evening of July 31, Second Panzer and Ninth armies began to withdraw to the Hagen position, immediately east of Bryansk. First Air Division covered their rear guards. It was the beginning of a retreat that would continue, with a few interruptions, all the way to Berlin.

Orel, Bryansk, the Desna River, Vyazma, Orsha, the Dnieper, the Sozh, Smolensk, Roslavl. All were names of the bloody battles in Army Group Center's westerly retreat. Sixth Air Fleet fought in every battle, rushing from danger point to danger point, crisis to crisis, growing progressively weaker, just like the rest of the Luftwaffe on the eastern front. It had invaded Russia with almost three thousand aircraft, but now strong forces were needed in the West and over the skies of the Fatherland. By early 1944, the Eastern air fleets could muster only 2,000 aircraft, and many of these were obsolete—some were even biplanes. The Eastern fleet's striking power was less than half of what it had been in 1941 and would decline even more rapidly thereafter.[60] Meanwhile, Russia had 8,800 military aircraft on the front, excluding reserves, and their strength was growing.[61] The veteran German fighter wings still continued to perform brilliantly. The 51st Fighter Wing ran its total number of victories to 8,000 on May 1, 1944, a feat that was duplicated by the 54th Fighter Wing "Gruenherz" on August 15. Two weeks later the pilots of JG 52 brought down their 10,000th enemy airplane—an astronomical figure! Nevertheless they were struggling against the tide, fighting the industrial might of most of the world. By the fall of 1944, the Luftwaffe on the eastern front was outnumbered 20 to 1.[62] Clearly the writing was on the wall.

Despite the enemy's technical and material superiority, which had existed as early as 1941, the Luftwaffe had maintained aerial superiority on some sectors and air parity on the others, largely due to the undeniable skill of its pilots. This situation, too, was changing, as had been demonstrated over the Mediterranean during the Battle of the Tunisian Bridgehead. Although he would remain the superior of the Soviet pilot for some time to come, the average German pilot of 1943 was simply not as good an aviator as his 1939–41 counterpart, who was beating everyone in sight except the R.A.F. during the Battle of Britain—and even that had been a close run. Before we examine his last battles, we must answer the question: Why did the quality of the German pilot decline?

Richard Suchenwirth called training "the Step-Child of the Luftwaffe."[63] This was certainly the case, especially after Hans Jeschonnek became chief of the General Staff. Easily the most important of the chiefs, Jeschonnek neglected training to an incredible degree. Indeed, he virtually renounced any claim to influence in this most vital area by making the pilot schools directly subordinate to the air fleet commanders. When the Luftwaffe was committed to war two and a half years ahead of schedule, Jeschonnek said: "We must conduct a short war: everything must therefore be thrown into action at the outset."[64] Jeschonnek blindly believed Hitler's assurances that it would be a short war, and he committed everything he had from the first day—even the instructor pilots. He knew that the Luftwaffe lacked both the men and material to fight a long war, so he sacrificed the long-term plans for development of the Luftwaffe for short-term gains, in effect mortgaging the future of the air force on the hope of a quick victory. When this victory did not materialize, the Luftwaffe found itself in deep, deep trouble.

The Office of the Chief of Training was created in February 1939. Its chief, Lt. Gen. Bernard Kuehl, realized that there were not enough pilot training schools to meet the requirements for the activation of new frontline units and for personnel replacements in the event of war. At that time Germany had only three bomber schools, one naval aviation school, and one school for fighter pilots. It took a full year to train a good fighter pilot and even longer to train bomber crews. Kuehl immediately requested authorization to establish new pilot training schools, but Jeschonnek turned down his request, stating that all resources were to be used for the activation of new frontline units.

The Training Office did not get control of the schools until after the Polish campaign, when Jeschonnek was finally convinced that the air fleet commanders had been too free in raiding the training establishments for the frontline units. Jeschonnek himself, however, seemed to view the training branch as some sort of reservoir of reserve pilots, to be dipped into whenever a crisis arose. He requisitioned Ju-52s and their instructor pilots for the Norwegian campaign, for the attack on Holland, and for the Balkans campaign, where they suffered tremendous losses. He raided the Training Command for Ju-52 and He-111 airplanes and crews to resupply Kholm and Demyansk in Russia in the winter of 1941–42. During the Stalingrad campaign he (and Goering) went to the well once too often and dealt the training arm a blow from which it never recovered.

In 1940, Lt. Col. Paul Deichmann, the chief of staff of the Training Office, came up with a plan to solve the problem, as far as the air transport branch was concerned.

Deichmann was an interesting man and a brilliant one. Very far sighted —one might say extremely so—he was the champion of the four-engine bomber after General Wever's death and became the champion of the training schools after that. Deichmann saw the necessity of creating a well-balanced, strategic air force more clearly than anyone on the General Staff of the Luftwaffe (except Wever), and he also argued against the Ju-88 when everyone else was calling it the "Wonder Bomber." He always seemed to be right. His problem was that he could never get anyone in authority to pay attention to his ideas.

Deichmann was born in Fulda, in the province of Hesse, on August 27, 1898. Educated at the prestigious Gross-Lichterfelde Cadet Academy (the closest thing Germany had to West Point), he was commissioned second lieutenant in the infantry in 1916 and led a platoon in the trenches on the western front. He became an air observer in 1917 and served in France and in the Baltic States until 1919, when he joined the Reichswehr. Deichmann transferred to the Air Ministry as a technical advisor in 1934 and remained on the Luftwaffe General Staff in Berlin until 1940, except for a part of 1937, when he commanded a bomber group at Erfurt.[65]

In 1940, just after the Norwegian campaign, he hit upon the idea of using old Ju-86s as trainers. This obsolete twin-engine aircraft had been used as a bomber in Poland but was then dropped from the armaments program without advanced warning to the German aircraft industry. Junkers, therefore, still had enough component parts on hand to make 1,000 airplanes. Furthermore, the Ju-86 had excellent flight characteristics and would make an excellent trainer. Deichmann drafted a plan to replace the Ju-52s taken from the training schools with Ju-86s. All that would be required was a small factory to assemble them. Although Milch approved the plan, Goering decided against it, apparently believing that the training schools would never again have to be raided for Ju-52s. He brushed aside Deichmann's arguments that the future demands for the Ju-52 at the front would be "tremendous."[66]

Shortly thereafter, the highly capable Deichmann left Berlin to become chief of staff of II Air Corps. Perhaps he was fed up with losing major arguments. In any event his subsequent career was distinguished. He succeeded Seidemann as chief of staff to Kesselring's OB South in Italy (1942–43) and was commander of the 1st Air Division in Russia (May-November, 1943). Later he led I Air Corps in Russia, Hungary, and Austria (November, 1943–April, 1945). In the last days of the war he directed Luftwaffe Command 4 in Austria, and he surrendered to the Americans at the end of the war. At last report he was living in Hamburg, a retired general of flyers.[67]

Goering and Jeschonnek did not raid the training establishment merely to obtain transports and transport instructor pilots—they took fighter and dive-bomber instructors as well. Jeschonnek was especially guilty, as he gradually changed the ratio of combat aircraft to trainers, transports, and reconnaissance aircraft. When the war broke out, the ratio was 57 to 43. By 1942 it was 75 to 25, and in 1944 it reached 88 to 12.[68] The training establishments simply no longer had the instructors or the aircraft to do their jobs properly. By 1944, British fighter pilots were receiving 360 hours of flight training before being sent to the combat units. American fighter pilot trainees were receiving forty hours more than that. New Luftwaffe fighter pilots were being sent to the

Gruppen with only 160 hours of flight time.[69] Then they were committed to combat in obsolete aircraft, facing American and British pilots with more than twice their experience, flying modern aircraft. The results were predictable: the Luftwaffe began to suffer higher combat losses and more accidents, especially upon landing. The quality of the new Luftwaffe pilot continued to deteriorate throughout the rest of the war.

✠

Deteriorating, also, was the Luftwaffe's military domination over the skies of the Reich itself. In January, 1943, the United States Army Air Force[70] made its first major bombing raid over the Reich. Its target was the U-boat base of Wilhelmshaven. The raid was partially successful, and the Eighth U.S. Air Force lost only three of the ninety-one aircraft participating in the daylight attack.[71] Although unimportant in itself, the Wilhelmshaven raid boded ill for the future, because the Americans were pouring the bulk of their industrial might against Germany. This attack also set a precedent that would remain almost uninterrupted until the end of the war: the Americans would engage in precision daytime bombing, while the British concentrated on nighttime raids against area targets. Even though this strategy evolved by accident, the strategy of nighttime area bombing and daytime precision bombing was to prove a devastating combination.

The R.A.F. resumed its nocturnal activities in January and February, 1943, with raids against Cologne and Nuremberg. The attacks did more damage to the surrounding countryside than to the cities themselves. In some places the civilian populations gathered in crowds and danced while they watched the fireworks displays provided by the air raids, but this was soon to change.[72] Gradually the R.A.F. raids increased in number, accuracy, and severity. On March 2, 1943, Bomber Command dropped 600 tons of bombs on Berlin, killing 700 civilians and leaving 35,000 homeless. Hitler was furious. He wanted to know what Goering was going to do in response to these terror tactics, but Goering was not available for an answer: he had scurried off to Rome in some haste—on a vacation.[73]

A mark of Goering's declining power was reflected in what happened to Rosette Korwan and her husband. Rosette, a Jewish actress, had been a close friend of Emmy Goering since they worked together at the Wiemar National Theater. After the Nazis banned Jewish performers, Rosette had lived on a small monthly stipend from Emmy. She passed up the opportunity to escape Nazi Germany, however, in order to be with her lover, whom she later married. In March 1943 he got into an altercation with an SS man, who arrested him. At Gestapo headquarters the SS discovered he was Jewish, but was not wearing his yellow star—a major criminal offense in the Third Reich. Rose telephoned Emmy, pleading with her to intercede on her husband's behalf. Alarmed, Emmy persuaded Hermann to intervene once more. Goering spoke to Heinrich Himmler about the couple. Although he refused to release Herr Korwan, the SS chief granted Rose's request to join her husband and promised to look after them. They would be sent to a "nice" camp, he said, and would be furnished with a private room and a servant to clean it for them. Instead, Himmler sent them directly to the gas chambers. He would never have dared to do such a thing to Frau Goering's friends at the height of the Reichsmarschall's power.[74]

Meanwhile, the bombing continued. The night of March 5–6 saw the beginning of what the British later called the Battle of the Ruhr. The Luftwaffe met the challenge with an assortment of technologically obsolete aircraft which had all been designed before the war. They were also short on trained pilots and air crewmen, while many of their instructors lay dead in the snows of Russia. Jeschonnek's short-sighted policies were now paying monstrous dividends. The first Anglo-American attack struck Essen with 442 heavy bombers. One hundred sixty acres of the city were devastated, and three-quarters of the buildings on another 450 acres were destroyed or seriously damaged by the bombs or the fires which they caused. Essen would be attacked four more times during the Battle of the Ruhr.[75]

Although the Allies concentrated against the Ruhr in March 1943, they did not limit their attentions to Germany's major industrial district. True, they blasted Essen, Duisburg, Duesseldorf, Geisenkirchen, Wuppertal, Dortmund, and Bochum, but they also attacked Berlin, Aachen, Stettin, Pilsen, Munich, Stuttgart, Frankfurt, and Nuremberg in strength. Hamburg was subjected to its first heavy bombing that month, while Nuremberg was set ablaze by 800 tons of bombs on the eighth. The next day Munich was heavily raided, and two days later Stuttgart was attacked. That day Hitler ordered Goering home from Rome. His presence did little good. On the night of March 15 Essen was hit again. This time the vital Krupp steelworks and armaments center was heavily damaged.

The raids continued until the thirtieth, when the Luftwaffe finally handed the R.A.F. a significant defeat. Seven hundred British bombers set out for Nuremberg that night. The German night fighters under General Kammhuber did not engage them until their fighter escorts, at the limit of their fuel range, turned back for home. The German fighters then attacked the British formations and shot down ninety-five bombers. Another dozen were so badly shot up that they later crashed or crash-landed in England. These heavy losses forced the British Bomber Command to temporarily suspend their attacks, but not for long. During the Battle of the Ruhr, Bomber

Command had flown 18,506 sorties and lost 872 aircraft. Another 2,126 had been damaged, for a total casualty ratio of more than 16 percent. Nevertheless, British production had proceeded at such a pace that the R.A.F. had almost 200 more bombers at the end of the battle than it had when it began.[76]

The temporary halt of massive British bombing did not stop them from launching minor raids, especially with their Mosquito bomber. A wooden-framed aircraft, it was faster than any German fighter and at least equally as maneuverable. It was employed in several roles but was most effective as a nuisance bomber. The Mosquitoes robbed the already tired German worker of his rest and served as a constant reminder that the enemy might strike anytime, anywhere. This fact would soon have its effect on German civilian morale.

U.S. precision bombing continued, mainly on the fringe of German airspace. On April 4 they killed more than 200 Parisians in an attack on the Renault factory and more than 200 Italians in an attack on Naples. The next day they struck the port city of Antwerp and killed more than 2,000 Belgian civilians. The British were also back in action, bombing Essen again. Throughout May there were violent attacks on the Ruhr. The R.A.F. dropped another 1,500 tons of bombs on Duisburg, Dortmund, and other cities, while a special squadron blew up two dams supplying much of the water to the Ruhr. Several R.A.F. Mosquitoes carried out a daylight raid on the Zeiss optical factory at Jena, in the center of the Third Reich, without suffering a single casualty.[77]

The attacks intensified in the last week of May. Dortmund took another 2,000 tons of bombs on the twenty-third, and Duesseldorf was hit by about the same force on the twenty-fifth. Two days later Wuppertal was attacked. Some 2,450 civilians were killed and about 118,000 left homeless in fifteen minutes of stark terror. On June 11 another 2,000 tons of bombs fell on Duesseldorf and another 100,000 people were left homeless. Fifteen hundred tons of bombs were dropped on Bochum the next day, and Oberhausen was severely bombed the day after that. In the third week of June, the R.A.F. deposited 2,000 tons of bombs on Krefeld, 1,640 tons on Muelheim and Oberhausen, 1,660 tons on Wuppertal, and 1,300 tons on Gelsenkirchen. In the two attacks on Wuppertal alone, 8,000 civilians were killed. And still the raids continued.[78] Cologne was raided on the night of June 28-29. Five hundred forty R.A.F. planes dropped 1,614 tons of bombs, killing 3,460 people and leaving 400,000 homeless in sixty terrifying minutes.[79]

Hitler ordered the fighter defense of the Reich increased in early July, 1943. The veteran 3rd Fighter Wing "Udet" (under Col. Wolf-Dietrich Wilcke) was recalled from the Russian front, II/JG 27 was transferred from

Italy to Weisbaden, and II/JG 51 "Moelders" was moved from Sardinia to Germany to defend the Munich area.[80] Other *Gruppen* would follow. By autumn there were five fighter divisions in Germany: the 1st under Doering defended Berlin and central Germany, the 2rd (Lt. Gen. Walter Schwaberdissen) headquartered at Stada and defended the German Bight on the North Sea coast, while Werner Junck's 3rd fought over Holland and the Ruhr. The understrength 7th and 8th were responsible for defending southern and eastern Germany, respectively.[81] The 4th and 5th Fighter Divisions were assigned to Sperrle's 3rd Air Fleet for the defense of occupied Europe. Goering also strengthened the Reich's flak defenses. By early 1944, there were no fewer than twelve flak divisions guarding German and associated

TABLE 15: ORDER OF BATTLE OF THE FLAK ARM BY DIVISION, EARLY 1944

Flak Division	Area of Responsibility
1st	Berlin
2nd (Mtz)	Russian Front
3rd	Hamburg
4th	Duesseldorf
5th	Southeastern Europe
6th (Mtz)	Russian Front
7th	Cologne
8th	Bremen
9th	Russian Front
10th (Mtz)	Russian Front
11th (Mtz)	Southern France
12th (Mtz)	Russian Front
13th	France (around Caen)
14th	Leipzig
15th (Mtz)	Russian Front
16th	France (around Lille)
17th (Mtz)	Russian Front
18th (Mtz)	Russian Front
21st	Southwestern Germany
22nd	Western Germany

Note: the 19th and 20th Motorized Flak Divisions had been destroyed in North Africa in 1943.
Source: Mitcham 1985, p. 519.

airspace, as opposed to the equivalent of five in late 1942. Table 15 shows the flak arm's order of battle in early 1944. Note that only eight of Germany's twenty extant flak divisions were at the front, while 60 percent guarded Nazi airspace. It was a terrible drain on the front.

Goering, as usual, did not blame himself for the disasters, but rather the "cowardice" of his fighter pilots, a statement no Allied bomber crewman would agree with. He also made the very serious mistake of trying to counter terror with terror, emphasizing German bomber production at the expense of fighter production. As a result, he was unable to defend against the next onslaught—one of the most powerful of the war.

The Battle of Hamburg began on the night of July 24, when 700 heavy R.A.F. bombers attacked the city, after other British aircraft released millions of strips of metal foil, totally neutralizing German radar. Only a dozen bombers were shot down as much of the city was destroyed and 1,500 civilians were killed. Over a hundred U.S. precision bombers appeared the next day, increasing the damage and hampering fire-fighting efforts. (The American contribution to the strategic bombing effort, though not to be minimized, did not rival the British air effort until 1944 and did not exceed it until the last quarter of that year; it never overshadowed it.)

The really devastating raid did not come until the night of the twenty-seventh, when 772 British bombers dropped 2,300 tons of bombs on the city. About half of these were incendiaries, half high explosives. The Hamburg Fire Department was already low on water from the previous two days, as north-central Germany was in the grips of a drought. The massive raid of the twenty-seventh killed many fire fighters and ruptured water mains. The heat was so intense that artificial firestorms were created. "The air brought in from the areas surrounding the major fires attained cyclonic force," Beck wrote later. "Ground-level Hamburg became the fire pan of a gigantic oven." Smoke rose to observable heights of four to five miles and many fire department units simply gave up fighting the uncontrollable blazes, concentrating on extricating trapped survivors instead.[82] Tens of thousands perished in the heat and hundreds of thousands fled the city in terror. Even the asphalt on the streets caught fire.

Two nights later the R.A.F. repeated the performance, dropping more than 2,000 tons of high explosive and incendiary bombs. That night the Luftwaffe shot down only twenty-eight bombers as Germany's second largest city died. The last raid, of only slightly less intensity, took place on August 2. In the four night raids of July 24–August 2, Hamburg suffered as much destruction as Britain endured throughout the entire war. The death total could only be estimated, but 50,000 is a commonly cited figure. Another 40,000 people were wounded. Half of the city's factories were destroyed and more than 50 percent of Hamburg's houses were destroyed by explosion or fire. More than a million homeless refugees fled into the interior, spreading fear and terror as they went. German war morale sagged for the first time. Munitions Minister Albert Speer predicted to Hitler that six more raids of this nature would end the war.[83] Fortunately for Germany, the Allies did not concentrate such air power against a single city until 1945, when they firebombed Dresden.

Goering did not dare show his face in Hamburg after the raid. He merely sent a letter of condolence to Gauleiter Karl Kaufmann and the population. It was never published because it would have caused a riot.[84]

✠

The enormous quantities of tin foil the R.A.F. dropped during the Battle of Hamburg effectively neutralized Kammhuber's Himmelbett system, which depended on radar to direct the fighters to their targets. Too inflexible and too dependent on ground direction, it was replaced by the "Wild Boar" (*Wilde Sau*) tactics invented by Maj. Hans-Joachim "Hajo" Hermann.

The brilliantly innovative Major Hermann had been born in Kiel on August 1, 1913, and had begun his combat career with the 4th Bomber Wing. Exceptionally successful in attacking British shipping during the war, he sank a dozen British vessels totalling about seventy thousand tons and was awarded the Knights Cross in 1940. Commander of III Group, 30th Bomber Wing, he transferred to the night fighters and organized the new 300th Fighter Wing, an experimental unit near Bonn, in mid-1942.[85]

Although Hermann was to personally shoot down nine U.S. bombers in the next two years, his main claim to fame lay in his endless innovations, of which the Wild Boar tactics were the most famous. They were based on the idea that the Allied night bombers could be silhouetted by lighting target areas with flares, searchlights, and flak. Then freelance, single-engine fighters flying at high altitudes could attack the bombers from overhead, using visual sighting exclusively. The tactics were so successful that two more Wild Boar wings—JG 301 and JG 302—were organized near Munich and Berlin, respectively. All three were controlled by the newly formed 30th Fighter Division, led by Major Hermann.[86] These tactics were soon adopted by the entire night fighter branch.

General Kammhuber was not at all in favor of the new tactics, but Colonel General Weise fully supported them, and he was backed by Hermann Goering. Kammhuber's stock at RLM was already low, because he had been pushing for a new model aircraft, specially designed for night fighting. In this he was opposed by Milch, who did not want to expend the raw materials or industrial workforce hours necessary to bring it into production.

These factors combined eventually led to Kammhuber's removal as general of night fighters.[87]

"Hajo" Hermann was eventually promoted to colonel and in December, 1943, was named inspector of aerial defense (*Luftverteidigung*). He was commander of the 9th Air Division in 1944 and, at the end of the war, was leader of Ram Command Elbe (*Rammkommando Elbe*), the German equivalent of the kamikaze pilots. Captured by the Russians in 1945, he spent the next decade in Soviet prisons.

Although more successful than the Himmelbett system, the Wild Boar tactics did not halt the R.A.F. bomber offensive. The "Battle of Berlin" began on July 24, 1943. During the first phase, which lasted until November 18, the Anglo-Americans launched thirty-three major raids. They concentrated against the capital city of the Reich, of course, but they also attacked Bochum, Duisburg, Gelsenkirchen, Wuppertal, Leverkusen, Essen, Duesseldorf, and Remscheild in the Ruhr, struck Hanover in more than 3,000 sorties, and hit Bremen, Kassel, Cologne, Frankfurt, Mannheim, Stuttgart, Munich, and Nuremberg with major aerial bombardments. Targets in France were also subjected to precision bombing, and Milan, Turin, and Genoa in Italy were victims of minor raids by the Fifteenth U.S. Air Force.[88]

The first major raid hit Berlin on August 1. Gauleiter Joseph Goebbels, who had neglected building air raid shelters, was at least wise enough to order the evacuation of children and nonessential personnel, and he constantly visited devastated sections of the city, keeping morale as high as was possible under the circumstances. Berlin, though largely reduced to ruins, was no repetition of Hamburg, even though 3,000 civilians died in the first two raids.[89]

Meanwhile, the Ninth U.S. Air Force joined the European air war. Operating from bases in North Africa, it attacked the Ploesti oilfields on August 1, with little success. Of the 178 B-24 "Liberators" involved, 50 were shot down and 55 others were seriously damaged by I/JG 4, IV/JG 27, and the Bulgarian Fighter Regiment, operating out of Rumania, Greece, and Bulgaria, respectively. On August 13 it was more successful, raiding the Messerschmitt Aircraft Works at Wiener Neustadt, near Vienna. Since there were no fighter defenses in Austria, the Luftwaffe was forced to create Fighter Command Austria (*Jafu Ostmark*) to counter the new threat—a further drain on the fighter arm. Then, on August 16, the Americans inaugurated shuttle bombing. Dozens of Flying Fortresses took off from England, bombed the Messerschmitt factory at Regensburg, and flew on to the American bases in North Africa before the Luftwaffe could react.[90]

On the night of August 17, the British turned their attentions to Peenemunde, the center of German V-weapons research activities. Forty of the 597 heavy bombers which attacked the facility were shot down, but 700 workers were killed, including many almost irreplaceable technicians. Professor Thiel, the rocket propulsion expert, and Chief Project Engineer Walther were among the dead.[91]

After the Hamburg raid, Goering met with Milch, Weise, Galland, and many other officers of the Luftwaffe General Staff. Even Col. Dietrich Peltz, the inspector of bomber forces, agreed that the bomber arm should at once relinquish its industrial priority so that Germany could produce more fighters. "Never before and never again did I witness such determination and agreement among the circle of those responsible for the leadership of the Luftwaffe," Galland recalled.[92] Personal animosity and ambition were put aside; everyone wanted to do everything possible to prevent a second national catastrophe of the scale of Hamburg. Even Goering was carried away. He rushed off to Fuehrer Headquarters to secure Hitler's permission for the Luftwaffe to give top priority to the defense of the Reich. Fighter production, he told the Fuehrer, must be emphasized, even at the expense of bomber production. There were apparently no surviving witnesses to the scene that followed in the Fuehrer's bunker, but Goering emerged sobbing. Hitler had rejected any radical changes in the air war; there would be no changeover from offensive to defensive tactics. Terror bombing against England would still be the answer to terror bombing against Germany; furthermore, Hitler said he had lost faith in the Reichsmarschall and the Luftwaffe. Completely shattered, Goering begged for another chance. Hitler consented. "The Fuehrer made me realize our mistake," he moaned to Galland and Peltz. "The Fuehrer is always right. We must deal such mighty blows to our enemy in the West that he will never dare to risk another raid like Hamburg . . ." Goering ordered Peltz to direct the aerial counterattack on England and hurried back to Rominten, East Prussia, to hunt.[93] The air war would take its inevitable course down the road to total defeat. If Hermann Goering could not see this (or refused to see it), Hans Jeschonnek finally saw it clearly. As a result, he took what he considered to be the appropriate step: he shot himself in the head.

✠

Chief of the General Staff of the Luftwaffe Col. Gen. Hans Jeschonnek was a child of his times and a victim of them. His youth had been ended by the First World War and much of his home province of Prussia had been gobbled up by the Poles under the Treaty of Versailles. After serving in a weak and restricted army for fourteen years, Lieutenant Jeschonnek was delighted to see Hitler come to power and begin to make Germany strong again. He was also pleased to be able to play a prominent role in this expansion. Unfortunately, he believed in Hitler totally. The Fuehrer had said that war would not come until 1942; all right, Jeschonnek thought, the war would not come until 1942. When the conflict broke out in 1939 instead, Jeschonnek knew that the Luftwaffe did not have the depth to fight a long war, especially on two fronts. But the Fuehrer assured him that it would be a short war. Jeschonnek's response was predictable: "Training units to the front!" We have seen the results.

Jeschonnek was a soldier and airman to his toes. Unlike Goering and many others, Jeschonnek had none of the plunderer in him. He never took anything from occupied countries. Indeed, his life-style has been characterized as Spartan. Possessing a strong intellect, he wrote memoranda which were often adopted into training manuals without modification, since there was nothing to change. And incidents such as this occurred years before he became chief of the Air General Staff. The problem was Jeschonnek was too much the soldier. His family (he had a wife and a daughter) did not play any decisive role in his life, and religion was even less important to him. Religion, to Jeschonnek, was "merely a silly and superficial social matter," in which he took no interest. "Thus," wrote Suchenwirth, "when the turning point of the war came to shatter his deepest confidence . . . Jeschonnek had absolutely no spiritual reserves upon which he could call." Basically he was a lonely, isolated man who could not open his heart to anyone.[94]

As chief of the General Staff, Jeschonnek made a number of serious mistakes. He was too firm an advocate of the dive-bomber, to the virtual exclusion of the horizontal bomber. He opposed the four-engine bomber. He was too enthusiastic about the Ju-88, which did not live up to expectations. He was too blind a believer in Hitler and National Socialism. He was convinced the Fuehrer would find a diplomatic solution to the "Danzig problem" without resorting to war. When the war started, Jeschonnek allowed the training wings to be committed as of Day One. He backed the Hitler Program against the Kammhuber Program, even though he knew the former was unrealistic.

Jeschonnek hid his unhappiness behind a mask of sarcasm, which alienated members of his staff. His relationship with General of Flyers Hans-Georg von Seidel, the chief of supply and administration, was particularly bad. Seidel, who was in charge of the organizations, armament, and maintenance and supply branches (General Staff Branches II, VI, and IV, respectively), was astute but caustic. Jeschonnek avoided him whenever possible, leading to a further fragmentation within the General Staff.[95]

Jeschonnek's blind obedience to Hitler also alienated Hoffmann von Waldau, the chief of operations (Branch I). Hoffmann was personable, urbane, aristocratic, and wise in the ways of the world. He was also one of the very few officers with whom Jeschonnek was on a first-name basis.[96] Their relationship cooled, however, especially after the United States entered the war. Except for Milch, Hoffmann von Waldau was just about the only member of the General Staff who recognized the military potential of the United States. Jeschonnek and Goering got rid of Hoffmann in the early spring of 1942 by naming him Air Commander Africa. While commanding X Air Corps, he was killed in an air accident in the Balkans on May 15, 1943. His death cost the Luftwaffe one of its brightest young generals. (He was succeeded by General Fiebig, who was named Luftwaffe Commander Southeast.)

Hans Jeschonnek's tenure as chief of the General Staff of the Luftwaffe was by no means a total failure. We must remember that, under his leadership, the Luftwaffe played a major (if not decisive) role in the conquest of Poland, Denmark, Norway, France, Belgium, Luxembourg, the Netherlands, Yugoslavia, Greece, and Crete. Although over-optimistic in June, 1940, he bore little responsibility for the loss of the Battle of Britain. He did, however, favor the Russian invasion and, when it failed in the winter of 1941–42, the Luftwaffe faced a war on three fronts.

Despite the increasing number of enemies arrayed against Germany, Jeschonnek did not insist that the air armaments industry increase its rates of production. His request for aircraft remained quite modest, especially in the 1939–41 period, when German industry was relatively unmolested by Allied bombers. Under Jeschonnek and Udet, the considerable production potential of the German aviation industry remained unused.

Jeschonnek's decline began in 1942, when the R.A.F. began pounding German cities. On June 1, 1942, the day after the raid on Cologne, Hitler summoned Jeschonnek to his East Prussian headquarters at Rastenburg and asked him how many British bombers had taken part in the assault. Jeschonnek replied that an estimated 200 aircraft penetrated the Luftwaffe's defenses, according to preliminary reports.

"The Luftwaffe had probably been asleep all night," the Fuehrer snapped, ". . . but I have not been asleep. I stay awake when one of my cities is under fire. And—" he screamed, working himself into a fine rage, "and I thank the Almighty that I can rely on my Gauleiter even if the Luftwaffe deceives me! Let me tell you what Gauleiter Grohe has to say! Listen—I ask you to listen carefully—THERE WERE A THOUSAND OR MORE ENGLISH AIRCRAFT—you hear—A THOUSAND . . . maybe more! Herr Goering, of course, is not here. Of course not . . ."[97]

Hitler's outbursts against Goering and the Luftwaffe grew more violent as the bombings continued. Goering, in keeping with his character, turned on Jeschonnek, attempting to make him the scapegoat for the Luftwaffe's failures. Hitler, however, shielded Jeschonnek from the Reichsmarschall. He knew where the real blame lay.

That summer the British began to launch raids of squadron size or less, using the small, fast Mosquitoes. They were so fast that the German fighters could not stop them. Guided by radar, they did little real damage, but they disrupted sleep, caused production disruptions, and would continue to harass the Germans for the rest of the war.

As the Hitler-Goering relationship deteriorated, the Fuehrer took to dealing directly with Jeschonnek. Goering—sensing a potential rival for power—took more and more to bypassing the chief of staff and issuing orders directly to the commands through Colonel von Brauchitsch or Ulrich Diesing, members of the "Little General Staff." The young Prussian now had difficulty in even obtaining an appointment with the Reichsmarschall. When he did, Goering usually just yelled at him. Jeschonnek, meanwhile, had to sit in on the Fuehrer conferences, at which Hitler's criticisms of the Luftwaffe became more and more bitter and frequently boiled over into rages. Jeschonnek endured them all like the gentleman he was. He just sat there, chalk-white, saying little or nothing. After one of his outbursts of temper, Hitler walked over to Jeschonnek and put his arm around his shoulder. "Of course," he said, "I didn't mean you at all."[98]

By 1943, Hans Jeschonnek was a worn-out man. He applied for a transfer, asking to command an air fleet. Goering, happy at the prospect of getting rid of Jeschonnek, readily consented. Hitler, however, said it was out of the question. He ordered the two Luftwaffe leaders to effect a reconciliation and start working together, but the new relationship lasted only about two weeks.[99] Jeschonnek felt he had only three choices left: denounce Goering to Hitler, resign as chief of staff, or commit suicide.

Jeschonnek had good grounds for resigning, because he was suffering from severe stomach pains and cramps. Such a step was too humiliating for the forty-year-old chief of staff, however. His comrades urged him to speak to Hitler about Goering, but Jeschonnek felt that he owed too much to the Reichsmarschall. On August l, 1943, however, during the Hamburg raids, he finally forced himself to take the necessary steps. He recommended to Hitler that he assume personal command of the Luftwaffe, as he had done with the army. He complained that the Reichsmarschall "is never available for consultation" and submitted a memorandum listing Goering's numerous errors.[100] Hitler, however, could not bring himself to dismiss his old crony.

Beneath Jeschonnek's hardened exterior lay an extremely vulnerable inner man. "Fundamentally, he was an extremely soft person," his secretary, Frau Kersten, said later, "but he didn't want to show it. He erected a wall around himself. In order to hide his inner vulnerability, he assumed a cool, slightly dissatisfied and seemingly sarcastic nature in public."[101]

On August 17, 1943, the Americans raided the ball-bearing works at Schweinfurt and the aircraft plants at Regensburg. Although the Luftwaffe appeared to have won a victory, because several enemy bombers had been shot down, the plants were heavily damaged, and the enemy had demonstrated his ability to penetrate to the deep interior of the Reich in broad daylight. That afternoon there was a terrible scene between Goering and his chief of staff. Jeschonnek then went for a ride on a skiff in Goldat Lake. He wanted to see a flight of ducks, he said. Then, in his quarters, he drank a bottle of champagne with his adjutant. That day was Jeschonnek's daughter's birthday. Meanwhile, more than 500 R.A.F. bombers blasted the V-weapons research and assembly site at Peenemuende.[102]

At 8 A.M. on August 18, Gen. Rudolf Meister, the chief of the Operations Branch, reported the extent of the damage to Jeschonnek. The chief of staff listened without emotion. When Meister left, Jeschonnek shot himself. He left two notes. One said: "I can no longer work together with the Reichsmarschall. Long live the Fuehrer." The second note said: "Diesing and Brauchitsch shall not be at my funeral."[103]

Hans Jeschonnek was buried near Fuehrer Headquarters at Rastenburg. Goering hushed up the suicide, circulating the story that he had died a natural death due to a hemorrhage of the stomach.

CHAPTER 13

Defeat on All Fronts

General of Flyers Guenther Korten replaced Jeschonnek as chief of the General Staff of the Luftwaffe. At the time he seemed to be the ideal choice. A Prussian and a strong Nazi, he was highly respected by Milch, and Adolf Hitler also thought a lot of him.

Korten, who had just turned forty-five, was quite experienced for his age. He had entered the service when World War I broke out as a sixteen-year-old Fahnenjunker in the engineers. He remained with this branch throughout most of his pre-Luftwaffe career. He received his pilot's training in 1925 as a "sports flyer" and was involved in the secret flight training in Russia in the late 1920s, with special emphasis in aerial photography. He joined the secret Luftwaffe as a captain in 1934, as a General Staff officer working for State Secretary Milch.

Korten's rise had been rapid. He was promoted to major in 1934, lieutenant colonel in 1937, colonel in 1939, major general in 1940, lieutenant general in 1942, and general of flyers the following year, for a total of six promotions in nine years. His assignments included commander of the 122nd Reconnaissance Group (1936–37), chief of staff to the Luftwaffe Commander in Austria (1938–40), and chief of staff of II Air Corps, 3rd Air Fleet and 4th Air Fleet (1940–42), before he became Luftwaffe Commander Don on August 25, 1942. Thereafter he commanded I Air Corps and (briefly) 1st Air Fleet before being summoned to Rastenburg to replace Jeschonnek.[1] He was succeeded as commander-in-chief of 1st Air Fleet by Kurt Pflugbeil.

General Korten was an advocate of strategic bombing. Like Hitler, he believed the answer to the British terror attacks was to counterattack. He also believed in a strong fighter defense for the Reich, even if it meant depleting the units at the front. Almost immediately after assuming his new duties, he transferred six fighter squadrons from the eastern front to Germany, and by November he was withdrawing bombers and crews from Russia to Germany, where they were to be retrained for strategic bombing against England.[2] As Russian strength grew, more units were transferred west. By January 1944, the Luftwaffe had lost air parity in the East.

Korten's strategic bombing ideas were attempted too late and with obsolete and inferior aircraft with inadequate bomb loads. (Most German twin-engine bombers carried a maximum of two tons of bombs, versus six for many of the Allied four-engine bombers.) Meanwhile, the Fifteenth U.S. Air Force struck from Italy and damaged the Wiener Neustadt aircraft factories in the Austrian Alps.[3] However on August 17, the week Korten became the fifth chief of the General Staff, the Luftwaffe finally rebounded with a series of significant victories over its American opponents.

That day, 376 U.S. heavy bombers from the Eighth Air Force took off from England and headed for the Messerschmitt plant at Regensburg and the ball-bearing plant at Schweinfurt on the Main River in northern Bavaria. Both targets were deep inside the Reich. The bombers were accompanied as far as Aachen by U.S. P-47 "Thunderbolt" fighters. The Luftwaffe waited until the short-range escorts had to return to base due to low fuel and then fell on the bombers, using Wild Boar tactics. Although Regensburg was extensively damaged and 400 Messerschmitt employees were killed, 60 American bombers were shot down and 138 seriously damaged: a 52 percent casualty ratio.[4]

The R.A.F. was also suffering from the new, free-for-all Luftwaffe fighter tactics. They lost fifty-six bombers on the night of August 24, although they smashed the southern section of Berlin, especially the suburb of Lankwitz. They came again on the night of the thirty-first, but their formations were attacked from as far afield as Denmark and central France and were largely dispersed by the time they reached the capital. Forty-seven more bombers were lost. The third attack in the series came on the night of September 2, and twenty-two more British Lancaster bombers were shot down. Damage to Berlin factories in this raid was minimal.[5]

A meaningful event for the Luftwaffe occurred on September 27, when British ground forces took the excellent Italian airports in the vicinity of Foggia. Within seventy-two hours the Fifteenth U.S. Air Force had set up residence within easy range of Austria. On October 1 it resumed daylight precision bombing on the Messerschmitt factories at Wiener Neustadt with devastating accuracy. "When the Americans lay down their carpet of bombs somewhere," Field Marshal Milch commented, "then anything beneath is pretty well matchwood." Wiener Neustadt was struck again on the second, and Frankfurt was attacked on October 4.[6]

The Eighth U.S.A.F. resumed its daylight attacks on the interior of the Reich on October 8, with raids on Bremen and Vegesack. Thirty bombers fell victim to Galland's fighters, who were now attacking the bombers from the forward hemisphere. This method of attack was invented by Col. Egon

Mayer and Maj. Georg-Peter Eder, the commanders of JG 2 "Richthofen" and II/JG 26, respectively. It required a great deal of skill and nerve, as the rate of closure was about 600 miles per hour, and there were incidents of collisions between American bombers and attacking Messerschmitts. But the new tactics, with their rapid and difficult angle of approach, kept the enemy waist and tail gunners from firing and gave the American forward gunners little time to react. Using this method, the twenty-six-year-old Mayer became the first pilot on the western front to score 100 victories. He had 102 confirmed kills when he met his death attacking a U.S. B-17 formation on March 2, 1944. The fearless Eder was luckier. Although he was shot down seventeen times and wounded twelve times, he shot down seventy-eight enemy airplanes (thirty-six of them four-engine bombers) and survived the war. He also destroyed three Sherman tanks and had eighteen unconfirmed kills.[7]

Meanwhile, the American raids continued. On October 9 attacks against Marienburg, Danzig, Gdynia, and Anklam resulted in the destruction of 90 percent of the Focke-Wulf aircraft works, at a cost of twenty-eight more American bombers. On October 10, thirty more U.S. bombers were shot down in an attack against Muenster by waves of attacking FW-190s, Me-109s, Me-110s, and Ju-88s. All twelve of the U. S. 100th Bombardment Group's B-17s were shot down. The Americans had lost eighty-eight bombers and almost nine hundred men in three days.[8]

October 14, 1943, was "Black Thursday" for the United States Air Force, which resumed its offensive by sending 291 bombers against the ball-bearing plant at Schweinfurt. This time almost the entire Reich fighter defensive force of 1,100 aircraft was concentrated within eighty-five miles of their flight path. The American fighter escort peeled off at the German border and the bombers were promptly attacked by waves of single- and twin-engine fighters firing rockets, machine guns, and 20mm and 30mm cannons. The German short-range fighters were close enough to their bases to refuel and return to the battle. The American bombers continued despite their heavy casualties and dropped their loads on the ball-bearing plant. As they returned to base they were subjected to renewed and repeated attacks. One eighteen-plane bomber formation could bring 200 heavy machine guns to bear on its attackers, so Galland also suffered casualties (twenty-five aircraft); nevertheless 60 bombers were shot down and 138 others seriously damaged—a 62 percent casualty rate. The Luftwaffe only lost thirty-eight fighters. It was a major defeat for the Allied airmen, who realized now that their daylight air superiority only extended over the fringes of German airspace.[9]

The Luftwaffe's Schweinfurt victory was marred by the destruction of the ball-bearing plant. Unlike during the previous raid, the flak commander failed to turn on the smoke generators in time, because he had wanted to test them first. Goering remarked that he intended to "round up the most monumental idiots" and add them to his staff "so that by consultation with them I can get some expert idea of what this or that idiot in the field might get up to."[10]

The Luftwaffe underwent another command shake-up in the fall of 1943. General Kammhuber, who opposed the Wild Boar tactics and who had gotten Goering into trouble with Hitler again by pressing for more fighter aircraft, among other things, was sent to Norway as commander of the 5th Air Fleet. Stumpff left Oslo and took charge of the newly created Air Fleet Reich. He replaced General Weise, who was rightly held as largely responsible for the Hamburg debacle. The XII Air Corps was redesignated I Fighter Corps and placed under General Beppo Schmid, the former chief intelligence officer of the Luftwaffe. Schmid was given the 1st, 2nd, 3rd, and 7th Fighter Divisions, while Field Marshal Sperrle's 3rd Air Fleet in France got II Fighter Corps (4th and 5th Fighter Divisions).[11] With this organization the Luftwaffe fought the second phase of the Battle of Berlin, which lasted from November 18, 1943, to March 24, 1944.

The first British attack was a heavy raid on Berlin, on the night of November 18, followed by similar attacks on the nights of the twenty-second and twenty-third. The raid on the twenty-second was particularly successful, as it killed 3,500 people, left another 400,000 homeless, destroyed Speer's Armaments Ministry Building and the army's Armaments Office. During this phase of the Allied air offensive, Berlin was attacked sixteen times (excluding harassment raids), and nineteen major attacks were conducted against other German cities. Ludwigshafen, Leverkusen, Frankfurt, Stettin, Brunswick, Magdeburg, Schweinfurt, Augsburg, Essen, and Nuremberg were all heavily bombed. In all, 20,224 sorties were flown, but 1,047 bombers were shot down by the Luftwaffe: an unacceptable casualty rate for the Allies.[12]

In late 1943, during this battle, the Luftwaffe made operational a device that improved the Ju-88R's night-fighting capabilities by injecting nitrous-oxide gas into its engine. This appreciably increased the R.A.F.'s casualty lists. For about a month in fact, beginning on December 20, they focused their attentions on the V-weapons launching sites in France instead of against German cities.[13] The respite was short-lived, however, because on January 11, 1944, the Americans resumed their strategic daytime assaults on German fighter factories. On that day 663 U.S. bombers attacked the factories at Halberstadt, Brunswick, Magdeburg, and Oschersleben. Most of their aircraft, however, were forced to turn back due to bad weather, allowing the defenders

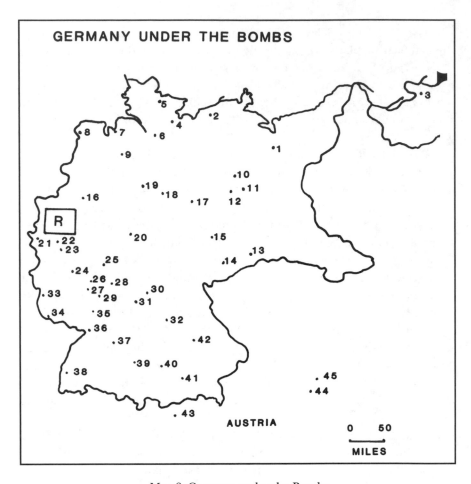

GERMANY UNDER THE BOMBS

Map 8: Germany under the Bombs

1. Stettin	13. Dresden	25. Giessen	36. Karlsruhe
2. Rostock	14. Chemnitz	26. Wiesbaden	37. Stuttgart
3. Koenigsberg	15. Leipzig	27. Mainz	38. Freiburg
4. Luebeck	16. Muenster	28. Frankfurt am	39. Ulm
5. Kiel	17. Magdelburg	Main	40. Augsburg
6. Hamburg	18. Brunswick	29. Darmstadt	41. Munich
7. Bremerhaven	19. Hanover	30. Schweinfurt	42. Regensburg
8. Wilhelmshaven	20. Kassel	31. Wursburg	43. Innsbruck
9. Bremen	21. Aachen	32. Nuremburg	44. Wiener-Neustadt
10. Oranienburg	22. Cologne	33. Trier	45. Vienna
11. Berlin	23. Bonn	34. Saarbrucken	
12. Potsdam	24. Koblenz	35. Mannheim	

R = The Ruhr (including Essen, Bochum, Geisenkirchen, Dortmund, Oberhausen, Munchen, Wuppertal, Elberfeld, and Dusseldorf) to concentrate against the remainder. The Eighth U.S.A.F. lost fifty-nine bombers and five fighter escorts against forty downed fighters for the Luftwaffe.[14] The United States could afford these losses, however, as American industry was producing two aircraft for every one shot down.

The R.A.F. was back in strength on the night of January 20, dropping 2,400 tons of bombs on Berlin. The next night they shattered Magdeburg. Despite the loss of 130 bombers in three nights, they kept coming, as did the Americans.[15]

The "Big Week" for Gen. Carl Spaatz's strategic air offensive began on February 20. The strategic group included the U.S. Eighth and Fifteenth air forces, commanded by Lt. Gen. James H. Doolittle and Maj. Gen. Nathan F. Twining, respectively. (The other American air forces in Europe—the Ninth and Twelfth—were now tactical units. The Twelfth was supporting Allied ground units in Italy, while the Ninth U.S.A.F. was preparing to support the D-Day invasion.) The objective of the strategic air offensive was ambitious in the extreme: destroy the Luftwaffe's capabilities to manufacture fighter aircraft. Between them the Eighth and Fifteenth U.S. air forces had sixteen wings of heavy bombers (1,028 Flying Fortresses and Liberators) plus 832 fighter escorts, augmented by sixteen Spitfire and Mustang squadrons on loan from the R.A.F. Their main target was the mammoth Messerschmitt complex near Leipzig, where 32 percent of all Me-109s were built, as well as eleven other targets, including the Ju-88, Ju-188, and Ju-52 plants at Bernburg, the Me-109 plants at Wiener Neustadt, the Messerschmitt factory at Regensburg, the Me-110 plants at Brunswick and Gotha, the FW-190 plants at Tutow and Oschersleben, and the He-111 bomber complex at Rostock.[16]

This time the Americans changed their tactics completely. They had with them large numbers of P-51 Mustangs, a long-range fighter capable of escorting the bombers all the way to their targets and back. The Americans were now looking for aerial battles instead of avoiding them.

On the first day, U.S. saturation bombing destroyed the Leipzig complex. By the time the Big Week ended on February 25 (five days earlier than planned, due to weather conditions), the U.S. air forces had dropped 10,000 tons of bombs on targets accounting for 90 percent of Germany's aircraft production. An additional 9,200 tons had been dropped at night on the ball-bearing centers of Stuttgart, Steyr, Schweinfurt, and others. The Anglo-Americans lost almost 300 bombers, but several plants were 75 percent destroyed. The Messerschmitt plant at Regensburg had been completely destroyed. Three hundred fifty completed but undelivered Me-109s had been lost at Leipzig alone; 200 more were destroyed at Wiener Neustadt and 150 more at other factories. Ju-88 production was cut in half and twin-engine fighter production was temporarily reduced to zero. Unfortunately, no reports on the decline in single-engine fighter production during Big Week seem to have survived the war.[17]

Still the raids continued. Galland reported: "Between January and April, 1944, our daytime fighters lost over 1,000 pilots. They included our best squadron, Gruppe and Geschwader commanders. Each incursion of the enemy is costing us some 50 aircrew. The time has come when our weapon is in sight of collapse.[18] OKL expressly forbade the withdrawal of fighter units from the eastern front, so Galland secretly ordered every *Gruppe* in Russia and Norway to give up one *Staffel* (i.e., one-third to one-fourth of its strength) for the defense of the Reich. Apparently these transfers were not noticed by the Luftwaffe High Command.[19] Once again, however, the frontline units were weakened.

Galland's expedient measures could not prevent the demise of the fighter arm. By the end of May, 1944, the Jagdwaffe had fewer than 250 single-engine fighters left for the defense of Germany. By that time, the Allies had 1,000 long-range fighters and thousands of bombers and short-range fighters to send against them.[20]

Goering's reaction to the American air offensive was typical. Right in the middle of the Big Week, he left for his castle at Veldenstein to begin a three-week leave. Of the Reichsmarschall at this time, Mosley wrote: "In the months that followed, Hermann Goering played little part in the darkening destiny of the German Reich. Like a suddenly ignited rocket, he would fizz unexpectedly through the sky, scattering sparks and making loud noises, and then he would be seen no more for weeks at a time."[21]

While Goering was vacationing at his family castle, the Americans bombed Berlin five times, on March 4, 6, 8, 9, and 22. The R.A.F. was also active, dropping more than 3,000 tons of bombs on Frankfurt on the night of the ninth alone.[22] Augsburg, Stuttgart, and Nuremberg were also heavily bombed, and thousands of tons of bombs were dropped on the V-weapons sites, then under construction in France and Belgium, as well as the U-boat bases in France. By the end of March, only 20,000 people remained in Cologne. Its prewar population had been 800,000.[23]

The advent of the Mustang was a turning point in the air war. It forced Galland and the other fighter commanders to engage the Allied bomber formations earlier in their approach routes. This, in turn, allowed the Allies to meet them with not only their Mustangs but with short-range Spitfires, Thunderbolts, and P-38 Lightnings as well. The attrition rate was soon beginning to tell, especially among the pilots. It was the loss of veteran aviators, more than any other single factor, that caused the demise of the Luftwaffe. Twenty-three-year-old Maj. Walter Nowotny, holder of the Knights Cross with Oak Leaves, Swords, and Diamonds, was shot down over Germany in one of the first Me-262 jets, with a host of Mustangs on his tail like "a pack of hounds" and was reported as killed in action on November 11, 1944. At the time of his death, Nowotny had 258 confirmed and 23 unconfirmed victories. Maj. Horst Ademeit, winner of 166 aerial combats, went down over Russia on August 8, 1944, killed by infantry fire; Col. Helmut Lent, one of the leading night fighters, had 110 kills when he died in action on October 7, 1944. The list goes on: Lt. Hans Beisswenger, 152 kills, died March 6, 1943; Maj. Kurt Braendle, 180 kills, died November 3, 1943; Lt. Anton Hafner, 204 victories, killed in action October 17, 1944, when he hit a tree during a low-level battle against the Russians; Capt. Joachim Kirschner, 188 kills, shot down over Croatia and captured by Communist partisans, who murdered him on December 17, 1943; Lt. Franz Schwaiger, 67 victories, killed by a Mustang pilot on April 24, 1944; Capt. Emil Lang, CO of II/JG 26, who once shot down seventy-two opponents in three weeks (including eighteen in one day—a record that still stands), 173 aerial victories, killed over France by U.S. Thunderbolts on June 29, 1944; Lt. Hans-Joachim Birkner, 117 kills, died when his engine failed during a takeoff from Krakow airfield in Poland, December 14, 1944; Col. Wolf-Dietrich Wilcke, commander of 3d Fighter Wing "Udet," 162 victories, shot down and killed by Mustangs on March 23, 1944; Col. Walter Oesau, commander of JG 1, 123 victories, killed by Lightnings over the Rhineland, May 11, 1944; Lt. Col. Hans Philip, 206 kills, shot down by Thunderbolts on October 8, 1943; Capt. Max Stotz, 189 kills, died on the eastern front, August 19, 1943; Albin Wolf, 144 kills, downed by anti-aircraft fire on the eastern front, 1944; Kurt Ueben, 110 victories, shot down by Thunderbolts, 1944; Maj. Joseph Wurmheller, 102 kills, died on the western front, June 22, 1944; Leopold Muenster, 95 kills, died in 1944 when he deliberately rammed a B-17; Capt. Heinrich Sturm, 158 aerial victories, killed on the eastern front, December 22, 1944.[24] And there were others: Stuka pilots with hundreds of destroyed armored vehicles to their credit, night fighters with dozens of victories, transport pilots who had braved the flak at Kholm, Demyansk, and Stalingrad, and bomber pilots with hundreds of sorties in their logbooks. The Luftwaffe, with its training system sacrificed to former expediencies, simply could not replace these men.

The Battle of Berlin ended with a British raid on Nuremberg. It was a Luftwaffe victory. Of the 795 Allied planes involved, 95 were shot down and 71 badly damaged. After that, Germany's cities were given a four-month respite while most of the allied air units turned their attention to the tasks of destroying the French transportation system, isolating and then sealing off the Normandy beachhead, supporting the D-Day invasion, and destroying the Nazi synthetic oil industry. There was no respite for the battered Luftwaffe, however. On Goering's orders, and at Hitler's insistence, it launched the so-called

"Baby Blitz" on London from January 21 to May 29, 1944. The British capital was struck by twenty-nine separate raids with an average strength of 200 aircraft per raid. When it began, the Attack Command England (Angriffsfuehrer England) had 462 operational aircraft. It had only 107 when the offensive ended, with nothing of substance accomplished.[25] There was, however, one major personal victory for Hermann Goering: he finally managed to rid himself of his deputy and would-be successor, Erhard Milch.

✠

"When Milch pisses," Paul Koerner said, "ice comes out."[26] In early 1943 Milch was at the peak of his influence at Fuehrer Headquarters and near the peak of his powers. He was state secretary of the Air Ministry, deputy commander-in-chief of the Luftwaffe, inspector general of the Luftwaffe, director of air armament, and chairman of the Board of Directors of Lufthansa. Now, he decided, was his chance to depose the Reichsmarschall and seize control of the Luftwaffe himself. The field marshal overestimated his new prestige, however, and overplayed his hand politically. On March 5 he dined with Hitler and recommended that Goering be forced to resign as C-in-C of the Luftwaffe. Whom he had in mind to replace the Reichsmarschall is not too difficult for us to guess.[27] Hitler, however, made no changes, and Goering's long-held suspicions were confirmed: Milch was out to replace him.

Not long after Stalingrad, Hitler revoked the Luftwaffe's industrial priority. A much greater percentage of Germany's available raw materials now flowed to the army, which used them to produce panzers, artillery, assault guns, shells, and other weapons. Many of Milch's formerly protected workers ended up in the ranks of the army, which was already undergoing severe manpower shortages at the front. By year's end, 90 percent of the aircraft industry was not able to work a second shift, due to a shortage of labor in the factories.[28]

Like many of the other field marshals, Milch no longer had the resources to accomplish his mission. He tried to compensate for his shortages in workers and material by speeding up the production of the V-1 rocket, whose development he had finally authorized in 1942.[29] Army Field Marshal Walter von Brauchitsch had called for its development long before. The V-weapons were successful but would come off the production lines too late to save Germany—or Milch, whose career began its inevitable decline.

After not seeing him for weeks, Goering summoned Milch to Rominten, his East Prussian hunting lodge, on July 2, 1943. In the presence of other generals and field marshals, the C-in-C and his deputy had an angry clash. At one point, Goering asked Milch if he actually thought that he (Goering) read

Milch's reports, which he called "rags." Milch coldly replied that if that were the case, it would be useless for him to make further trips as inspector general of the Luftwaffe. The Reichsmarschall replied that he need not bother, as far as he was concerned. Milch, furious and clearly out of favor, returned to Berlin.[30] His influence continued to diminish.

In July 1943, the R.A.F. levelled Hamburg. On August 2, after inspecting the damage, Milch bluntly cried to Dr. Goebbels: "We have lost the war!"[31] In vain did Milch try to convince Goering and Hitler to concentrate their fighter strength for the defense of the Reich, instead of at the front. He was also unable to prevent further manpower raids on the Luftwaffe's reserved workers. He had another terrible row with Goering at the latter's mansion, Karinhall, in October. Goering was becoming more and more jealous and suspicious of Milch, as Hitler began to criticize both the Reichsmarschall and the Luftwaffe more and more severely.

Goering, of course, realized that Milch was again angling to replace him. In 1943 he told General Kreipe: "First he wanted to play the part of my crown prince. Now he wants to be my usurper."[32] In late 1943, he began to curb Milch's power again by creating the Office of the Chief of Personnel Armament, which consolidated all Luftwaffe personnel matters under one bureau. Goering's old comrade from the Great War, Col. Gen. Bruno Loerzer, was named to fill the post. The new chief was directly subordinate to Goering. Worse than this for Milch, a new star was rising in the Nazi heirarchy. Albert Speer, the former architect, had been named minister of armaments and war production after Dr. Fritz Todt was killed in an air crash on February 8, 1942.[33] Speer was showing true genius in this post, and he was gradually eclipsing Milch. Karl-Otto Saur, Speer's chief assistant, was taking over Luftwaffe plants and diverting air force resources to other uses.

Milch's ambitious aircraft production program also went aground in late 1943, when the worst drought in ninety years hit occupied Europe. Hydroelectric power losses caused serious declines in the output of nitrogen, high-grade steel, synthetic fuel, and aluminum. Oil importation also dropped parallel with the level of the Danube River. Germany's oil came from Rumania by barge. The low water level forced the barges to reduce their loads from 700 tons per trip to 300. The 144,000 tons of petroleum Germany received in October 1943, declined to 80,000 tons the following month.[34] Without this supply of energy, Milch was unable to meet his goals, at a time when his prestige badly needed the boost—for Milch sensed that his days in power were numbered.

In desperation, like Udet before him, Milch gambled. In November, he ordered Volkswagen to begin mass production of the Fi-103 flying bomb, despite severe technological problems in the prototypes. This was the same type of gamble Udet had taken with the Ju-88 and Me-210 in the winter of 1940–41, and with the same result. Two thousand of the flying bombs were partially finished when it was discovered that their structure was too weak.[35] Precious man-hours and resources had been wasted—again.

Milch now began to give ground, hoping to retain at least part of his power. On February 23, 1944, he agreed to the creation of the Fighter Staff. Its objective was to disperse and reorganize fighter aircraft production in tunnels, caves, and bomb-proof factories. Karl-Otto Saur would be in charge of the new organization. This step represented a major concession and loss of power for Milch, but at least now, with Saur in charge, he would no longer be able to raid aircraft factories for workers.[36]

On November 26, 1943, a demonstration of the Me-262—one of the first jets—was held at Insterburg Airfield. Hitler, in the presence of Goering and Milch, asked if the Me-262 could carry bombs. Before anyone could stop him, Professor Willy Messerschmitt answered that they could carry one 1,000- or two 500-kilo bombs without any trouble (i.e., without design modification). Neither Goering nor Milch said anything. Goering may not have known that this projection was wrong, but Milch certainly did; nevertheless he remained silent, for he did not wish to incur the Fuehrer's disfavor. As a result of the new requirement, jet aircraft production had to be set back several months.[37] The Me-262 fighter-bomber would not be ready when the Allies landed in Normandy on June 6, 1944.

Milch attended a Fuehrer conference on January 4, 1944. It was the first one he had been invited to in months—a sure indication of disfavor in Nazi Germany. Hitler discussed his plans for repelling the Allied invasion, and the use of the Me-262 as a fighter-bomber figured prominently in those plans. No doubt fearing for his increasingly deteriorating position, Milch again kept his mouth shut, letting Hitler think the Me-262 would be available as a fighter-bomber, when he knew it would not be.[38]

For Erhard Milch, the day of reckoning for his silence came at the Berghof on the afternoon of May 23, 1944. Col. Edgar Peterson, the director of Luftwaffe Research Establishments, was briefing Hitler on the Me-262 program. Goering, Speer, Saur, Milch, and Galland were also present. Peterson referred to the jet as a fighter. Hitler interrupted, saying he thought the Me-262 was coming out as a high-speed bomber. How many, the Fuehrer wanted to know, had been manufactured as bombers? All eyes turned to Milch, who was finally forced to admit that none had been. Hitler was stunned. After an awkward silence, Milch explained to the Fuehrer that the Me-262 could not carry bombs without extensive design modifications, and even then bombs weighing over about 1,000 pounds could not be used.

Hitler exploded. He wanted a fighter-bomber. He had expected a fighter-bomber. He had been led to believe that he would receive a fighter-bomber.

He had been deceived. He subjected Milch, Goering, and Galland to a torrent of verbal abuse. He upbraided them as unreliable, insubordinate, and even treasonable. Milch tried to speak again, but Hitler shouted him down. He then turned away from Milch and refused to speak to him during the rest of the conference. When Milch left for Berlin that evening, his career was wrecked. Shortly afterwards, Hitler withdrew his directive earmarking Milch as Goering's successor.[39] The Allied invasion was now only two weeks away.

As a result of this conference, Hitler transferred the entire jet program away from the Fighter Branch and gave it to the general of bomber forces. "The fighter arm and the defense of the Reich, which had seen in the jet fighter the savior from an untenable situation, now had to bury all hopes," Galland commented.[40] Hitler did not authorize the creation of the first jet fighter wing until Reichsfuehrer-SS Heinrich Himmler (who was meddling in Luftwaffe affairs) recommended it. This wing, JG 7, was formed under the command of Col. Johannes Steinhoff in November, 1944—too late to have any influence on the air war, or on Erhard Milch's career.[41]

Now that Milch no longer had the support of the Fuehrer, Goering wasted no time in stripping him of his power. On May 27 he agreed to transfer the entire air armaments program from Milch to Saur. On June 20, in Hitler's presence, Goering ordered Milch to resign as director of air armaments. He would also have to resign as secretary of state for aviation, although he would retain his post as inspector general of the Luftwaffe, to keep the news of their intragovernmental dispute from becoming public. Milch resigned the next day. On June 30, 1944, Milch made a bitter farewell speech to his staff, in which he blamed the reorganization on the intrigues and obstructionism of Speer and Saur and on the Allied bombing campaign—not because of any failure on the part of the Luftwaffe or the Office of Air Armaments. Milch now went into semiretirement in his lakeside hunting lodge.[42]

Speer named Milch his deputy for armaments and war production and plenipotentiary for armaments in the Four Year Plan. Hitler agreed to this move, and Goering did not object, but the appointment was tokenism, without any real power. Milch took it as an indication of Speer's guilty conscience for his role in Milch's downfall.[43] It was not like Erhard Milch to blame himself for anything.

After the July 20, 1944, attempt on Hitler's life failed, Milch sent him a message of congratulations. He even called the conspirators "vermin" on the witness stand at Nuremberg.

Milch continued to make inspection trips until October 1, 1944, when his car skidded at high speed on the road near Arnhem, ran into the woods and hit a tree. Milch woke up in the hospital, with broken ribs and lung damage. He lay immobilized in his hunting lodge until early 1945, but showed up unexpectedly at Karinhall on January 12, to congratulate Goering on his fifty-second birthday. The Reichsmarschall was surprised and very unpleasant. Three days later Milch found out why: he received a week-old letter from Goering, dismissing him from his last office, inspector general of the Luftwaffe.[44] He was placed in Fuehrer Reserve and remained there for the rest of the war.

✠

Erhard Milch was not the only high-ranking member of the Luftwaffe to fall from power in 1944. Field Marshal Hugo Sperrle, the commander-in-chief of the 3rd Air Fleet, was sacked as well—and with considerably more justification.

Sperrle became more and more disillusioned over Hitler's and Goering's conduct of the war, and this may have accelerated his own lack of interest in the war. Lt. Gen. Hans Speidel, the chief of staff of Erwin Rommel's Army Group B in France in 1944, remembered: "Sperrle was a man of unusual vitality; but the more clearly he saw the unholy disorder in Hitler's leadership, the more he expended his energies in bitter sarcasm. He tried to work with us in a comradely manner whenever he could, especially since he shared the political views of Rommel."[45]

Sperrle seems to have become more and more vain and indolent the longer he stayed in France. Considering himself a great gourmet and with a stomach to prove it, he became more interested in fine foods and wines and gambling than in the operations of his air units. His prejudice against women in the service also grew to almost insane proportions. It should have been obvious to anyone that Germany had a worker shortage by 1943. Obviously, if more women could be employed in rear-area duties, more men could be released for duties in the combat zone. Sperrle did not see things that way, however. When a female military operator answered his calls, he would throw the telephone to the floor and scream. Once, as he was out walking with Lt. Gen. Hermann Plocher, Sperrle saw a female dressed in fatigues enter a mess hall.

"Do I see right?" Sperrle asked, incredulously. "Is that a woman going into the mess hall where our heroes eat?"

Yes, Plocher replied. In fact, he knew the woman. She was a German agent who had just returned from a very dangerous mission behind enemy lines.

The field marshal, realizing that he had made a fool out of himself, was at a loss for words. He sputtered for a few moments and then said: "I know. That's what I mean. She should be eating in the General's mess."[46]

At least Hugo Sperrle was flexible.

The 3rd Air Fleet had no chance of defeating the U.S. and British air forces, who began paving the way for the Allied invasion in April 1944. As of

**TABLE 16: ORGANIZATION AND STRENGTH, 3D AIR FLEET,
MAY 31, 1944**

Unit	Aircraft Types	Strength	Operational
Air Fleet Units:			
5th Group	Night Fighters	33	17
123rd Group	Long-range recon	59	30*
13th Group	Short-range recon	30	16
Trans units	Transports	64	31
II Fighter Corps:			
4th Fighter Div	Day fighters	104	71
	Night fighters	57	29
5th Fighter Div	Day fighters	69	48
II Air Corps	Close-spt aircraft	73	55
IX Air Corps	Long-range bombs	326	150
X Air Corps	Antishipping a/c	23	20
2nd Air Div	Torpedo bombers	53	30
Totals	Fighters (all)	425	266
	Bombers (inc. antiship and torpedo)	402	200
	Transport aircraft	64	31
	Total:	891	497

*Includes long-range aircraft of 5th Group

Source: Ellis I, p. 567

May 31, Sperrle had only 891 aircraft, of which 497 were serviceable.[47] Table 16 shows his exact organization and strength. His few, understrength units faced a vast aerial armada of some fourteen thousand combat aircraft. The enemy's primary objective prior to D-Day was to seal off the battlefield and isolate Seventh Army in Normandy from its supplies and reinforcements. To accomplish this task, the French railroad network had to be smashed. Before the Allied air offensive began, the German transportation staff was running more than one hundred supply trains a day to the armies in France. By the end of April, it was only running forty-eight; and by the end of May, only twenty trains per day were operating throughout France. Rail traffic was at a standstill as all bridges over the Seine, Oise, and Meuse rivers had been destroyed or seriously damaged. By April 30 some 600 supply trains were backlogged in Germany, unable to proceed; in France, the Allied air forces were destroying up to 113 locomotives per day.[48] General Esposito wrote:

"Allied air attacks had weakened the railroad transportation system in France to the point of collapse."[49] The French highway system was in similar straits. On June 3, 1944, the Luftwaffe Operations Staff reported:

> In the area of northern France and Belgium—the zone of the invasion in the narrower sense of the word—the systematic destruction that has been carried out since March of all important junctions of the entire network—not only the main lines—has most seriously crippled the whole transport system (railway installations, including rolling stock). Similarly, Paris has been systematically cut off from long distance traffic, and the most important bridges over the lower Seine have been destroyed one after another. . . In the "intermediate zone" between the German and French-Belgian railway system "all the important through stations . . . have been put out of action for longer or shorter periods . . . In May the first bridge over the Rhine—at Duisburg—was destroyed 'according to plan' in a large scale attack."[50]

The report concluded that the rail network in the western region had been completely wrecked and that "the Reichsbahn authorities are seriously considering whether it is not useless to attempt further repair work."[51]

On D-Day, June 6, 1944, Normandy resembled a strategic island. Rommel was completely unable to bring up his panzer units quickly enough to launch a counteroffensive. Meanwhile, the Allies, with more than 5,400 fighters and 3,500 bombers, absolutely dominated the airspace above the battle zone, destroying tanks, strongpoints, supply installations, and gun emplacements. To oppose them, Sperrle had only two operational day fighter wings—JG 2 "Richthofen" and JG 26 "Schlageter."[52] Sperrle's units were only able to operate on the fringes of Eisenhower's air umbrella. His operations against the Allied naval forces were equally devoid of success.

In the critical period from June 7 through 16, for example, the Allies lost just sixty-four naval vessels. The Luftwaffe accounted for only five of these. During the period June 6–August 31, 1944, the Allies landed 2,052,299 men, 438,471 vehicles, and 3,098,259 tons of supplies in Normandy. They were supported by the 4,101 aircraft of the British Bomber, Air Defense, and Coastal commands, the British Second Tactical Air Force, and the Eighth and Ninth U. S. air forces. Meanwhile, the poorly trained pilots of the 3rd Air Fleet and Air Fleet Reich lost 644 airplanes destroyed and 1,485 damaged in flight accidents not involving combat. In combat operations they lost 3,656 airplanes (2,127 of them by 3rd Air Fleet).[53] Clearly, after five years of war, the Allies had finally achieved air superiority not only over the battlefield, but over the pilots of the Luftwaffe as well. In fact, in the latter part of June 1944, Goering met with Sperrle and promised him 800 fighter planes. Sperrle thought for a moment and then told the Reichsmarschall that he had not more than 500 fighter pilots available to fly them.

After failing to reinforce 3rd Air Fleet prior to the invasion-when Germany still had a small chance of success—Goering rushed twenty-three groups of fighters to the invasion sector after the landings were an accomplished fact. Units sent to Normandy by June 12 included III/JG 1; II/JG 2; II and III/JG 3; I and II/JG 5; II/JG 11; I and II/JG 27; II/JG 53; and I/JG 301. Most of these units were taken from home air defense, and all were ground to bits within weeks.[54] The Luftwaffe thus weakened the air defense of the Reich by committing irreplaceable fighter units to a battle of attrition, without significantly affecting the outcome of the battle in the West. One fighter pilot bitterly commented that the fighter arm followed the last shell crater.

Two weeks after D-Day, II Fighter Corps was reporting "fighter operations now only conditionally possible. Effective reconnaissance and fighter operations entirely ruled out for the invasion area. Thirty Anglo-American airfields constructed and operational in the bridgehead."[55] About the same time, the operations officer of the 3rd Air Fleet reported a general enemy air superiority of 20 to 1, which increased to 40 to 1 during major operations.[56] Baron Heinrich von Luettwitz, the commander of the 2nd Panzer Division, reported: "The Allies have total air supremacy. They bomb and shoot at anything that moves, even single vehicles and persons. Our territory is under constant observation . . . The feeling of being powerless against the enemy's aircraft . . . has a paralyzing effect . . ."[57]

Because of the massive enemy air superiority, the Allies gradually ground Rommel's divisions to bits. The Desert Fox himself was critically wounded by an enemy fighter-bomber on July 17. On July 25, 1,507 heavy bombers, 380 medium bombers, and 559 fighter bombers dropped more than 4,150 tons of bombs on the Panzer Lehr Division. Lt. Gen. Fritz Bayerlein reported 70 percent casualties, and virtually all of his tanks were destroyed.[58] The next day American armor poured through the hole in the German lines. Field Marshal Guenther von Kluge (Rommel's replacement) had positioned his reserves in the wrong place and reacted too slowly, and the Battle of Normandy was lost.

When the Anglo-Americans broke out of the Normandy bridgehead, most of the Luftwaffe ground service and signal units simply headed east as rapidly as they could. Hitler charged them with running away (with considerable justification) and held Sperrle responsible. This was the last straw. On August 19 he relieved Sperrle of his command and replaced him with Col. Gen. Otto Dessloch. A month later, on September 22, he downgraded 3rd Air Fleet and redesignated it Luftwaffe Command West.[59]

Sperrle was very much embittered after the fall of France and was no longer considered fit for important assignments. He was unemployed for the rest of the war. After the collapse of Nazi Germany, some sources, including Field Marshal Milch and General Speidel, charged that Sperrle was a scapegoat for Goering's failures in the West.[60] Field Marshal Rommel, however, expressed disappointment over the Luftwaffe in France as early as the end of 1943,[61] and David Irving described Sperrle as "indolent and harmful."[62] Suchenwirth noted that in 1944 Sperrle was unaccustomed to the rigors of war and attributed at least part of his failure in France to that fact.[63] Maj. Lionel F. Ellis, the Official British historian, summed it up well when he wrote of the Luftwaffe's battle in Normandy:

> Greatly outnumbered by the Allied air forces they had, perhaps, been as active as their strength and supremacy of Allied air forces allowed, but their resulting effort was of little account to the Allied armies. Their most effective operations were the dropping of mines in the shipping-infested waters of the assault area. The commander of the Third Air Fleet, Field Marshal Hugo Sperrle, had held that appointment during the whole of the German occupation of France, 'living soft' in Paris. He does not seem to have had any lively reaction when the Allies landed and none of his subordinates is distinguishable in the air fighting in Normandy. The war diaries of the army commands in the West have few references of the Luftwaffe that are not critical and they give no indication that Sperrle had any voice in shaping the conduct of operations.[64]

Field Marshal Sperrle was captured by the British on May 1, 1945.[65] He was tried at Nuremberg for war crimes, but on October 27, 1948, he was acquitted of all charges. Officially denazified June 9, 1949,[66] he moved to Munich. Here he lived quietly (although bitter and depressed) until his death on April 2, 1953.[67] He was buried in Munich on April 7.[68]

As the Luftwaffe's position continued to deteriorate, General Korten was, predictably, in trouble with Hermann Goering. Their former close relationship had cooled by late 1943 as the Reichsmarschall lashed out at Korten, just as he had done with Jeschonnek. Korten privately confided to Milch that he planned to resign by August 1944, at the latest. On July 20 he attended a Fuehrer conference at Rastenburg. Also present was army colonel Count Claus von Stauffenberg, the chief of staff of the Replacement Army, a leader in the anti-Hitler conspiracy. The one-armed, one-eyed count had a bomb in his briefcase. He set it to detonate and then left the room.

When the bomb exploded, General Korten was leaning over the table, pointing to a map. He was probably within four feet of the bomb when it went off. Hitler, the target of the assassination, was painfully but not seriously injured. Although initially reported as only slightly wounded, Korten was in fact very seriously injured.[69] A wooden splinter from the table had lodged in his abdomen, and for five days he hung between life and death.[70] He expired on July 25, 1944, only two days after his promotion to colonel general.[71] Karl Bodenschatz, Goering's liaison officer to Fuehrer Headquarters, was also seriously wounded in the legs by the blast.

Hitler proposed that Korten be succeeded by Col. Gen. Ritter von Greim, but Goering would not hear of it, so he appointed Lt. Gen. Werner Kreipe instead. The Reichsmarschall also took the opportunity to rid himself of Korten's chief of operations, Maj. Gen. Karl Koller, whom he did not like, and replace him with Maj. Gen. Eckhardt Christian.[72]

Kreipe was another young officer who had risen rapidly. Born in Hanover in 1904, he was too young to serve in World War I. He enlisted in the 6th Prussian Artillery Regiment in 1922 and first came under fire in November 1923, when, as a young Nazi, he participated in Hitler's Beer Hall Putsch. Commissioned in 1925, he did his flight training in Bavaria from 1928 to 1930. He joined the Luftwaffe in 1934 as a captain and was assigned to the Command Office of RLM as a General Staff officer. Later he worked under Milch and accompanied him to France and Britain prior to the start of the war.

Promoted to major in 1937, Kreipe was commander of the 122d Reconnaissance Group when the war broke out. In the next five years he climbed to the rank of lieutenant general and was promoted to general of flyers on September 1, 1944, one month after he became the sixth chief of the Luftwaffe General Staff. In the meantime he served as commander of the 2d Bomber Wing in the French campaign of 1940 and in the early stages of the Battle of Britain (1940), was on Sperrle's staff (1940), was chief of the Development Office at RLM (1940–41), and was Sperrle's chief of operations from February to November, 1941. Promoted to lieutenant colonel in 1940, he went to Russia in November, 1941, as chief of staff of I Air Corps. He later served as chief of staff of Korten's Luftwaffe Command Don before returning to Berlin as chief of training.[73]

Kreipe would probably have made an excellent chief of staff had he been left to his own devices. Hitler, however, was now interfering in the internal affairs of the Luftwaffe, as he had been doing with the army since 1938. He had not done this in the early years of the war—until Goering had proven himself incompetent. By 1944, however, Hitler was hamstringing the Luftwaffe. Stumpff, for example, complained that he could not move even a single AA gun without permission from Rastenburg. Kreipe tried to alleviate this situation. An enthusiastic supporter of the Me-262 jet fighter, Kreipe also tried to get Hitler to reverse himself on the issue of using the Me-262 as a fighter-bomber. The result was several heated arguments between the Fuehrer and the young chief of staff. By this point in the war, Hitler wanted only yes-men around him, and this the youthful Hanoverian definitely was not. On August 30, Kreipe noted in his diary: "In growing temper he [Hitler] made short work of me. Now I was stabbing him in the back as well! Irresponsible elements in the Luftwaffe like Milch and Galland talked me into it!"[74]

In mid-September, 12,000 civilians were killed in a half-an-hour raid that destroyed that heart of Darmstadt. As a result, Hitler considered replacing Goering with Col. Gen. Ritter Robert von Greim. He was so angry at the Luftwaffe that he banned General Kreipe from Fuehrer Headquarters, although how he managed to blame Kreipe for this disaster is anybody's guess. Since Goering was now afraid to go near Hitler and only appeared at Rastenburg when summoned, and General Bodenschatz was still recovering from his wounds, a command vacuum existed between the Luftwaffe and the High Command. Only General Christian represented the air force at Fuehrer Headquarters.

The Hitler-Kreipe arguments climaxed on September 18, when the chief of staff was asked to submit his resignation.[75] Oddly enough, Kreipe's career did not end here. He remained at his post for several weeks, until a suitable replacement could be found. Then, on December 5, 1944, he became commandant of the Air War Academy in Berlin, which was responsible for training Luftwaffe General Staff officers. After the war he was employed by the West German Traffic Ministry.[76]

The seventh and last chief of the General Staff of the Luftwaffe was General of Flyers Karl Koller, who replaced Kreipe on November 27. Goering's first choice for the post had been Col. Gen. Kurt Pflugbeil, the commander of the 1st Air Fleet in Russia, but his reply to the offer had been uncompromising: he refused to accept the job under any circumstances.[77] Perhaps Pflugbeil later regretted this decision. He surrendered his air fleet to the Russians in May 1945, and died in a Soviet prison camp ten years later. He never saw Germany again.

Karl Koller was born in Bavaria in 1898 and entered the army when World War I broke out. He was sixteen years old at the time. Nevertheless he became a pilot in 1917 and flew on the western front. Discharged in 1919, he joined the Bavarian State Police in 1920 and remained there for sixteen years. He reentered the service as a major in the Luftwaffe in 1936, attended the Air War Academy, became operations officer of Luftwaffe Group 3 (later 3rd Air Fleet) in 1938, and was moved up to chief of staff of the 3d in 1941. After serving on the eastern front, he became chief of operations at OKL in 1943. Despite his solid but rather undistinguished record, Koller had been promoted rapidly: lieutenant colonel (1939), colonel (1941), major general (1943), and general of flyers (November 27, 1944). He bypassed the rank of lieutenant general altogether.[78]

The uninspiring Koller's tenure as chief of the General Staff was undistinguished, but it is doubtful that even a brilliant, charismatic leader could have made much difference against the vast air armada that was leveling the German cities and grinding her depleted ground divisions into bits. The cities of the Reich were given a respite in April and early May, and to a lesser extent until after D-Day, for the Anglo-American air units were busy pulverizing the French transportation system and sealing off the Normandy battlefield. However, they still managed to concentrate against the German oil industry and, after D-Day, they resumed their raids on German cities on an unprecedented scale.

The destruction of the German oil industry began on May 12, 1944, when 935 heavy bombers of the Eighth U.S. Air Force, with massive British and American fighter support, bombed the German synthetic oil plants at Zwickau, Merseburg-Leuna, Bruex, Luetzkendorf, Bohlen, and others.[79] In all, twenty synthetic oilworks were attacked. They had a total production capacity of 374,000 tons of fuel per month, including 175,000 tons of aviation fuel.[80] Forty-six bombers and ten Allied fighters were shot down, but Luftwaffe fighter losses were almost as high, and all the oil plants were destroyed or severely damaged.[81]

On May 23, Albert Speer and his "crisis manager," Hans Kehrl, met with Goering and Hitler. Calling the flak defenses ineffective, they set forth the dire consequences for the German war effort if effective fighter protection was not provided for the defense of the fuel industry. The Fuehrer and Reichsmarschall remained unconvinced. Within three weeks they stripped the Reich of the bulk of its fighter defense and sent it to Normandy, but the raids against the fuel industry continued. "The loss of the struggle for oil refineries was the 'Stalingrad' of the German war production," Beck wrote later.[82]

By the end of May, German oil production had declined significantly. By September, not a single synthetic oil plant was in full operation. After that, production increased slightly, but Germany's oil famine continued until the very end, seriously affecting and sometimes dictating ground operations, especially among panzer units. Things were equally bad in the air. Synthetic output of aviation fuel, which had been 175,000 tons per month in the spring, was down to 12,000 tons per month by September, 1944, and the Ploesti oilfields in Rumania had been captured by the Russians. The oil shortage caused what Franklin called the "virtual collapse" of the night fighter arm. The statistics bear out this comment: the night-flying British Bomber Command suffered 11 percent losses in June. By August this figure was down to 3.7 percent, and the following month it suffered an even smaller casualty rate. Allied bombing, however, intensified. From July through August, 1943, the Bomber Command and Eighth U.S. Air Force had dropped 44,500 tons of bombs. Over the same period in 1944, they dropped more than 200,000 tons, not including the considerable efforts of the Fifteenth U.S. Air Force.[83]

The situation became so bad that, on September 5, Hitler went into a tirade in which he enumerated the lies he had been told about production figures and aircraft performance year after year. He ended the outburst by announcing his decision to disband the Luftwaffe as a separate arm of the service. Only a private discussion with Goering changed his mind, and only then because the Reichsmarschall managed to provide new parachute regiments to plug the gap then existing between the Seventh Army and the North Sea.[84] Goering himself only managed to keep his job because he was Hitler's designated successor and the Fuehrer could never quite forget the dashing World War ace who had fallen beside him at the Feldherrnhalle more than twenty years before.

Because of Hitler's increasingly hostile attitude, Goering took to imitating General Galland. When Hitler was mad at him (which was more often than not those days), he would appear at Fuehrer Headquarters for conferences he could not avoid dressed very simply, without decorations, and with a terrible-looking hat perched on his head.[85]

Hitler was, in fact, growing more and more publicly critical of Goering and expressing himself more and more rudely. "Goering!" he yelled at one conference, "Your Luftwaffe isn't worth a damn! It doesn't deserve to be an independent branch of the service any more. And that's your fault! You're lazy!" Tears of shame streamed down Goering's cheeks, but he couldn't think of anything to say.[86]

✠

As the enemy armies advanced on both the eastern and western fronts, a deep sense of gloom descended across Germany. "No longer was there any relief from the hardships of the overly strenuous work, the fear of the next bombing raid, the struggle to keep outworn clothing wearable . . ." Beck recorded.[87] The cities were characterized by ruins and rubble, lice, and rats. The danger of strafing was now added to the peril of bombing, and the distances from the enemy air bases to the German cities were so short that raids were now frequently conducted in the early morning, at the lunch hour, and in the mid-afternoon. The enemy now had so many airplanes that they attacked any convenient target, including individual farmhouses and cattle in the fields. Meanwhile, Gen. of Fighter Forces Adolf Galland came up with a plan to turn the tables on the Allied bombers in one massive stroke.

Lt. Gen. Adolf Galland was the leading figure among the German fighter pilots in the second half of the war. Born in Westerholt, Westphalia, in 1912, he was the descendent of a family of Huguenots who fled France to escape religious persecution. This accounts for his French name. An early glider enthusiast, he enrolled in Alfred Keller's German Air School (in reality a secret air force pilots' training base) at Braunschweig in 1932. After crashing a plane and injuring an eye, he should have been washed out of the program for failing his flight physical. He memorized the eye chart, however, and passed every subsequent exam. He completed his advanced flight training in Grotaglia, Italy, and briefly served as a flight instructor for the secret Luftwaffe. Assigned to the 10th Infantry Regiment and the Dresden War Academy in 1934, he underwent officer training and was commissioned Leutnant on January 1, 1935.

Second Lieutenant Galland did his fighter pilot's training in 1935 and was posted to the Richthofen wing (later JG 2), where he served as pilot, training officer, and technical officer. Sent to Spain in May, 1937, he commanded 3/J/88—the close support squadron of the Condor Legion. Because this unit was equipped with obsolete He-51 biplanes, he scored no victories in the civil war. He was a squadron commander in II/LG 2 when the war broke out, and, as part of Richthofen's division, flew Hs-123 ground attack aircraft in support of the panzer spearheads during the Polish campaign. He was promoted to captain on October 1, 1939.

Galland transferred to the 27th Fighter Wing in the winter of 1939–40 and, after scoring several victories in France, assumed command of III/JG 26 in June, 1940. He was promoted to major and awarded the Knights Cross on July 19, 1940. He was named commander of the 26th Fighter Wing on August 22, 1940.

Adolf Galland distinguished himself as a fighter pilot and a wing leader on the western front in 1940 and 1941. On May 1, 1941, he shot down his seventieth victim and was himself shot down. Picked up by a liaison airplane, he returned to his base, ate a hurried lunch, took off again, and was shot down again—twice in one day! This time he injured his ankle when he bailed out. He was picked up by French peasants and taken to a hospital.[88]

During his career, Adolf Galland shot down 104 airplanes, most of them British. he succeeded Moelders as general of fighter forces in November, 1941, and was only thirty years old at the time of his promotion to major general (November 11, 1942)—the youngest general in the Wehrmacht at the time.[89]

General Galland was a persistent advocate of heavier concentration on fighter production. The number of fighters as a percentage of all aircraft manufactured was 30.2 percent in 1941, virtually the same as 1939 (30.1 percent), when the war broke out. Gradually this figure increased, to 35.8 percent in 1942, 43.9 percent in 1943, 62.2 percent in 1944, and 65.4 percent in 1945.[90] This was too slow for Galland, who believed in 1940 that more fighters should be produced. Galland also strongly advocated the use of jets as fighters, not fighter-bombers. Politically Galland allied himself with Erhard Milch, who believed as he did—a move hardly designed to ingratiate himself with Hermann Goering.

In the fall of 1944, Galland hit upon the idea of creating a huge fighter reserve of 2,000 aircraft under the command of I Fighter Corps. He planned to unleash them all in a surprise attack against the Allied bomber formations on a single day. Galland predicted that they could destroy at least 400 enemy bombers in one swoop and possibly destroy the morale of the Allied airmen and their leaders in the process. In September, 1944, he pulled the 4th, 76th, and 7th Fighter Wings back to the Reich for rebuilding and placed JG 1, 16, 11, and 17 in reserve. If combined with JG 3, 300, and 301 of Air Fleet Reich, this would give him ten fighter wings for the attack. At that time Luftwaffe Command West had only four fighter wings (JG 2, 26, 27, and 53) and there were only four operational wings on the entire eastern front (JGs 5, 51, 52, and 54).[91]

Galland's plan was a desperate one, but so was Germany's military situation in the latter part of 1944. Although he probably would not have broken the back of the Allied bomber offensive, Galland would almost certainly have succeeded in inflicting heavy casualties on the Allied air forces and perhaps made them more cautious about bombing the Third Reich. On November 12 he was ready and awaiting only a favorable opportunity to strike. He never got the chance. On November 20, Goering took his fighter reserves away from him. Leaving only JG 300 and 301 for the defense of the Reich, the Fat One committed the reserves to the support of the army, which was about to launch the Battle of the Bulge. As a result, the irreplaceable fighters were wasted against nondecisive ground targets. Hitler's last offensive in the West began on December 16 and had shot its bolt by December 25. Casualties among the fighter squadrons were all out of proportion to the damage they inflicted. "The Luftwaffe received its death blow in the Ardennes," Galland moaned.[92] He was right. The war was lost.

The Luftwaffe's last offensive, Operation "Bodenplatte," took place on January 1, 1945, when all available units attacked Allied airfields in the Netherlands, Belgium, and Luxembourg. They destroyed or seriously damaged 800 enemy airplanes, but lost 150 themselves, including some of their best surviving pilots. By now the Allies could absorb the blow, but the Luftwaffe could not.

✠

Naturally, Goering continued to blame others for the failure of the Luftwaffe. In early October 1944, for example, he met with wing, group, and squadron commanders in the great hall of the Reichs Air Defense School at Gatow. Without preliminaries he launched directly into an attack on the fighter pilots. "I've spoiled you," he roared at them. "I've given you too many decorations. They've made you fat and lazy. All that about the planes you'd shot down was just one big lie . . . A pack of lies, I tell you! . . . You didn't make a fraction of the kills you reported." He called the fighter pilots cowards, malingerers, and liars.[93]

Col. Johannes Steinhoff wrote later that ". . . for sheer cynicism and arrogance he outdid himself."[94] As a result of these insults, a group of fighter pilots—led by Col. Guenther Luetzow and Colonel Steinhoff, plotted to appeal to Hitler to have Goering replaced. The Reichsmarschall got wind of the conspiracy, however, and responded as he always did. In January, 1945, he sacked Luetzow, the commander of the 4th Air Division; Steinhoff, the commander of the 7th Fighter Wing; Col. Hannes Trautloft, the commander of JG 54; and Col. Eduard Neumann, the fighter commander, Italy. Adolf Galland, who was openly sympathetic to the conspirators, was also sacked. He was replaced by Gordon M. Gollob, a former instructor pilot in the Austrian air force.

Gollob, born in Vienna in 1912 as Gordon McGollob, was an officer of Scottish descent who changed his name at the order of OKL in 1938. He flew Me-110s in Poland, Norway, and the Battle of Britain and became a ME-109 pilot in late 1940. He distinguished himself on the eastern front in 1941, where he once shot down nine enemy airplanes in a single day. After a tour of duty at the Luftwaffe research and testing base at Rechlin (December 1941 to May 1942), he returned to Russia as commander of JG 77 (May to October, 1942) and from then until April 1944, was on the staff of the Fighter Command 3 in Paris and was with Fighter Command 5 on the English Channel. Deeply involved in the new fighter projects, including the jet and rocket-propelled aircraft, he headed a special fighter staff under Galland during the Battle of the Bulge. In his career he personally shot down 150 enemy aircraft 144 of them in the East.[95] Despite his great technical ability and skill as an aviator, he was, of course, unable to do anything to affect the outcome of the air war after his appointment as General der Jagdwaffe in January, 1945.

A month later, Speer told Hitler of the "mutiny of the fighter pilots" and the Fuehrer ordered Goering to give Galland a unit. Given no choice, Hermann turned over the 44th Fighter Unit (JV 44) to the general. This unit was a jet fighter squadron—a formation usually commanded by lieutenants or captains. Colonels Steinhoff and Luetzow joined the 44th as pilots, without commands of their own. Galland ended the war with 103 kills, while Steinhoff had 149. When Colonel Luetzow was killed in action in the last week of the war, he had 103 aerial victories. After the war, Steinhoff became commander of the West German Air Force, and many Americans saw him escorting President Reagan when he paid tribute to German World War II dead at the military cemetery at Bitburg. Galland moved to Argentina and helped Juan Peron organize the Argentine air force (1947–55). He was running his own aerospace consulting business in Bonn at last report.[96]

✠

Like the fighter pilots, the rest of the Luftwaffe was also disillusioned with Goering, who was by now only a shell of his former self. Due to the collapse in the West, in which most of the Luftwaffe ground organization simply took to its heels, Goering ordered the arrest of three air administrative area commanders: General of Flak Artillery Dr. Eugen Weissmann, General of Flyers Wilhelm Wimmer, and General of Flyers Karl Drum. Hitler—and therefore Goering—demanded the death penalty. The evidence in the cases was inconclusive, however, and the judge, General Baron von Hammerstein, resisted the pressure of the Reichsmarschall to find them guilty and execute them. Goering did extract one death penalty, however: General of Flyers Bernhard Waber was shot for illicitly adding to his personal property. The Luftwaffe was outraged. Who was Goering, the greatest art thief in history, to execute *anyone* for looting? Air force morale fell even lower as a result of the incident.[97]

✠

The Luftwaffe was driven from the sky in the last months of 1944, as Germany's cities were reduced to rubble. With their newly won bases in France, the U.S. and Royal air forces had little trouble assuming absolute air supremacy. A good example of how they used it is seen in what happened to Dueren. On November 16, this little city between Aachen and the Rhine was struck by 2,703 tons of bombs in a single raid. Ninety-five percent of the town was destroyed. In the last three months of 1944, Bomber Command alone dropped 163,000 tons of bombs, compared with 40,000 tons in the same period the year before. Some 53 percent of the total bomb load fell on German cities, including Duisburg, Essen, Cologne, and Duesseldorf, all of which were struck with more than 38,000 tons of bombs each in fewer than 100 days. Other cities devastated in the same period included Ulm, Stuttgart, Karlsruhe, Heilbronn, Freiburg, Ludwigshaven, Saarbruecken, Nuremberg, Munich, Bonn, Kolbenz, Bremen, Wilhelmshaven, Brunswick, Osnabrueck, and Giessen. The Eighth U.S. Air Force, meanwhile, dropped an even greater tonnage of bombs, concentrating 39 percent of its effort against synthetic oil plants at Gelsenkirchen, Merseburg-Leuna, Castrop, Sterkrade, Hanover, Harburg, Hamburg, Bottrop, Misburg, Bohlen, Zeitz, Leutzkendorf, and others. The Fifteenth U.S. Air Force attacked the oil plants in the South, at Floridsdorf, Korneuberg, Vienna, and Linz.[98] The loss of life was incredible. An estimated 500,000 to 600,000 Germans were killed by bombs in the 1940–45 period—about ten times the number of civilians killed in Britain during the war. Between February 1 and April 21, 1945, Berlin was subjected to eighty-three separate heavy bombings.[99] By January, 1945, the Eighth U.S.A.F. alone was sending out 1,500 bombers a day. Magdeburg and Chemnitz were shattered on February 6, but Dresden got the worst of it. On February 13 it was fire-bombed with 650,000 incendiaries. The city burned for a week, and the firestorms could be seen for 200 miles. Since the city was packed with refugees from the East, the death total could only be guessed at, but it was estimated at 135,000—more than twice as many as were killed in England during the entire war—all dead in a single raid.[100]

Meanwhile, the Luftwaffe pilots and thinning ranks of veteran aces continued to do their duty, flying out day after day, despite overwhelming odds. A great many of the veteran flyers, old before their time, were lost in 1945. Lt. Otto Kittel of JG 54, a winner of 267 aerial victories, was shot down by a Soviet IL-2 on February 14, only a week before his twenty-eighth birthday; Rudi Linz, 70 kills, was shot down by a Spitfire, as was Wilhelm Mink (72 victories). Friedrich Haas of JG 52, 74 kills, was shot down by a MIG, while his wing mate, Franz Schall, 137 kills, died in a crash landing. Gerhard Hoffmann, winner of 125 aerial combats, simply failed to return from a mission, and his fate is still unknown. Maj. Heinrich Ehrler, 204 kills, died on the eastern front on April 6, 1945. Colonel Luetzow, flying a jet, attacked a B-17 formation over Donauwoerth on April 23, 1945, and was never seen again. Col. Erich Leie, 118 victories, was commander of JG 77 on March 7, 1945, when he was killed by a YAK pilot. Nor were they the only casualties among the aces. Col. Kurt Buehligen, commander of JG 2 "Richthofen," had 112 kills when he was shot down and captured on the eastern front in early 1945. Col.

Gerhard Schoepfel, commander of JG 6 and winner of 40 victories, was captured in Czechoslovakia. Capt. Karl Schnoerrer, 46 kills, was shot down over Hamburg on March 30 and lost his left leg. Col. Johannes "Macki" Steinhoff attempted to take off on a hastily repaired runway on April 8, when his Me-262 hit a partially filled bomb crater and his landing gear was ripped off. Steinhoff was severely burned in the ensuing fire and spent months in a burn unit. His eyelids were completely burned away and he did not close his eyes until 1969, when an R.A.F. surgeon made new eyelids for him, from skin taken from Steinhoff's arm.[101] Hans-Ulrich Rudel, the leading Stuka pilot of the war, had his leg blown off during an attack on a Soviet tank in 1945. And there were many others.

As the Luftwaffe died and the Third Reich fell apart, Hermann Goering's world crumbled also. His hunting lodge at Rominten had already been burned to prevent its falling into Russian hands. On January 31, 1945, with the Russians already near, Emmy Goering left Karinhall with the female servants and four trucks full of art treasures. Hermann stayed on, however, guarding his beloved home with a parachute division. He saw Hitler very seldom now, and when he did the Fuehrer screamed curses and insults at him. Albert Speer visited him at Karinhall in mid-February. He described Goering as one of the few persons in Hitler's entourage who saw things "realistically and without illusions." Speer tried to get Goering to join him, Guderian, and some others in confronting Hitler with an ultimatum to end the war. Goering replied that he understood Speer's feelings, but he had been with Hitler too many years and had gone through too much with him to break loose now.[102]

A few days later, Hitler ordered the paratroopers moved from Karinhall to positions south of Berlin. Goering supervised the packing of his favorite drinking glasses and the remaining art treasures: paintings, tapestries, and rugs. He shot his four favorite bison from his private zoo, shook hands with his forest workers, and set off for Bavaria. His adjutant, Col. Berndt von Brauchitsch, son of the army field marshal, said he never looked back once. A few hours later the parachute engineers fired the demolition charges. Karinhall, including the mausoleum, went up in smoke and flames.[103]

As the war came to a close, Goering seemed to become more and more indifferent to his personal fate. He began to visit the front, until Hitler ordered him to stop. He even tried to start negotiations with the British through Swedish intermediaries, but this effort came to nothing.[104]

Hitler and Goering met for the last time at the Fuehrer Bunker in Berlin on April 20, 1945, Hitler's fifty-sixth and final birthday. He called upon Hitler to abandon Berlin and escape to the south on the last road still open between the advancing Germans and the Americans. Hitler refused to leave the capital. Goering then suggested that someone from the Luftwaffe—either he or Chief of the General Staff Karl Koller—should move further south, since the Allies were on the verge of cutting Germany in two. "You go, then," Hitler answered coolly. "I need Koller here." The two shook hands without showing any emotion and parted forever.[105]

Before he could get out of Berlin, Goering was caught in an air raid. He ducked into a public bomb shelter, where he was warmly received by the occupants. He joked with them about calling him Mayer, a reference to a famous speech he had made in the early days of the war, saying that people could call him by a Jewish name if a British bomber ever reached Germany. Strangely enough, Goering was always popular with the common people of Germany and kept their affection right up to the end. They were always delighted by his portly figure, his comical good humor, his numerous and often outrageous uniforms and other costumes, and his childlike delight in medals. Even on his infrequent visits to bombed-out cities, the homeless residents came out to cheer him. One gets the impression that they never quite took him seriously, or else never held him responsible for his actions.

Hermann Goering played one last scene in the final act of the Third Reich. At noon on April 23, General Koller reported to him at Berchtesgaden. He informed the Reichsmarschall of Hitler's intention to commit suicide which, of course, came as no surprise to Goering. Koller suggested that now was the time for him to take charge of the government and begin peace negotiations. Goering was leery. He spoke of Bormann as his "deadly enemy" who would call him a traitor if he acted. On the other hand, Goering did not want to be accused of sitting idly by in Germany's hour of disaster.

Goering summoned Hans Lammers, the state secretary of the Reichs Chancellery, for legal advice. Lammers told him the Fuehrer decree of June 29, 1941, made Goering Hitler's successor if he died or his deputy (and acting head of state) if the Fuehrer became incapacitated. Everyone present agreed that to be cut off in Berlin and preparing to commit suicide was tantamount to being incapacitated, for Hitler would lose the ability to communicate to military and civilian authorities—ergo, he would not be able to govern. Goering then sent a carefully worded telegram to Berlin. "In view of your decision to remain in the fortress of Berlin," it began, "do you agree that I take over at once the total leadership of the Reich, with full freedom of action at home and abroad as your deputy, in accordance with your decree of June 29, 1941?" Goering went on to state that if he had not heard from Hitler by 10 P.M. that night, he would assume Hitler had lost his freedom of action and would take charge of the government.

Hitler said nothing at all when he first received the telegram. His initial reaction was totally lethargic. It only took Bormann a short while, however, to convey a totally false meaning to the dispatch. "Goering is engaged in treason," he announced.[106] Within a half an hour he had fanned Hitler into a white heat. The Fuehrer railed against Goering, whom he called a corrupt drug addict, a usurper, and a traitor. He ordered Goering arrested and sent him a message saying, "What you have done warrants the death penalty," but he promised to spare Goering further punishment if he would resign all of his offices immediately, on the pretext that he had suffered a heart attack. The next day German radio announced the news of Goering's resignation. He was replaced as commander-in-chief of the Luftwaffe by Field Marshal Ritter Robert von Greim. Hitler had sacked his last field marshal.

Goering's arrest only lasted a few days, for Hitler committed suicide in Berlin on April 30. "Now I'll never be able to convince him that I was loyal to the end," Goering moaned. His wife's reaction was much more dramatic. When she heard the news, Emmy Goering had a heart attack.[107]

Goering had a few, last days of freedom before he surrendered to U.S. Brig. Gen. Robert J. Stack near Fischhorn, Austria, on May 8. He spent them at Mauterndorf Castle, which he had inherited from his godfather, Ritter von Epenstein, several years before. The Reichsmarschall was sure that he was under Eisenhower's personal protection and would soon be able to negotiate the terms of Germany's surrender. He was soon disillusioned. He was flown to the U.S. Seventh Army's interrogation center at Augsburg, where he was stripped of his diamond ring, his *Pour le Merite* and Grand Cross, his marshal's baton, and his epaulets. He was soon dining on U.S. Army C rations.[108]

Goering was tried as a major war criminal at Nuremberg in 1946. He was weaned from paracodeine, lost about one hundred pounds, and made a good show of his defense by almost everyone's account. "No one," Lord Birkett wrote in his private notes, "appears to have been quite prepared for his immense ability and knowledge, and his thorough mastery and understanding of every detail of the captured documents . . . Suave, shrewd, adroit, capable, resourceful, he quickly saw the elements of the situation, and, as his confidence grew, his mastery became more apparent."[109] Still, he must have known a successful legal defense was impossible. He said that he maintained his loyalty to the Fuehrer at all times, although he did not approve of the murders and the atrocities of the Nazi regime. He even weakly asserted that he did not believe that Hitler was aware of the full extent of the crimes of some of his subordinates.[110] He was convicted and, on October 1, sentenced to death by hanging.

Although his old bravado was gone, Goering's physical courage did not desert him, and he maintained a facade of nonchalance to the last. In his final letter to his wife, he even told her that there would be statues of Hermann Goering all over Germany in fifty or sixty years.[111]

At about 10:40 P.M. on the night of October 15, 1946, two hours before he would have been hanged, Goering swallowed a vial of cyanide poison which he had smuggled into prison with him. Early the next morning his body, along with those of the other executed war criminals—Field Marshal Keitel, SS Chief Ernst Kaltenbrunner, Alfred Rosenberg, Hans Frank, Wilhelm Frick, Juluis Streicher, Arthur Seyss-Inquart, Fritz Sauckel, and Alfred Jodl—were secretly taken to a Munich crematorium. The ashes were then placed in a car, which deposited them in an anonymous lane somewhere in the countryside near Munich.[112]

CHAPTER 14

Ritter Von Greim:
The Last Field Marshal

Hitler's last field marshal was born in Bayreuth, the home of Wagner, on June 22, 1892. In many ways his tragedy was representative of both his generation and of the Luftwaffe. The son and grandson of a Bavarian army officer, he followed in his ancestors' steps and joined the Royal Bavarian Army as an officer-cadet on July 14, 1911. He was initially assigned to a railway battalion. Robert von Greim was commissioned second lieutenant on October 28, 1912, and was transferred to the artillery.[1]

Lieutenant von Greim served with the 8th Field Artillery Regiment as a battery officer and adjutant from 1913 to August, 1915, and served on the western front. Then he was assigned to the 204th Artillery Observation Detachment as a forward observer—a very dangerous job indeed on the western front in 1915. After about a year of this hazardous duty he volunteered for an even more dangerous job: he applied for assignment as an army aviator. Duly accepted, Greim was posted to the flight school at Schleissheim, where he underwent pilot's training. He was promoted to first lieutenant on January 20, 1917.[2]

Greim returned to France and soon proved to be an excellent fighter pilot and a born leader. Despite his relatively junior seniority and rank, he became squadron leader of the 34th Jagdstaffel (fighter squadron). He later commanded the 10th Fighter Group in March and April, 1918, and then Fighter Group "Greim," which controlled all fighter forces; signed to the German Second Army, a post he held until the end of the war.[3]

Greim shot down twenty-eight enemy aircraft in the First World War. The King of Bavaria awarded him the Knights Cross of the Bavarian Military Order of Max Joseph, which carried with it the title "Ritter" (knight). He was also decorated with the *Pour le Merite* (the "Blue Max") on October 8, 1918, less than six weeks before the fall of the Second Reich.[4]

Lieutenant von Greim returned to the squadron at Schleissheim after the war but left the army with the honorary rank of captain on March 31, 1920. Like so many other young Germans after the collapse of the Kaiser's

Empire, Greim was truly a member of the lost generation. He seemed to be drifting, searching for his place in life. He studied law at the University of Munich, but there is no evidence that he ever graduated. Later he became a stunt pilot with Ernst Udet.

Greim met Adolf Hitler in 1919 or 1920 and soon became an enthusiastic Nazi. Like so many Germans of the era, he found its combination of nationalism and socialism too attractive to resist. Always a romantic, he had found a cause in which he could believe. Greim almost worshipped the former corporal and continued to do so until the end. In March 1920, during the Kapp Putsch, he took Hitler on his first flight, from Munich to Berlin. The weather was so turbulent that Hitler became sick and kept vomiting. When they landed, the future Fuehrer swore that he would never, never fly again.[5]

After the Allied Armistice Commission confiscated his airplane, Greim became a bank official for a time, but then returned to civil aviation. From August 1924 to May 1927, he was in Canton, China, organizing military aviation for Chiang Kai-shek's Nationalist Air Force. He returned to Germany that summer and by October 1 was director of the Bavarian Air Sport Society and manager of a private flying school at Wuerzburg, Nuremberg, and Munich. Later, the Wuerzburg school became an official Luftwaffe transport pilots' school. In 1928 he was reportedly engaged in studying the medical aspects of flying, possibly for the Reichswehr.[6] He officially reentered the army on January 1, 1934, although this fact could not be made public because it was a violation of the Treaty of Versailles. He was the commander of the secret Luftwaffe flight school at Wuerzburg, which operated under the camouflaged name of "Advertisement Units."[7] On April 1, 1934, Greim (now a major) became commander of the 132nd Fighter Group, the first Luftwaffe fighter unit, which was established at Doeberitz, near Berlin. It was part of the Richthofen *Geschwader* (later JG 2) and included three fighter squadrons equipped with Ar-65 and He-51 biplanes. A year later, when Hitler lifted the veil of secrecy surrounding the Luftwaffe, Greim was named inspector of fighters and dive bombers.[8]

Greim's rise in the Luftwaffe was rapid. He had talent, experience, the right kind of background, and the right political convictions. He was promoted to lieutenant colonel (September 1, 1935), was named inspector of equipment and safety devices (February 10, 1936), and was promoted to colonel on April 1, 1936. He received a prized appointment on June 1, 1937, when he was named chief of the Personnel Section (later Office) of the German Air Ministry—in effect, chief of personnel of the Luftwaffe. He was promoted to major general on February 1, 1938, and became a member of the German Academy for Aerial Research that same year.[9]

Major General Ritter von Greim switched from staff to line on February 5, 1939, when he assumed command of the 5th Air Division. This unit did not take part in the Polish campaign but was nevertheless upgraded to V Air Corps in late 1939 or very early 1940. Greim's promotion to lieutenant general was dated January 1, 1940,[10] so it is probable that this was the date on which the 5th Air was officially upgraded.

The invasion of France was Greim's first major campaign in the Second World War. He initially headquartered near Stuttgart and operated against northeastern France, on the southern flank of the main ground thrust, mostly with bomber units. He did a thorough job of disrupting the French transportation and supply systems and helped prevent the French from achieving a timely concentration against the "Panzer Corridor," the German breakthrough to the sea. Greim did not take part in the Dunkirk debacle. He was awarded the Knights Cross on June 2 and was promoted to general of flyers during the multitudinous promotions of July 19, 1940. He was only forty-eight years old.[11]

During the Battle of Britain, Greim's V Air Corps directed the 51st, 54th, and 55th Bomber Wings, which were equipped with Ju-88 and He-111 bombers. As in France, he was subordinate to Sperrle's 3rd Air Fleet.[12] He performed his duties in an acceptable manner, but without winning any special laurels.

Up until this point, Greim had achieved credible results, but without achieving any special distinction. In May 1941, however, Greim's command was shifted to the East and reinforced with the 3rd Fighter Wing (equipped with Me-109 fighters). His aircraft crossed the Soviet frontier on June 22, in support of Rundstedt's Army Group South.[13] He spent the rest of the war—and virtually the rest of his life—in more or less constant action on the eastern front. Few airmen distinguished themselves on the Russian front to the degree that Greim did. From June 22 to 25 alone his units flew 1,600 sorties against seventy-seven Russian airfields, destroying 774 Soviet aircraft on the ground and 136 in the air. By July 3, Greim was able to report that his corps had destroyed more than 1,000 enemy aircraft on the ground. Fifth Air Corps supported Kleist's 1st Panzer Group in the crossing of the Sluch, in the Battle of Uman (where 103,000 Soviets were captured and 317 tanks and 858 guns were captured or destroyed), and in the Battle of Kiev, which resulted in the surrender of 667,000 Russian soldiers in September 1941. He supported Rundstedt's armored spearheads in the opening of the bridgehead at Dnepropetrovsk, in destroying three Soviet divisions at Novo-Moskovsk, and in the rolling up of the Soviet Dnieper flank in the Zaporozhve vicinity. His units blasted Soviet columns and troop concentrations and smashed Russian railroad lines, materially delaying the Communist resupply and reinforcement efforts and preventing them from stabilizing the southern sector of the eastern front. He then paved the way for the encirclement of large Soviet formations against the

Sea of Azov, where more than 100,000 Red soldiers and hundreds of tanks were captured.[14]

Greim lost aerial supremacy on the southern sector in late September, 1941, when almost all of his fighter units were transferred north to take part in the Battle of Moscow. He nevertheless continued to send his bombers and dive-bombers far behind Russian lines, interdicting their rail communications around and east of Kharkov. From September 23 to October 12, 95 Soviet trains (including 4 ammunition and 4 fuel trains) were completely destroyed and another 288 were heavily destroyed. Russian railroad traffic was cut in sixty-four places, and Soviet marshal Timoshenko was forced to abandon several ground counterattack plans because his ravaged logistical system could not support them. Greim also repeatedly and successfully attacked the Soviet tank factory at Kramatorsk (one of the most important tank factories in the Soviet Union in 1941) and smashed the large Red aircraft plant at Voronezh.[15]

Greim was forced to give up his last fighter unit (the III Group of the 52d Fighter Wing) on October 22. Fifth Air Corps still pressed its attacks, even without fighter protection, and played a major role in the capture of Kharkov, Kurst, and the Donets Industrial Basin. Following the fall of Kharkov, Greim's units destroyed 79 railroad trains and damaged 148 others in the attacks between the Donets and the Don. They also continued bombing and dive-bombing attacks against Soviet troop concentrations, roads, and tactical positions, in support of the Sixth and Seventeenth armies. In late October, Greim was given the mission of supporting Kleist's 1st Panzer Group (later First Panzer Army) in its drive on Rostov.[16]

"General Mud" took over on November 6, forcing Kleist to temporarily halt his offensive. The Russians then made a major effort to get their rolling stock out of the region. For the first time trains consisting entirely of locomotives (forty to sixty per train) were spotted by the Luftwaffe. In a seventeen-day period—much of it poor flying weather—Greim's pilots destroyed 12 trains and 51 locomotives and damaged another 32 trains and 161 locomotives. Some of Greim's fighters were restored to him during this period, and they shot down 65 Russian aircraft in 578 sorties. The Reds were unable to prevent the destruction of much of the rolling stock in southern Russia.[17]

On November 12, the 54th and 55th Bomber Wings, which had been in combat since May 1940, were withdrawn to Germany to rest and refit. Only one group of the 55th was left behind, reducing Greim's total bomber strength to fewer than ten aircraft. He continued to support Kleist's advance with Stukas and fighters.[18] Rostov fell on November 23, but the Soviets counterattacked almost immediately with fourteen fresh divisions, as well as strong tank and air support.[19] They advanced over the frozen Don River delta and retook the city on November 28. Greim then covered Kleist's retreat from Rostov.[20]

On November 30, 1941, Greim, his headquarters, and several of his combat units were transferred to Belgium, with the idea of organizing a mine-laying air corps for use against the United Kingdom. Within a week, however, the Soviet winter offensive was unleashed from the Baltic to the Black Sea. The High Command of the Luftwaffe quickly decided to split V Air Corps in half. One part, under Col. Hermann Plocher, the corps chief of staff, remained in Belgium. The other half, under Greim, was redesignated Special Staff Crimea (Sonderstab Krim) and returned to 4th Air Fleet, where its mission was to help Manstein repulse the imminent Russian advance from the Kerch Peninsula and maintain the siege of Sevastopol.[21]

At Karinhall on January 7, 1942, Reichsmarschall Goering personally briefed Greim on the Crimean situation,[22] which was this: Manstein's Eleventh Army was besieging powerful Russian forces at Sevastopol, but the Soviet bridgehead on the Kerch Peninsula had not been eliminated. Soon the Kerch Strait would be frozen solid, and the Reds would be able to transport immense quantities of supplies and reinforcements to the Crimea and take Manstein in the rear, possibly forcing him to lift the siege and even abandon the Crimea. This Greim was to help prevent.[23]

Greim arrived at his new headquarters at Poltava on January 15. His units included the 77th Dive-Bomber Wing (minus I Group); III Group, 51st Bomber Wing; I Group, 100th Bomber Wing; a fighter squadron of the 77th Fighter Wing; and Col. Wolfgang von Wild's Air Command South, a miscellaneous collection of torpedo-bomber, air/sea reconnaissance, and anti-amphibious squadrons.[24]

Greim's main problem was the low operational strength of his units, caused by the intense cold. Fighter and dive-bomber groups, normally twenty to thirty operational aircraft, were down to twelve to fifteen aircraft, while bomber groups were down to six or seven aircraft. Ground organization was faulty, and the necessary supplies were absent.[25]

Manstein had already repulsed one Soviet advance in late December. On January 15—the day Greim arrived—he anticipated the Soviets by attacking their bridgehead on the Kerch, despite the fact he was outnumbered two to one. The Reds counterattacked on the nineteenth, halting Manstein's advance at Parpach. Greim performed valuable service by attacking Red strongpoints, artillery positions, and troop and armored concentrations, as well as dock installations in their rear, all against strong Red Air Force fighter units, equipped with lend-lease aircraft. The squadrons of Special Staff Crimea flew 1,089 sorties between January 19 and February 18 and destroyed 23 Soviet aircraft in aerial combat, 44 more on the ground, sank 25,000 tons of shipping, bombed Red port installations at Kerch and Kamysk Burum, and destroyed 335 Soviet vehicles (some of them horse-drawn supply wagons), 14 trains, 14 artillery batteries, a fuel depot, and a supply depot. Greim's total losses were two He-111 bombers.[26]

In early February the Brussels group of the V Air Corps staff, including Colonel Plocher, returned to the eastern front, where it assisted in the withdrawal of Richthofen's VIII Air Corps from the central sector ("Combat Zone Center"). In mid-February, Special Staff Crimea was ordered dissolved; Greim and his group joined Plocher's group at Smolensk soon after, reuniting V Air Corps Headquarters. Six weeks later, on April 1, V Air was expanded and redesignated Luftwaffe Command East, an air fleet-level headquarters. Greim was now responsible for the air and flak support of Army Group Center. Special Staff Crimea was replaced by IV Air Corps, and the plans for creating a mine-laying corps in the West were quietly abandoned.[27]

Luftwaffe Command East initially consisted of the 18th Flak Division (Maj. Gen. Richard Reimann), 12th Flak Division (Maj. Gen. Ernst Buffa), 1st Air Division (Maj. Gen. Alfred Buelowius), 2d Air Division (Maj. Gen. Stefan Froehlich), and Air Administrative Commands II (headquartered at Posen and Warsaw) and Moscow, headquartered at Smolensk.[28]

Johannes Steinhoff described Greim as a "virile, likable Bavarian [who] positively radiated steadfastness."[29] The big, blue-eyed, broad-shouldered commander was called "Papa" Greim by his men, who adored him. With his imposing physical presence, friendly disposition, and spectacles, he must have seemed like a father figure to them.[30] Whatever the reason, he seemed to be able to get the maximum effort from his few, understrength units. His mission in the spring of 1942 was to support Field Marshal Guenther von Kluge's Army Group Center. Hitler's strategy for the East in 1942 called for a major offensive on the southern sector. Kluge's tasks were secondary: hold his lines and, insofar as possible, deceive the Soviets into thinking that the main German offensive would come in the central, not the southern, sector. Kluge has never been given sufficient credit for the brilliant manner in which he accomplished this task, even though it had unpleasant side effects for Army Group Center. Stalin, deceived into thinking the main German blow would fall here, concentrated the bulk of his divisions against Kluge's depleted regiments.

The most dangerous positions on the central sector were those of the Ninth Army (Col. Gen. Walter Model), which was exposed to attack from three sides in the Rzhev salient. The Soviets tried to pinch off the salient (and not for the first time) on April 13 and 16, but failed, thanks largely to the 2nd Air and 12th Flak Divisions. The Soviets suffered heavy losses in this battle.[31]

Throughout 1942 Luftwaffe Command East flew from one tactical crisis to another, for Army Group Center's front was too long and lacked sufficient artillery, antitank guns, and tanks, as most of the panzer divisions had been sent south or were rebuilding in France. Also, Greim lacked the necessary aircraft, for Loehr's 4th Air Fleet to the south had priority for replacements. There could be no question of waging strategic aerial warfare; Greim concentrated instead on interdiction raids against Russian railroads, attempting to slow the Soviet buildup against Army Group Center. Later, in late May, he concentrated against the Red Guards Cavalry Corps of General Below, which had penetrated behind Fourth Army southeast of Smolensk and south of Vyazma. He was unable to completely stop the Russian airlift to Below.

Luftwaffe Command East was greatly outnumbered by the Red Air Force, but it was able to maintain air parity due to the superior skill of its pilots and even managed to win a few significant tactical victories. In late July, for example, Soviet ground forces pushed to the outskirts of Rzhev. Greim committed the 1st Air Division to the battle, and its dive-bombers inflicted heavy losses on the Russians. Meanwhile, the 51st Fighter Wing, under Lt. Col. Karl-Gottfried Nordmann, established air superiority in Ninth Army's sector. The battle lasted well into October, but all Communist attempts to seize Rzhev were turned back with heavy losses.[32]

In November, 1942, the Battle of Stalingrad reached its climax. It drew both Luftwaffe and army units into the inferno like a magnet. From August 17 to November 29 Luftwaffe Command East was reduced from eleven bomber groups to seven, from five and one-third fighter groups to four and one-third, and lost its only antitank and ground attack squadrons. It was allowed, however, to keep its three dive-bomber groups. Most or all of these units ended up on the southern sector. Despite these losses, Greim had to help contain the Russian breakthrough between Bely and Velikiye-Luki. Greim directed the air operations from a command train commuting between Vitebsk and Nevel. He committed his glider units to resupply Velikiye-Luki, which was surrounded by the Russians. He delivered flame throwers and antitank guns to the garrison and provided close air support for Army Group Center's unsuccessful relief attempt, which bogged down within two miles of the town. Only 180 of the 7,000 men surrounded at Velikiye-Luki escaped.[33]

The unrelenting battle of attrition on the central sector continued in 1943, especially in the zones of the Third Panzer and Ninth armies, from Velikiye-Luki to Rzhev. The Germans were pushed back toward Vitebsk, but in general managed to hold their lines. Whenever possible, Greim energetically attacked the Russian railroad system, to hamper their attempts to resume the offensive. The bombings severely damaged the Soviet supply depots at Kalinin, Toropets, and Velikopolye. In February the Second Army and Second Panzer Army came under heavy attacks in the Kursk-Orel sector. Greim concentrated all available units on the threatened zone and shot down as many as 38 Soviet airplanes and destroyed up to 116 tanks per day, until the Russians gave up the offensive in late March. Meanwhile, the other air units covered the evacuation of the Rzhev salient during the first two weeks in March. This operation shortened Kluge's line by about 120 miles and released ten divisions for use elsewhere.[34] As it frequently did, the Luftwaffe acted as a sort of fire brigade for the ground forces in time of crisis, until the rainy season arrived in April and halted almost all military operations.

Greim used the weather-imposed lull to rehabilitate his flying units and also to attack Russian railroad facilities, supply bases, airfields, and industrial installations deep in the Soviet rear. For his tactical successes Greim received a number of rewards from Hitler, who held him in high esteem. On February 16 he was promoted to colonel general, and on April 4 the Fuehrer personally decorated him with the Oak Leaves to the Knights Cross.[35] On May 11 Luftwaffe Command East was formally upgraded and became the 6th Air Fleet.[36]

Meanwhile, Hitler and his generals launched what turned out to be their last major offensive on the eastern front. Their objective was to sever the Kursk salient at its base. The results we have seen. From that point on, all roads led back to Berlin for the battered Army Group Center and the depleted 6th Air Fleet which supported it.

Despite fighting odds of 4.4 to 1 and greater, Greim remained fanatically loyal to the Nazi cause. One prisoner taken in 1944 said he was becoming "more important and more fanatic" and "the outstanding Number One man in the Luftwaffe."[37] There can be little doubt that he had a talent for inspiring his men. "Few commanders were more popular among German airmen than Greim," General Plocher wrote after the war.[38]

On June 22, 1944, the Soviets struck Army Group Center (now under Field Marshal Ernst Busch) with 2,500,000 men.[39] They were supported by 2,318 fighters, 1,744 ground attack aircraft, 1,662 bombers, 431 night bombers, and 179 reconnaissance aircraft—a total of 6,334 airplanes.[40] Greim met this vast armada with 775 machines: an 8.2 to 1 inferiority. To make matters worse, 6th Air Fleet was ill-constituted to meet such an attack, as it had only 100 ground attack aircraft and 100 single-engine fighters, and Greim's 370 long-range bombers were of little tactical value. Ironically, Greim had given up fifty fighters to Air Fleet Reich only the month before.[41]

Greim could do nothing to prevent the wholesale destruction of Army Group Center. Twenty-eight German divisions were smashed or totally destroyed, and some 350,000 men were killed, wounded, or missing.[42] Sixth

Air Fleet also lost heavily in pilots, aircraft, and flak guns during the debacle. The forward air bases were also overrun, forcing 6th Air back to unprepared, unstocked bases in Poland and East Prussia. Greim did receive some reinforcements as he fell back, but they did not make much difference and probably did not equal his losses. Overall, the Luftwaffe strength on the eastern front declined from 2,085 aircraft in June to 1,760 by July 31.[43]

For his part in the disaster, Field Marshal Busch was sacked, despite the fact that he was a fanatical Nazi. Hitler, however, attached no blame to Greim, even though he had failed to detect the magnitude of the Soviet buildup. On August 31, 1944, he invested Ritter von Greim with the Knights Cross with Oak Leaves and Swords,[44] making him one of the most decorated men in German history. Very few men held the Oak Leaves and Swords *and* the *Pour le Merite.*

Hitler considered Greim, along with Richthofen and Kesselring, to be the best Luftwaffe generals. In 1944 he began to look for a possible successor to Goering as supreme commander of the air force. Kesselring, who was conducting a brilliant ground campaign in Italy, could not be spared, and Richthofen was seriously ill with the tumor that would eventually kill him. The Fuehrer, therefore, began to look upon Greim as a possible C-in-C of the Luftwaffe. On July 20, 1944, in the attempt on Hitler's life, Luftwaffe Chief of Staff Guenther Korten was mortally wounded. As soon as the confusion died down, Hitler proposed that Greim be named his successor. On July 24, however, the Reichsmarschall appointed Gen. Werner Kreipe instead. The reason Goering passed over Greim was simple: he mistrusted the air fleet commander, correctly guessing that Hitler might be tempted to take the next logical step and name Greim commander-in-chief of the Luftwaffe.[45]

Goering was right to fear Greim. In mid-September, after 12,000 civilians were killed in an Allied air raid that destroyed the center of Darmstadt, Hitler actually spoke of the possibility of making Greim C-in-C of the air force.[46] On September 21, the Fuehrer interviewed Greim and offered him the post of deputy commander-in-chief of the Luftwaffe. According to the terms Hitler proposed, Greim would be de facto supreme commander, and Goering would be little more than a figurehead. Greim discussed the offer with Himmler, Bormann, and SS general Hermann Fegelein (chief SS liaison officer to the Fuehrer) over the next two weeks,[47] before Goering worked up the nerve to confront Greim on October 3. He was in a "towering rage" when he met the colonel general at Karinhall that day. Greim recalled later that Goering was "so angry as to appear to have taken leave of his senses. In the cloud-cuckoo-land of his hunting lodge, he was once more the mighty creator of the Luftwaffe."[48] After a vicious tongue-lashing, the "Fat One" ordered Greim to return immediately to his air fleet, which was now in

Poland. When Kreipe called on Goering later, he found the Reichsmarschall "completely broken." Goering complained bitterly that Greim was a traitor and that "they" were trying to get rid of him behind his back.[49]

Goering's move spoiled Hitler's plans and left him with only two choices: acquiesce to Goering's order or sack the Reichsmarschall. Either alternative was poor. If he replaced Goering—the number two man in Nazi Germany and a man who had been with him since 1922—it would be an admission to the entire world of the desperate straits in which the Third Reich found itself. The other choice was to leave Goering in charge, and he had already proven he was incapable of running the air war. Dissatisfied, the Fuehrer decided to do nothing for the time being.[50] By late October, however, he was again considering replacing Goering with Greim.[51] His criticisms of the Luftwaffe became more and more bitter after the Greim idea failed.[52]

Perhaps as a consolation prize, Hitler officially cited Greim a second time for the services of his flak units and for his outstanding leadership as commander of the 6th Air Fleet soon after he returned to the East.[53] This action may have been taken to ensure that Goering took no steps against Greim, as he had against Field Marshal Milch when that officer became a threat to his position. If so, it worked. The Reichsmarschall may have been hostile to the Ritter, but he never brought up the possibility of replacing him, despite the deteriorating situation in the East.

Greim was in mental turmoil in the winter of 1944–45. Still a believer in Hitler, he felt torn between this loyalty and his loyalty to Germany and the Luftwaffe. On the evening of January 13, 1945, Col. Guenther Luetzow and Col. Johannes Steinhoff, the commanders of the 1th Air Division and the 7th Fighter Wing, respectively, turned up at his headquarters at Lodz, Poland. These two young officers had shot down more than 250 enemy aircraft between them. Now they wanted to induce Greim into a plot to replace Goering as C-in-C of the Luftwaffe by personally appealing to Hitler for his removal. "Papa" Greim invited them to sit down by the fireplace. In the glow of the dying embers, he listened in silence as they presented their case. When they had finished, he gave vent to some of his personal anguish:

> Gentlemen, I ask you to appreciate what a wretched position all this has put me in. I who have served the Reichsmarschall faithfully all of these many years. Who has believed in the Fuehrer—and, damn it, still believe in him. At least I try to . . . You've no idea of the things I have to force myself to sign. One simply has to believe—I mean one needs this faith like a rock in order to survive it all. What you go through in your units I have here a hundred times over . . . And the lookout for my air fleet becoming daily more hopeless. No,

gentlemen—you're asking too much of me. I can't become a traitor.
I just can't. And least of all against Hermann Goering. Do you
understand that? I can't do it![54]

His voice then failed him and, choked with emotion, he sank down into
his armchair, his fists pressed against his forehead.

As the officers left, Greim warned them that the high command already
knew of their plans. Since he considered their motives honorable, Greim
tried to protect them from Goering's wrath, but to no avail. The Reichsmarschall relieved both men of their commands, along with several of their
confederates. He even threatened to have the outspoken Luetzow shot.[55]

After East Prussia was cut off from the rest of Germany during the Russian advances of early 1945, 6th Air Fleet concentrated in Czechoslovakia. On
April 7, 1945, the 4th Air Fleet (still fighting on the southern sector of the
eastern front) was downgraded to Luftwaffe Command 4 and absorbed by
Greim's command.[56] This move gave Greim responsibility for the air battles
over eastern Germany, Poland, Slovakia, Bohemia, Moravia, and Croatia.[57] In
the second week of April a further command consolidation took place.
Greim's 6th Air Fleet absorbed Luftwaffe Command West and VII Air Corps,
while Stumpff's Air Fleet Reich absorbed Luftwaffe Command Northeast
(formerly II Air Corps), 14th Air Division, and 1st and 2nd Fighter Divisions.
Thus the Luftwaffe was divided into two major commands, with Stumpff concentrating against the Anglo-Americans. Greim's veteran ground attack formations continued to fight the Russians, but he had only 2,200 aircraft of all
classes to bring against 15,000 Soviet airplanes, and most of the best German
pilots were already dead. Teenage Luftwaffe pilots were being thrown into
battle with only forty hours of training flight time. Nevertheless, when the
Soviets began their final push across the Oder on April 16, Greim managed
to fly 1,000 sorties against it. This level of resistance could not be maintained
for long against the Red Air Force's 6.8 to 1 aerial superiority. Besides, Greim
was running out of aviation fuel. By April 25, when Berlin was completely
surrounded, the Communists had total aerial supremacy over the capital of
the Reich.[58]

On April 23, Goering sent his famous message to Hitler, asking the
Fuehrer if he (Goering) should assume leadership of the Reich (see Chapter 13). Hitler responded by relieving Goering of his command and ordering his arrest. The Fuehrer then summoned Greim to Berlin.

When Hitler's message arrived on April 24, Greim was at his headquarters in Munich. A less fanatical man would have ignored the dispatch, for flying to Berlin was little short of suicide. After all, not a single operational
airfield remained in German hands in the dying city. Greim, however, left at
once for the capital of the Reich. He was accompanied by Hanna Reitsch,

another fanatical Nazi and a famous stunt pilot, who was one of the few women to hold the Iron Cross. The next morning they arrived at the Luftwaffe testing and research base at Rechlin, where they intended to board a helicopter and land in the garden of the chancellery. The only helicopter at Rechlin was damaged, however, so the pair appropriated a FW-190 and ordered its pilot, a sergeant, to fly them to Gatow. Hanna was stuffed in the tail of the two-seat fighter as the general and sergeant hedge-hopped Russian flak to Gatow. Here, the next morning, Greim and Reitsch boarded an old Arado-60 (Ar-60) training plane and flew at treetop level toward Hitler's bunker. Over the Tiergarten in Berlin an antiaircraft shell shattered Greim's foot. Hanna Reitsch took over the controls and landed the aircraft in a shell-potted street on the east-west axis near the chancellery—a neat piece of flying indeed.[59] Greim, in terrible pain, was carried to the Fuehrer Bunker.

At first it was feared that Greim's foot might have to be amputated. Hitler welcomed him as his wound was being dressed for surgery. "I have called you here because Hermann Goering has betrayed both me and the Fatherland," he exclaimed. "Behind my back he has made contact with the enemy. I have had him arrested as a traitor, deprived him of all of his offices, and removed him from all organizations. That is why I have called you." He then promoted the startled commander to commander-in-chief of the Luftwaffe, with the rank of field marshal.[60]

The surgeons managed to save the new marshal's foot, and Hitler had him put to bed in a room opposite the Fuehrer conference room. At 10 P.M. that night German radio announced Greim's promotion to the world. Also that night Hitler visited him, gave him a suicide capsule, and ordered him to concentrate the few remaining jet squadrons around Prague.[61] On April 27 or 28, Gen. Karl Koller, the last chief of the General Staff of the Luftwaffe, telephoned Greim from OKW Headquarters, then located in the woods near Fuerstenberg. Greim told him:

> Just don't lose hope! Everything will still turn out all right. My contact with the Fuehrer and his strength has strengthened me like a dip in the fountain of youth. The Fuehrer sat at my bedside for quite a while and discussed everything with me. He retracted all of his accusations against the Luftwaffe. He is aware of what our service branch has accomplished. His reproaches are aimed solely at Goering. He had the highest praise for our forces! This made me exceedingly happy.[62]

The romantic Greim, it seems, had been affected by the dream world of the Fuehrer Bunker. Elsewhere, real events took their course. On the night of April 28–29 Russian tanks were reported concentrating south of Potsdamer

Platz, massing for the assault on the chancellery. Hitler came to Greim's room and slumped down on his bed. The only hope left, he said, was the relief attack Gen. Walter Wenck was launching. He ordered Greim to support it with every aircraft he had. He instructed the wounded marshal and Fraulein Reitsch to fly out of Berlin in the Arado trainer and to direct the Luftwaffe attack. Both begged to be allowed to sacrifice themselves with Hitler in the bunker, but Hitler was adamant. They were needed at Luftwaffe Headquarters, he said. Hitler also ordered Greim to arrest Himmler for high treason. The Reichsfuehrer-SS had attempted to open negotiations with the Allies behind his back, the Fuehrer said.[63]

That day—the morning of April 29—Greim and Hanna Reitsch flew out of Berlin and miraculously escaped through a hail of Russian small-arms fire. They landed at Grand Adm. Karl Doenitz's headquarters at Ploem, where they saw Himmler and told him that Hitler had denounced him for treason. The next day, with the Russians only a few hundred yards away, Adolf Hitler committed suicide in Berlin. Shortly before his death, Hitler appointed Admiral Doenitz as his successor.

Doenitz, who considered Greim a "fine man and officer," wanted to keep him as C-in-C of the Luftwaffe. Greim declined, however. On May 2, at Ploem, he spoke very bitterly to the grand admiral, because, as Doenitz recalled, "the idealism and devotion to duty of the soldiers who believed they had been serving a noble cause should have ended in so dire a catastrophe. He did not wish, he said, to go on living, and we parted, deeply moved."[64]

Immediately after Hitler's death, the Luftwaffe forces in the north suspended all operations against the Western Allies. Greim made his way back to the south, probably on May 3, where fighting against the Russians continued. Here, in northern Austria and Bohemia, the Luftwaffe made its last stand. It had only 1,500 aircraft left, and the flight units were in remnants, disorganized and demoralized, and almost without fuel, as the supply and transportation systems had virtually ceased to function. Greim managed barely fifty sorties a day until May 8, when Germany finally surrendered.[65]

Greim was utterly demoralized and disillusioned. He was ill, in pain, on crutches, and all of his dreams were shattered. In May he was taken prisoner and sent to a hospital in Salzburg. Here, on May 24, true to his word, Ritter von Greim committed suicide, probably using the pill that Hitler had given him in the bunker, three weeks before. He was fifty-three years old.[66]

APPENDIX 1

Table of Equivalent Ranks

Luftwaffe	United States Army Air Corps
Reichsmarschall (Goering)	None
Field Marshal (Generalfeldmarschall)	General of the Army
Colonel General (Generaloberst)	General
General (General der Fliegers, etc.)	Lieutenant General
Lieutenant General (Generalleutnant)	Major General
Major General (Generalmajor)	Brigadier General
Colonel (Oberst)	Colonel
Lieutenant Colonel (Oberstleutnant)	Lieutenant Colonel
Major (Major)	Major
Captain (Hauptmann)	Captain
First Lieutenant (Oberleutnant)	First Lieutenant
Second Lieutenant (Leutnant)	Second Lieutenant
Fahnenjunker/Fahnrich	None[1]

---

1. Roughly equivalent to Officer-Cadet or officer candidate.

Luftwaffe	Royal Air Force[2]
Reichsmarschall (Goering)	Marshal of the Royal Air Force
Field Marshal (Generalfeldmarschall)	Air Chief Marshal
Colonel General (Generaloberst)	Air Chief Marshal
General (General der Fliegers, etc.)	Air Marshal
Lieutenant General (Generalleutnant)	Air Vice Marshal
Major General (Generalmajor)	Air Commodore
Colonel (Oberst)	Group Captain
Lieutenant Colonel (Oberstleutnant)	Wing Commander

Luftwaffe	Royal Air Force[2]
Major (Major)	Squadron Leader
Captain (Hauptmann)	Flight Lieutenant
First Lieutenant (Oberleutnant)	Flying Officer
Second Lieutenant (Leutnant)	Pilot Officer

---

2. Source of R.A.F. Equivalent Ranks: Hanfried Schliephake, *The Birth of the Luftwaffe* (Chicago: Henry Regnery, 1971), p. 80.

APPENDIX 2

Chain of Command of Luftwaffe Aviation Units

Oberkommando der Luftwaffe (OKL) (High Command of the Luftwaffe)

Chef des Generalstabes der Luftwaffe (Chief of the General Staff of the Air Force)

Luftflotte (Air Fleet)

Fliegerkorps (Air Corps)

Fliegerdivision (Air Division)

Geschwader (Wing) (R.A.F. Group)

Gruppe (Group) (R.A.F. Wing)

Staffel (Squadron)

Kettle (Section) (called "Schwarm" in fighter units)

APPENDIX 3

Strengths of Luftwaffe Units

Unit	Composition	Rank of Commander
OKL	All Luftwaffe Units	Reichsmarschall
Air Fleet	Air Corps and Air and Flak Divisions	General to Field Marshal
Air Corps	Air and Flak Divisions plus various misc. units	Major General to General
Air Division	2 or more wings	Colonel to Major General
Wing	2 or more groups	
	100 to 120 aircraft	Major to Major General
Group	2 or more squadrons	
	30 to 36 aircraft	Major to Lt. Colonel
Squadron	2 or more sections	
	9 to 12 aircraft	Lieutenant to Captain
Section	3 or 4 aircraft	Lieutenant

APPENDIX 4

Glossary of Luftwaffe Terms

Erganzungsgruppen: training groups.

Fernaufklaerungsgruppe: a long-range reconnaissance squadron; abbreviated (F) or FAG. The 1 (F) 123 would be the 3rd Squadron, 123rd Long-Range Reconnaissance Group.

Fliegerdivision: an air division. Gradually replaced by the air corps in operational situations, but never entirely so.

Fliegerfuehrer: special air command, usually under air fleet command. Although primarily concerned with antishipping or weather reconnaissance operations, they sometimes controlled fighter, bomber, and dive-bomber units. For purposes of this book, the term is used to designate the commanders or their commands (i.e., Fliegerfuehrer Afrika is translated as Air Commander Africa or Air Command Africa).

Fliegerkorps: an air corps.

Fliegerverbindungsoffiziere ("Flivos"): air force liaison officers attached to army units; responsible for coordinating reconnaissance, close air support, and other missions.

Flugwetterdienst: the Air Force Meteorological Service.

Geschwader: an air wing, the largest mobile, homogenous formation in the Luftwaffe.

Gruppe: a group; the basic combat and administrative aviation unit of the Luftwaffe. Largely self-contained, the entire gruppe was usually based at a single airfield. It could be detached from its parent wing (geschwader). Gruppen were abbreviated II/KG 77 (II Group, 77th Bomber Wing), I/JG 3 (I Group, 3rd [Single-Engine] Fighter Wing), etc.

Jagdfuehrer: "Fighter Commander." Abbreviated "Jafu," this division-level headquarters controlled fighter units in its area (Jafu Ostmark, for example, controlled fighter units in Austria and is translated "Fighter Commander Austria" or "Fighter Command Austria").

Jagdgeschwader: a single-engine fighter wing, abbreviated JG 1, JG 2, etc.

Jagdkorps: an air corps consisting entirely or almost entirely of fighter units.

Kampfgeschwader: a bomber wing, abbreviated KG 1, KG 2, etc. Lehrdivision: a testing division, responsible for testing the latest types of aircraft, antiaircraft defenses, and air signal units.

Luftgau: corps-level air administrative districts responsible for administration and supply organizations, as well as recruiting, mobilization, and training; they had specific territorial responsibilities over set geographical areas. Luftgau functioned under the Air Ministry (Goering) and were designated by Roman numerals (Luftgau III) or locations (Luftgau Norwegen, or Air Administrative District Norway).

Luftwaffe Command: a headquarters intermediate in status between air fleet and air corps; included downgraded air fleets (3d Air Fleet became Luftwaffe Command West in 1944, 2nd Air Fleet became Luftwaffe Command South in late 1944, and 4th Air Fleet became Luftwaffe Command 4 in 1945, for example).

Nachtjagdgeschwader: a night fighter wing, abbreviated NJG 1, NJG 2, etc.

Nachtschlachtgruppe: a night harassment wing. Established in 1944, they consisted of obsolete aircraft (Ar-65s, He-50s, etc.). Abbreviated NS 1, NS 2, etc.

Nahaufklaerungsgruppe: a short-range reconnaissance unit, abbreviated NAGr, or (H). 1 (H) 32 would be 1st Squadron, 32d Reconnaissance Group (Short-Range).

OKL (Oberkommando der Luftwaffe): The High Command of the German Air Force. The command organ of the Luftwaffe. Directed by Goering, the day-to-day operations of O.K.L. were supervised by the chief of the General Staff of the Luftwaffe.

OKW (Oberkommando der Wehrmacht): The High Command of the Armed Forces. Directed by Field Marshal Wilhelm Keitel, this organization was nominally the immediate superior of OKL. Goering, however, refused to cooperate with Keitel, making the OKL, in fact, an independent body.

RDL (Reichsministerium der Luftfahrt): The Ministry of Aviation. Controlled civil aviation and supply, administration, and technical matters for the Luftwaffe.

RLM (Reichsluftfahrministerium, or Reichsluftfahrt Ministerium): The German Air Ministry. Initially in charge of all Luftwaffe functions, many of its responsibilities were later taken over by OKL.

Schlachtgeschwader: a ground attack and antitank wing; used primarily on the eastern front.

Schnellkampfgeschwader: a ground attack wing; used primarily on the eastern front.

Seenotdienst: the sea rescue service. During the war it saved the lives of many pilots on both sides.

Stabs-Schwarm: the staff section of a geschwader (wing); normally contained three to six aircraft.

Staffel: a squadron; the smallest operational Luftwaffe unit. Normally commanded by a captain or a lieutenant. It included a full-time adjutant. The signal, technical, and navigation branches of the staffel were supervised by flying officers in their spare time. Abbreviated 1, II/JG 77 (1st Squadron, II Group, 77th Fighter Wing), 3, I/KG 100 (3rd Squadron, I Group, 100th Bomber Wing), etc.

Stukageschwader: a Ju-87 "Stuka" wing. Abbreviated StG 1, StG 2, etc.

Zerstoerergeschwader: (literally, "Destroyer Wing"); a twin-engine fighter wing, abbreviated ZG 1, ZG 2, etc.

Other Leading Luftwaffe Personalities

Aschenbrenner, Lt. Gen. Heinrich. World War I infantry officer. Became a pilot in the 1920s and spent six weeks with the Russian 20th Air Force Brigade in 1931. Later served as air attaché at the German embassy in Moscow (1939–40) and was chief signals officer with Kesselring's 2nd Air Fleet (1940–42). From 1942 until the end of the war he was chief signals officer at Luftwaffe Command Headquarters, except for a period of temporary duty as chief signals officer with 5th Air Fleet (1943).

Axthelm, Gen. Walter von. Bavarian. Flak expert. Led I Flak Corps in France and Russia (1940–42). Later became inspector general of the flak branch, a post he had at the end of the war. Promoted to general of flak artillery on April 1, 1944.

Baumbach, Lt. Col. Werner. Born in Coppenburg, Oldenburg area, 1916, Baumbach was the only bomber pilot to receive the Knights Cross with Oak Leaves and Swords. He commanded KG 30 in 1942 and later worked with Dr. Speer, his close personal friend, on the remote-controlled bomber project. After the war he wrote *Zu Spaet?* (*Too Late?*), one of the best early books on the Luftwaffe. He emigrated to Argentina with his wife and son in 1948 and, became a technical adviser to industrial firms. At the age of thirty-six he crashed and drowned in the Rio de la Plata.

Below, Col. Nikolaus von. Luftwaffe adjutant to Adolf Hitler from June 16, 1937, to April 29, 1945.

Beust, Col. Baron Hans-Henning von. A veteran of the Condor Legion, Beust was commander of III/KG 27 from 1940 until May 29, 1942, and then led the wing in the Stalingrad campaign. Hospitalized for infantile paralysis from October 1943 until April 1944, he was chief of staff to the general of bomber forces from September 24, 1944, until January 1, 1945, and was then named general of bomber forces.

Brauchitsch, Col. Bernd von. Son of Field Marshal Walter von Brauchitsch, the commander-in-chief of the army (1938–41). A member of the General

Staff of the Luftwaffe, Bernd commanded I/StG 76 and IV (Stuka) Group, 1st Destroyer Wing, in 1940 and was Goering's personal adjutant and a member of the "Little General Staff" for most of the war.

Buelowius, Gen. Alfred. Joined Prussian army, 1912. Discharged as a captain in 1919. Joined Luftwaffe, 1933. Served with bomber and dive-bomber schools until 1942. Served with VIII Air Corps in Russia (1942). Named commander, Luftwaffe Command North, September 1942, and commanding general, 1st Air Division, in Russia (October 1942). Commander of various air administrative areas, December 1944, to the end of the war. Promoted to general of flyers, 1945.

Christ, Col. Torsten. Operations officer of the Condor Legion for much of the Spanish civil war, Christ would have made general officer rank except for an aversion to flying, which resulted from an air accident which disfigured his face. He held a variety of General Staff posts during World War II and was chief of supply at OKL at the end of the war.

Deichmann, Gen. Paul. Infantry officer and aerial observer in World War I. Served as chief of staff, II Air Corps, in the French campaign (1940), Battle of Britain (1940-41), Russia (1941), and the Mediterranean (1941–42). Chief of staff of OB South (Kesselring), August 1942 to June 1943. Briefly commander of IV Air Administrative Command in Austria (1943). Later chief of staff, 3d Air Fleet (Sperrle), 1943–44. Ended the war as general of flyers and commander, I Air Corps, on the eastern front (1945).

Dessloch, Col. Gen. Otto. Pilot and observer in German air service, World War I. Commander, 6th Air Division (1939). Commander, II Flak Corps (1940–41) and I Flak Corps (1942). Commander, 4th Air Fleet, Russian front, 1943–44. Replaced Sperrle as commander, 3d Air Fleet in France, August, 1944. Returned to command of the 4th Air Fleet on the eastern front in late 1944. Replaced Field Marshal Ritter von Greim as commander, 6th Air Fleet, on April 29, 1945, and held this command at the end of the war. Promoted to colonel general on March 1, 1944.

Doerstling, General of Flyers Egon. Chief of the Office of Procurement under Udet and later chief of supply for the Luftwaffe, he was in charge of administrative area commands in Holland and Austria from August 1943 until the end of the war.

Drum, Gen. Karl. Entered service, 1913. Served as an infantry officer and flight observer in World War I. Entered the clandestine General Staff after the war. Rose to chief of the inspectorate of aerial reconnaissance forces and operations, Reich Air Ministry. Named chief of staff to Luftwaffe General with the commander-in-chief of the army, 1939. Chief, Air Support Command, Army Group South (1941–42). Later commander-in-chief,

OKW Force in Holland, commander of the 11th Luftwaffe Field Division, and commander, Luftwaffe Administrative Area Western France. Ended the war as a general of flyers. Worked for the United States Air Force Historical Branch after the war.

Fiebig, Gen. Martin. Specialist in close air support operations who rose to the rank of general of flyers. Trained in Russia, late 1920s, as a close support expert. Commander, 1st Air Division, Russia (1941–42). Succeeded Richthofen as commander, VIII Air Corps (1942). Played prominent role in the Stalingrad relief operation (1942–43). Named commander, II Air Corps (1943). This headquarters was upgraded to Luftwaffe Command Northeast in April, 1945, and was operating on the eastern front at the end of the war. He was executed by the Yugoslavians after the war.

Foerster, General of Flyers Helmuth. Highly decorated flying officer, World War I. Reentered service as a lieutenant colonel in the Luftwaffe, March 1, 1934. Named commander, Bomber Wing "General Wever," 1936. Commanded an air division in Poland (1939). Chief of staff, 5th Air Fleet in Norway, 1940. Member, French-German Peace Commission, 1940. Later OKW commander in Serbia (1941) and commander, I Air Corps, eastern front (1941–October, 1942). Chief of administration, Reich Air Ministry (1942–45). Pensioned as a lieutenant colonel in 1952.

Hartmann, Maj. Erich. The leading ace of World War II, Hartmann shot down 352 aircraft—348 on the eastern front. He was commander of the 52d Fighter Group when he was captured by the Russians in 1945 after his airfield was overrun. He remained in Russian captivity until the mid-1950s. Hartmann held the Oak Leaves, Swords, and Diamonds to the Knights Cross.

Heidrich, General of Paratroopers Richard. An infantry officer in World War I and during the Reichswehr period, Heidrich was commander of the 514th Infantry Regiment when he transferred to the Luftwaffe in 1939. He distinguished himself as a paratrooper commander, leading the 3rd Parachute Regiment (1940–42), 7th Air Division (1942–43), 1st Parachute Division (1943–44), and I Parachute Corps (1944–45). Heidrich is especially famous for his defense of Monte Cassino in Italy in 1944.

Holle, Col. Gen. Alexander. Enlisted as a private, November, 1915. Served with 13th Infantry Regiment during World War I and with 16th Infantry Regiment between the wars. Admitted to General Staff, 1931. Transferred to Luftwaffe, 1934. Commander, 1st Wing, 3rd Dive-Bomber Group, 1938–40. Named chief of staff, IV Air Corps, January 1940. Rose rapidly thereafter. Served as commander, 26th Bomber Group, chief of staff, Air Command North (East), chief of the Luftwaffe Staff in Greece, commander, X Air Corps, and commander, Luftwaffe Command West (formerly 3d Air

Fleet) (1944). Holle was commander, IV Air Corps, in Denmark from December, 1944, to the end of the war. Junck, Maj. Gen. Werner. Commander, 3d Fighter Division, on western front (1940-43). Played prominent role as a fighter commander during the Battle of Britain. Later commanded the II Fighter Corps (1944).

Meindl, Gen. Eugen. A prominent member of the Luftwaffe's parachute corps, Meindl commanded the 112th Mountain Artillery Regiment (1938–40) and distinguished himself at Narvik. Later he commanded the ad hoc Division Meindl on the northern sector of the Russian front (1941–42). Meindl was commander of the 1st Luftwaffe Field Division in early 1942 and directed the XIII Air Corps (1942–43) and was in charge of assembling new Luftwaffe field divisions, which consisted of utilizing air force personnel as infantrymen—with disastrous results. In late 1943 he was named commander of the II Parachute Corps and distinguished himself in the Battle of St. Lo in Normandy (June–July, 1944). He was severely wounded at Falaise in August, but later returned to command of the II Parachute and led it until the end of the war.

Meister, Gen. Rudolf. A World War I aerial observer, Meister served in a Freikorps flying detachment in 1919 and joined the Reichswehr. He underwent military aviation training in Russia, 1928–30, and joined the Luftwaffe General Staff in the mid-1930s. Meister was chief of staff of I Air Corps (1939–40), chief of staff, VIII Air Corps (October 1940 to March 1942), chief of Operations Branch at OKL (June to September, 1943) and commander, IV Air Corps (from June to October, 1944). Later that month he was named commander, Luftwaffe Forces in Denmark. He served as chief of the Luftwaffe Personnel Office from December 1944 until the end of the war.

Nowotny, Maj. Walter. Commander of the first jet wing to operate against the Allies, Nowotny had shot down 255 aircraft on the eastern front. He was opposed to the early commitment of the Me-262 pilots on the western front because he felt his pilots were inadequately trained, but his advice was ignored by the Luftwaffe High Command. On November 8, 1944, he scored his 258th kill, but was himself shot down and killed by American fighters as he attempted to return to base. He was a holder of the Knights Cross with Oak Leaves, Swords, and Diamonds.

Peltz, Maj. Gen. Dietrich. Born in 1914, Peltz joined the Luftwaffe in 1935 and was commander of a dive-bomber squadron in 1939. He transferred to the heavy bombers in 1940 and was a wing commander by 1941. He directed a dive-bombing school at Foggia, Italy, in 1941, and commanded I Group, 60th Bomber Wing, in the Mediterranean in 1942, operating against Allied convoys bound for North Africa. Peltz was appointed inspector for bomber aircraft in December 1942, and was placed in charge of bomber attacks against England in March 1943. He assumed command of IX Air Corps on the western front in September 1943, despite his relatively junior rank. Peltz directed II Fighter Corps in support of Hitler's Ardennes Offensive in late 1944/early 1945 and was then returned to the command of IX Air Corps, with the mission of converting long-range bomber units into fighter units. He apparently fell into Russian hands at the end of the war and disappeared.

Pflugbeil, Col. Gen. Kurt. A World War I flier and Freikorps veteran, he underwent bomber training in Russia in 1928, was attached to the Italian air force, and was transferred to the Luftwaffe in 1935. He commanded an air corps in 1939 and directed an air administrative command in France and Belgium (1940). Pflugbeil commanded the IV Air Corps (August, 1940–September, 1943), primarily on the Russian front. Later he commanded the 1st Air Fleet (later Luftwaffe Command Courland) in northern Russia (1943–45). Pflugbeil was offered the post of chief of the General Staff of the Luftwaffe, but categorically refused to accept it. He died in May 1955, in a Soviet prison.

Pickert, Lt. Gen. Wolfgang. Served on the eastern and western fronts in World War I. Joined the flak artillery arm of the Luftwaffe in 1935 and became inspector of flak forces, Reich Air Ministry, 1937. He was commander of the Rhine-Ruhr Air Defense District (1939–April, 1940) and chief of staff, I Flak Corps, in France. Until May 1942, he was chief of staff, Air Fleet Reich. Pickert led the 9th Flak Division in Russia (May 1942–1944) and was commander of III Flak Corps on the western front (1944–45). He was named commander of flak forces, OKL, in March 1945, and surrendered in Italy in April, 1945.

Plocher, Lt. Gen. Hermann. Commissioned 1922. Pilot training, 1925. Joined Luftwaffe as captain, 1935. He served in Spain (1936–38), was chief of staff of the Condor Legion (1937–38), and later chief of staff of the V Air Corps in France and Russia (1940–42). Plocher was chief of staff of Luftwaffe Command East and 6th Air Fleet (Greim) in Russia (1942–43) and commanded the 19th Luftwaffe Field Division (1943), the 4th Air Division (1943), and the 6th Parachute Division on the western front (1944–45). He also served as chief of staff of the 3d Air Fleet (Sperrle) from October 1943 to July 1944. He wrote three excellent monographs on the air war in Russia for the United States Air Force Historical Branch in the 1960s.

Pohl, Gen. Ritter Maximilian von. Served as German air attaché to Rome and chief liaison officer to the Italian air force, 1941–42. Pohl was promoted to general of flyers on February 1, 1942. He succeeded Baron von Richthofen as commanding general, Luftwaffe Command South, in November 1944, and directed Luftwaffe units in Italy until the end of the war.

Rohden, Maj. Gen. Hans-Detlef Herhudt von. Served in World War I, then joined the General Staff. Transferred to Luftwaffe in 1935. In 1939 he commanded a bomber group in Schwerin and was chief of staff of the IX Air Corps in the West (1940). He was chief of staff of 4th Air Fleet on the Russian front (1941–42) but was relieved of his post by Milch. Later he became chief of staff of the 1st Air Fleet on the northern sector of the eastern front and an instructor at the Luftwaffe War Academy. He served as chief of the 8th (Military Science) Branch of the General Staff of the Luftwaffe in 1944 and 1945. After the war, Rohden was known for his historical writings on the history of air power. He died in 1952.

Rudel, Col. Hans-Ulrich. An incredibly brave man and skillful pilot, Rudel was the leading Stuka pilot of World War II. In four years' service on the Russian front, he destroyed more than 700 Soviet tanks and armored vehicles—enough to equip an entire armored corps. He continued operating against the Russians, even after one of his legs was shot off. Both Hitler and Goering ordered him to stop flying, but he ignored them. Faced with the choice of court-martialing Rudel or letting him get away with direct disobedience of a Fuehrer order, Hitler let Rudel have his way, and he continued to fly until the end of the war. He surrendered to the Allies after Hitler's suicide and later migrated to Argentina. Rudel was promoted to colonel on January 1, 1945, and was commander of the 2nd Ground Attack Wing. He was the only holder of the Golden Knights Cross with Oak Leaves, Swords, and Diamonds, a medal created just for him. He was only twenty-nine years old in 1945.

Ruedel, Col. Gen. Otto Guenther. Inspector of antiaircraft artillery for the Luftwaffe in 1936, Ruedel became the first general of flak artillery in 1939. He was chief of air defense for the Luftwaffe (1937–43) and was promoted to colonel general in 1943. He was chief of the Luftwehr (air arm) of the Reich Aviation Ministry in 1945.

Schlemm, General of Flyers Alfred. A noted Luftwaffe ground commander, Schlemm commanded the H Luftwaffe Field Corps on the Russian front (1942) and the I Parachute Corps in Italy (1944). He played a major role in containing the Anzio bridgehead south of Rome in early 1944.

Seidel, Gen. Hans-Georg von. A General Staff officer in World War I, Seidel left the army in 1920 as a captain of cavalry. He joined the Luftwaffe as a major in 1934, was promoted to major general the day the war started, and was promoted to lieutenant general in July, 1940. He became quartermaster of the Luftwaffe by June, 1941, and was primarily responsible for equipping the Luftwaffe for the winter war of 1941–42. Due to his foresight, and that of Milch, air force personnel were prepared for the Russian winter and did not suffer to the degree that the soldiers did. He was promoted to general of flyers on December 1, 1942, and apparently commanded X Air Corps in 1944 and 1945.

Waber, Gen. Bernard. Fought in World War I as a member of the Austrian army. Integrated into the Luftwaffe, 1938, after Austria was absorbed by the Third Reich. Waber commanded Air Administrative Area VIII in Poland (1939–41) and Air Administrative Command Kiev in Russia (1941–43). He was promoted to general of flyers in March 1942. In 1944, as Luftwaffe commander of the Northern Balkans, he was court-martialed for black market activities and for personally engaging in large-scale looting. He was executed by a firing squad on February 6, 1945. His death caused great indignation within the Luftwaffe, primarily because Hermann Goering confirmed the sentence. Goering, of course, was the greatest looter of the Second World War, and the execution of Waber was considered an act of rank hypocrisy.

Weise, Col. Gen. Hubert. A distinguished flak artillery officer, General Weise led the I Flak Corps in France in 1940 with considerable skill. For his services he was promoted to colonel general on July 19, 1940. Later, as "Luftwaffe Commander Center," he was in charge of all defense units in the Reich from 1942 to late 1943. At the end of the war, Weise was chief of the Flak Technical Branch of the Air Ministry. He had previously served as the commander of Luftgau III in 1938.

Wimmer, Gen. Wilhelm. This technologically competent General Staff officer was chief of the Technical Department of the Luftwaffe until June, 1936, and significantly contributed to the early technological superiority of the German Air Force. Unfortunately Hermann Goering could not stand him and replaced him with Ernst Udet—a move which may well have cost Germany the war. Wimmer briefly commanded Air Group I (later 1st Air Fleet) prior to the invasion of Poland, but most of his wartime service was as commander of Air Administrative Area Belgium and Northern France (September 1940 to 1944)—a relatively insignificant assignment. He was unemployed after his territory was overrun by the Allies.

The Principal German Aircraft, 1935–45

Arado Ar-65. A single-seat fighter and a biplane. First warplane of the Luftwaffe. First flew, 1931. Entered the service in 1933, in violation of the Treaty of Versailles. The first fighter units of the Luftwaffe were equipped with this aircraft. Used as an advanced trainer until 1940.

Arado Ar-66. Primary trainer. Entered the service, 1933, also in violation of the Treaty of Versailles. Hundreds produced. Later used to equip night harassment groups (NSGr) on the eastern front (1944–45).

Arado Ar-196. Two-seat naval reconnaissance aircraft. This seaplane was equipped with two 20mm cannon and three machine guns. Outclassed by Allied fighters. Operated primarily in the Bay of Biscay (off the western coast of France), the Mediterranean islands, and the Black Sea. 435 produced.

Arado Ar-234 "Blitz." Single-seat bomber. The first jet bomber. First flight, June 15, 1943. First operational delivery to the Luftwaffe: September, 1944. 214 produced. Problem with aircraft: lack of fuel in the fifth year of the war. Ar-234s destroyed the bridge at Remagen in March, 1945.

Buecker Bu-133 "Jungmeister." The "Young Man" was an aerobatic aircraft developed in 1935 and delivered to the Luftwaffe in 1936. The Luftwaffe purchased several hundred as aerobatic trainers but did not use them in combat.

Buecker Bu-181 "Bestmann." Single-engine trainer; also used as a utility aircraft, transport, and glider tug. About six thousand built in World War II.

DFS-230. An assault glider, originally ordered by Ernst Udet from Deutsches Forschungsinstitut fuer Segelflugzeug as a military transport glider. About one thousand were delivered to the Luftwaffe, almost all before 1941. The DFS-230 was used in the May 10, 1940, assault against Eben Emael, a critical fortress in Belgium, with complete success. It was later used in the assault on Crete, where the gliderborne troops suffered heavy casualties, but again was successful. DFS-230s were also used in Otto Skorzeny's successful effort to rescue Mussolini from a mountaintop hotel in 1943. The employment of the DFS-230 became less and less frequent as the Luftwaffe lost command of the air after 1940.

Dornier Do-17. Nicknamed "the Flying Pencil" because of its slender body, it was originally designed as a civil transport. It was first purchased by the Luftwaffe in 1936 as a medium bomber and was in combat in Spain by 1937. It could carry an internal load of about one ton of bombs. Successful in Poland, France, and the Balkans, they proved vulnerable to the R.A.F. fighters and were relegated to a training role by the end of 1941, although some were still used on the western front. They were equipped with only three machine guns.

Dornier Do-19. Known as the "Ural Bomber," this four-engine bomber was designed to carry 3,500 pounds of bombs and had a range of about one thousand miles, as opposed to 750 miles for the He-111. Only one prototype ever flew. The aircraft was cancelled in April, 1937, after the death of General Wever. Dornier Do-24. A trimotor reconnaissance flying boat. About two hundred used by the Luftwaffe during the war. It was used in all coastal sectors. The Do-24 was an excellent flying boat and was adopted by several foreign countries after the war. It was still in production in the mid-1960s.

Dornier Do-215. A modification of the Flying Pencil, this aircraft had six machine guns and a more powerful engine than the Do-17. It was still vulnerable to modern fighters. About one hundred were purchased by the Luftwaffe, some of which were used in a reconnaissance role. Production of this aircraft was terminated in early 1941.

Dornier Do-217. Medium twin-engine bomber. Maximum bomb load: 8,800 pounds, including 3,300 external. Most models had six machine guns. The Luftwaffe purchased 1,730 of these aircraft between 1940 and late 1943, when production was terminated. Problems: too complex electronically. It also suffered from structural strain. A fast aircraft, some Do-217s were used as night fighters in 1943.

Fieseler Fi-156 "Storch." A single-engine, two- or three-seat aircraft with a fixed landing gear, it was remarkably versatile. About 2,700 were produced for the Luftwaffe from 1937 to 1945. It was used as a communications, liaison, command, and reconnaissance aircraft.

Flettner Fl-282 "Kolibri." The first helicopter in mass production, the "Hummingbird" was in service from 1942, mainly in the 40th Transport Squadron. The pilot had no enclosed cockpit. The Fl-282 was used as an observation aircraft.

Focke-Wulf FW-58 "Weihe." A twin-engine utility aircraft, the "Kite" was used for communications, training, light transport, or as an ambulance. About

4,500 were purchased by the Luftwaffe between 1937 and 1942. It could deliver one and a half tons of cargo but had a range of less than 500 miles.

Focke-Wulf FW-189 "Uhu." A twin-engine, three-seat reconnaissance aircraft, the "Owl" was known for its toughness and excellent handling, which frequently allowed it to avoid enemy fighters. About 850 were delivered to the Luftwaffe between 1940 and the fall of 1944.

Focke-Wulf FW-190. A single-seat, single-engine fighter or fighter-bomber, it was faster than any Allied fighter when it made its appearance in combat in early 1941. It had heavy armament, including up to four machine guns and two Mauser cannons firing through the propeller hub. Besides being a formidable weapon, it was tough enough to be used on the forward dirt strips near the front. It was designed to replace the Me-109 (which it did, but never completely), but many were diverted to the eastern front to replace the vulnerable Ju-87 "Stuka. " Its principle defect was that its performance deteriorated rapidly at high altitudes. One of its main missions after 1942 was close air support on the eastern front, where most air battles took place only a few hundred feet above the ground, rather than above 24,000 feet, as in the West. Twenty thousand FW-190s were delivered to the Luftwaffe, mainly between 1943 and 1945.

Focke-Wulf FW-200 "Condor." Maritime reconnaissance bomber and transport. Range: 2,200 miles. Bomb load: 2.3 tons. Originally designed as long-range commercial transport for Lufthansa, prewar Condors set speed records on transoceanic flights. However, they suffered from structural weaknesses, including wing and fuselage failures. Nevertheless, the Condor was first used operationally in June 1940, against British shipping. Very successful at first, the Allies countered it by introducing Catapult-Armed Merchantman (CAM) fighters, as well as escort carriers and long-range coastal aircraft. The Condor was forced into a purely transport role (primarily on the eastern front) by mid-1944. Total production for the Luftwaffe was 276.

Gotha Go-145. A single-engine, two-seat biplane, the Go-145 was used as a primary trainer by the Luftwaffe throughout the war. Many were used to equip night harassment squadrons on the eastern front after 1942. About 10,000 were produced.

Heinkel He-45, He-46, and He-50. These two-seater, single-engine biplanes were used as reconnaissance-bombers and advanced trainers. They had a maximum airspeed of only 180 miles per hour and were very vulnerable; nevertheless they were used on the eastern front as night harassment aircraft from 1942 until 1944.

Heinkel He-51. Three major models of this single-seat, single-engine biplane were produced: the He-51A-1 (a single-seat fighter), the He-51B-2 (a reconnaissance seaplane), and the He-51C (a land-based, ground attack aircraft). First flown in 1932 and produced in 1933, the first He-51 was delivered to the Reichswehr in 1934, in violation of the Treaty of Versailles. They were used by the Condor Legion in Spain, and a few saw action in Poland in 1939. Some were still used as advanced trainers as late as 1943.

Heinkel He-59. A twin-engine, two-seat biplane, the He-59 was used as a seaplane, in coastal mining and rescue operations, and in ground attack and reconnaissance missions. First delivered to the army in 1932, the last delivery to the Luftwaffe took place in 1936. Its most famous operation took place in May, 1940, when ten He-59Cs landed sixty men on the Waal River in Rotterdam. These soldiers captured the city's main bridge and played a significant part in the early capitulation of Holland. Some He-59s were still conducting mining operations off the Atlantic coast in 1943.

Heinkel He-70. A three-seat reconnaissance monoplane, used by the Condor Legion in Spain. The Luftwaffe cancelled production in 1938 because of the introduction of more modern aircraft. Some He-170s (modified He-70s) were used on the eastern front in 1941.

Heinkel He-72 "Kadett" A two-seat biplane, used as a primary trainer from 1934 until the collapse of the training program in late 1944.

Heinkel He-111. A twin-engine medium bomber with a maximum speed of about 250 miles per hour, a 4.2-ton payload, and a range of 745 miles. The main German bomber for most of the war, it was also used as a transport in emergency situations, such as the Stalingrad relief operation. Armed with three machine guns, the He-111 experienced great success in Spain and Poland, but proved highly vulnerable to modern R.A.F. fighters in 1940. It was nevertheless in production until late 1944, largely because of the failure of the Luftwaffe Technical Branch and the German aircraft industry to produce a suitable replacement. About 5,600 were manufactured for use by the Luftwaffe.

Heinkel He-162 "Salamander." A single-engine interceptor, known as the "Volksjaeger" (People's Fighter), it first flew in December 1944, and the first He-162s reached the squadrons in January 1945. About three hundred had been delivered by the end of the war, and about eight hundred were on the assembly lines. Because of Germany's deteriorating military position, the He-162 was rushed into production and was consequently plagued with problems, including hydraulic difficulties, landing gear problems, and a tendency of the wings to collapse in flight. Even those which flew were of little use, since most of the veteran pilots were already dead, and many of the He-162 pilots were inexperienced volunteers from the Hitler Youth.

Heinkel He-177. A two-propeller, four-engine heavy bomber designed to replace the He-111. It was faster than the He-111 and was capable of carrying 6.6 tons of bombs. First flown in November 1939, it suffered from technological difficulties throughout its career, largely because of the ridiculous OKL/Technical Office requirement that the heavy bomber had to be capable of diving. Some 1,400 were delivered to the Luftwaffe, beginning in March 1942, although they were never satisfactory. The engines frequently caught fire, even in normal flight.

Heinkel He-178. The first jet. An experimental aircraft, it was first flown in 1939. Neither Milch or Udet were interested in it, however, and it was not mass produced. The only prototype was destroyed when Allied bombs struck the Berlin Air Museum in 1943.

Heinkel He-219. A two-seat, twin-engine night fighter which became operational in November 1943, this aircraft was fast and extremely maneuverable. Only 219 of them had been delivered in 1944 when, for some unknown reason, OKL ordered their production stopped.

Heinkel He-277. A four-engine heavy bomber, secretly developed by Heinkel without the permission of Hermann Goering. The first prototype flew in late 1943, and several others flew in succeeding months. It was apparently a superior aircraft. On July 3, 1944, however, the project was cancelled and the German aircraft manufacturer was ordered to produce nothing but fighters and fighterbombers.

Henschel Hs-123. Single-seat biplane used as a dive-bomber and close support aircraft in the early days of the Luftwaffe. Although the last delivery was made in 1938, this obsolete aircraft was used in the Balkans and on the eastern front until the end of 1944.

Henschel Hs-126. A single-engine, two-seat reconnaissance aircraft. First produced in 1936, it was manufactured until January 1941. About eight hundred were used by the Luftwaffe. Vulnerable to modern fighters, the Hs-126 was employed on the eastern front and in the Balkans in reconnaissance, antipartisan, and night harassment operations until the end of the war.

Henschel Hs-129. Inferior, underpowered, single-seat, close support aircraft. More than eight hundred were produced before production was cancelled in late 1942. They were used mainly on the eastern front.

Henschel Hs-130. A high-altitude bomber which reached heights of more than 40,000 feet. It was developed too late in the war to be mass produced. Junkers Ju-52. Tri-engine passenger and freight aircraft, occasionally used as a bomber. It could carry 1.5 tons of freight, or about seventeen passengers. Originally built for Lufthansa in 1930, it was perhaps the premier transport aircraft of its day. It was adopted by many foreign air forces and civilian aviation firms and was manufactured for the Spanish air force as late as 1975. About five thousand served in the Luftwaffe during the war. The Ju-52 was the mainstay of the Luftwaffe's transport branch throughout the conflict. Junkers Ju-86. Twin-engine bomber, except for the R-model (Ju-86R), which was a reconnaissance airplane. First produced in 1936, it carried about one ton of bombs and three machine guns for defense. It performed well in Spain and Poland but was obsolete by 1940. It was used on the eastern front after that date. About one thousand were produced for the Luftwaffe.

Junkers Ju-87 "Stuka." A single-engine dive-bomber and ground attack airplane, the Ju-87 was one of the most famous airplanes in the history of military aviation and the most feared airplane in the early years of the war. It had two seats: one for the pilot in front and one in the rear for the gunner, who faced aft. It was usually armed with a one-ton bomb and twin machine guns or cannons under the wings, with a third machine gun in the rear of the cockpit. Some models carried a single 1,000-pound bomb under the center of the fuselage and four 500-pound bombs under the wing. The B-model had a range of 373 miles and a maximum speed of about 240 miles per hour. Later models had a range of up to 620 miles. It entered production in 1935. The Ju-87 was highly effective in Poland, France, the Balkans, and the eastern front but was too slow when operating against modern Allied fighters. It suffered such heavy losses in the Battle of Britain that it had to be withdrawn. After 1942, when the quality of the Red Air Force began to improve, the Ju-87 was replaced by the FW-190. Production of the Stuka was terminated in 1944, although some continued to serve in night attack units until the end of the war. About 5,000 were produced.

Junkers Ju-88. Developed in 1936 as a dive-bomber, the Ju-88 was used in a variety of roles, including level bombing and close ground support, as well as antitank, night fighting and reconnaissance operations. About 15,000 were produced in the war. Some models of the Ju-88 could carry up to 3.3 tons of bombs. Structurally sound and highly maneuverable, its performance was severely cut because the Technical Office added the requirement that it be able to dive. It also lacked defensive armament (carrying only three machine guns) and was therefore vulnerable to Allied fighters. Nevertheless it proved superior to the Me-110 as a night fighter, and it appeared primarily in that role in the last years of the war. Production of the Ju-88 did not halt until its factories were overrun.

Junkers Ju-188. A twin-engine bomber. Production of the Ju-188 began in 1941 and continued until 1944, when resource shortages forced its termination. A good medium bomber, it carried 3.3 tons of bombs and four or five machine guns, depending on the model. About one thousand were produced in the war.

Junkers Ju-288. A part of the "B-Bomber" program, this twin-engine medium bomber consumed too many valuable resources and had several developmental problems. Although about twenty-five prototypes were produced, it never reached the production lines. The Ju-288 was scrapped by Hermann Goering upon the recommendation of Erhard Milch.

Messerschmitt Me-108. An excellent four-seat, single-engine communications, ambulance, and utility aircraft, the Me-108 was in production from 1934 to 1944. About one thousand were used on all fronts throughout the war.

Messerschmitt Me-109. This single-seat, single-engine fighter was the most important airplane used by the Luftwaffe in the Second World War. Thirty thousand of them were produced between 1937 and 1945—more than any other type of aircraft used by the German Air Force. Armed with two or three machine guns, the Me-109 was hampered by poor lateral control at high speeds and was technologically inferior to the British Spitfires and Hurricanes and the American Mustang, but not grossly so. It nevertheless continued to operate on all fronts until the end of the war, largely because the German aircraft industry and the Luftwaffe Technical Branch were unable to produce a suitable replacement in sufficient numbers. Many of the Me-109s were employed in a fighter-bomber role.

Messerschmitt Me-110. A two-seat, twin-engine day fighter, it was designed to escort German bombers. It was also occasionally used as a ground attack aircraft. It performed well in Poland and France but proved too vulnerable to Spitfires and Hurricanes during the Battle of Britain. The Me-210 was designed to replace it, but when it proved to be a failure the Luftwaffe had no choice but to continue manufacturing this obsolete aircraft until the end of the war. Total production was about six thousand.

Messerschmitt Me-163. A single-seat jet interceptor, the revolutionary "Komet" was rushed into production in early 1944, despite numerous technological and production difficulties. It had a maximum speed of almost six hundred miles per hour. However, it had no landing gear (it took off on a jettisonable trolley and landed on a skid) and was almost as dangerous to its pilots as to enemy aircraft. Its propellants were highly volatile and tended to explode on landing. The Me-163s devastated several American bomber formations in the last year of the war, but entirely too many Komets (and their pilots) were lost due to accidents. About 370 were used by the Luftwaffe during the war.

Messerschmitt Me-210. Designed to replace the Me-110, this twin-engine, two-seat fighter suffered from numerous technological difficulties, including severe flight instability and landing-gear malfunctions. Luftwaffe pilots considered this aircraft a death trap. Production was nevertheless started in 1942, before it had been adequately tested. Three hundred fifty had been manufactured before production of this flawed aircraft was terminated. Great hopes had been placed in the Me-210, and its failure was a severe blow to the Luftwaffe's war effort.

Messerschmitt Me-262. A single-seat jet fighter/fighter-bomber, this aircraft first flew in April, 1941. It might have won the air war for Germany, but its development was hampered by the disinterest of Milch, Udet, and others. It first reached the squadrons in September 1944. About thirteen hundred were produced during the war, but only about one hundred ever flew in combat, due to a lack of fuel and the near-collapse of the German transportation network. With a maximum speed of 540 miles per hour, it was a formidable weapon in combat.

Messerschmitt Me-321 "Gigant." This heavy cargo glider could carry a 24.5 ton payload or a company of infantry. Production began in mid-1941 and was terminated in early 1944.

Notes

CHAPTER 1: THE SECRET AIR FORCE

1. Matthew Cooper, *The German Air Force, 1933–1945* (London: Jane's, 1981), p. 9 (hereafter cited as "Cooper").
2. Robert Manvill and Heinrich Fraenkel, *Goering* (New York: Simon and Schuster, 1962), p. 27 (hereafter cited as "Manvill and Fraenkel"); Leonard Mosley, *The Reich Marshal: A Biography of Hermann Goering* (New York: Doubleday and Co., 1974; reprinted., New York: Dell Publishing Co., 1975), pp. 23–26 (hereafter cited as "Mosley"); "General Officers of the German Air Force," Air University Archives, Document EO 11652, Maxwell Air Force Base, Montgomery, Alabama, n.d. (hereafter cited as "Gen. Off.s, GAF").
3. Manvill and Fraenkel, p. 26.
4. Ibid, pp. 44–46.
5. Floyd Gibbons, *The Red Knight of Germany* (New York: Doubleday and Co., 1927; reprinted., New York: Bantam Books, 1959), pp. 190–209.
6. Mosley, pp. 47–53.
7. Manvill and Fraenkel, p. 37.
8. Herbert M. Mason, Jr., *The Rise of the Luftwaffe* (New York: Dial Press, 1973), p. 132 (hereafter cited as "Mason").
9. Richard Suchenwirth, "The Development of the German Air Force," *United States Air Force Historical Studies Number 160*. Harry R. Fletcher, ed. United States Air Force Historical Division, Aerospace Studies Institute (Maxwell Air Force Base, Montgomery, Alabama: Air University Archives, 1968) (hereafter cited as "Suchenwirth MS 'Development of GAF'").
10. Wilberg Personnel Extract, Air University Archives, Maxwell Air Force Base, Montgomery, Alabama.
11. Mosley, pp. 269–71.
12. Wilberg remained on active duty until November 20, 1941, when he was killed in an air accident in Belgium.
13. Paul Schmidt, *Hitler's Interpreter* (London: Heinemann, 1951), pp. 30–32; Manvill and Fraenkel, p. 136.
14. Robert Wistrich, *Who's Who in Nazi Germany* (New York: MacMillan Publishing Co., 1982), p. 209 (hereafter cited as "Wistrich"). The future state secretary's full name was Erhard Alfred Richard Oskar Milch (Milch Personnel Extract).
15. According to German Colonel Killinger (Auswerte Stelle-West), comments to British interrogators (C.S.D.I.C. [U.K.], S.R.G.G. 1243 [C], dated 22 May 1945) on file at the Historical Research Center, Air University Archives, Maxwell Air Force Base, Montgomery, Alabama. Dozens of these interrogations are on file and hereafter shall be cited as "Interrogation of . . ." followed by the name of the

officer and the date of the interrogation, when given. Some of the captives were surprisingly frank—even outspoken—in their remarks.

16. Interrogation of Colonel Killinger, 22 May 1945.

17. Richard Suchenwirth, "Command and Leadership in the German Air Force," *United States Air Force Historical Studies Number 174*. United States Air Force Historical Division, Aerospace Studies Institute (Maxwell Air Force Base, Montgomery, Alabama: Air University, 1969) (hereafter cited as "Suchenwirth MS 'Command'").

18. David Irving, *The Rise and Fall of the Luftwaffe: The Life of Field Marshal Erhard Milch* (Boston: Little, Brown and Company, 1973), p. 5 (hereafter cited as "Irving, *Milch*"); Milch Personnel Extract.

19. Suchenwirth MS "Command"; Irving, *Milch*, pp. 5—8; Milch Personnel Extract.

20. Irving, *Milch*, pp. 8–9. His promotion was dated August 18, 1918—three years to the day after his promotion to first lieutenant (Milch Personnel Extract).

21. Ibid, pp. 9–10.

22. Suchenwirth MS "Command."

23. Irving, *Milch*, p. 11.

24. Ibid, pp. 12–14. Suchenwirth stated that Milch did not join Junkers until 1923, but Irving's date seems more likely (Suchenwirth MS "Command").

25. Irving, *Milch*, p. 22; Suchenwirth MS "Command."

26. Irving, *Milch*, pp. 24–25. According to his personnel extract, Milch joined the Nazi party in January, 1930.

27. Interrogation of Colonel Killinger.

28. Irving, *Milch*, p. 29; Suchenwirth MS "Command."

29. Willi Frischauer, *The Rise and Fall of Hermann Goering* (Boston: Houghton Mifflin Company, 1951), p. 99 (hereafter cited as "Frischauer"); Mosley, p. 209; Bella Fromm, *Blood and Banquets* (New York: Harper and Row, 1942), 106.

30. Irving, *Milch*, pp. 36–37; Mason, p. 110.

31. Suchenwirth MS "Development of the GAF."

32. Cyril March, ed., *The Rise and Fall of the German Air Force, 1933–1945* (London: Her Majesty's Stationery Office, 1948; reprint ed., New York: St. Martin's Press, 1983), p. 11 (hereafter cited as "March").

33. Irving, *Milch*, pp. 36–37; Mason, p. 110.

34. Suchenwirth MS "Development of the GAF."

35. Ibid; March, p. 8.

36. In 1938, after the Luftkreise had been set up and were functioning well, Goering sent all three of these men back into retirement. All three were recalled to service by Field Marshal Walter von Brauchitsch, the commander-in-chief of the army, when the war broke out. Hans Halm commanded Wehrkreis VIII (VIII Military District in Silesia) until May, 1942, when he permanently retired as a general of infantry. Edmund Wachenfeld commanded Wehrkreis VII (Bavaria) until his retirement as a general of artillery on March 1, 1943. He died in Munich in 1958. Leonhard Kaupisch led an ad hoc corps into combat in Poland and, as commander of XXXI Army Corps, directed the German occupation of Denmark and was subsequently military governor of that country. He retired in 1942 as a general of artillery and died in Weimar in 1945. Wolf Keilig, *Die Generale des Heeres* (Friedberg: Podzun-Pallas-Verlag, 1983), pp. 124, 164, and 358–59 (hereafter cited as "Keilig").

37. Robert Goralski, *World War II Almanac, 1931–1945* (New York: G. P. Putnam's Sons, 1981), p. 33.

CHAPTER 2: COMMAND FRAGMENTATION

1. Andreas Nielsen, "The German Air Force General Staff," *United States Air Force Historical Studies Number 173*. United States Air Force Historical Division, Aerospace Studies Institute (Maxwell Air Force Base, Montgomery, Alabama: Air University, 1952) (hereafter cited as "Nielsen MS").
2. Ibid.
3. Kenneth Macksey, *Kesselring: The Making of the Luftwaffe* (New York: David McKay Company, 1978), pp. 17–18 (hereafter cited as "Macksey"); Gen. Off.s, GAF.
4. Macksey, pp. 23–28; Richard Brett-Smith, *Hitler's Generals* (Novato, California: Presidio Press, 1977), p. 236.
5. Gen. Off.s, GAF; Macksey, pp. 34–39.
6. Macksey, pp. 37–45; Gen. Off.s, GAF.
7. Albert Kesselring, *Kesselring: A Soldier's Record* (Westport, Connecticut: Greenwood Press, 1970), p. 14.
8. Gen. Off.s, GAF.
9. Telford Taylor, *Sword and Swastika: Generals and Nazis in the Third Reich* (New York: Simon and Schuster, 1952; reprinted., Chicago: Quadrangle Books, 1969), p. 248 (hereafter cited as "Taylor, *Sword and Swastika*").
10. Cooper, p. 68.
11. Richard Suchenwirth, "Historical Turning Points in the German Air Force War Effort," *United States Air Force Historical Studies Number 189*. United States Air Force Historical Division, Aerospace Studies Institute (Maxwell Air Force Base, Montgomery, Alabama: Air University, 1969) (hereafter cited as "Suchenwirth MS 'Turning Points'").
12. Cajus Bekker, *The Luftwaffe War Diaries* (New York: Ballantine Books, 1969), p. 328 (hereafter cited as "Bekker").
13. Suchenwirth MS "Turning Points."
14. Suchenwirth MS "Development of the GAF."
15. Mosley, p. 176.
16. Ibid, pp. 261–63.
17. Irving, *Milch*, pp. 50–54; Suchenwirth MS "Command."
18. Cooper, pp. 16–17.
19. Ibid, p. 19.
20. Ibid.
21. Suchenwirth MS "Command."
22. Ibid.
23. Irving, *Milch*, pp. 47 and 53.
24. Udet Dienftlaubahn, Air University Archives: *Ernst Udet, Ace of the Iron Cross*, Stanley M. Ulanoff, ed. (New York: Arco Publishing Company, 1981), p. 2 (hereafter cited as "Udet").
25. Udet, pp. 3–18; Udet Dienftlaubahn.
26. Colonel Ulanoff's translation (op cit, Footnote 24) is very good, except that he states in his introduction that Goering forced Udet to commit suicide. As we shall see, this is not correct.
27. Ibid, pp. xv–xvi and 143; Udet Dienftlaubahn. Udet's Pour le Merite was awarded on April 9, 1918.
28. Udet, pp. 91–94.
29. Udet Dienftlaubahn.
30. Irving, *Milch*, pp. 120–21, 143–44, and 243.
31. Suchenwirth MS "Command."

32. Felmy Personnel Extract, Air University Archives.
33. Mason, p. 249.
34. Suchenwirth MS "Command"; Irving, *Milch*, pp. 67–68; Cooper, pp. 78–79; Mason, p. 251.
35. Kammhuber Personnel Extract.
36. Suchenwirth MS "Command"; Irving, *Milch*, pp. 67–68; Cooper, pp. 78–79; Mason, p. 251.

CHAPTER 3: SPAIN: THE FIRST BATTLE

1. Raymond L. Proctor, *Hitler's Luftwaffe in the Spanish Civil War* (Westport, Connecticut: Greenwood Press, 1983), pp. 12—4 and 32–33 (hereafter cited as "Proctor").
2. Bruce R. Pirnie, "First Test for the War Machine," *World War II*, Volume 1, Number 5 (January, 1987), pp. 44–45 (hereafter cited as "Pirnie").
3. Karl Drum, "The German Air Force in the Spanish Civil War," *United States Air Force Historical Studies Number 150*, United States Air Force Historical Division, Aerospace Studies Institute (Maxwell Air Force Base, Montgomery, Alabama: Air University, 1965) (hereafter cited as "Drum MS").
4. Proctor, pp. 60–61.
5. Gen. Off.s, GAF; Wistrich, p. 294.
6. Cooper, p. 4.
7. Gen. Off.s, GAF.
8. Drum MS.
9. Gen. Off.s, GAF.
10. Drum MS.
11. Ibid. Henke was killed shortly thereafter.
12. Ibid.
13. Proctor, p. 65.
14. Drum MS.
15. Proctor, p. 84.
16. Ibid, p. 66.
17. Ibid, pp. 94–95.
18. Harry R. Fletcher, "Legion Condor: Hitler's Military Aid to Franco, 1936–1939," Unpublished M.A. Thesis (Madison, Wisconsin: University of Wisconsin, 1961), pp. 121–22 and 137 (hereafter cited as "Fletcher").
19. Hermann Plocher, "The German Air Force Versus Russia, 1941," *United States Air Force Historical Studies Number 153*, United States Air Force Historical Division, Aerospace Studies Institute (Maxwell Air Force Base, Montgomery, Alabama: Air University, 1965) (hereafter cited as "Plocher MS 1941").
20. Lt. Lothar von Richthofen, younger brother of the Red Baron, was shot down and seriously wounded on March 13, 1918. He spent most of the rest of the war in hospitals or on convalescent leave. He married Countess Doris von Keyserling, the daughter of one of the Kaiser's advisors, in 1919. They had a daughter, but were separated soon after. Lothar was killed in an air accident on July 4, 1922 (Gibbons, pp. 176–77).
21. Gen. Off.s, GAF; Plocher MS 1941.
22. Gen. Off.s, GAF.

23. Wistrich, p. 248; Snyder, p. 296. Also see Samuel W. Mitcham, Jr., *Triumphant Fox: Erwin Rommel and the Rise of the Afrika Korps* (Briarcliff Manor, New York: Stein and Day, 1984), p. 67 (hereafter cited as "Mitcham 1984").
24. Gen. Off.s, GAF.
25. Drum MS.
26. Ibid.
27. Cooper, p. 49.
28. Fletcher, pp. 196–97.
29. Fletcher, pp. 109 and 197–98; Drum MS.
30. Drum MS; Fletcher, p. 198.
31. Proctor, pp. 117–18.
32. Pirnie, p. 48.
33. Fletcher, pp. 147–48.
34. Drum MS.
35. Proctor, pp. 76–77, 124, and 158.
36. Gen. Off.s, GAF.
37. Ibid.
38. Proctor, p. 216.
39. Fletcher, pp. 185–95.
40. Proctor, pp. 187–206, 210.
41. Keilig, p. 357; Taylor, *Sword and Swastika*, pp. 138 and 389.
42. Drum MS.
43. Fletcher, pp. 109 and 197-98; Drum MS. These figures exclude about eighteen reconnaissance aircraft.
44. Dale M. Brown and the editors of Time-Life Books, *The Luftwaffe* (Alexandria, Virginia: Time-Life Books, 1982), p. 19 (hereafter cited as "Brown").
45. Fletcher, pp. 203–4.
46. Fletcher, pp. 206–8; Drum MS.
47. Roger J. Bender, *The Luftwaffe* (Mountain View, California: R. James Bender Publishing Company, 1972), p. 130.
48. Proctor, p. 253.
49. Drum MS.
50. Bekker, p. 562; Proctor, pp. 260–63.
51. Proctor, p. 259. Proctor, a retired U.S. Air Force lieutenant colonel, is a professor of history at the University of Idaho. In this author's opinion, his Hitler's Luftwaffe in the Spanish Civil War is the definitive work produced thus far on the Condor Legion.
52. Suchenwirth MS "Command."

CHAPTER 4: THE BUILDUP AND THE OUTBREAK OF THE WAR

1. Suchenwirth MS "Command."
2. Mason, pp. 260–61.
3. The Luftwaffe divisional commanders in 1939 were Ulrich Grauert (1st), Loerzer (2d), Putzier (3d), Keller (4th), Greim (5th), Dessloch (6th), and Student (7th) (Walter A. Musciano, Messerschmitt Aces [New York: Arco Publishing Company, 1982], p. 5 [hereafter cited as "Musciano"]). Lt. Gen. Helmut Foerster commanded the Lehrdivision (training division).

4. Suchenwirth MS "Development of the GAF."
5. Tony Wood and Bill Gunston, *Hitler's Luftwaffe* (Secaucus, New Jersey: Chartwell Books, 1984), pp. 182-84 (hereafter cited as "Wood and Gunston"); Suchenwirth MS "Development of the GAF."
6. Suchenwirth MS "Development of the GAF."
7. Wilhelm Speidel, "The Luftwaffe in the Polish Campaign," *United States Air Force Historical Studies Number 151*, United States Air Force Historical Division, Aerospace Studies Institute (Maxwell Air Force Base, Montgomery, Alabama: Air University: 1956) (hereafter cited as "Speidel MS").
8. Ibid.
9. Ibid.
10. Ibid.
11. Robert M. Kennedy, *The German Campaign in Poland* (1939), United States Department of the Army Pamphlet 20–255 (Washington, D.C.: Department of the Army, 1956), pp. 53–54 (hereafter cited as "Kennedy").
12. Speidel MS.
13. Ibid.
14. Ibid.
15. Brown, pp. 26–27.
16. Speidel MS.
17. Kennedy, p. 102.
18. Brown, p. 32.
19. Speidel MS.
20. Brown, p. 32.
21. Speidel MS.

CHAPTER 5: BLITZKRIEG

1. Len Deighton, *Blitzkrieg: From the Rise of Hitler to the Fall of Dunkirk* (New York: Alfred A. Knopf, 1979), pp. 187–88; Brown, pp. 52–53 (hereafter cited as "Deighton").
2. David Irving, *Hitler's War* (New York: The Viking Press, 1977), p. 79 (hereafter cited as "Irving 1977").
3. Kammhuber Personnel Extract, Air University Archives.
4. Albert Kesselring, *Kesselring: A Soldier's Record* (Westport, Connecticut: Greenwood Press, 1970), pp. 44–47 (hereafter cited as "Kesselring").
5. Irving 1977, p. 79.
6. Falkenhorst commanded the Army of Norway until it was absorbed by the 20th Mountain Army on December 18, 1944. He was living in Detmold in 1957 (Keilig, p. 85).
7. Earl F. Ziemke, "The German Northern Theater of Operations, 1940–1945," *United States Department of the Army Pamphlet 20-271* (Washington, D.C.: United States Department of the Army, 1959), p. 37 (hereafter cited as "Ziemke 1959"); Cooper, p. 109.
8. Ziemke 1959, p. 36.
9. Roger Edwards, *German Airborne Troops, 1936–45* (New York: Doubleday and Company, 1974), p. 71 (hereafter cited as "Edwards").
10. Ziemke 1959, p. 88.
11. Plocher MS 1941; March, p. 64; Cooper, p. 110.
12. Cooper, p. 112.

13. Pertinax [pseudo. Andre Geraud], *The Gravediggers of France* (New York: Doubleday and Company, 1944), p. 42 (hereafter cited as "Pertinax").

14. Ibid, p. 17.

15. Ibid, p. 11.

16. Jacques Benoist-Mechin, *Sixty Days That Shook the West: The Fall of France* (New York: G. P. Putnam's Sons, 1963), p. 40 (hereafter cited as "Benoist-Mechin").

17. Heinz Guderian, *Panzer Leader* (New York: E. P. Dutton, 1957; reprint ed., New York: Ballantine Books, 1967), p. 72 (hereafter cited as "Guderian"); Pertinax, pp. 25–26.

18. A. Goutard, *The Battle of France, 1940* (New York: Ives Washburn, 1959), p. 34 (hereafter cited as "Goutard"); Irving, *Milch*, p. 89; Cooper, p. 112.

19. Deighton, pp. 199–200.

20. Benoist-Mechin, p. 75.

21. Goutard, p. 134.

22. Ibid, p. 133.

23. Ibid.

24. Musciano, p. 13.

25. Lionel E. Ellis, *The War in France and Flanders, 1939–40* (London: Her Majesty's Stationery Office, 1953), pp. 55–56 (hereafter cited as "Ellis").

26. Deighton, p. 233.

27. Ellis, p. 57.

28. Bekker, pp. 60–64.

29. Cooper, p. 113; Kesselring, p. 59; Benoist-Mechin, p. 67.

30. Musciano, pp. 13, 77–78.

31. Deighton, p. 269.

32. Leonard Mosley and the editors of Time-Life Books, *The Battle of Britain* (Alexandria, Virginia: Time-Life Books, 1977), pp. 26–27 (hereafter cited as "Mosley et al").

CHAPTER 6: THE AIR WAR AGAINST BRITAIN, 1939–42

1. Coeler Personnel Extract, Air University Archives.

2. Coeler was subsequently commander of the XIV Air Corps and the Air Transport Branch (from October 15, 1944). He was placed in Fuehrer Reserve on February 5, 1945 (Coeler Personnel Extract).

3. Geisler Personnel Extract.

4. Mosley et al, pp. 18–20.

5. Irving, *Milch*, pp. 91–92.

6. Mosley et al, pp. 18–20.

7. Ibid, p. 20.

8. Nielsen MS.

9. Mosley et al, p. 53.

10. Cooper, p. 129.

11. Brett-Smith, p. 139.

12. Cooper, pp. 129–32.

13. Musciano, p. xiv.

14. Cooper, pp. 131–32.

15. Irving, *Milch*, p. 99. Cooper (p. 136) lists the British strength as 492 operational aircraft.

16. Cooper, p. 137; Irving, *Milch*, p. 99.

17. Irving, *Milch*, pp. 100–101; Mosley et al, p. 99; Cooper, pp. 143–44.
18. Musciano, pp. 5 and 85–86.
19. "Cooper, p. 146.
20. Ibid, p. 147.
21. Ibid.
22. Mosley et al, p. 117.
23. Telford Taylor, *The Breaking Wave* (New York: Simon and Schuster, 1967), p. 158 (hereafter cited as "Taylor, *Breaking Wave*").
24. Irving, *Milch*, p. 101.
25. Macksey, p. 88.
26. Cooper, pp. 152–54; Bekker, 240–41; Irving, *Milch*, pp. 104–5; Len Deighton, *Fighter* (New York: Alfred A. Knopf, 1977; reprinted., New York: Ballantine Books, 1979), pp. 251–52 (hereafter cited as "Deighton, *Fighter*").
27. Plocher MS 1941.
28. Interrogation of Adolf Galland, 6 June 1945.
29. Interrogation of Erhard Milch, 6 June 1945.
30. Adolf Galland, *The First and the Last* (New York: Henry Holt and Company, 1954; reprint ed., New York: Ballantine Books, 1987), p. 142 (hereafter cited as "Galland").
31. Schmid Personnel Extract.
32. Plocher MS 1941.
33. Winston S. Churchill, *Their Finest Hour* (Boston: Houghton Mifflin Company, 1949), p. 331.
34. Cooper, p. 154.
35. Taylor, *Breaking Wave*, p. 204.
36. Galland, pp. 46, 78.
37. Walter Kreipe, "The Battle of Britain," in *The Fatal Decisions*, William Richardson and Seymour Freidin, eds. (London: Michael Joseph, 1956), p. 18.
38. Musciano, p. 20.
39. Cooper, pp. 173–75.
40. Musciano, p. 42.
41. Interrogation of Lieutenant General Veith, May, 1945.
42. Wistrich, pp. 294–95.
43. Deighton, *Fighter*, p. 248; Mosley et al, p. 56.
44. Irving, *Milch*, p. 201.
45. Paul Joseph Goebbels, *The Goebbels Diaries*, Louis P. Lochner, ed. (New York: Doubleday and Company, 1948; reprinted., New York: Universal-Award House, 1971), p. 315 (hereafter cited as "Goebbels").
46. Williamson Murray, *Strategy for Defeat: The Luftwaffe, 1933–1945* (Maxwell Air Force Base, Montgomery, Alabama: Air University Press, 1983), p. 197 (hereafter cited as "Murray").
47. Coeler Personnel Extract.
48. March, p. 104; Cooper, pp. 125–26.
49. Harlinghausen Personnel Extract, Air University Archives.
50. Bekker, pp. 369–79; Cooper, pp. 126 and 178.
51. Harlinghausen Personnel Extract; Proctor, p. 260.
52. Kessler Personnel Extract.

CHAPTER 7: THE BALKANS CAMPAIGN

1. Peter Young, *World War, 1939–45* (New York: Thomas Y. Crowell Company, 1966), p. 94 (hereafter cited as "Young").
2. Robert Goralski, *World War II Almanac, 1931–1945* (New York: G. P. Putnam's Sons, 1981), pp. 136–41 (hereafter cited as "Goralski").
3. Ibid, p. 145.
4. I. S. O. Playfair, *The Mediterranean and the Middle East,* Volume II: *The Germans Come to the Aid of Their Ally* (London: Her Majesty's Stationery Office, 1960), p. 85 (hereafter cited as "Playfair II").
5. Bekker, pp. 229–30.
6. United States Department of the Army, "The German Campaigns in the Balkans (Spring, 1941)," *United States Department of the Army Pamphlet 20-260* (Washington, D.C.: Military Historical Division, 1953), pp. 20–24 (hereafter cited as "DA Pam 20–260"), p. 50.
7. Ibid, p. 49; Cooper, p. 197.
8. DA Pam 20-260, p. 50.
9. Playfair II, p. 81.
10. DA Pam 20-260, p. 80.
11. Ibid, pp. 81–91.
12. Playfair II, p. 96.
13. Ibid.
14. DA Pam 20-260, pp. 105–7.
15. Karl Gundelach, "The Battle for Crete, 1941," in H. A. Jacobsen and J. Rowder, *Decisive Battles of World War II: The German View* (New York: G. P. Putnam's Sons, 1965), p. 102 (hereafter cited as "Gundelach"); DA Pam 20-260, pp. 107–9.
16. Playfair II, p. 105.
17. DA Pam 20-260, pp. 118–20.
18. Ibid, p. 124; Gundelach, p. 117. Cooper (p. 199) put XI Air Corps' strength at 700 Ju-52s and 80 gliders.
19. Fourth Air Fleet, "The Invasion of Crete," Luftwaffe report dated 28 November 1941. Translated by the British Air Ministry, 1947, and on file at the Air University Archives (hereafter cited as "Fourth Air Fleet Report, 'Crete'").
20. DA Pam 20-260, p. 124.
21. Fourth Air Fleet Report, "Crete."
22. Cooper, p. 199.
23. Edwards, p. 83.
24. Gundelach, pp. 111–16.
25. Gundelach, pp. 117 and 120–21.
26. Edwards, pp. 91–93.
27. Gundelach, pp. 124–25; Edwards, p. 95; Bekker, pp. 270–76.
28. Bekker, p. 276.
29. Ibid, pp. 278–80.
30. Ibid, pp. 280–82.
31. Ibid, p. 282.
32. Ibid, pp. 282–83.
33. DA Pam 20-260, p. 141.
34. Bekker, p. 548.
35. Gundelach, p. 130.
36. Da Pam 20-260, p. 141.

37. Gundelach, pp. 130–31.
38. Gen. Off.s, GAF.

CHAPTER 8: RUSSIA, 1941: THE LAST BLITZKRIEG

1. Nicholas Bethell and the editors of Time-Life Books, *Russia Besieged*, World War II series, Volume 6 (Alexandria, Virginia: Time-Life Books, 1980), pp. 22–23 (hereafter cited as "Bethell et al").
2. Goralski, pp. 123–25.
3. Adolf Hitler, *Mein Kampf* (Munich: Verlag Frz. Eher Nachf., 1925; reprint ed., Boston: Houghton Mifflin Company, 1971), pp. 641–47.
4. Murray, pp. 70–71.
5. United States Department of the Army, "The German Campaign in Russia—Planning and Operations (1940–42)," *United States Department of the Army Pamphlet 20-261a* (Washington, D.C.: United States Department of the Army, 1955), p. 22 (hereafter cited as "DA Pam 20-261a").
6 Suchenwirth MS "Command."
7. Plocher MS 1941.
8. Kesselring, p. 93.
9. Irving, *Milch*, pp. 116–17.
10. Suchenwirth MS "Command."
11. Ibid.
12. Irving, *Milch*, p. 121.
13. DA Pam 20-261a, p. 37.
14. Hermann Plocher, "The German Air Force Versus Russia, 1943," *United States Air Force Historical Studies Number 155*, United States Air Force Historical Division, Aerospace Studies Institute (Maxwell Air Force Base, Montgomery, Alabama: Air University, 1965) (hereafter cited as "Plocher MS 1943"); Suchenwirth MS "Development of the GAF"; Cooper, p. 27; Richard Brett-Smith, *Hitler's Generals* (Novato, California: Presidio Press, 1977), p. 129 (hereafter cited as "Brett-Smith").
15. Brett-Smith, p. 130. First Air Division was upgraded to I Air Corps in the winter of 1939–40.
16. "Stellenbesetzung Hoeherer Kommandeuer der Luftwaffe" (Maxwell Air Force Base, Montgomery, Alabama: Air University Archives) (hereafter cited as "Stellenbesetzung"); Plocher MS 1941.
17. Plocher MS 1941.
18. Stellenbesetzung; Plocher MS 1941. Pflugbeil died in Russian captivity on May 31, 1955.
19. Stellenbesetzung; Plocher MS 1941.
20. Plocher MS 1941.
21. DA Pam 20-261a, p. 42.
22. R. J. Overy, *The Air War, 1939–45* (Briarcliff Manor, New York: Stein and Day, 1980), p. 62 (hereafter cited as "Overy").
23. Plocher MS 1941.
24. Overy, p. 62.
25. DA Pam 20-261a, p. 42.
26. Werner Baumbach, *The Life and Death of the Luftwaffe* (New York: Coward-McCann, 1960; reprint ed., New York: Ballantine Books, 1972), p. 136 (hereafter cited as "Baumbach").

27. Cooper, p. 223.

28. Hermann Plocher, "The German Air Force Versus Russia, 1942," *United States Air Force Historical Studies Number 154*, United States Air Force Historical Division, Aerospace Studies Institute (Maxwell Air Force Base, Montgomery, Alabama: Air University, 1965) (hereafter cited as "Plocher MS 1942").

29. Brett-Smith, p. 137.

30. Bekker, p. 552.

31. Plocher MS 1941.

32. Ibid.

33. Cooper, p. 223; Plocher MS 1941.

34. Goralski, p. 164.

35. Cooper, p. 222.

36. Albert Seaton, *The Battle for Moscow* (Briarcliff Manor, New York: Stein and Day, 1971; reprint edition, New York: Playboy Press Paperbacks, 1980), p. 39 (hereafter cited as "Seaton, Moscow"); Plocher MS 1941.

37. Guderian, p. 134.

38. Plocher MS 1941.

39. Ibid.

40. Ibid.

41. Brett-Smith, p. 141.

42. Stellenbesetzung.

43. Plocher MS 1941.

44. Frau von Richthofen, the widow of the baron, never consented to have her husband's diary published in full because of the many derogatory personal references Richthofen made in it about people with whom he dealt. Lieutenant General Plocher read it and found it disappointing, as it dealt mainly with personalities and was gossipy, and it did not yield any insights into Richthofen's military operations (Harry R. Fletcher, personal communication: December 19, 1984).

45. Plocher MS 1941.

46. Figures on this battle differ slightly. DA Pam 20-261a (p. 44) puts the Russian losses at 290,000 men, 2,500 tanks, and 1,400 guns captured. Lucas placed the Soviet losses at 324,000 men, but agrees with the DA pamphlet on the number of tanks and guns destroyed or captured. Seaton (p. 125) also quotes the German estimates placing Soviet losses at twenty-two rifle divisions and the equivalent of seven tank divisions and six mechanized brigades. The 3rd and 10th and the bulk of the 13th Soviet armies were destroyed, along with elements of the 4th and 11th armies. See James Lucas, *War on the Eastern Front, 1941–45* (Briarcliff Manor, New York: Stein and Day, 1979; reprint ed., New York: Bonanza Books, 1979), p. 176 (hereafter cited as "Lucas").

47. Plocher MS 1941.

48. Lucas, p. 176; Seaton, p. 130.

49. Plocher MS 1941.

50. Ibid.

51. Franz Halder, *The Private War Journal of Generaloberst Franz Halder, Chief of Staff of the Supreme Command of the German Army, 14 Aug 39–24 Sep 42* (Washington, D.C.: Department of the Army, Office of the Chief of Military History, 1950), July 13, 1941 (hereafter cited as "Halder Diary").

52. Plocher MS 1941; Cooper, p. 227.

53. Plocher MS 1941.
54. Ibid.
55. Ibid.
56. Plocher MS 1941; also see Bekker, pp. 319–25.
57. Musciano, pp. 88-89; Galland, pp. 78–80; Moelders Personnel Extract.
58. Galland, p. 78.
59. Musciano, p. 89.
60. Paul Carell, *Hitler Moves East, 1941–43* (Boston: Little, Brown and Company, 1964; reprint ed., New York: Bantam Books, 1966), p. 266 (hereafter cited as "Carell 1966").
61. Bekker, p. 322.
62. Hans Ulrich Rudel, *Stuka Pilot* (New York: Ballantine Books, 1958; reprint ed., New York: Bantam Books, 1979), pp. 31–43 (hereafter cited as "Rudel").
63. Bekker, pp. 322–23.
64. Rudel, pp. 31–43 and 53.
65. Ibid.
66. Bekker, p. 324.
67. Plocher MS 1941.
68. Carell 1966, pp. 269–70.
69. Plocher MS 1942.
70. Plocher MS 1941.
71. Ibid.
72. Overy, p. 62.

CHAPTER 9: THE FALL OF ERNST UDET

1. Cooper, p. 29.
2. Suchenwirth MS "Command."
3. Baumbach, pp. 14–17.
4. Cooper, p. 271.
5. Wood and Gunston, p. 210.
6. General a.D. Marquardt, "Die Stuka-Idee hat der deutsche Luftwaffe den Untergang gebracht" ("The Dive-Bomber Concept as the Ruin of the German Air Force"), Karlsruhe Document Collection.
7. Mason, p. 255.
8. Cooper, p. 71.
9. Suchenwirth MS "Command."
10. Suchenwirth MS "Turning Points."
11. Suchenwirth MS "Command."
12. Mason, p. 258.
13. Wood and Gunston, p. 188.
14. Bekker, p. 555.
15. Cooper, p. 71.
16. Suchenwirth MS "Command."
17. Mason, p. 256.
18. Cooper, p. 54.
19. Mason, p. 256.
20. Suchenwirth MS "Command."
21. Ibid.
22. Ibid.

23. Ibid.
24. Ibid.
25. Brett-Smith, p. 132.
26. Suchenwirth MS "Command."
27. Ibid.
28. Brett-Smith, p. 131.
29. Suchenwirth MS "Command."
30. Cooper, p. 278.
31. Suchenwirth MS "Command"; Baumbach, p. 17.
32. Ibid. Lucht was retired with a pension on January 1, 1943, and went to work as the manager of the Messerschmitt Works at Regensburg. He was killed—apparently during an Allied bombing raid—in the last weeks of the war. Ploch, an aerial observer in World War I, had served in the secret air force based at Lipetsk, Russia, in the 1920s and was fluent in Russian. He had further trouble with Milch, however, and was permanently retired on November 30, 1942.
33. See Irving, *Milch*, for an excellent and more detailed description of Milch's accomplishments in the air armaments field.
34. Gen. Karl Koller, quoted in A.D.I.K. Report Number 348/1945, British Air Ministry (on file at the Air University Archives, Maxwell Air Force Base, Montgomery, Alabama).
35. Brett-Smith, p. 109.

CHAPTER 10: THE RUSSIAN FRONT, 1942–43
1. Plocher MS 1941.
2. Ibid.
3. Plocher MS 1942.
4. Plocher MS 1941.
5. Ibid.
6. Cooper, p. 240.
7. Plocher MS 1941 and 1942.
8. Fritz Morzik, "German Air Force Airlift Operations," *United States Air Force Historical Studies Number 167*, United States Air Force Historical Division, Aerospace Studies Institute (Maxwell Air Force Base, Montgomery, Alabama: Air University, 1961) (hereafter cited as "Morzik MS"); Plocher MS 1942.
9. Carell 1966, p. 438.
10. Morzik MS; Plocher MS 1942.
11. Morzik Personnel Extract.
12. Morzik MS.
13. Plocher MS 1942.
14. Ibid; Morzik MS.
15. Overy, p. 65; Plocher MS 1942.
16. Gen. Off.s, GAF.
17. Erich von Manstein, *Lost Victories* (Novato, California: Presidio Press, 1982), p. 235 (hereafter cited as "Manstein").
18. Seaton, Moscow, p. 259.
19. Plocher MS 1942.
20. Ibid.
21. Manstein, pp. 236-38; Seaton, Moscow, p. 259.
22. Plocher MS 1942.

23. Carell 1966, pp. 501–4; Seaton, Moscow, p. 263. Both Carell and Seaton cite Soviet sources, which are probably conservative.
24. Plocher MS 1942.
25. Carell 1966, pp. 501–4; Plocher MS 1942; Seaton, Moscow, p. 263.
26. Plocher MS 1942.
27. Ibid.
28. Seaton, p. 264; also see Carell 1966, pp. 504–11.
29. Carell 1966, p. 511.
30. Plocher MS 1942.
31. March, p. 113.
32. Bekker, p. 390.
33. Ibid, pp. 391–93; March, p. 113.
34. March, p. 114.
35. Bekker, p. 398; Carell 1966, pp. 466–67.
36. Bekker, p. 398.
37. Ibid; March, p. 115; Carell 1966, p. 467.
38. Cooper, p. 245.
39. Galland, pp. 87–88.
40. Plocher MS 1942.
41. Ibid.
42. Gen. Off.s, GAF.
43. Cooper, pp. 245–46; Plocher MS 1942.
44. Plocher MS 1942.
45. Ibid.
46. Cooper, p. 247.
47. Plocher MS 1942.
48. Cooper, pp. 245–46.
49. Plocher MS 1942.
50. Seaton, Moscow, p. 291.
51. Plocher MS 1941.
52. John Shaw and the editors of Time-Life Books, *Red Army Resurgent*, World War II series, Volume 20 (Alexandria, Virginia: Time-Life Books, 1979), p. 137 (hereafter cited as "Shaw et al").
53. Plocher MS 1942.
54. Ibid, citing Richthofen Diary, entry of November 1–2, 1942.
55. Irving, *Hitler's War*, p. 285.
56. Plocher MS 1942.
57. Ibid.
58. Seaton, *Moscow*, pp. 306–7.
59. Rudel, p. 73.
60. Plocher MS 1942.
61. Mosley, p. 334.
62. Plocher MS 1942.
63. Kurt Zeitzler, "Stalingrad," in *The Fatal Decisions*, William Richardson and Seymour Freidon, eds. (London: Michael Joseph, 1956), pp. 144–45.
64. Plocher MS 1942.
65. James D. Carnes, "A Study in Courage: General Walther von Seydlitz' Opposition to Hitler," Unpublished Ph.D. Dissertation (Tallahassee, Florida: Florida State University, 1976), p. 147.
66. Plocher MS 1942.

67. Irving 1977, p. 457.
68. Ibid.
69. Cooper, p. 251.
70. Morzik MS.
71. Ibid.
72. The Ju-90 was a four-engine, 750 horsepower, long-range commercial transport. The Ju-290 was a modified Ju-90 with a longer fuselage and a 1,700 horsepower engine. The FW-200 "Condor" was a Lufthansa long-range transport that was never made suitable for a military transport (Plocher MS 1942).
73. Morzik MS.
74. Ibid.
75. Plocher MS 1943.
76. Morzik MS.
77. Earl F. Ziemke, *Stalingrad to Berlin: The German Defeat in the East.* United States Department of the Army, Office of the Chief of Military History (Washington, D.C.: United States Government Printing Office, 1966), pp. 61 and 75 (hereafter cited as "Ziemke").
78. Plocher MS 1942.
79. Ibid.
80. Ibid.
81. Irving 1977, p. 458.
82. Seaton, Moscow, p. 328.
83. Morzik MS.
84. Ibid.
85. Irving, *Milch*, pp. 184–87.
86. Ibid, p. 196.
87. Plocher MS 1943; Morzik MS.
88. Irving, *Milch*, p. 197.
89. Morzik MS.
90. Irving, *Milch*, p. 197.
91. Plocher MS 1942.
92. Ibid.
93. Morzik MS.
94. Plocher MS 1942.
95. Morzik MS.
96. Plocher MS 1942.
97. Irving 1977, p. 485.
98. Gen. Off.s, GAF.
99. Plocher MS 1942.
100. Mosley, p. 359.

CHAPTER 11: THE BOMBINGS BEGIN, 1942

1. Galland, p. 127.
2. Sir Charles Webster and Noble Frankland, *The Strategic Air Offensive against Germany, 1939–1945* (London: Her Majesty's Stationery Office, 1961), Volume II, pp. 392–93 (hereafter cited as "Webster and Frankland").
3. Ibid; Manvill and Fraenkel, pp. 260–61; Noble Frankland, *Bomber Offensive: The Devastation of Europe* (New York: Ballantine Books, 1970), pp. 42–43 (hereafter cited as "Frankland").
4. Goebbels, p. 183.

5. Ibid, pp. 216–18; Webster and Frankland II, pp. 393–94.
6. Earl R. Beck, *Under the Bombs: The German Home Front, 1942–1945* (Lexington: University of Kentucky Press, 1986), p. 3 (hereafter cited as "Beck").
7. Cooper, pp. 185–86; Beck, pp. 1–2.
8. Beck, pp. 8–9.
9. Webster and Frankland II, pp. 406–8.
10. Brett-Smith, p. 138.
11. Cooper, p. 191.
12. Ibid.
13. Irving, Milch, p. 147.
14. Ibid, pp. 147–48.
15. Ibid, pp. 147–48, citing Burton H. Klein, *Germany's Economic Preparations for War* (Cambridge, Massachusetts: Harvard University Press, 1959), pp. 198f.
16. Cooper, p. 184.
17. Ibid, pp. 57–58 and 184.
18. Beck, p. 97.
19. Cooper, p. 58.
20. Jerry Scutts, *Luftwaffe Night Fighter Units, 1939–45* (London: Osprey Publishing, 1978), pp. 3–4 (hereafter cited as "Scuffs").
21. Martini was born in Lizsa, Poland, on September 20, 1891, and entered the imperial German Army as a Fahnenjunker (officer-cadet) in the 1st Telegraph Battalion in March, 1910. He was associated with signal units throughout his career. He served as a signal officer in World War I with a Freikorps outfit fighting against the Poles in 1919, and in the Reichsheer, before being transferred to the RLM as a major in 1933. He was chief of the Signals Office of the Luftwaffe General Staff by 1934 and was promoted to major general in 1938. He was named general der luftnachrichtentruppen (general of air signal troops) on September 20, 1941—his fiftieth birthday. He was the chief Luftwaffe signals expert throughout the war (Martini Personnel Extract, Air University Archives).
22. Scuffs, p. 7.
23. Cooper, p. 184.
24. Doering, a native of Ribbehardt, Pomerania, later commanded 3d Fighter Division until 1944, when he became chief of the Central Office at RLM. He was promoted to lieutenant general on October 1, 1941 (Doering Personnel Extract, Air University Archives).
25. Webster and Frankland II, pp. 414–15.
26. Ibid, p. 416.
27. Beck, p. 9.
28. Cooper, pp. 192–93.
29. Suchenwirth MS "Command."
30. Galland, pp. 134–35.
31. Manvill and Fraenkel, pp. 266–67.
32. Musciano, p. 57.
33. Cooper, pp. 263–66.

CHAPTER 12: THE TIDE TURNS, 1943

1. Irving, *Milch*, p. 112; Playfair II, pp. 1–9.
2. Froehlich Personnel Extract.
3. Playfair II, p. 171.

4. See Mitcham 1984, pp. 95–116, for a detailed description of this battle.
5. Cooper, p. 203.
6. Brett-Smith, p. 114.
7. Froehlich Personnel Extract.
8. Cooper, p. 212.
9. Plocher MS 1941.
10. I. S. O. Playfair and C. J. C. Molony, *The Mediterranean and Middle East*, Volume IV, *The Destruction of the Axis Forces in Africa* (London: Her Majesty's Stationery Office, 1966), p. 171 (hereafter cited as "Playfair and Molony IV").
11. Brett-Smith, p. 133.
12. Loerzer Personnel Extract.
13. Playfair and Molony IV, pp. 471-72.
14. Seidemann Personnel Extract.
15. Playfair and Molony IV, p. 417.
16. Cooper, pp. 216–17.
17. Ibid; Playfair and Molony IV, p. 417.
18. Proctor, pp. 260-61; Harlinghausen Personnel Extract.
19. Seaton, *Moscow*, p. 348.
20. Ibid, p. 349.
21. Plocher MS 1943.
22. Ibid.
23. Ibid.
24. Gen. Off.s, GAF.
25. Murray, p. 164.
26. Brett-Smith, p. 136.
27. Cooper, p. 288; March, p. 258.
28. Cooper, p. 289.
29. Albert N. Garland and Howard McG. Smyth, *Sicily and the Surrender of Italy*, Office of the Chief of Military History, United States Army in World War II, Mediterranean Theater of Operations (Washington, D.C.: United States Government Printing Office, 1965), p. 83 (hereafter cited as "Garland and Smyth").
30. Cooper, pp. 289–90.
31. Ibid.
32. Murray, p. 165.
33. Kesselring, p. 237.
34. Irving 1977, p. 572; Cooper, pp. 290–91; Murray, pp. 1645.
35. Irving, Milch, p. 232.
36. Kesselring, p. 251.
37. Cooper, pp. 330–31.
38. Ibid, p. 371.
39. Gen. Off.s, GAF.
40. Brett-Smith, p. 371; Irving 1977, p. 628, citing Richthofen Diary.
41. Louis L. Snyder, *Encyclopedia of the Third Reich* (New York: McGraw-Hill Book Company, 1976), p. 296 (hereafter cited as "Snyder"); Gen. Off.s, GAF.
42. Musciano, pp. 52–53.
43. See Raymond F. Toliver and Trevor J. Constable, *The Blonde Knight of Germany* (New York: Doubleday and Company, 1970) for the details of Hartmann's incredible career.
44. Musciano, pp. 126–28.

45. Four of Rall's victories were against Americans. After the war he became a lieu-
    tenant general in the West German Air Force and was deeply involved in
    developing weapons systems for the Lockheed F-104 jet for NATO. Three of
    Nowotny's kills, five of Batz', nine of Graf's, and twenty of Hafner's were against
    the Western Allies. All of Barkhorn's and Kittel's victories took place in the East.
    Bekker, pp. 561–63; Musciano, pp. 52–53 and 131–33.
46. Musciano, pp. 52–53.
47. Plocher MS 1943.
48. Ibid.
49. Ibid.
50. Ibid.
51. Ibid.
52. Ibid. In addition to his air units, Dessloch controlled the I Flak Corps (Lt. Gen.
    Richard Reimann) and Luftwaffe Administrative Area Command Kiev (Gen. of
    Flyers Bernard Waber).
53. Musciano, p. 53; Plocher MS 1943.
54. Irving 1977, p. 533.
55. Plocher MS 1943.
56. Musciano, p. 54.
57. Plocher MS 1943.
58. Ibid.
59. Ibid.
60. Ibid.
61. Seaton, *Moscow*, pp. 399–400.
62. Musciano, pp. 54–55.
63. Suchenwirth MS "Command."
64. Cooper, p. 96.
65. Deichmann Personnel Extract, Air University Archives.
66. Suchenwirth MS "Turning Points."
67. Deichmann Personnel Extract.
68. Cooper, p. 261.
69. Suchenwirth MS "Turning Points."
70. Hereafter referred to as the United States Air Force. Although it did not become
    an independent branch of the service until 1947, I will refer to it as the United
    States Air Force for the sake of convenience.
71. Ziemke, p. 118; Musciano, p. 57; Frankland, p. 59.
72. Beck, p. 46.
73. Frankland, p. 119; Mosley, pp. 362–63.
74. Mosley, pp. 363–64.
75. Frankland, pp. 59–60.
76. Irving, *Milch*, pp. 207–8 and 273; Frankland, p. 61.
77. Irving, *Milch*, p. 215.
78. Ibid, pp. 215–16.
79. Beck, pp. 61–62.
80. Musciano, p. 58.
81. Galland, p. 144; Musciano, p. 59.
82. Beck, pp. 68–70.
83. Albert Speer, *Inside the Third Reich* (New York: MacMillan, 1970), p. 283 (here-
    after cited as "Speer"); Frankland, p. 69; Irving, *Milch*, pp. 227–29.

84. Galland, p. 174.
85. Musciano, p. 134.
86. Scutts, pp. 16–17; Musciano, pp. 58–59.
87. Scutts, p. 22; Galland, pp. 148–49. The aircraft Kammhuber wanted manufactured, the He-219 "Owl," had been fully tested and had several advantages over the Me-110, including a longer range and a smaller crew. Although fast and extremely maneuverable, only about 220 of them were manufactured during the war. Ironically, this was the only aircraft to experience any success against the Mosquito (Wood and Gunston, pp. 190–92).
88. Frankland, p. 71.
89. Helmut Heiber, *Goebbels* (New York: E. P. Dutton, 1972; reprint ed., New York: Da Capo Press, 1972), pp. 296–99 (hereafter cited as "Heiber").
90. Musciano, pp. 58–59.
91. Frankland, pp. 72–74.
92. Galland, p. 174.
93. Mosley, pp. 368–69.
94. Suchenwirth MS "Command."
95. Ibid.
96. Ibid.
97. Frischauer, p. 196.
98. Suchenwirth MS "Command."
99. Ibid.
100. Brett-Smith, p. 140.
101. Suchenwirth MS "Command."
102. Ibid.
103. Ibid.

CHAPTER 13: DEFEAT ON ALL FRONTS

1. Korten Personnel Extract.
2. Irving, *Milch*, p. 213.
3. Ibid, p. 231.
4. Glenn B. Infield, *Big Week* (New York: Pinnacle Books, 1974), pp. 45–48 (hereafter cited as "Infield"); Irving, *Milch*, p. 233; Beck, pp. 72 and 85.
5. Heiber, p. 296; Irving, *Milch*, pp. 234–35.
6. Infield, p. 46.
7. Musciano, pp. 79–81.
8. Irving, *Milch*, p. 244; Infield, p. 46.
9. Gordon A. Harrison, *Cross-Channel Attack*, Office of the Chief of Military History, United States Army in World War II, The European Theater of Operations (Washington, D.C.: United States Government Printing Office, 1951), pp. 210–11 (hereafter cited as "Harrison"); Infield, pp. 45–48; Irving, *Milch*, p. 246; Beck, pp. 84–85; Musciano, p. 60. The Eighth U.S.A.F. also raided Bremen, Danzig, Marienburg, and Muenster in October, 1943. They lost another 148 aircraft and nearly 1,500 aircrewmen in these raids.
10. Irving, *Milch*, p. 247.
11. Galland, p. 166.
12. Frankland, p. 71.
13. Irving, *Milch*, p. 261.

14. Ibid, p. 267.
15. Ibid, pp. 267–68.
16. Infield, pp. 82 and 96.
17. Ibid, pp. 199–203.
18. Ibid, pp. 202–3.
19. Galland, p. 144; Musciano, pp. 61–62.
20. Musciano, pp. 61–62.
21. Mosley, p. 369.
22. Frankland, p. 81; Irving, *Milch*, p. 272.
23. Galland, p. 191.
24. Bekker, pp. 537–38 and 561–63; Musciano, p. 63.
25. Friedrich Ruge, "The Invasion of Normandy," in *The Decisive Battles of World War II: The German View*, H. A. Jacobsen and J. Rohwer, eds. (New York: G. P. Putnam's Sons, 1965), pp. 323–29; Samuel W. Mitcham, Jr., *Rommel's Last Battle* (Briarcliff Manor, New York: Stein and Day, 1983), p. 40.
26. Mosley, p. 343.
27. Irving, *Milch*, pp. 201–3.
28. Ibid, p. 166.
29. Ibid, p. 160.
30. Ibid.
31. Ibid, p. 230.
32. Brett-Smith, p. 115.
33. Speer, pp. 192–93.
34. Irving, *Milch*, pp. 254–55.
35. Ibid, p. 266.
36. Ibid, pp. 271–74.
37. Ibid, p. 257.
38. Ibid, p. 265.
39. Ibid, pp. 281-82; Suchenwirth MS "Command."
40. Galland, p. 282.
41. Ibid, p. 287.
42. Irving, *Milch*, p. 285; Suchenwirth MS "Command."
43. Suchenwirth MS "Command"; Irving, *Milch*, p. 286.
44. Irving, *Milch*, p. 291.
45. Hans Speidel, *Invasion 1944* (Chicago: Henry Regnery Company, 1950; reprint ed., New York: Paperback Library, 1968), p. 46 (hereafter cited as "Speidel Invasion").
46. Harry R. Fletcher, personal communication, December 19, 1984.
47. Lionel F. Ellis, *Victory in the West*, Volume I, *The Battle of Normandy* (London: Her Majesty's Stationery Office, 1962), p. 567 (hereafter cited as "Ellis I").
48. Speidel, *Invasion*, pp. 46–47; Harrison, pp. 225 and 228–30; J. F. C. Fuller, *The Second World War, 1939–45* (New York: Duell, Sloan and Pearce, 1949). p. 294.
49. Vincent J. Esposito, ed., *A Concise History of World War II* (New York: Frederick A. Praeger, 1964), p. 80.
50. Ellis I, p. 111.
51. Ibid.
52. Musciano, p. 62.
53. Ellis I, pp. 245, 478, and 488–91.
54. Musciano, p. 62.

55. Paul Carell, *Invasion: They're Coming!* (New York: E. P. Dutton, 1963; reprint ed., New York: Bantam Books, 1964), p. 179 (hereafter cited as "Carell *Invasion*").
56. Ibid.
57. Galland, p. 233.
58. Martin Blumenson, *Breakout and Pursuit*, Office of the Chief of Military History, United States Army in World War II, The European Theater of Operations (Washington, D.C.: United States Government Printing Office, 1961), p. 234.
59. Joseph Schmid, "The Employment of the German Luftwaffe against the Allies in the West, 1943–45," *United States Air Force Historical Studies Numbers 158–160*, Volume X, "Command Structure in the West, 1 Jan 43-22 Sep 44," United States Air Force Historical Division, Aerospace Studies Institute (Maxwell Air Force Base, Montgomery, Alabama: Air University, 1955).
60. Speidel, *Invasion*, p. 46; Milch Interrogation. Also see Brett-Smith, p. 127.
61. David Irving, *The Trail of the Fox* (New York: Thomas Congdon Books, E. P. Dutton, 1977).
62. Irving, *Milch*, p. 336.
63. Suchenwirth MS "Command."
64. Ellis I, p. 490.
65. Interrogation of Milch and Sperrle, Air University Archives.
66. Brett-Smith, p. 127.
67. Otto E. Moll, *Die deutsche Generalfeldmarschaelle, 1939–1945* (Rastatt-Baden: Erich Pabel Verlag, 1961), p. 245.
68. Wistrich, p. 294.
69. James Forman, *Code Name Valkyrie* (New York: S. G. Phillips, 1973; reprint ed., New York: Dell Publishing Company, 1975), pp. 181 and 197.
70. Peter Hoffmann, *The History of the German Resistance, 1933–1945* (Cambridge, Massachusetts: The M.I.T. Press, 1977), pp. 402–5.
71. Korten Personnel Extract.
72. Eckhardt Christian was only thirty-seven years old in 1944. He entered the service as a naval cadet in 1926 and served as a signal and flak artillery officer. He joined the Luftwaffe in 1933 and trained as an aerial observer and bomber pilot before attending the Air War Academy for General Staff training in 1938. He commanded II and III Groups, KG 26, during the Battle of Britain and was continuously occupied in various staff posts with OKW and OKL thereafter. He was promoted to major general on September 1, 1944, and named chief of the Operations Branch of the Luftwaffe three days later. He held the post until the end of the war (Christian Personnel Extract).
73. Kreipe Personnel Extract, Air University Archives.
74. Irving, *Milch*, p. 289.
75. Cooper, p. 368.
76. Kreipe Personnel Extract.
77. Suchenwirth MS "Command"; Plocher MS 1943.
78. Koller Personnel Extract, Air University Archives.
79. Frankland, p. 119.
80. Beck, p. 131.
81. Frankland, p. 119.
82. Beck, p. 130.
83. Frankland, pp. 122–24.
84. Irving 1977, p. 703.

85. Suchenwirth MS "Command."
86. Ibid.
87. Beck, p. 151.
88. Musciano, pp. 95–99; Galland Personnel Extract.
89. Galland Personnel Extract.
90. Bekker, p. 556; Galland, p. 13.
91. Galland, p. 249.
92. Ibid, pp. 259–61.
93. Johannes Steinhoff, *The Final Hours* (Baltimore, Maryland: The Nautical and Aviation Publishing Company of America, 1985), p. 58 (hereafter cited as "Steinhoff").
94. Ibid, p. 59.
95. Gollob Personnel Extract; Musciano, p. 64; Bekker, p. 561.
96. Musciano, pp. 95–99.
97. Suchenwirth MS "Command."
98. Frankland, pp. 127–28, 134, and 136; Irving 1977, p. 734.
99. Ziemke, p. 477.
100. See David Irving, *The Destruction of Dresden* (New York: Holt, Rinehart and Winston, 1964), for the full story of the firebombing of Dresden.
101. Musciano, pp. 64–65, 78–79, 81–82, 99–100, 106, and 119; Bekker, p. 562; Steinhoff, pp. 159–164.
102. Speer, p. 427.
103. Mosley, p. 375.
104. Suchenwirth MS "Command."
105. Ibid.
106. Speer, p. 482.
107. Mosley, p. 384.
108. Goralski, p. 406; Mosley, pp. 387–89; Suchenwirth MS "Command."
109. Manvill and Fraenkel, pp. 10–11.
110. G. M. Gilbert, *Nuremberg Diary* (New York: Farrar, Straus and Cudahy, 1947; reprint ed., New York: Signet Books, 1961), pp. 172–99.
111. Snyder, p. 124.
112. Mosley, pp. 429–30.

CHAPTER 14: RITTER VON GREIM: THE LAST FIELD MARSHAL

1. Gen. Off.s, GAF.
2. Ibid.
3. Ibid.
4. Ibid; Plocher MS 1941.
5. John Toland, *Adolf Hitler* (New York: Random House, 1976; reprint ed., New York: Ballantine Books, 1977), p. 133.
6. Gen. Off.s, GAF.
7. Ibid.
8. Ibid; Cooper, p. 4.
9. Gen. Off. s, GAF.
10. Ibid.
11. Ibid; Bekker, pp. 152 and 159.
12. Bekker, p. 545.

13. Ibid, p. 551.
14. Plocher MS 1941.
15. Ibid.
16. Ibid.
17. Ibid.
18. Ibid.
19. Goralski, p. 182.
20. Plocher MS 1941.
21. Ibid.
22. Ibid.
23. Manstein, pp. 217-31, and Carell 1966, pp. 319-21.
24. Plocher MS 1942.
25. Ibid.
26. Ibid.
27. Plocher MS 1941 and 1942.
28. Plocher MS 1942.
29. Steinhoff, p. 84.
30. Ibid.
31. Plocher MS 1942.
32. Ibid.
33. Ibid; Paul Carell, *Scorched Earth: The Russian-German War, 1943–44* (Boston: Little, Brown and Company, 1966; reprint ed., New York: Ballantine Books, 1971), pp. 316–34 (hereafter cited as "Carell 1971").
34. Plocher MS 1942.
35. Gen. Off. s, GAF.
36. Plocher MS 1943.
37. "General Ritter von Greim," document on file at the Air University Archives, Maxwell Air Force Base, Alabama.
38. Plocher MS 1941.
39. Carell 1971, p. 567.
40. T. N. Dupuy and Paul Martell, *Great Battles of the Eastern Front* (Indianapolis/New York: Bobbs-Merrill Company, Inc., 1982), p. 157.
41. Murray, pp. 285–86.
42. Carell 1971, p. 596. Some of these men later made their way back to German lines in Poland, but not many.
43. Murray, p. 286.
44. Gen. Off. s, GAF.
45. Irving, *Milch*, pp. 288 and 335.
46. Irving 1977, p. 708.
47. Ibid, p. 714.
48. Steinhoff, p. 91.
49. Suchenwirth MS "Command."
50. Ibid; Irving 1977, p. 714.
51. Irving 1977, p. 728.
52. Suchenwirth MS "Command."
53. Gen. Off.s, GAF.
54. Steinhoff, pp. 91–92.
55. Ibid, pp. 91–92 and 109.
56. Cooper, p. 374.

57. Adolf Galland, K. Ries, and R. Ahnert, *The Luftwaffe at War, 1939–1945*, David Mondey, ed. (Chicago: Henry Regnery Company, 1972), p. 243.
58. Cooper, pp. 374–75.
59. Snyder, p. 127; William L. Shirer, *The Rise and Fall of the Third Reich* (New York: Simon and Schuster, 1960), pp. 1118–19 (hereafter cited as "Shirer"). The Snyder and Shirer accounts differ slightly, but not in substance.
60. Shirer, pp. 1118–19.
61. Irving, *Hitler's War*, pp. 813–14.
62. Suchenwirth MS "Command."
63. Snyder, p. 127; Irving 1977, p. 879.
64. Karl Doenitz, *Memoirs: Ten Years and Twenty Days* (Cleveland and New York: World Publishing Company, 1959), p. 454.
65. Cooper, p. 376.
66. Wistrich, p. 105; Brett-Smith, p. 132; Gen. Off.s, GAF.

Bibliography

Baumbach, Werner. *The Life and Death of the Luftwaffe.* New York: Coward-McCann, 1960.

Beck, Earl R. *Under the Bombs: The German Home Front, 1942–1945.* Lexington: University of Kentucky Press, 1986.

Bekker, Cajus. *The Luftwaffe War Diaries.* New York: Ballantine Books, 1969 (originally published as *Angriffshoehe 4000* by Gerhard Stalling Verlag, Hamburg: 1964; edited and translated by Frank Ziegler).

Bender, Roger J. *The Luftwaffe.* Mountain View, California: R. James Bender Publishing Company, 1972.

Benoist-Mechin, Jacques. *Sixty Days That Shook the West: The Fall of France.* New York: G. P. Putnam's Sons, 1963.

Bethell, Nicholas, and the editors of Time-Life Books. *Russia Besieged.* World War II series, Volume 6. Alexandria, Virginia: Time-Life Books, 1980.

Bewley, Charles. *Hermann Goering and the Third Reich.* New York: Devin-Adair, 1962.

Blumenson, Martin. *Breakout and Pursuit.* United States Army in World War II, The European Theater of Operations. Office of the Chief of Military History, United States Department of the Army. Washington, D.C.: United States Government Printing Office, 1961.

———. *Salerno to Cassino.* United States Army in World War II, Mediterranean Theater of Operations. Office of the Chief of Military History, Department of the Army. Washington, D.C.: United States Government Printing Office, 1969.

Brett-Smith, Richard. *Hitler's Generals.* Novato, California: Presidio Press, 1977.

British Air Ministry. A.D.I.K. Report Number 348/1945. On file, Maxwell Air Force Base, Montgomery, Alabama: Air University Archives.

Brown, Dale M. and the editors of Time-Life Books. *The Luftwaffe.* Alexandria, Virginia: Time-Life Books, 1982.

Caidan, Martin. *Black Thursday.* New York: E. P. Dutton, 1960; reprint ed., New York: Ballantine Books, 1966.

———. *The Night Hamburg Died.* New York: Ballantine Books, 1960.

Carell, Paul. *Hitler Moves East, 1941–1943.* Boston: Little, Brown and Company, 1964. Reprint edition, New York: Bantam Books, 1966.

———. *Invasion: They're Coming!* New York: E. P. Dutton, 1963. Reprint edition, New York: Bantam Books, 1964.

———. *Scorched Earth: The Russian-German War, 1943–1944.* Boston: Little, Brown and Company, 1966. Reprint edition, New York: Ballantine Books, 1971.

Carnes, James D. "A Study in Courage: General Walther von Seydlitz' Opposition to Hitler." Unpublished Ph.D. Dissertation. Tallahassee, Florida: Florida State University, 1976.

Chant, Christopher, Richard Humble, William Fowler, and Jenny Shaw. *Hitler's Generals and Their Battles.* New York: Chartwell Books, 1976.

Chant, Christopher, ed. *The Marshall Cavendish Illustrated Encyclopedia of World War II.* New York: Marshall Cavendish Corporation, 1972.

Chapman, Guy. *Why France Fell: The Defeat of the French Army in 1940.* New York: Rinehart and Winston, 1968.

Churchill, Winston S. *Their Finest Hour.* Boston: Houghton Mifflin Company, 1949.

Clark, Alan. *Barbarossa: The Russian-German Conflict, 1941–45.* New York: William Morrow and Company, 1965.

Cooper, Matthew. *The German Air Force, 1933–1945.* London: Jane's Publishing Company, 1981.

Davidson, Eugene. *The Trial of the Germans.* New York: The MacMillan Company, 1966.

Deichmann, Paul. "German Air Force Operations in Support of the Army." United States Air Force Historical Studies. Maxwell Air Force Base, Montgomery, Alabama: Aerospace Studies Institute, Air University.

Deighton, Len. *Blitzkrieg: From the Rise of Hitler to the Fall of Dunkirk.* New York: Alfred A. Knopf, 1979.

———. *Fighter.* New York: Alfred A. Knopf, 1977. Reprint edition, New York: Ballantine Books, 1979.

Doenitz, Karl. *Memoirs: Ten Years and Twenty Days.* Cleveland and New York: World Publishing Company, 1959.

Drum, Karl. "The German Air Force in the Spanish Civil War." *United States Air Force Historical Studies Number 150.* Maxwell Air Force Base, Montgomery, Alabama: United States Air Force Historical Division, Aerospace Studies Institute, Air University, 1965.

Dupuy, T. N. and Paul Martell. *Great Battles on the Eastern Front.* Indianapolis/New York: Bobbs-Merrill Company, Inc., 1982.

Edwards, Roger. *German Airborne Troops, 1936–1945.* New York: Doubleday and Company, 1974.

Ellis, Lionel F. *Victory in the West. Volume I: The Battle of Normandy.* London: Her Majesty's Stationery Office, 1962.

———. *Victory in the West.* Volume II: *The Defeat of Germany.* London: Her Majesty's Stationery Office, 1968.

———. *The War in France and Flanders, 1939–40.* London: Her Majesty's Stationery Office, 1953.

Esposito, Vincent J., ed. *A Concise History of World War II.* New York: Frederick A. Praeger, 1964.

Faber, Harold, ed. *Luftwaffe: A History.* New York: Quadrangle/The New York Times Book Company, 1977.

Fletcher, Harry R. "Legion Condor: Hitler's Military Aid to Franco, 1936–1939." Unpublished M.A. Thesis, University of Wisconsin, Madison, 1961.

———. Personal communication, 1984.

Folttmann, Josef, and Hanns Moeller-Witten. *Opfergang der Generale.* Berlin: Verlag Bernard and Graefe, 1959.

Forman, James. *Code Name Valkyrie.* New York: S. G. Phillips, 1973. Reprint edition, New York: Dell Publishing Company, 1975.

———. *Nazism.* New York: Dell Publishing Company, 1980 (originally published by Franklin Watts, New York, 1978).

Fourth Air Fleet, "The Invasion of Crete." Luftwaffe report dated 28 November 1941. Translated by the British Air Ministry, 1947.

Frankland, Noble. "Bombing: The R.A.F. Case." History of the Second World War, Part 79. New York: Marshall Cavendish, 1973.

———. *Bomber Offensive: The Devastation of Europe.* New York: Ballantine Books, 1970.

Frischauer, Willi. *The Rise and Fall of Hermann Goering.* Boston: Houghton Mifflin Company, 1951.

Fromm, Bella. *Blood and Banquets.* New York: Harper and Row, 1942.

Fuller, J. F. C. *The Second World War, 1939–45.* New York: Duell, Sloan and Pearce, 1949.

Gackenholz, Hermann. "The Collapse of Army Group Center in 1944. " *Decisive Battles of World War II: The German View.* H. A. Jacobsen and J. Rowher, eds. New York: G. P. Putnam's Sons, 1965.

Galante, Pierre. *Operation Valkyrie: The German Generals' Plot against Hitler.* New York: Harper and Row, 1981.

Galland, Adolf. *The First and the Last.* New York: Henry Holt and Company, 1954. Reprint edition, New York: Bantam Books, 1987.

Galland, Adolf, K. Ries, and R. Ahnert. *The Luftwaffe at War, 1939–1945.* David Mondey, ed. Chicago: Henry Regnery Company, 1972.

Garland, Albert N., and Howard McG. Smyth. *Sicily and the Surrender of Italy.* United States Army in World War II, The Mediterranean Theater of Operations. Office of the Chief of Military History, Department of the Army. Washington, D.C.: United States Government Printing Office, 1965.

Gibbons, Floyd. *The Red Knight of Germany.* New York: Doubleday, Page and Company, 1927. Reprint edition, New York: Bantam Books, 1959.

Gilbert, G. M. *Nuremberg Diary.* New York: Signet Books, 1961 (originally published by Farrar, Straus and Cudahy, New York, 1947).

Girbig, Werner, and Hans Ring. *Jagdgeschwader 27.* Munich: Motorbuch Verlag, 1971.

Goebbels, Paul Joseph. *The Goebbels Diaries.* Louis P. Lochner, ed. New York: Doubleday and Company, 1948. Reprint edition, New York: Universal-Award House, 1971.

Goerlitz, Walter. *Paulus and Stalingrad.* Westport, Connecticut: Greenwood Press, 1974.

Goralski, Robert. *World War II Almanac, 1931–1945.* New York: G. P. Putnam's Sons, 1981.

Gosztony, Peter, ed. *Der Kampf um Berlin 1945 in Augenzeugenberichten.* Duesseldorf. Rauch, 1970.

Goutard, A. *The Battle of France, 1940.* New York: Ives Washburn, 1959.

Guderian, Heinz. *Panzer Leader.* New York: E. P. Dutton, 1957. Reprint edition, New York: Ballantine Books, 1967.

Gundelach, Karl. "The Battle for Crete 1941." *Decisive Battles of World War II: The German View.* H. A. Jacobsen and J. Rohwer, eds. New York: G. P. Putnam's Sons, 1965.

Halder, Franz. *The Private War Journal of Generaloberst Franz Halder, Chief of Staff of the Supreme Command of the German Army, 14 Aug 39–24 Sep 42.* Washington, D.C.: Department of the Army, Office of the Chief of Military History, 1950.

Harrison, Gordon A. *Cross-Channel Attack.* United States Army in World War II, European Theater of Operations. Office of the Chief of Military History, Department of the Army. Washington, D.C.: United States Government Printing Office, 1951.

Hart, B. H. Liddell. *The German Generals Talk.* New York: Quill, 1979.

———. *History of the Second World War.* New York: G. P. Putnam's Sons, 1972.

Heckstall-Smith, Anthony, and H. T. Baille-Grohman. *Greek Tragedy*. New York: W. W. Norton and Company, 1961.

Heiber, Helmut. *Goebbels*. New York: E. P. Dutton, 1972. Reprint edition, New York: Da Capo Press, 1972.

Held, Werner, and Holger Nauroth. *The Defense of the Reich*. London: Arms and Armour Press, 1982.

Hitler, Adolf. *Mein Kampf*. Munich: Verlag Frz. Eher Nachf., 1925. Reprint ed., Boston: Houghton Mifflin Co., 1971.

Hoehne, Heinz. *Canaris*. New York: Doubleday and Co., 1979.

Hoffmann, Peter. *The History of the German Resistance, 1933–45*. Cambridge, Massachusetts: The M.I.T. Press, 1977.

Horne, Alister. *To Lose a Battle: France, 1940*. Boston: Little, Brown and Company, 1969.

Howe, George F. *Northwest Africa: Seizing the Initiative in the West*. U.S. Army in World War II, The Mediterranean Theater of Operations. Washington, D.C.: United States Department of the Army, 1957.

Infield, Glenn B. *Big Week*. New York: Pinnacle Books, 1974.

Irving, David. *The Destruction of Dresden*. New York: Holt, Rinehart and Winston, 1964. Reprint edition, New York: Ballantine Books, 1965.

———. *Hitler's War*. New York: The Viking Press, 1977.

———. *The Rise and Fall of the Luftwaffe: The Life of Field Marshal Erhard Milch*. Boston: Little, Brown and Company, 1973.

———. *The Trail of the Fox*. New York: Thomas Congdon Books, E. P. Dutton, 1977.

———. *The War Path: Hitler's Germany, 1933–1939*. New York: Viking Press, 1979.

Jacobsen, Hans-Adolf, and J. Rohwer, eds. *Decisive Battles of World War II: The German View*. New York: G. P. Putnam's Sons, 1965.

Janssen, Gregor. "The Effect of the Bombing." *History of the Second World War*, Part 79. New York: Marshall Cavendish, 1973.

Keilig, Wolf. *Die Generale des Heeres*. Friedberg: Podzun-Pallas-Verlag, 1983.

Kennedy, Robert M. "The German Campaign in Poland (1939)." *United States Department of the Army Pamphlet 20-255*. Washington, D.C.: Department of the Army, 1956.

Kesselring, Albert. *Kesselring: A Soldier's Record*. Westport, Connecticut: Greenwood Press, 1970.

Kiriakopoulos, G. C. *Ten Days to Destiny: The Battle for Crete, 1941*. New York: Franklin Watts, 1985. Reprint edition, New York, Avon Books, 1986.

Klein, Burton H. *Germany's Economic Preparations for War*. Cambridge, Massachusetts: Harvard University Press, 1959.

Knoke, Heinz. *I Flew for the Fuehrer*. New York: Holt, Rinehart and Winston, 1953. Reprint edition, New York: Bantam Books, 1979.

Kreipe, Walter. "The Battle of Britain," in *The Fatal Decisions*. William Richardson and Seymour Freidin, eds. London: Michael Joseph, 1956.

Kriegstagebuch des Oberkommando des Wehrmacht (Wehrmachtfuehrungsstab). Frankfurt-am-Main: Bernard and Graefe Verlag fur Wehrwesen, 1961.

Lee, Asher. *The German Air Force*. London: Duckworth, 1946.

Lucas, James. *War on the Eastern Front, 1941–1945*. New York: Bonanza Books, 1979. Originally published by Stein and Day, Briarcliff Manor, New York, 1979.

Macksey, Kenneth. *Kesselring: The Making of the Luftwaffe*. New York: David McKay Company, 1978.

Manstein, Erich von. *Lost Victories*. Novato, California: Presidio Press, 1982.

Manvill, Robert, and Heinrich Fraenkel. *Goering.* New York: Simon and Schuster, 1962.

March, Cyril, ed. *The Rise and Fall of the German Air Force, 1933–1945.* Royal Air Force Historical Branch. London: Her Majesty's Stationery Office, 1948. Reprinted., New York: St. Martin's Press, 1983.

Marquardt, General a.D. "Die Stuka-Idee hat der deutsche Luftwaffe den Untergang gebracht" ("The Dive-Bomber Concept as the Ruin of the German Air Force"). Karlsruhe Document Collection.

Mason, Herbert M., Jr. *The Rise of the Luftwaffe.* New York: Dial Press, 1973.

Mitcham, Samuel W., Jr. *Hitler's Field Marshals and Their Battles.* Briarcliff Manor, New York: Stein and Day, 1987.

———. *Hitler's Legions: The German Army Order of Battle, World War II.* London: Martin Secker and Warburg, 1985. Originally published by Stein and Day, Briarcliff Manor, New York, 1985.

———. *Rommel's Desert War.* Briarcliff Manor, New York: Stein and Day, 1982.

———. *Rommel's Last Battle.* Briarcliff Manor, New York: Stein and Day, 1983.

———. *Triumphant Fox: Erwin Rommel and the Rise of the Afrika Korps.* Briarcliff Manor, New York: Stein and Day, 1984.

Moll, Otto E. *Die deutschen Generalfeldmarschaelle, 1939–1945.* Rastatt-Baden: Erich Pabel Verlag, 1961.

Morzik, Fritz. "German Air Force Airlift Operations. " *United States Air Force Historical Studies Number 167.* United States Air Force Historical Division, Aerospace Studies Institute. Maxwell Air Force Base, Montgomery, Alabama: Air University, 1961.

Mosley, Leonard, and the editors of Time-Life Books. *The Battle of Britain.* Alexandria, Virginia: Time-Life Books, 1977.

Mosley, Leonard. *The Reich Marshal: A Biography of Hermann Goering.* New York: Doubleday and Company, 1974. Reprint edition, New York: Dell Publishing Company, 1975.

Murray, Williamson. *Strategy for Defeat: The Luftwaffe, 1933–1945.* Maxwell Air Force Base, Montgomery, Alabama: Air University Press, 1983.

———. "Vaunted Air Power Overwhelmed." *World War II,* Volume 2, Number 1 (May, 1987).

Musciano, Walter A. *Messerschmitt Aces.* New York: Arco Publishing Co., 1982.

Nielsen, Andreas. "The German Air Force General Staff." *United States Air Force Historical Studies Number 173.* United States Air Force Historical Division, Aerospace Studies Institute. Maxwell Air Force Base, Montgomery, Alabama: Air University, 1952.

Overy, R. J. *The Air War, 1939–1945.* Briarcliff Manor, New York: Stein and Day, 1980.

Pertinax [pseudo. Andre Geraud]. *The Gravediggers of France.* New York: Doubleday and Company, 1944.

Pirnie, Bruce R. "First Test for the War Machine." *World War II,* Volume 1, Number 5 (January, 1987).

Playfair, I. S. O. *The Mediterranean and the Middle East.* Volume II: *The Germans Come to the Aid of Their Ally.* London: Her Majesty's Stationery Office, 1960.

———. *The Mediterranean and Middle East.* Volume III: *British Fortunes Reach Their Lowest Ebb.* London: Her Majesty's Stationery Office, 1960.

Playfair, I. S. O., and C. J. C. Molony. *The Mediterranean and Middle East.* Volume IV: *The Destruction of the Axis Forces in Africa.* London: Her Majesty's Stationery Office, 1966.

Plocher, Hermann. "The German Air Forces Versus Russia, 1941." *United States Air Force Historical Studies Number 153*. United States Air Force Historical Division, Aerospace Studies Institute. Maxwell Air Force Base, Montgomery, Alabama: Air University, 1965.

———. "The German Air Force Versus Russia, 1942." *United States Air Force Historical Studies Number 154*. United States Air Force Historical Division, Aerospace Studies Institute. Maxwell Air Force Base, Montgomery, Alabama: Air University, 1965.

———. "The German Air Force Versus Russia, 1943." *United States Air Force Historical Studies Number 155*. United States Air Force Historical Division, Aerospace Studies Institute. Maxwell Air Force Base, Montgomery, Alabama: Air University, 1965.

Price, Alfred. *Luftwaffe Handbook, 1939–1945*. New York: Charles Scribner's Sons, 1977.

Proctor, Raymond L. *Hitler's Luftwaffe in the Spanish Civil War*. Westport, Connecticut: Greenwood Press, 1983.

Richardson, William, and Seymour Freidin, eds. *The Fatal Decisions*. London: Michael Joseph, 1956.

Rommel, Erwin. *The Rommel Papers*. B. H. Liddell Hart, ed. New York: Harcourt, Brace and Company, 1953.

Rudel, Hans Ulrich. *Stuka Pilot*. New York: Ballantine Books, 1958. Reprint edition, New York: Bantam Books, 1979.

Ruge, Friedrich. "The Invasion of Normandy," in *The Decisive Battles of World War II: The German View*. H. A. Jacobsen and A. Rohwer, eds. New York: G. P. Putnam's Sons, 1965.

Rust, Kenn C. *The 9th Air Force in World War II*. Fallbrook, California: Aero Publishers, 1970.

Schliephake, Hanfried. *The Birth of the Luftwaffe*. Chicago: Henry Regnery Co., 1972.

Schmid, Josef. "The Employment of the German Luftwaffe Against the Allies in the West, 1943–45." *United States Air Force Historical Studies Numbers 158–160*. Volume X: "Command Structure in the West, 1 Jan 43–22 Sep 44." United States Air Force Historical Division, Aerospace Studies Institute. Maxwell Air Force Base, Montgomery, Alabama: Air University, 1955.

Schmidt, Paul. *Hitler's Interpreter*. London: Heinemann, 1951.

Scutts, Jerry. *Luftwaffe Night Fighter Units, 1939–45*. London: Osprey Publishing, 1978.

Seaton, Albert. *The Battle for Moscow*. New York: Playboy Press Paperbacks, 1981 (originally published by Stein and Day, Briarcliff Manor, New York, 1980).

———. *The Russo-German War, 1941*. New York: Praeger Publishers, 1970.

Shaw, John, and the editors of Time-Life Books. *Red Army Resurgent*. Volume 20, *World War II*. Alexandria, Virginia: Time-Life Books, 1979.

Shirer, William L. *The Rise and Fall of the Third Reich*. New York: Simon and Schuster, 1960.

Snyder, Louis L. *Encyclopedia of the Third Reich*. New York: McGraw-Hill Book Company, 1976.

Speer, Albert. *Inside the Third Reich*. New York: The MacMillan Company, 1970.

Speidel, Hans. *Invasion: 1944*. Chicago: Henry Regnery Company, 1950. Reprint edition, New York: Paperback Library, 1968.

Speidel, Wilhelm. "The Luftwaffe in the Polish Campaign." *United States Air Force Historical Studies Number 151*. United States Air Force Historical Division, Aerospace Studies Institute. Maxwell Air Force Base, Montgomery, Alabama: Air University, 1956.

Stahl, Peter W. *The Diving Eagle: A Ju-88 Pilot's Diary.* London: William Kimber, 1984.

Steinhoff, Johannes. *The Final Hours.* Baltimore, Maryland: The Nautical and Aviation Publishing Company of America, 1985.

"Stellenbesetzung Hoeherer Kommandeure der Luftwaffe." Maxwell Air Force Base, Montgomery, Alabama: Air University Archives. Unpublished document.

Suchenwirth, Richard. "Command and Leadership in the German Air Force." *United States Air Force Historical Studies Number 174.* United States Air Force Historical Division, Aerospace Studies Institute. Maxwell Air Force Base, Montgomery, Alabama: Air University, 1969.

———. "The Development of the German Air Force." *United States Air Force Historical Studies Number 160.* Harry R. Fletcher, ed. United States Air Force Historical Division, Aerospace Studies Institute. Maxwell Air Force Base, Montgomery, Alabama: Air University, 1968.

———. "Historical Turning Points in the German Air Force War Effort." *United States Air Force Historical Studies Number 189.* United States Air Force Historical Division, Aerospace Studies Institute. Maxwell Air Force Base, Montgomery, Alabama: Air University, 1969.

Taylor, Telford. *The Breaking Wave.* New York: Simon and Schuster, 1967.

———. *The March of Conquest.* New York: Simon and Schuster, 1968.

———. *Sword and Swastika: Generals and Nazis in the Third Reich.* New York: Simon and Schuster, 1952. Reprint edition, Chicago: Quadrangle Paperbacks, 1969.

Toland, John. *Adolf Hitler.* New York: Random House, 1976. Reprint edition, New York: Ballantine Books, 1977.

Toliver, Raymond F., and Trevor J. Constable. *The Blonde Knight of Germany.* New York: Doubleday and Company, 1970. Reprint edition, New York: Ballantine Books, 1971.

Townsend, Peter. *Duel of Eagles.* New York: Pocket Books, 1972. Originally published by Simon and Schuster, New York, 1971.

Udet, Ernst. *Ace of the Iron Cross.* Stanley M. Ulanoff, ed. New York: Arco Publishing, 1981.

United Kingdom C.S.D.I.C. G.G. (Interrogation) Reports. On file at the Historical Research Center, Air University Archives, Maxwell Air Force Base, Montgomery, Alabama. Interrogations of Colonel Killinger, Field Marshal Milch, Field Marshal Sperrle, Major General Stahl, and Lieutenant General Veith.

United States Department of the Army. "The German Campaigns in the Balkans (Spring, 1941)." *United States Department of the Army Pamphlet 20-260.* United States Army Military History Division. Washington, D.C.: United States Department of the Army, 1953.

———. "The German Campaign in Russia—Planning and Operations (1940–1942)." *United States Department of the Army Pamphlet 20-261a.* Washington, D.C.: United States Department of the Army, 1955.

United States Military Intelligence Service. "Order of Battle of the Italian Army." Washington, D.C.: United States War Department General Staff, October, 1943.

Webster, Sir Charles, and Noble Frankland. *The Strategic Air Offensive against Germany, 1939–45.* 4 Volumes. London: Her Majesty's Stationery Office, 1961.

Wistrich, Robert. *Who's Who in Nazi Germany.* New York: MacMillan Publishing Company, 1982.

Wood, Tony, and Bill Gunston. *Hitler's Luftwaffe.* Secaucus, New Jersey: Chartwell Books, 1984.

Young, Peter. *World War, 1939-45*. New York: Thomas Y. Crowell Co., 1966.

Young, Peter, ed. *The Marshal Cavendish Illustrated Encyclopedia of World War II*. 11 Volumes. Freeport, New York: Marshall Cavendish Corporation, 1981.

Zeitzler, Kurt. "Stalingrad," in *The Fatal Decisions*. William Richardson and Seymour Freidon, eds. London: Michael Joseph, 1956.

Ziemke, Earl F. "The German Northern Theater of Operations, 1940-1945." *United States Department of the Army Pamphlet 20-271*. Office of the Chief of Military History. Washington, D.C.: United States Department of the Army, 1959.

————. *Stalingrad to Berlin: The German Defeat in the East*. United States Department of the Army, Office of the Chief of Military History. Washington, D.C.: United States Government Printing Office, 1966.

PERSONNEL EXTRACTS USED:

Aschenbrenner, Heinrich
Axthelm, Walter von
Baumbach, Werner
Below, Nikolaus von
Beust, Baron Hans Henning von
Bodenschatz, Karl Heinrich
Brauchitsch, Bernd von
Buelowius, Alfred
Christ, Torsten
Christian, Eckhardt
Christiansen, Friedrich
Coeler, Joachim
Deichmann, Paul
Dessloch, Otto
Doering, Kurt von
Doerstling, Egon
Felmy, Hellmuth
Fiebig, Martin
Foerster, Helmut
Froehlich, Stefan
Galland, Adolf
Geisler, Hans Ferdinand
Gollob, Gordon M.
Grauert, Ulrich
Harlinghausen, Martin
Hermann, Hajo
Hoffmann von Waldau, Otto
Jeschonnek, Hans
Kammhuber, Joseph
Kessler, Ulrich
Koller, Karl
Korten, Karl
Kreipe, Werner
Loehr, Alexander
Loerzer, Bruno
Lucht, Roluf

Martini, Wolfgang
Meister, Rudolf
Milch, Erhard
Moelders, Werner
Morzik, Fritz
Nielsen, Andreas
Plocher, Hermann
Schmid, Joseph "Beppo"
Seidel, Hans-Georg von
Seidemann, Hans
Speidel, Wilhelm
Steinhoff, Johannes
Wilberg, Helmut

Index

Stackpole Military History Series

Real battles. Real soldiers. Real stories.

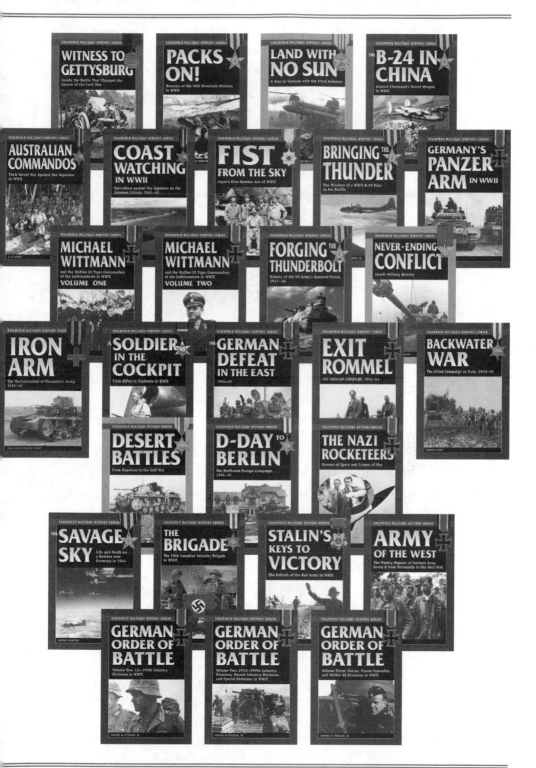

Stackpole Military History Series

LUFTWAFFE ACES
GERMAN COMBAT PILOTS OF WORLD WAR II

Franz Kurowski,
translated by David Johnston

Whether providing close-support for the blitzkrieg, bombing enemy cities and industrial centers, or attacking Allied fighters and bombers during both day and night, the Luftwaffe played a critical role in World War II and saw some of the most harrowing combat of the war. Franz Kurowski puts readers in the cockpit with seven of Germany's deadliest and most successful pilots.

$19.95 • Paperback • 6 x 9 • 400 pages • 73 b/w photos

WWW.STACKPOLEBOOKS.COM
1-800-732-3669

Stackpole Military History Series

MESSERSCHMITTS OVER SICILY
DIARY OF A LUFTWAFFE FIGHTER COMMANDER
Johannes Steinhoff

Driven from their North African bases, the Luftwaffe
regrouped on Sicily in early summer 1943 as the Allies
prepared to invade the island. Despite crushing odds, the
pilots of the 77th Fighter Wing took to the skies and
attempted to ward off waves of Allied bombers and
fighters. Wing commander Johannes Steinhoff chronicles
those frantic months when the Luftwaffe fought to stay
alive and engaged in fierce aerial combat.

$17.95 • Paperback • 6 x 9 • 288 pages • 17 b/w photos

WWW.STACKPOLEBOOKS.COM
1-800-732-3669

Stackpole Military History Series

FLYING AMERICAN COMBAT AIRCRAFT OF WWII

1939–45

Robin Higham, editor

From bombing raids in the flak-filled skies over
Germany and Japan to cargo runs above the snowy
Himalayas and wheeling dogfights in nimble fighters,
American aircraft contributed to victory in all theaters
of World War II. Written by the former aviators
themselves, these riveting accounts take the reader
into the cockpits of such storied and beloved
warplanes as the B-17 Flying Fortress, the P-40
Kittyhawk, the P-51 Mustang, and many more.

$19.95 • Paperback • 6 x 9 • 368 pages • 73 b/w photos

WWW.STACKPOLEBOOKS.COM
1-800-732-3669

Stackpole Military History Series

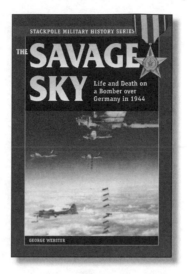

THE SAVAGE SKY
LIFE AND DEATH ON A BOMBER OVER GERMANY IN 1944
George Webster

The life expectancy of an American B-17 crew in Europe
during World War II was eleven missions, yet crews had to
fly twenty-five—and eventually thirty—before they could
return home. Against these long odds the bomber crews of
the U.S. 8th Air Force, based in England, joined the
armada of Allied aircraft that pummeled Germany day after
day. Radioman George Webster recounts the terrors they
confronted: physical and mental exhaustion, bitter cold at
high altitudes, lethal shrapnel from flak, and German
fighters darting among bombers like feeding sharks.

$16.95 • Paperback • 6 x 9 • 256 pages • 21 photos

WWW.STACKPOLEBOOKS.COM
1-800-732-3669

Stackpole Military History Series

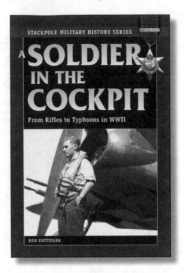

A SOLDIER IN THE COCKPIT
FROM RIFLES TO TYPHOONS IN WORLD WAR II
Ron Pottinger

In October 1939, barely a month after World War II
erupted in Europe, Ron Pottinger was conscripted into the
British Army as a rifleman in the Royal Fusiliers. A year
later, amidst pilot shortages due to losses during the Battle
of Britain, he transferred to the Royal Air Force, where he
began flying the 7.5-ton Hawker Typhoon fighter. He flew
dozens of dangerous ground-attack missions over occupied
Europe through bad weather, heavy flak, and enemy
fighters before being shot down in early 1945 and ending
the war in a German prisoner of war camp.

$16.95 • Paperback • 6 x 9 • 256 pages • 91 photos

WWW.STACKPOLEBOOKS.COM
1-800-732-3669

Stackpole Military History Series

FIST FROM THE SKY
JAPAN'S DIVE-BOMBER ACE OF WORLD WAR II
Peter C. Smith

Known as the "god of dive-bombing," Takashige
Egusa was one of the Imperial Japanese Navy's most
legendary pilots of World War II. In December 1941
he led an eighty-plane attack force against Pearl
Harbor and, two weeks later, assaulted the American
gun batteries on Wake Island. After a series of missions
in the Indian Ocean, Egusa was badly burned at
Midway in 1942. A warrior to the last, he returned
to duty, only to be killed on a desperate raid on
enemy aircraft carriers in the Marianas.

$16.95 • Paperback • 6 x 9 • 192 pages • 70 b/w photos

WWW.STACKPOLEBOOKS.COM
1-800-732-3669

Stackpole Military History Series

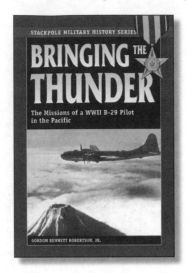

BRINGING THE THUNDER
THE MISSIONS OF A WWII B-29 PILOT IN THE PACIFIC
Gordon Bennett Robertson, Jr.

By March 1945, when Ben Robertson took to the skies above Japan in his B-29 Superfortress, the end of World War II in the Pacific seemed imminent. But although American forces were closing in on its home islands, Japan refused to surrender, and American B-29s were tasked with hammering Japan to its knees with devastating bomb runs. That meant flying low-altitude, nighttime incendiary raids under threat of flak, enemy fighters, mechanical malfunction, and fatigue. It may have been the beginning of the end, but just how soon the end would come—and whether Robertson and his crew would make it home—was far from certain.

$19.95 • Paperback • 6 x 9 • 304 pages • 36 b/w photos, 1 map

WWW.STACKPOLEBOOKS.COM
1-800-732-3669

Stackpole Military History Series

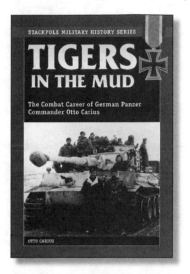

TIGERS IN THE MUD
THE COMBAT CAREER OF GERMAN PANZER
COMMANDER OTTO CARIUS

Otto Carius,
translated by Robert J. Edwards

World War II began with a metallic roar as the
German Blitzkrieg raced across Europe, spearheaded
by the most dreadful weapon of the twentieth century:
the Panzer. Tank commander Otto Carius thrusts the
reader into the thick of battle, replete with the
blood, smoke, mud, and gunpowder so common
to the elite German fighting units.

$19.95 • Paperback • 6 x 9 • 368 pages
51 photos • 48 illustrations • 3 maps

WWW.STACKPOLEBOOKS.COM
1-800-732-3669

Stackpole Military History Series

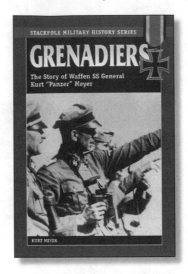

GRENADIERS
THE STORY OF WAFFEN SS GENERAL
KURT "PANZER" MEYER
Kurt Meyer

Known for his bold and aggressive leadership, Kurt
Meyer was one of the most highly decorated German
soldiers of World War II. As commander of various
units, from a motorcycle company to the Hitler Youth
Panzer Division, he saw intense combat across Europe,
from the invasion of Poland in 1939 to the 1944
campaign for Normandy, where he fell into Allied
hands and was charged with war crimes.

$19.95 • Paperback • 6 x 9 • 448 pages • 93 b/w photos

WWW.STACKPOLEBOOKS.COM
1-800-732-3669

Stackpole Military History Series

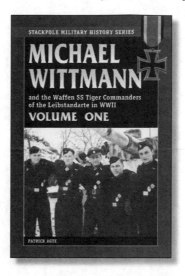

MICHAEL WITTMANN AND THE WAFFEN SS TIGER COMMANDERS OF THE LEIBSTANDARTE IN WORLD WAR II
VOLUME ONE
Patrick Agte

By far the most famous tank commander on any side in
World War II, German Tiger ace Michael Wittmann destroyed 138
enemy tanks and 132 anti-tank guns in a career that embodies the
panzer legend: meticulous in planning, lethal in execution, and
always cool under fire. Most of those kills came in the snow and mud
of the Eastern Front, where Wittmann and the Leibstandarte's
armored company spent more than a year in 1943–44 battling the
Soviets at places like Kharkov, Kursk, and the Cherkassy Pocket.

$19.95 • Paperback • 6 x 9 • 432 pages • 383 photos • 19 maps • 10 charts

WWW.STACKPOLEBOOKS.COM
1-800-732-3669

Stackpole Military History Series

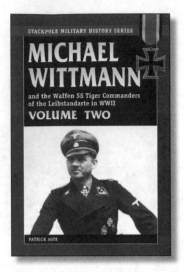

MICHAEL WITTMANN AND THE WAFFEN SS TIGER COMMANDERS OF THE LEIBSTANDARTE IN WORLD WAR II
VOLUME TWO
Patrick Agte

Barely two months after leaving the Eastern Front,
Michael Wittmann and the Leibstandarte found themselves in
Normandy facing the Allied invasion in June 1944. A week after D-Day,
Wittmann achieved his greatest success, single-handedly destroying
more than a dozen British tanks and preventing an enemy
breakthrough near Villers Bocage. He was killed several months later
while leading a Tiger battalion against an Allied assault. The
Leibstandarte went on to fight at the Battle of the Bulge and in
Hungary and Austria before surrendering in May 1945.

$19.95 • Paperback • 6 x 9 • 400 pages • 287 photos • 15 maps • 7 charts

WWW.STACKPOLEBOOKS.COM
1-800-732-3669